LIVING

ROOM

LECTURES

Texas

Film

Studies

Series

Thomas

Schatz,

Editor

LIVING ROOM LECTURES

The Fifties Family in Film and Television

Nina C. Leibman

UNIVERSITY OF TEXAS PRESS   *Austin*

Requests for permission to reproduce material from this work
should be sent to Permissions, University of Texas Press,
Box 7819, Austin, TX 78713-7819.

⊗ The paper used in this publication meets the minimum
requirements of American National Standard for Information Sciences
—Permanence of Paper for Printed Library Materials, ANSI Z39.48-1984.

Library of Congress Cataloging-in-Publication Data

Leibman, Nina C. (Nina Clare), 1957–
    Living room lectures : the fifties family in film and television /
Nina C. Leibman. — 1st ed.
        p.   cm. — (Texas film studies series)
    Filmography: p.
    Includes bibliographical references (p.   –   ) and index.
    ISBN 0-292-74683-0 (cloth). — ISBN 0-292-74684-9 (paper)
    1. Television and family—United States.   2. Family in motion
pictures.   I. Title.   II. Series.
    PN1992.8.F33L45   1995
    791.43′655—dc20   94-36606

With love for Ken,
and for our children,
Philip and Laura

Contents

Acknowledgments

While it is impossible to thank everyone who crossed my path since I began studying film and television ten years ago, there are some special people who deserve mention here. First, my professors at UCLA were always supportive, encouraging, and inspiring. In particular, I'd like to thank the quintessential dissertation chair, Nicholas Browne, for keeping me on my scholarly toes with just the right blend of criticism and praise. I owe him a tremendous debt.

My thanks to the many individuals listed at the end of this book who granted me interviews or wrote me letters. In particular, I am grateful to Barbara Billingsley for opening her heart and for making me lunch, to Paul Petersen and Shelley Fabares for their warmth and humor, and to Mrs. June MacMurray, who babysat while I questioned her husband. Thanks also to Mrs. Eugene Rodney and to Arnold Becker for allowing me to reproduce excerpts of primary materials.

At the University of Texas Press, Frankie Westbrook and Betsy Williams have been wonderfully helpful, while Thomas Schatz's enthusiasm and suggestions have been nothing short of tremendous. Thanks also to Mimi White for her inspirational comments on an earlier version of this book.

Most important, my love and gratitude go to my husband, Ken Donney, for his constant faith, his intellectual insights, and his continual good humor as we juggled two careers, two babies, and two thousand diapers in the midst of completing this project.

LIVING

ROOM

LECTURES

Introduction

A quick quiz: A young boy, convinced that his family doesn't understand him, runs off seeking financial independence, life's truths, and an opportunity to prove to his father that he is a responsible adult. He encounters enormous disappointment, ultimately learns that his father really does love him, and returns to a more elevated position in the family. Name the narrative: (a) *East of Eden,* (b) *The Donna Reed Show,* (c) *Father Knows Best,* or (d) all the above. My discovery that the correct answer is "all the above" inspired this study. I was already well aware that representations of the trials and tribulations of family life flourished in film and television throughout the mid-to-late 1950's. I was equally aware of a vague sense of dysfunction within television's supposedly ideal and harmonious familial clans—that the twenty-six-minute episodes revolved around a lot more than selecting the perfect prom dress. And while previous scholarly work had demonstrated the film and television industries' competitive and cooperative strategies on a corporate or business level, I began to wonder whether there was evidence of a further connection in the content of their fiction. These three areas of curiosity gave birth to this study.

The introduction of television significantly transformed American cultural life and reorganized American entertainment and its central genres, an impact felt most strongly from the mid-1950's through the early 1960's. During this time the three major networks established and extended their dominance of the broadcasting structure; the major film studios entered the television production field and became the primary suppliers of television product; production personnel traversed the slippery slope back and forth from the large-screen medium to the small; television viewing reached its most widespread penetration; and schedules, ratings practices, and regulatory forces were formalized into a normative process that would last through the cable revolution of the 1980's. My goal in writing this book is to provide

1. Smiling faces obscured the undercurrent of anxiety permeating domestic "comedies" like *Leave It to Beaver*. (Copyright Universal.)

insight into the competitive and cooperative strategies of the film and television industries in the late 1950's and early 1960's by conducting a dual examination of the industries' material and textual practices. In the first part of this book I examine and analyze the film and television industries as they developed and responded to pressures emanating from their structural identities, their regulatory guidelines, and their perceptions of audience. In the second part I articulate a link between these practices and their textual outcomes by analyzing the representation of American family life within one of the decade's most popular genres, the family melodrama. I do so by organizing the wealth of domestic melodramas produced during this period according to consistent thematic and stylistic preoccupations, then explaining these narrative tendencies as necessitated by the complementary requirements of the film and television industries.

In the mid-1950's through the early 1960's, at the same time that the family melodrama gained its greatest popularity in both television and film, both industries experienced major transformations and entrenchment of practices. Initially, any institutional distinctions can be read against a backdrop of the profound impact and aftermath of the Paramount decisions filed by the U.S. Supreme Court in 1948 and 1949, which coincided with the commercial development of the television industry. During this period the major studios were still reeling from the effects of those decisions, which forced them, among other things, to divest themselves of their theaters, to fire hundreds of studio personnel, to decrease their output, and to streamline their appeal.[1] The Paramount decisions made it more difficult for the majors to collude and to wield monopoly power, which in turn allowed new competitive forces (independent production, foreign films, nonmajor studio production, etc.) to enter the arena. In addition, after 1948, the major studios severely curtailed the numbers of their in-house productions. This drop in output can be attributed to many factors: a decrease in demand engendered by a decline in expendable income; cost-saving practices necessitated by the loss of guaranteed screens; possible coordination among the majors; and perhaps most significantly, the growing availability of television.[2] The late 1950's saw the most dramatic increase in television viewing and the sharpest decrease in movie attendance ever. By 1956, when 34,900,000 families had television sets, weekly movie attendance dropped to 47,000,000 (slightly more than half its peak audience in 1946).[3] In that same year average daily viewing of television was estimated at five hours per day.[4] In response to its declining audience, and as a way to restructure its former mass orientation toward a more specific one, the film industry conducted its first full-scale demographic survey. The survey revealed that individuals under thirty constituted 72 percent of the movie audience but only 50 percent of the general population, an assessment that continues to orient film product toward a youth market.[5] During this same period the television industry focused on fulfilling the same mass needs that the film industry was quickly abandoning. (Not until 1963, when the A. C. Nielsen company—in answer to *advertiser* demands—began more refined audience studies, did the networks abandon the mass market for a more splintered one.) In the mid-to-late 1950's, then, with quite different audience goals and with distinct demographic realities, the film and television industries began to carve out their separate content turf, resulting, ironically, in a predisposition toward the same genre—the domestic family melodrama.

The mid-1950's were pivotal years of intense corporate competition and cooperation between the studios and the television industry, as each tried to comprehend the other's role in the production, marketing, and critical evaluation of small-screen product produced by big-screen factories. In 1954 Disney studios signed an agreement with ABC to provide a filmed program based on the amusement park it was building. Other major studios ventured into dramatic series production; Columbia was the first, with *Father Knows Best,* followed in 1955 by 20th Century–Fox and Loew's.[6] That same year

RKO sold its entire film inventory for television viewing, undermining the major studios' hitherto solid opposition to meeting the new industry's demand for product.[7] It was also the year that Warner Bros. produced for ABC *Warner Brothers Presents,* a rotating series of three distinct dramas, each ending with a twelve-minute promotional film for current theatrical releases.[8]

As Christopher Anderson points out, the Warner Bros.–ABC deal typifies the anxieties and practices that characterized the nascent business relationships between the film and television industries.[9] James L. Baughman, focusing on the Warner Bros.–ABC agreement, notes that by the mid-1950's the film industry diminished its vociferous attacks on television as it became aware of several factors, including the success of film spectaculars, a leveling off of audience loss, and the marketing opportunity that television provided.[10] The Warner Bros.–ABC deal was an economic blueprint for making use of idle studio lots and unemployed film technicians and for avoiding the networks' cash outlay for expensive and established broadcast stars. The mid-1950's were particularly crucial for the television industry because television's aesthetic terms were then being established.[11] The public dialogues among journalists, government agencies, sponsors, the networks, and the studios created an arena in which the so-called elite, live, New York anthology dramas were pitted against the supposedly inferior mass-produced telefilms. William Boddy notes that "the shift in dramatic formats was only one of many programming changes in the mid-1950's: prime-time programming also shifted from New York to Hollywood, from anthology programs to continuing-character series, and from the dramatic model of the legitimate theatre to that of genre-based Hollywood entertainments."[12] More than anything, Boddy's work documents, from an interpretive perspective, the 1950's battle over textual content and television's programming domain. Over time, as David Marc argues, the majors encouraged studio-name recognition in conjunction with programs or genres just as they had during the classic Hollywood era for feature films. In his study of Columbia's Screen Gems, Marc analyzes how studios' characterization as the "homes" of particular adventure series or sitcoms worked to solidify television's formulas and genres and simultaneously to promote the Hollywood studios.[13]

While private negotiations continued through the early 1950's, the film industry publicly depicted television as an increasing threat, an economic villain both undermining American entertainment and stealing the theatrical audience. Although the studios' claims of victimization were highly exaggerated,[14] the real loss of audience did inspire the film industry to employ a number of combative strategies during the 1950's. Some of these strategies concerned the actual viewing experience; the decade saw a proliferation

of innovative techniques designed to differentiate the theater-going experience from the home-viewing one, including formats such as Cinerama,
CinemaScope, and Smell-O-Vision.[15] The film industry also maintained
institutional clout through economic supremacy, controlling past theatrical
releases, stars' contracts, and studio space.[16] The majors tried to beat the
broadcasters via alternative programming forms such as theater or subscription television—in effect, doing television without the set.[17] Ultimately,
however, the film industry fought the television threat by becoming its
heaviest supplier and a consistent advertiser, and by using it as a testing
ground for genres, screenplays, and personnel.

Scholarly efforts to date have united in debunking the myth that the major
studios simply *feared* television, asserting instead that the hegemonic battles
between the film industry and the broadcasting industry were complicated
by their mutual needs to use one another for self-promotion and economic
survival. But while much has been written about the technological and the
institutional histories of the visual media, especially in terms of corporate
battles and industrial warfare, my interest is in a more subtle confirmation
of the conflicted relationship between the two. This project establishes links
between the two media in their distinctive representations of American
family life through an examination of specific texts along the axis of genre
production.

Traditionally, film and television's domestic melodramas have been analyzed separately;[18] indeed, they are usually viewed as quite different generic
expressions. Thomas Elsaesser, Jackie Byars, Thomas Schatz, and others
whose work focuses on film define the family melodrama generally as a narrative concerned with domestic problems and celebrations, in which social
dilemmas are reconfigured into familial ones and where solutions to these
dilemmas are located in a reaffirmation of familial love, all portrayed in a
hyperbolic style and mode of presentation in which the mise-en-scène, cine-
matographic properties, and sound are exaggerated to a point of stylistic self-
consciousness. In the succeeding chapters I argue that when television's half-
hour "comedies" are reexamined against this definition—shorn of their laugh
tracks and the critical assertion that these programs are indeed "funny"—
these series bear the unmistakable generic markers of domestic family melodrama, characterized by the same familial strife and reconciliation that form
the foundation of the feature-film domestic melodrama. This unexpected
generic similarity between the film and television texts invites an investigation of the popularity of this genre in both film and television production
during this decade.

The family and its domestic anxieties had long been a dominant narrative focus for feature film, stretching back to the silent films of D. W. Griffith (*Broken Blossoms* [1919] and *Way Down East* [1920] are prime examples). With the advent of sound, film delved even deeper into the causes and consequences of familial struggle, frequently featuring class issues or contemporary social problems. The 1930's films of John Stahl such as *Magnificent Obsession* (1935) and *Imitation of Life* (1934) were typical of so-called women's weepies. (Indeed, such was their popularity and impact that Douglas Sirk created an entire *oeuvre* with his remakes of these films in the 1950's.) These maternal melodramas were counterbalanced in the 1940's by the supremely successful boy-coming-of-age escapades of Mickey Rooney's *Andy Hardy* and its sequels and by the radio tale of "Henry Aldrich."

In the 1950's, when studio production as a whole was decreasing, a new type of drama began to dominate major studio output, a drama in which representations of family life began a strange and pronounced journey into stylistic excess, patriarchal omnipotence, and the depiction of controversial social issues. As I discuss in the chapters which follow, these family films called into question the very existence of the family while simultaneously offering it as the answer to all society's ills. Characterized by representations of contemporary, American, and middle-class families, this new type of drama explored and exploded generation gaps, replaced maternal love and sacrifice with neglectful fathers who became "sensitized" by film's end, and transmuted into familial arguments and resolutions all the 1950's questions revolving around racial strife, economic clashes, teen sexuality, and the dangers of blind conformity. This new wave of domestic dramas began in 1954, when eight family melodrama features were released. Generic penetration climbed steadily, peaking in 1956, 1957, and 1958 with twenty-two, twenty-seven, and thirty-seven films, respectively, and then plunged downward quite suddenly. By 1963 only eighteen domestic melodramas were released; by 1964 the genre was represented by a mere three examples. This is not to say that the genre disappeared; rather, the terms of its existence were drastically rearticulated so that as the notion of "family" became much more fluid, it was more explicitly castigated and less frequently offered as a panacea for the problems of the day.[19]

The mid-1950's are also recognized as the time when another genre was born, distinct from, but related to, the modern domestic melodrama: the "teenpic." The focus of much critical study of late, the teenpic exists as a concrete relic of the birth of teen culture in the United States. Featuring youthful cast members and rock-and-roll music, and focusing on teenage angst and relationships and the generation gap, the teenpic addressed domestic problems from the point of view of the youth, to the exclusion of any parental voice at all. Jon Lewis, Thomas Doherty, and David M. Considine all cite *The Blackboard Jungle* (1955) as what Lewis calls the "prototypical youth problem/school problem film."[20] Other teenpics ranged from the horror jokes of *I Was a Teenage Werewolf* (1957) to musical extravaganzas like *Rock, Rock, Rock* (1956) to *Beach Party* (1963) high jinks. What separates them from the films explored in this study is their lack of familial identification, parental conflict, or even intergenerational interaction. In most of these films, the youths exist in an adolescent vacuum, encountering the older generation only as teachers, shopkeepers, or police officers. Films that include the older population—such as *Rebel without a Cause* (1955), *A Summer Place* (1959), and *Splendor in the Grass* (1961)—transgress the boundary of the single-point-of-view teenpic to become quintessential examples of the 1950's domestic melodrama.

The ebb and flow of family melodrama on television exactly parallels the pattern in film. Before 1954, television's depiction of family life could hardly be classified as contemporary domestic melodrama. Either the families depicted were working class (*Life of Riley, The Honeymooners*) or urban (*The Danny Thomas Show*), or the shows themselves were star-based situational comedies (*I Love Lucy, Burns and Allen*). Regardless of configuration, the shows' narratives were traditional situation-comedy in which characters were victims of confusion and complication, jokes were broad and even slapstick, and verbal wordplay or performance was central. While these programs did provide a context and a foundation for the series which followed, they lacked an emphasis on familial love and relationships, moral transgression, and lessons learned that was to come with the studio-produced family melodramas of the mid-to-late 1950's. By the end of the decade, these shows had declined in both popularity and advertising desirability.

Columbia's Screen Gems was the first major studio to produce an original domestic melodrama when *Father Knows Best* premiered in 1954. The success of *Father Knows Best* and *The Adventures of Ozzie and Harriet* created a host of imitators (such as *Dennis the Menace, Leave It to Beaver, The Tom Ewell Show, December Bride, Love & Marriage, The Dennis O'Keefe Show, Bachelor Father*, and *Pete and Gladys*), so that by the late 1950's more than 60 percent of the domestic and family comedies on the air were middle class and suburban.[21] (See Table 1.) A word of clarification needs to be added about *The Adventures of Ozzie and Harriet*, which actually predates *Father Knows Best* by two years. *The Adventures of Ozzie and Harriet* had been broadcast on the radio since 1948; when it moved into television it was produced simultaneously in both media, sometimes relying on the radio script verbatim for the television show. Although *Father Knows Best* also began on the radio, its

Table 1 Network Comedy Production, 1951–1964

Year	Family[a] (no./%)	Domestic[b] (no./%)	Family/ Domestic (%)	Other[c] (no./%)	Total Comedies (no.)
1951	3/42	2/29	71	2/29	7
1952	5/25	3/15	40	12/60	20
1953	8/38	3/15	53	10/47	21
1954	10/37	3/11	48	14/52	27
1955	9/47	2/11	58	8/42	19
1956	5/33	2/13	46	8/54	15
1957	10/56	3/16	72	5/28	18
1958	6/40	5/33	73	4/27	15
1959	3/20	6/40	60	6/40	15
1960	4/20	10/50	70	6/30	20
1961	7/33	9/43	76	5/24	21
1962	8/30	7/26	56	12/44	27
1963	6/30	5/25	55	9/45	20
1964	5/16	5/16	32	21/68	31

[a]Family comedies are situation comedies in which the source of humor is the complications that arise when a series of events plagues a set of characters. (See Newcomb, *TV: The Most Popular Art,* pp. 25–58.) Not restricted to suburbia, family comedies usually take place in urban environs (*Make Room for Daddy*), are star based (*I Love Lucy*), or feature working-class characters (*The Life of Riley*).
[b]Domestic comedies are those which revolve around middle-class nuclear families living in suburbia and feature a professional father (doctor, accountant, etc.) and a full-time, stay-at-home mother. Humor is found in the interrelationships of the family members.
[c]Other comedies are programs such as *The Gale Storm Show*, about a cruise director, *The Bob Cummings Show,* about a photographer, and *The Phil Silvers Show*, a military comedy.
I make these distinctions to emphasize the importance of family life in situation comedies in general, and to underscore the eventual dominance that domestic comedy (aka domestic melodrama) achieved during the late 1950's.

form was quite dissimilar to that of its small-screen successor—the title ended with a question mark, the father bore little resemblance to the sagacious confidant of the television series, and, with the exception of Robert Young, it had a different cast. Thus, while *The Adventures of Ozzie and Harriet* merely added pictures to its already popular radio show, the television premiere of *Father Knows Best* was the introduction of a vastly altered series. In addition, it is somewhat difficult to regard *The Adventures of Ozzie and Harriet* as the genesis for the domestic melodrama in its early years because of its continuing debt to its radio history. When the show began on radio,

2. During the 1950's *The Adventures of Ozzie and Harriet* (pictured), along with *Father Knows Best,* served as prototypes for television's domestic melodramas. (Copyright All American Television/ Western International Syndication.)

Ozzie played a bandleader; often, he and Harriet performed orchestral inter-ludes between the comedy sketches. Gradually, the musical numbers were de-emphasized as the vignettes grew in prominence, leaving the listener to infer that these were simple stories of a bandleader at home. When the pro-gram left radio in 1954, it began to deal with more complex stories of familial interaction, updating its stage set—Ozzie and Harriet got a queen-sized bed!—so that the teleplays more closely resembled domestic melodramas than vaudeville-type routines.

Just as 1963 marked the decline in production of theatrical family melo-dramas, this year also marked the beginning of a period of transformation for television formats. *Leave It to Beaver* and *Father Knows Best* both ceased first-run production. *The Donna Reed Show* changed its family structure from a biological one to an adoptive one, as Shelley Fabares (Mary) left the series and the Stones adopted an orphan girl. On *The Adventures of Ozzie and Harriet*, Ricky married Kris, and the program began to focus on the trials and tribulations of a young married couple. The once-infrequent configura-tion of single-parent households now became the TV standard with *Flipper, The Lucy Show,* and *The Farmer's Daughter,* while the families that remained became either supernatural (*My Living Doll, Bewitched, My Favorite Martian*) or rural (*The Beverly Hillbillies* and *Petticoat Junction*).

In the chapters ahead, I delineate the elements of the popular genre of domestic melodrama in both film and television, review and analyze evidence of institutional pressures upon producers of melodrama, and describe and evaluate fictional renderings of social enclaves and issues. While scholarly attention to the family melodrama genre during this period has heretofore been limited to a few feature films, an understanding of that genre in a more expansive context invites movement beyond the films of Sirk, Minnelli, and Kazan to locate the same structures and dilemmas in the films starring Hayley Mills or Doris Day, films which reveal a pattern of stylistic and narrative concerns similar to those unearthed when closely examining the television texts.

Chapter 1 establishes the constituent elements of the family melodrama genre, locating the genre in its historical roots. Within this chapter, I construct a more refined and expanded generic framework in which to place the film and television texts.

Why, during this decade, did the genre attain such popularity, a popularity grounded in an extremely specific rendering of family life for a quite rigidly defined period of time? Why such similar story lines in both film and television when the two industries were intent on emphasizing their individuality? There are many possible interpretations for narrative consistency between the two media. Some scholars (e.g., Joseph Campbell or Roland Barthes) might postulate that "the family" is a myth, a creation for the maintenance and psychic well-being of society. Whatever their superficial differences, both film and television are similarly involved in a form of sophisticated mythmaking, relying on transhistorical modes of storytelling which traditionally focus on areas of social concern. Another account might posit a "reflection theory," noting that the television and film industries merely mirror reality. During the Eisenhower administration there was enormous emphasis on family. (Indeed, as president, Eisenhower established a government commission to study family life.) Perhaps film and television's preoccupation with domestic melodrama was nothing more than a fictionalizing of the headlines of the day, a reflection of societal fears and concerns. While each of these interpretations is undoubtedly true on one level, I am not interested in analyzing these texts as indices of the social milieu or as representations of the collective unconscious. The conflation of events and practices ("encrustations," to use Tony Bennett's term) made direct linkage between fictionalized representations and their social context too speculative for this study. Thus, I decided to go directly to the material means of production. As David Bordwell, Kristin Thompson, and Janet Staiger did in their study of classic American cinema, I limited my concerns to the relationship between "texts" and the film and television industries: What exactly compelled these industries to represent family life in the way that they did and for such a short period of intense activity? I began, then, by examining documents which revealed evidence of conscious and unconscious cooperation and competition between the two industries in relation to the presentation of the family, a complex interrelation that John Ellis characterizes as "exchange, a relationship of mutual dependence whose terms are constantly shifting."[22]

To uncover the terms of this "exchange," I drew on extensive archival data, including the production files of the Production Code Administration, letters from production personnel, interoffice memos, publicity folders, communications with fans, trade journals, and personal papers and letters. In addition, I conducted numerous interviews. Part 1 documents these findings, with particular emphasis on the technological restrictions, perceptions of audience, and regulatory factors that played a crucial role in formulating studio and network output.[23]

I have used these materials to articulate a relationship between institutional factors and the representation of the family in film and television, accounting for similarities and differences in the presentation of the family and clarifying one point of connection between the two industries. I should note here that I have not attempted anything as reductive as a one-to-one accounting. It is hardly likely, for example, that *My Three Sons* revered the aged Bub and Uncle Charley because its primary sponsor was Quaker Oats (whose boxes were adorned with a benevolent elderly Quaker). But neither have I ignored the real demands made by sponsors, advertising agencies, networks, and producers that helped steer the programs toward specific goals and solutions.

John Ellis has argued that the film and television industries exist in a relationship of "mutual dependence," each doing what the other is forbidden to do for various regulatory, financial, or technical reasons.[24] Locating the industries' common ground of genre allowed me to conduct a double exploration of sorts: first, to analyze and discern the means by which each industry asserted its claim on the audience; and second, to discover and organize the redundant fictionalized familial problems of the day.

In Part 2, then, I explore and analyze one common feature of that mutual dependency—the family melodrama of the mid-1950's through the early 1960's, examining over 100 feature films and more than 500 television episodes. Using textual analysis as an approach, I consider the various sys-

tems of meaning production—narrative structure, visuals, dialogue, mise-
en-scène—with an eye toward repetitions, gaps, and contradictions.[25] The
approach might best be characterized as a "nearly" close textual analysis, in
which I scanned the images for stylistic patterns, dissected the narratives for
structural motifs, or analyzed the sound for its support or subversion of the
visual image, but did not examine subtleties—the use of mirrors, for example—that a less-thorough selection of texts might have allowed. Throughout, my approach was informed by the traditions of poststructuralist ideological analysis and feminist analysis, particularly that operating on the
principles of Louis Althusser, E. Ann Kaplan, and Linda Williams.[26]

The management of so many texts suggested the adoption of some type of
framework with which to structure these approaches. Not particularly interested in a statistical content analysis, I focused on patterns and repetitions.
This accounts for the organization of chapters in Part 2 by questions of
power, gender, and economics, the three perspectives by which I was best
able to sort and analyze the myriad textual examples. There is some categorical overlap here; power, in particular, is often predicated on either gender or economics.[27] This did not prove debilatory, however, as the narratives
usually emphasized one theme over another, especially in terms of narrative
events and dialogue.

On the surface, the portrayals of the angst-filled Starks, Trasks, and Stampers of *Rebel without a Cause, East of Eden,* and *Splendor in the Grass* seem
completely at odds with television's seemingly secure Andersons, Cleavers,
and Nelsons. Part 2, however, illustrates the very real similarities these film
and television texts share in terms of familial crises and resolutions as well
as their differences in terms of ideology and controversy.

The two parts of the book thus function to construct a more complete
history of the film and television media during a complicated decade of both
institutional differentiation and generic overlap, toward an ultimate goal of
understanding how the fictionalized family came to be the common arena of
interest and exploitation.

PART ONE

Contextual Explanations

1 The Melodramatic Territory

Although critics operate on an implicit awareness of the genre of family melodrama, very few have concerned themselves with a distinct description of its boundaries. In addition, most articles dealing with melodrama exclude all but a few theatrical films (choosing to focus on the products of Sirk, Kazan, Ray, and Minnelli) and neglect the countless more obscure films that center family concerns as subject—movies such as *Blue Denim* (1959), *A Summer Place* (1959), and *A Hatful of Rain* (1957). More important, 1950's television programs dealing with the family have yet to escape their previous delineation as "situation comedy," although they bear a remarkable generic resemblance to their feature film counterparts. This chapter functions, then, to expand the definition of the family melodrama as genre, based on a consistent use of generic elements as well as compatibility with the classic melodramatic tradition discussed by Peter Brooks, John G. Cawelti, and Thomas Elsaesser. It is in the formulation and review of the domestic melodrama's characteristics that the inclusion of previously neglected texts (such as television's "situation comedies" and the Doris Day or Hayley Mills feature films) becomes so obvious. It is important to note that the inclusion of the television programs into the family melodrama genre owes an initial debt to Horace Newcomb's definition of these shows as "domestic comedies." It was Newcomb who originally divided the less rigorous term of television "comedy" into the two distinct areas of situation comedy and domestic comedy. Newcomb's generic elements for domestic comedy (a strong sense of place, an emphasis on warmth, a narrative trajectory based on moral dilemma and instructive resolution) when combined with the generic prescriptions for family melodrama, function to support these television texts as family melodrama.[1]

The Melodramatic Tradition

Peter Brooks' *The Melodramatic Imagination* and John G. Cawelti's *Adventure, Mystery, and Romance*[2] offer a critical foundation for understanding the domestic melodrama. Importantly, the characteristics categorized by them are evident in the 1950's film and television texts, and operate to identify these texts as part of the melodramatic tradition. Both authors locate the melodrama's origin in nineteenth-century France. The authors list a number of properties which define the expressionistic nature of the melodramatic text within this historical setting.[3] To better chart the consistencies of these characteristics, I have separated them into three large conceptual categories: morals and aesthetics, systems of representation and expression, and the structured world.

Morals and Aesthetics

Both authors note that in the realm of traditional melodrama the moral plane was bound by a tension between realism and hyperbole. The plots of these early dramas dealt with the mundane routine of everyday domestic life, yet the characters' reactions to—and the stylistic depiction of—various plot elements were exaggerated or extreme. The world itself is "normal," but the events which take place in it, the characters' responses to these events, and the actors' interpretations of these characters are extended and enlarged.

A second characteristic of traditional melodrama is its self-reflexivity. Brooks notes that "melodrama at heart represents the theatrical impulse itself: the impulse toward dramatization, heightening, expression, acting out."[4] Just as actors exaggerate the everyday, so the characters within the drama itself are circumscribed by an overplay of emotion. Because of its expressive nature, both writers see melodrama as a "victory over repression." For Brooks this has a number of repercussions. First, melodrama involves characters who confront one another with their "true feelings." Melodrama involves the "rhetorical breaking-through of repression," in which characters express what spectators fear to utter aloud. For Brooks, the pleasure of melodrama consists in this very confessional mode.[5] Second, Brooks observes that much of what is expressed in melodrama is not always verbal. Instead, due to the heightened emotion of the subject, Brooks sees melodrama as a "text of muteness" in which "words, however unrepressed and pure . . . appear to be not wholly adequate to the representation of meanings, and the melodramatic message must be formulated through other registers of the sign."[6] The emotions are often so strong they cannot be expressed in verbal language, but find their voice in gestures, facial movements, postures, moans, and tears. Cawelti, too, notes melodrama's ability to get beneath superficiality to latent meanings: "Typically, the melodramist [sic] tries to makes us feel that we have penetrated what shows on the surface to the inside story; he offers what appears to be the dirt beneath the rug."[7]

While the aesthetic world of melodrama revolved around hyperbole, expressionism, and gestures, the moral world was one circumscribed by virtue.[8] In essence, Brooks and Cawelti both argue that melodrama replaced the church as the forum for the ongoing dialectic between good and evil in that the narratives revolved around a moral dilemma. In these tales, the heroine was identified by her sexual purity and judged by her tenacity in maintaining (or at least attempting to maintain) her innocence.

From the mid-nineteenth century to the 1930's, melodrama's moral world experienced a gradual evolution—away from the triumph of a virtuous individual via an intervention by God, and toward a self-determined success over the seductions of easy wealth or pleasure. The world was expanded beyond the stock, stereotypical characters of the nineteenth-century morality plays to include both a critique and appreciation of twentieth-century society and the individual's place in that society. Each story tried to expose through various character types and stock situations the struggle between warring moral systems.

As David N. Rodowick notes, "an extreme polarization of values remained constant (e.g., good vs. evil, virtue vs. corruption, heroism vs. villainy, etc.), and despite a variety of situations and predicaments, the structure of conflict was essentially the same, preserving the moral order from a largely external threat."[9]

Melodrama's preoccupation with maidenhood eventually changed as well, giving way to a vision of women as active participants in the enunciation of both family life and the place of humanity within the domestic sphere.[10] The central moral dilemma was thus no longer whether a woman could defend her virtue (or, more commonly, have it defended for her) but whether she was (or should be) virtuous to begin with, and more important, whether the proper expression for her chastity should be as the domestic heart of the nuclear household. This configuration of melodrama is particularly obvious in the novels of Hardy and Dickens and the silent films of Griffith.

Systems of Representation and Expression

Because melodrama is concerned with expression, there is often a conflation between form and substance. The plot of melodrama is mired in self-revelation and accusation, so that, quite consistently, the techniques the actors use to represent their characters are often the same means by which the characters represent their interior states. There is, on the part of the actors and the characters they play, a continual unlayering of the text's meaning (a text that Brooks calls the "text of the moral occult"), in which the confessional mode is quite self-conscious and explicit.

As melodrama developed throughout the nineteenth and twentieth centuries, it was still overwhelmingly concerned with this "moral occult," and plots continued to revolve around castigation and confession. Particularly during the 1930's and the development of the Actors Studio "method," there came to be a reverberation between the actor's goal of getting at the "truth" of a character and the character's goal of getting at the "truth" of a relationship. Additionally, melodrama evolved into an even more self-conscious fictional experience, in terms of both what it expressed, and how it expressed it. The first and most pronounced change has been characterized by Thomas Elsaesser as a personalization of the social. In melodrama's earliest days, the individual was seen primarily as a channel of God, someone through whom various ethical forces were embodied and expressed. By the beginning of the twentieth century, the individual was regarded as a social participant, someone who comes to stand for various cultural forces, and whose dilemmas and decisions personify topical social contradictions in an attempt to circumvent or overpower them.[11]

The key system of representation for melodrama since its inception has been the metaphor, in which color-coded sets, props, and specific locales (graveyards, bedrooms, mansions) are laden with cultural and intertextual significance, and in which music functions as narrative cue, emotional emphasis, and structural break. Characters register as metonymic figures (the virgin, the villain, the hero), whose relationships with one another provide a narrative shorthand for the crises and resolutions of the melodramatic text.

The second and third avenues of transformation into melodrama's more modern incarnation revolve around this representative device of metaphor and rest in the genre's metamorphosis from a written medium to a visual one. Film melodrama, according to Elsaesser, has raised the stakes of literary melodrama. For Elsaesser (and others) traditional melodrama functions along a dual continuum of form and content—that is, while the form of enunciation serves the story (the music, the simplistic characters, the excessive acting), it also has a life of its own in which the "rhythms" of its presentation are often as important as its substance. This creates an ambiguity (music as both structural and thematic component) that is expanded with the multi-sensory experience of cinematic and televisual melodrama.

In addition, modern melodrama has gained additional emotional potency by its condensation from the written to the visual form:

> When . . . we call something melodramatic, what we often mean is . . . a foreshortening of lived time in favor of intensity—all of which produces a graph of much greater fluctuation. . . . It is easy to see how in the process of having to reduce 7 to 9 hours' reading matter to 90-odd minutes, such a more violent "melodramatic" graph almost inevitably produces itself, short of the whole thing becoming incoherent.[12]

The very fact that so much narrative and emotional activity must be crammed into a much shorter span of comprehension renders every word, gesture, metaphor, and symbol that much more potent and laden with meaning.

The Structured World

Traditional melodrama is structured around an oxymoronic conflation of grand activities and everyday routine. Grimsted, in discussing eighteenth-century playwright August von Kotzebue, notes melodrama's propensity for injecting pedestrian domestic activities with overtones of extreme emotional significance:

> Kotzebue's domestic plays presented not just the ordinary, but the ordinary closely involved with the unusually pathetic. While the table was being set and the socks knitted, his heroines were also in the midst of some heartrending experience, such as yearning for the young officer in the picture frame.[13]

Conflict is located in the battles between spiritually superior individuals and representatives of a social world gone bad by its secularization. These emotional wars are waged and won on a playing field of chance, coincidence, and peripety. This reliance upon peripety forms the second key component of melodrama's structured world. Unlike the protagonists in tragedy, in which the individual experiences an evolutionary growth determined by self-awareness and interaction with the world, the protagonists of melodrama are reactive, forced to grapple with the unexpected. One grandiose revelation produces a chain of repercussions and misunderstandings which grows proportionately to the protagonists' reactions to them. As each event builds upon reaction, and each reaction builds upon its predecessor, the melodramatic struggle becomes a Gordian knot of mistaken identity, undelivered messages, and thwarted romances, resolvable only via the intervention and reliance on the sudden reversal of these events—a nick-of-time rescue, a discovery of a long-lost bloodline, a wealthy benefactor.

Finally, the traditional melodramatic world is structured around an individual and her or his resistance to corruption. The individual is pitted against the unseen forces of degradation and despair, as well as more tangible enemies in the form of dastardly villains and unscrupulous landowners. The resolution of traditional melodrama, then, rests in the triumph of the individual over insincerity, self-deception, and a corrupt society.

Modern[14] melodrama remains indebted to grandiose and everyday events, as well as to peripety, but its focus has expanded to encompass a greater number of individuals. Modern melodrama focuses not on the struggle between the protagonist and God, but on the presentation of the hero/heroine in light of the larger social community. In Cawelti's "social melodrama" these characters consist of an assortment of often disconnected individuals who share both a social world and a conflict between materialism and personal acceptance.[15] The spectator reads the various successes or failures of these individuals as evidenced by their moral value system in opting for, or rejecting, the decent over the dollar. The purpose of modern melodrama is still the triumph of the individual over adversity—only the adversary is no longer the black devil specter of an Antichrist, or even a threat to personal health or virtue. Now the conflict is located between the individual and society, and victory is not evidenced by society changing, but by the individual learning to cope.

The operation of peripety in the socially anxious environment of modern melodrama renders the narrative resolution at once more incredible and more subversive. As Ellis notes:

> Other films propose impossible solutions in rather different ways. It is a characteristic of melodrama that it is capable of producing situations that cannot receive a satisfactory resolution: both desire and social constraint cry out to be appeased in this genre. Hence those films which have a transparently "stuck on" happy ending in which husband and wife, who have hated each other throughout, are reunited as a conventional caring couple at the film's closure. Sometimes the case is not even as clear as this, with a film declining into incoherence under the pressure of its own contradictions.[16]

The structure of modern melodrama revolves around an unsolvable contradiction—the effort of the protagonist to succeed in a difficult or undesirable world. This world is characterized by explicit allusion to its verisimilitude—its connection with reality.[17] As Christine Gledhill has written, melodrama's invariable deployment of familial values across sub-genres attests to a psychic overdetermination in the conjunction of social and personal, charging the idea of home and family with a symbolic potency. This surfaces in a persistently nostalgic vein. As David Grimsted and Martha Vicinus note, melodrama's challenge lies not in confronting how things are, but rather in asserting how they ought to be.[18]

In sum, then, we can categorize the traditional melodrama (in its various evolutionary phases) as one in which morality and virtue dominate as themes and goals, in which metaphorical systems operate as the primary means of representation, and in which texts confront both the mundane and the fantastic through a prism of contradiction, coincidence, and peripety.

Choosing a Sample/Sampling that Choice

Armed with the general characteristics of twentieth-century melodrama, I selected and viewed an exhaustive array of examples as a means of explicating a more thorough definition of the 1950's family problem text, and even more important perhaps, as a means of redefining previously classified "comedies" as seminal examples of a newer postwar type of family melodrama. At this junction, I think it crucial that the reader understand the rationale for the texts included here, with the proviso that it was only with the immersion into such a multitude of texts that many of the characteristics delineated emerged with such startling clarity and consistency.

For the world of television, 100 episodes were viewed and analyzed from each of the following series:

The Adventures of Ozzie and Harriet, ABC, October 1952–September 1966.

Father Knows Best, CBS, October 1954–March 1955; NBC, August 1955–September 1958; CBS, October 1958–September 1962;[19] ABC, October 1962–April 1963.

Leave it to Beaver, CBS, October 1957–September 1958; ABC, October 1958–September 1963.

The Donna Reed Show, ABC, October 1958–September 1966.

My Three Sons, ABC, September 1960–September 1965; CBS, September 1965–August 1972.

These particular domestic prime-time series were selected on the basis of their cross-representation both of all three major networks and of a number of major production studios, their popularity, and their tremendous longevity. (All five programs have been in syndication continuously since ceasing

first-run production.) For purposes of analysis, it was equally important
select a group of texts with different areas of narrative or character emphas
In its transformation from the radio question *Father Knows Best?* to the e
phatic declaration of the television series, *Father Knows Best* (the most cri
cally acclaimed) heralded the type of domestic program in which the sa
cious and benevolent father solved the family crises. *The Adventures of Oz
and Harriet* is particularly intriguing in its conflation of a "real" family int
fictional world and in the multi-media connections it emphasizes (Ozzie a
Harriet's big-band past, Ricky's music career, David and Ricky's theatri
film appearances).[20] While the program's initial run exceeded the period
study, analysis revealed that, like *The Donna Reed Show* and *My Three So*
the run of the series was fragmented by distinct production changes or ch
acter replacements, which coincided identically with the study's 1954–1
focus. From 1954 to 1963 the series aired solely on television, stories revolv
around the nuclear Nelson household, and Ozzie was given a never-defir
white-collar occupation. Its synchronous radio transmission of the first t
years and its threefold stories of the families of Ricky, David, and Oz
which characterized the program from 1963 onward remarkably bracket
1954–1963 period of study.

My Three Sons was selected as representative of a new type of family c
figuration—the single-parent household—that was to become the norm
the mid-1960's (*Gidget, The Ghost and Mrs. Muir, The Courtship of Edd
Father, Julia,* etc.). Although *Bachelor Father* preceded it, *My Three Sons*
chosen because of its longevity and popularity, and because of the analyti
significance of its reconfiguration of "Mother" into the two avuncular ch
acters: Bub and Uncle Charley. Like *The Adventures of Ozzie and Harriet* a
The Donna Reed Show, the program altered its structure significantly dur
the course of its years-long existence. In 1965, two character changes
curred: William Frawley (Bub) and Tim Considine (Mike) left the progr
and their characters were replaced with Uncle Charley, and adopted
Ernie. In addition, the program shifted networks, changed from black a
white to color, and changed sponsorship, with subsequent influence on
narrative focus of the program. For these reasons, only the years 1960–1
were analyzed.

Leave It to Beaver was chosen as exemplary of the child-centered explc
of a loveable, troublesome child. I chose *Leave It to Beaver* over, for examp
Dennis the Menace because it was the prototype for this narrative configu
tion and because its longevity has been remarkable and nearly cultlike.
Donna Reed Show is one of the few (nonwidow) domestic comedies t
claimed to center the mother figure; the position of Donna Reed as b

producer and star of her series seemed particularly relevant to an institutional study with generic emphasis. Interestingly (and I discovered this only after the shows' selection), all of the programs boasted a "real-world" connection, in either story ideas (Roswell Rogers, Nate Monaster, Ozzie Nelson, Peter Tewksbury, Joe Connelly, and Bob Mosher all credit their scenarios to their own family experiences) or in terms of production personnel (the real-life Nelsons played "themselves"; Donna Reed was married to the co-producer of her program, Barry and Stanley Livingston played friends and then brothers on *My Three Sons*). This connection to a living culture became extremely important in understanding the marketing strategy of the networks and production companies, especially in terms of the family representations they encouraged.

Selection of the 89 feature films was based on their similar narrative preoccupation with the contemporary American middle-class family, but the boundaries of the categorization proved more elastic, primarily because the film industry is less intent on duplicating itself than is series television. The film industry sought to capitalize on the sensationalism or topicality of 1950's controversy, but with various twists in order to entice a paying audience. Thus, the filmic melodramas presented contemporary issues in the thinly disguised setting of a historical period (*East of Eden* is an obvious example), or masked stories of social commentary as "comedies" (*The Parent Trap* and divorce; *The Thrill of It All* and career women).

In assessing these texts as family melodrama, a number of characteristics proved essential; it is these conventions and stylistic elements that I wish to highlight here. Generic definition incurs the risk of undue broadness or specificity, as well as conflation of genre with director or studio. Relying on previous work by Schatz, Jane Feuer, Rick Altman, and others, I present a series of somewhat structured categories through which to locate the various conventions of melodrama. It should be understood that the components of all of these categories are drawn from the underlying foundations of the melodramatic tradition itself as outlined above.

Narrative Patterns

Thomas Elsaesser noted the predilection in family melodrama for reconfiguring all social conflict and contradiction into familial issues; the centrality of the family is a crucial defining characteristic of 1950's domestic melodrama.[21] Not only are the problems family problems, but those situations which are not explicitly the domain of the nuclear unit are transformed into familial terms. Additionally, the solution to these problems is rendered in the context of family life, eliding class, race, and geographic factors which might contribute equally toward both the creation and the resolution of the conflict. By the 1950's the world of melodrama had changed from a world of stereotypical individuals to one of familial societies in which the family was rendered as the crucial factor in social development, and outside influences were available only as they made themselves present within the familial sphere. Jackie Byars neatly summarizes the debt this structure owes to previous generic forms:

> The family melodrama emerged in the early fifties. Elements of the "women's films" and the family comedies combined to produce a discernibly different sort of film focused on the family. . . . Familial conflicts [previously] had enhanced plots centered around external complications but had not furnished the dominant narrative conflict; now family crises began to take on centrality in the melodrama.[22]

The preoccupation with familial concerns granted the family a supremacy as the locus of both problem and solution and a currency of definition separate from mere stylistics. Not only do these films center on familial concerns in general, but a series of patterns of representation exists that allows categorization by central problem, in which the trajectories of pain and resolution distinguish the family problem films and television programs as individual expressions of overlapping concerns. While earlier texts presented a drama circumscribed and defined by stereotypes and metonymic individuals—the virgin/villain/hero—and while the later "social" melodramas presented the individual at odds with society, these new films redefined society strictly in terms of the family. The key system of discourse was now the family, the arena was the household, and social problems were made apparent only as they affected or influenced the familial structure. Gender positioning, issues of power, and economic concerns are thus located and revealed in a pronounced interplay of family dynamics.

Second, the narrative trajectory moves from exterior consequences to a presentation of interior states as the children (usually sons) relinquish their asocial behavior and voice their love and responsibility for, and dependence on, the father. Current events became metonymized within the various characters and the implicit dictum is that social ills are best solved within the family situation. For example, problems of integration are resolved through intermarriage, the commingling of families personalizing the ethnic/racial problem and recuperating it under the more personal headings of father-son conflict, pride, and cooperation. Juvenile delinquency is blamed on paternal apathy; its solution is paternal love.

A third narrative pattern paradoxically conditions paternal-filial bonding upon the fathers' mortal illness. It is only with his father's impending death that the son is allowed to ascend to a position of responsibility and maturity, in essence becoming the caretaker for his ailing parent, and finding emotional liberation with his father's ever-increasing fallibility. As will become clear in further chapters, this common generic emphasis on patriarchy and paternalism is specified further with the genre's predilection for distinct narrative dilemmas. Indeed, it is possible to chart these highly repetitive narrative preoccupations among the various films (and programs), revealing a statistical preference for stories of adolescent coming-of-age (40 percent of the family films screened), marital problems (34 percent of the films), and remarriage and courtship dilemmas (17 percent of the films).[23]

Like their feature-film counterparts, the television programs also centered on familial conflict and solution, but with a more optimistic perspective. Where feature film families are rife with tension and animosity, their television incarnations are depicted as idealized versions of family life, often pitted against outsider, dysfunctional units. Narrative solution depends on absolution and a reappropriation into an operative nuclear group, a less harsh answer than the film world's call for the elimination of all troublemakers. The television texts are infused with a cross-series system of troublesome binary choices: self-promotion versus friendship, greed versus thrift, middle-class informality versus the restrictiveness of wealth, homemaking selflessness versus careerist isolation, and familial togetherness versus economic self-promotion.[24] The solution of each of these dilemmas is found through confrontation, recognition of patriarchal rights, and acquiescence.

In both the film and the television texts, the 1950's melodramas were infused with idiosyncratic fifties' ideological messages. Topical issues were recuperated into family problems, as racism, juvenile delinquency, and mental illness were reconfigured as either father-son conflicts (conveniently solved with the resolution of the paternal-filial bond), generational snafus (resolved by a thoughtful reappropriation into mainstream consumerism), or gender animosities (unraveled by heterosexual love and matrimony). Importantly, however (and this becomes more clear in the discussions which follow), it is possible to conclude that the television programs provide a reversal of the narrative foundation of the feature films; in film, the social world becomes the familial, while in television, the familial world operates as an allegory for the social. In both cases the domestic unit is the primary focal point, but its relationship with society diverges.

Looking at narrative patterns, particularly with a view to understanding the emphasis placed on familial interaction, proved crucial in the selection of films for this study. For example, the simple existence of a character embodying social conflict, or the presentation of a generation gap, did not necessarily qualify a film or television program as family melodrama, as defined here. In order to fulfill generic constraints, a text had to foreground conflict as a *familial* disorder and resolve any and all dilemmas via a restitution of some sort of nuclear unit. This means that a number of teen-oriented films (the "Beach Party" series) cannot be classified as family melodrama, because they lack the parental voice. Films such as these include many *Beach Party* imitators, juvenile-delinquent films, and rock-and-roll "flicks." Only if a rock-and-roll film centered on the parents' objections or a confrontation between generations was it possible to call it family melodrama (*Rock, Rock, Rock*).

To be a family-problem film means also to focus on the internal conflagrations of the nuclear unit—parents at war with their children, children caught in custody battles, multigenerational conflicts over loyalty. Marital-affair films in and of themselves rarely fit the category of family melodrama, because their narrative trajectories have more to do with thwarting social convention than recognizing the shaky supremacy of the familial unit. Story lines featuring strictly marital dilemmas, then, were defined as family melodrama only if the couple was predominantly concerned with having children or the loss of a child, or if the conflict related to a spouse's memory of childhood dysfunction (*Tunnel of Love* [1958], *The Shrike* [1955]). Plots revolving only around extramarital affairs (*The Interns* [1962], *The Carpetbaggers* [1964], *The Man with the Golden Arm* [1956]) were not considered family problem films.

Inevitably, there is a gray area: texts whose narrative structures are dominated by familial anxiety and reconciliation, but whose stylistics render the texts at odds with the basic generic model. These generic hybrids will prove intriguing for future study, but cannot be incorporated logically into an analysis of the domestic melodrama in its purest sense. Such films and television programs include the melo-musical (*Bye Bye Birdie* [1963], *Meet Me in St. Louis* [1948], and perhaps even *The Sound of Music* [1965]), the melo-western (*Winchester 73* [1950], *How the West Was Won* [1962]), and the melo-sitcom (*The Brady Bunch* [1969–1974], which is based on an essential melodramatic concept of the widowed-blended family, for whom, however, the majority of plots center on the confusion/complication/alleviation structure of traditional situation comedy).

In addition to foregrounding the family, the domestic melodrama enacts other generically crucial narrative patterns. One such narrative pattern, somewhat subordinate to or inclusive of the structural valuation of the

nily unit, has to do with the family members themselves. It is in its trans-
rmation into a tale of patriarchal-filial bonding that the 1950's domestic
elodrama most significantly differs from its predecessors. Over the course
its development, the family melodrama has focused on different family
embers as the significant point of identification and conflict. Early tales of
tcasts and orphans gave way to sagas of maternal sacrifice and grief. These
aternal melodramas were particularly common during the 1930's and 1940's
both film and radio, with Barbara Stanwyck, Claudette Colbert, and even
arlene Dietrich giving voice to the martyrdom of motherhood, while radio
ap opera producer Irna Phillips espoused the importance of mother love
d sanctity for the broadcast medium. By the 1950's the terms of familial
volvement and acceptance had changed extraordinarily toward a forum for
ternal-filial affection, to the near or total exclusion of the mother figure.
1e consistency with which the role of the father was emphasized both ex-
icitly and implicitly was perhaps the most crucial transformation in the
velopment of the family-melodrama genre and provides yet another com-
on denominator between the film and television texts. The upcoming
apters on gender and power detail the stakes of this change and the varia-
ns it traversed.

A final structural component of these domestic melodramas rests in the
ea of dramatic resolution. If these texts foreground the family and family
ve as the solution to a myriad of problems, the *means* to both the narrative
ises and their answers rests in the melodramatic device of peripety. For, in
elodrama, characters do not act upon various natural or social environ-
ents in order to bring about change; rather, they react to uncontrollable
rces around them. The plot of each text is set in motion and resolved by
treme acts of fate or coincidence, and it is this dependence upon change
fortune which operates to circumvent the mimetic appearance of family
e. In *East of Eden* (1954), *Cat on a Hot Tin Roof* (1958), and *Splendor in the
ass*,[25] the fathers' sudden illnesses render them dependent on their here-
fore no-good sons, enabling the sons to offer support. In *All That Heaven
lows* (1955), Ron Kirby's fall enables Carey to tend to him, nurselike, rather
an as an equal sexual partner. The sudden appearance of Norma Veil in
1ere's Always Tomorrow* (1956) convinces Cliff of both his own antagonism
ward his family and their need for him. World War I lets Aron Trask escape
a battlefield (*East of Eden*); Pop's sudden need for money exposes Johnny's
roin addiction in *A Hatful of Rain* (1957); Jett Rink's overnight oil discovery
talyzes mayhem and celebration in *Giant* (1956); Buzz's shocking death in
e "chicken race" in *Rebel without a Cause* results in Jim and Judy's run from
e law, while Plato's ultimate demise provides the fodder for the resolution

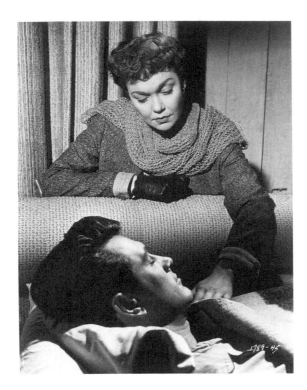

3. The melodramatic device of peripety dictates that Ron (Rock Hudson) must fall from a cliff at the exact moment Carey decides to declare her love for him. At the end of 1955's *All That Heaven Allows*, she can thus be little more to him than his nurse. (Copyright Universal.)

in the Stark family. Within all the films, stock-market crashes, declarations of war, oil wells, deaths, and sudden reversals in fortune sustain the peripetous device so prevalent in earlier forms of melodrama.

The television programs also rely on fantastic surprise and coincidence—often to test the moral character of the participants. In *Leave It to Beaver*, for example, the fifth-grader wins a sports car, Wally is suddenly visited by a girl to whom he's been sending dishonest letters, and a five-dollar check for a lawn-mowing job bounces. In *Father Knows Best*, the Andersons encounter an orphan boy at the same time as a childless couple expresses its desire to start a family; Betty's fencing match coincides with her last chance to take her baby-sitting charge camping, and Jim goes to a flower shop owned by a woman who mistakenly thinks he is her secret suitor. *The Adventures of Ozzie and Harriet* is so dominated by peripety that each episode is clearly structured in distinct, yet mutually dependent, parallel plots with the conclusion resting on a successful blending of the two narrative strands. In *My Three Sons* and *The Donna Reed Show*, peripety functions as both cause and resolution of family problems. Steve Douglas reluctantly agrees to go on a rock-and-roll talent show with his sons only to discover that a client will witness his humiliation because the client's own son is on the show. Fate provides the solution, just as it provided the crisis, when both the Douglas family and young Rhineheart lose and the client sees this as an opportunity to bond with Steve over the sacrifices parents make for their children. At the exact moment that Donna begins to express her resentment for Alex's lack of appreciation for her temporary assistance in his office, a child falls ill and the couple must work together as doctor and nurse (husband and wife) in order to restore the child's health and, concurrently, the health of their marriage. The continual interruption of narrative action by phone calls and doorbells, all of which function to provide crisis or resolution, underscores the fatalistic coincidence inherent in the melodramatic form and stressed in the family programs.

The narrative structure of the 1950's family melodrama is thus predicated, first, by a centrality of family and family issues; second, by an omnipotence placed upon the family unit as site of both problem and solution; third, by an emphasis upon the father as the validation for a successful narrative resolution; and fourth, by a reliance upon peripety as the underlying mode of resolution.

Character Types

Unlike some genres which rely on particular character types for their primary definition (the western, the gangster film, the film noir), the domestic melodrama contains characters and stereotypes not necessarily exclusive to it. Obviously, families abound in all genres, and the depiction of mothers, fathers, sisters, and brothers in a film or television program does not signify that that text is family melodrama. The pivotal distinguishing feature of family melodrama rests in both the quantity and quality of its family members. First, most, if not all, family melodramas link the activities and anxieties of at least two distinct familial groupings. In film, a troubled family is paralleled by a doomed or extraneous family; in television, the central idealized starring family is compared and contrasted with the troubled guest-starring family or the marginally dysfunctional supporting family. In both texts, the family *as* family is a character in itself, referred to reverentially in the third person, and explicitly recognized as greater than the sum of its parts.

In 1950's family melodrama in particular, a number of maternal and paternal character types emerge repeatedly. These types and their function in the narrative are analyzed extensively in the forthcoming chapter on gender; I

4. Mrs. Bartlett (Marsha Hunt) is a typically ineffectual mother in 1959's *Blue Denim*. Here, her son Arthur (Brandon de Wilde) attempts to reveal his girlfriend's pregnancy. Mrs. Bartlett's naïveté and stupidity blind her to his dilemma; she happily recommends he read a manual on the facts of life. (Copyright 20th Century–Fox.)

review them here as yet another series of indicators for generic exclusivity. The character perhaps most important to the 1950's melodrama is the evil, absent, or superfluous mother. These maternal figures exist in both film and television texts in various gradations of malevolence or stupidity, and distinguish the 1950's melodramas from their 1930's and 1940's predecessors, which typically revered the mother-figure. In 1950's films, the mothers are typically portrayed either as judgmental, harsh, undemonstrative, and cold or as smothering, diabolical, and aberrantly attracted to their sons. Mothers not rendered as malicious are depicted as completely out of touch with their children and their children's emotional needs, as physically unavailable (through careerism or even death), or as naive to the point of mental instability.

The ineffectuality of mothers is complemented by the competence of fathers, a portrayal quite distinct from earlier presentations of family life in both film and television. Family melodrama in 1940's film often eliminated the father figure entirely or diminished his importance to the emotional well-being of the children,[26] while television's earlier examples of fatherhood depicted the head of the household as little more than a bumbling fool, dependent upon his wife and children for his successes and failures. Family

elodrama of the 1950s reverses the conventions—granting narrative su-
remacy to the patriarch and positing his sagacious benevolence as attain-
ble goal (film) or exemplary reality (television). In 1950's film melodrama
he text often follows the process of a father's emotional maturation: a for-
erly reticent dad learns to express his love for his children, take charge of
s wife, and steer his family toward an authoritarian paradise with himself
head. Television's focus on the father is even more pronounced: the very
tles of some of the programs underscore his importance (e.g., *Father Knows
est, My Three Sons*),[27] while other programs rely on narrative contrivances
signed to remind the characters and the viewers of the supremacy of the
ther. Television dads are wise and funny, well-educated and nurturing, lov-
g and demanding, omnipotent and omnipresent.

Characteristic portrayals of teenagers and adolescents also mark the 1950's
mily melodrama as distinct from earlier incarnations or from other con-
mporaneous genres. In both the film and television texts, youth are far
ore serious—operating as the voice for status-quo norms and desires,
nting their emotional wrath, calling for adult intervention. Additionally,
ere is a great deal more attention paid to the young; previously, melodrama
- family programs marginalized teens and teenage problems, depicting the
ung as symptomatic of their parents' ills, or as the tangible burdens that
e parents must provide for. Here, the young form their own subculture
d it is their very characterization as a social group distinct from, but emo-
onally dependent on, the family unit that functions in underscoring the
nre.

Finally, it is the characters that are omitted from the family melodrama
at further work to clarify its defining features. For the most part, family
elodramas boast neither large crowd scenes nor supporting players. The
rrative is limited to the relationships among a few people: the family, its
iends and relatives, and—very occasionally—professional social groups
signed to support the supremacy of the family unit (social workers, teach-
s, and psychologists). Missing from the texts are Hollywood's familiar
able of male authority figures—police officers, doctors, office workers, cor-
rate bigwigs—all of whom are replaced by fathers and father figures.

hemes

/ith its evolution into 1950's family problem films and television programs,
elodrama underwent moderate thematic transformation. While domestic
elodrama's dominant themes continued to be the valorization of love and
mily over success and society, the virtue of self-sacrifice, the dangers of

familial neglect, and the importance of truth and confession, a number of transformations occurred to adjust it to changing societal norms or concerns. Nineteenth-century melodrama's focus on an individual's fight for virtue became a valuation of the patriarchally structured family unit, each family member acquiring his or her proper hierarchical position in relation to the family's father. Whereas nineteenth-century melodrama's moral concern centered on a heroine protecting her virtue, by the 1950's the moral world was redefined to include a sense of self-discovery; the 1950's hero was charged with guarding, protecting, valuing, and recognizing his self-awareness. The formerly linear progression of the virtue-morality play thus evolved into a cyclical accounting of relationships within a closed, familial world. Characters were challenged to confront their own goals and desires and to reconcile them with the needs of their family first and of society second. Melodrama's literary tradition of forcing the choice of individuality over materialism was thus altered into a choice between mental instability and familial acceptance, as the 1950's texts work toward the thematic conclusion that to lose one's family is to lose one's mind.

These themes will be explored more thoroughly in the forthcoming chapters dealing with power, gender, and economics. I wish here to sketch those patterns which demanded such further research and clarification, and more importantly, to demonstrate how these themes operate in establishing generic boundaries. Detailed descriptions of the texts are prohibited by scholarly expediency; nevertheless, it is possible to locate moments which illustrate the various elements of the melodramatic model. Perhaps the most potent remnant of Brooks' and Cawelti's models of the traditional melodrama is to be found in the emphasis of the 1950's texts on the "moral occult." Each of these films and television programs is concerned, to a large extent, with uncovering the "true" feelings of the characters. The subjects of these narratives make explicit their desire for familial closeness, attention, and love while at the same time underscoring the need to talk about these feelings. Dialogue thus serves two purposes—to render the subjects' feelings in terms of content, and to demonstrate a sort of cinematic "talking cure," via the form in which these emotions are declared.

For example, in *East of Eden, Giant, A Hatful of Rain, Five Finger Exercise* (1962), *Fear Strikes Out* (1957), *From the Terrace* (1960), *Rebel without a Cause, Splendor in the Grass,* and countless other films of this era, all the sons express their need to be loved on their own terms. The dialogue is replete with lines like "Talk to me!" "Why don't you look at me?" "Can't you see me as I really am?" "I've tried so hard to please you." "I only wanted you to love me." "Help me." Female characters are no less expressive of their own emotional needs. The mother figures in *Suddenly Last Summer* (1959), *Return to Peyton Place* (1961), *Five Finger Exercise, Stranger in My Arms* (1959), and *All Fall Down* (1962), make explicit their jealousy over their grown sons' love interests. In *All Fall Down,* Annabelle claims, "It hurts me to see Berry Berry in love. It hurts when the boy you love loves somebody else"; Violet Venable repeats, "Violet and Sebastian, Sebastian and Violet; we were quite a couple; we never needed anyone else ever." Deanie in *Splendor in the Grass,* Echo in *All Fall Down,* Carey in *All That Heaven Allows,* Mollie in *A Summer Place,* Alison in *Peyton Place* (1957) and *Return to Peyton Place,* and Maggie in *Cat on a Hot Tin Roof* all make patent their desire for sexual fulfillment. In *There's Always Tomorrow, Peyton Place, Imitation of Life* (1959), and *Hilda Crane* (1956) the career woman bares her lonely, family-desiring soul. Narrative constructs of careerism, or pre-marital sexuality, or the generation gap are subordinated in all of these cases to the dominant thematic goal of confession and absolution. These films are identifiable as family melodrama because they argue explicitly and implicitly that the road to familial restitution is paved with a verbalization of inner need.

These emotional outbursts are equally prevalent in the television texts (though often lost behind a laugh track), and indeed function to demarcate these programs as part of the family melodrama genre. On *Father Knows Best* the two daughters, Betty and Kathy, are particularly adept at expressing angst and emotional confusion. In "Dilemma for Margaret" (1955–1956), an episode about Betty's school-club initiation, for example, Betty adroitly characterizes the peculiar conditional love her parents hold for her, as she sobs hysterically, "It's not fair for you to put me on the spot like this!" In "Kathy's Big Deception" (1959–1960), 12-year-old Kathy, stricken over her awkward development, stares into a mirror, shrieking, "You're ugly! You're fat and ugly and I hate you!"

On *Leave It to Beaver,* the characters frequently make explicit their inner feelings or fears; Beaver worries about his academic prowess, Wally frets about girls, and both boys question their father's love for them. Eddie Haskell, the smarmy neighbor boy, functions like a mischievous id, mocking social convention, questioning middle-class values, and criticizing Beaver and his activities. While Eddie rarely exposes his own psyche, his provocations catalyze the Cleaver children into lengthy speeches of familial allegiance and glorification. In *The Donna Reed Show,* Jeff is forever accusing his father of paternal neglect as the elder Stone rushes off on various medical emergencies; Donna's dissatisfaction with her secondary role as a full-time homemaker is verbalized in terms of insecurity, demoralization, and humiliation. *My Three Sons* is constructed almost exclusively on a narrative

pattern of malfeasance, discovery, confession, and absolution, culminatir
with the various sons, Bub, and occasionally Steve Douglas owning up
their sense of maternal loss or their various insecurities about wome
schoolwork, or professional status. In *The Adventures of Ozzie and Harri*
the moral occult is most often apparent in episodes devoted to praising t
patriarch—narratives such as "Ozzie's Night Out" (1953–1954), "Ozzie t
Treasurer" (1956–1957), and "The Motorcycle" (1958–1959), which explicit
center the duties of fatherhood and Ozzie's prowess at them; each episo
ends with either Ozzie's wife or friends baring their respective souls in
declaration of how much they depend on Ozzie's wisdom, strength, and co
sistency of judgment.

In keeping with the criteria of the moral occult, not only do these stat
ments represent inner feelings, the feelings themselves deal with a high
significant dilemma which society usually deems should be repressed. Thu
on their way to affirming the consistent themes of family versus society, c
reerism versus domestication, and the power of love, these shows present a
array of consistent threats to the familial unit which are eventually va
quished by the characters' self-expression. Particularly dominant are tho
themes which deal with the ardent attachment between fathers and sons, t
incestuous maternal desire for the son, and the sexual or careerist needs
women. In the television programs, the thematic emphasis is upon tho
very elements which serve to define and reinforce the ideal consuming famil
Speeches in every episode underscore one or more of the following points: t
superiority of the middle class, the required subjugation of housewives, t
omnipotence of fathers and father-love, the fairness of the American syste
of capitalism, and the necessity of gender-bound roles and attributes. At t
same time, characters actively suppress any interests which might interfe
with the successful functioning of these value systems.

Religion, once the thematic foundation of nineteenth-century melodram
has not been eliminated from the 1950's texts, but it is no longer recognizab
as religion. Family ritual and the celebration of family traditions is a new
sacred phenomenon, an area beyond transgression, revered and reserved
separate from the bounds of the emotional strife of the stories. For exampl
nearly all the films discussed herein present some depiction of Christma
New Year's Eve, or a birthday. The holiday is crucial for its reiteration of t
family as the dominant unit for such celebration, while at the same time
underscores the divisiveness of these particular families and how such di
harmony challenges the sanctity of both family life and the particular cel
bration. As Nöel Carroll has noted:

Christmas is the day on which our culture celebrates the completion of its mythic first family. Because Christmas exists in large measure as a mass fantasy—inextricably bound up with childhood associations of the warmth, generosity, and security of the family—the holiday is one of the most potent symbols in Hollywood's arsenal. . . . Christmas induces regression, rekindling childlike beliefs in social stability and community that grow out of idealizations of the family.[28]

Exclamations of "Don't ruin Christmas," "Can't we at least get along for one day? It's Christmas," and so on, abound in *All That Heaven Allows, Giant, All Fall Down* and *Splendor in the Grass.* When Christmas is unavailable, the films center on a birthday (usually that of the patriarch) to demonstrate the same perseverance (and impossibility) in setting aside differences and proving love. The ritual days are exhibited as "other," as special, and those characters who refuse to indulge in the ritual of happiness and celebration are deemed transgressive, impossibly unhappy, or mentally ill. In a structural sense, the ritual day often functions as a turning point in the story—emphasizing either parental-filial conflict or familial hypocrisy. It is usually on this day that all the unspoken emotional conflicts are aired and the text of muteness is made most patent.[29]

Television series all boast special programs for Christmas, whose importance is underscored by their meta-ritualistic nature, by which a particular Christmas episode gains potency by its trans-yearly airing—appearing over and over through the years during Christmas week.[30] But ritual behavior is not limited to Christmas: episodes are generally constructed around various meals (most importantly breakfast and dinner) during which familial crises and resolutions are literally "tabled."

Stylistic Elements

Interestingly, it is melodrama's aesthetic world which has changed the least. The 1950's family-problem film and its domestic counterpart on television are categorized as melodrama initially because of their adherence to melodrama's two main aesthetic criteria—the importance of gesture and metaphor as a means of transmitting interior states, and the extensive use of hyperbole.

Family-problem films and television programs both express the text of the moral occult and transcend it. Although these characters verbalize their inner feelings, those feelings are not socially approved and the form in which the feelings are expressed (weeping, moaning, screaming) is equally casti-

5. The text of muteness is exemplified in scenes like this one from 1955's *East of Eden,* in which Cal (James Dean) is so overwrought with emotion that he can confront his father (Raymond Massey) only with a vocabulary of gestures, moans, grimaces, and cries.

gated by society. Thus the characters perform triple cathartic duty: they express both themselves and the normatively prohibited, and they do so via a prohibited means of expression. The melodramatic means of expression is best characterized by Brooks' text of muteness. It is typical of a melodramatic text to present the most crucial of revelations or emotional outpourings in a highly exaggerated and nearly incomprehensible emotive style. Cal Trask of *East of Eden* and Jim Stark of *Rebel without a Cause* are pictures of adolescent angst and hysteria. When each must confront his father, the overwhelming emotions are impossible to deal with; James Dean, who plays both characters, relies upon moans, silent tears, stifled screams, and physical contact to transmit his interior state, and Dennis Hopper follows a similar pattern in *Giant.* Warren Beatty relies more on primal shouts to display his tear-filled anxiety in *All Fall Down* and *Splendor in the Grass,* as does Paul Newman in *Cat on a Hot Tin Roof* and *From the Terrace.* Natalie Wood and Eva Marie

Saint register their newly discovered sexuality via sighs and gasps; Elizabeth Taylor, Katharine Hepburn, and Angela Lansbury make patent their frustrations via shrieks and semicoherent ramblings.[31] The acting technique of showing rather than saying, coupled with the "unspeakable" nature of the characters' desires, necessitates the need for gesture in place of explicit language. For example, in *Rebel without a Cause,* when Jim Stark begs his father for help, the simple cry for aid ("Help me!") becomes emotionally exaggerated by the actor's weeping and literally pulling himself up by leaning on his father's shoulders.

For the television programs the text of muteness is no less potent. In *Father Knows Best* the three Anderson children—Betty, Bud, and Kathy—express their true feelings alternately through tears, hiding, and a combination of foot-stomping, running away, and door-slamming. In *My Three Sons,* when Chip, the youngest son, feels upset about his deceased mother, he gets a stomach ache; Mike, the eldest, storms out of the room while an aural hallucination expresses his anger; Robbie waves his arms about in hopeless frustration, amid groans and castigations of his family's misunderstanding. On *The Adventures of Ozzie and Harriet,* it is the patriarch who is most often at a loss for words. Caught in an embarrassing, humiliating, or potentially challenging situation, Ozzie stumbles and mumbles until rescued by the verbal acuity of either his wife or his sons. The boys' anxiety, less severe than that of some of their television counterparts, nevertheless reveals itself through nonverbal declarations—racing off on a motorcycle, singing a song, and the ubiquitous door-slamming. On *Leave It to Beaver,* Beaver scuffs his feet, whines, and runs away, while his elder brother, Wally—like Bud— seeks seclusion. On *The Donna Reed Show,* daughter Mary—like Betty— runs upstairs in tears, unable to express her heartfelt passions, while brother Jeff seeks isolation or—like Robbie—the comfort of gestures and mournful accusations. June Cleaver wrings her hands, Margaret Anderson furrows her brow, and Donna Stone bites her lip—each indicating the unspoken through a reliance on gesture.[32]

The melodramatic element of hyperbole reveals itself in film most interestingly in terms of narrative crises. Over one-third of the eighty-nine films closely analyzed for this book contain a psychologist/analyst or an ersatz analytical situation. In *Splendor in the Grass, Fear Strikes Out, Home Before Dark* (1958), *David and Lisa* (1962), *Suddenly Last Summer,* and *The Days of Wine and Roses* (1962), the central characters are, at one time or another, institutionalized. Psychiatrists and/or social workers are either an active or a promised part of the narrative in *A Hatful of Rain, The Three Faces of Eve*

(1957), *Crime in the Streets* (1956), *Dino* (1957), *The Unguarded Moment* (1956
The Cobweb (1955), *Please Don't Eat the Daisies* (1960), *Tunnel of Love,* an
Lonelyhearts (1958). In other films friends or social representatives take o
the role of therapist, analyzing a mentally anguished protagonist and his c
her unconscious motivations: in *All That Heaven Allows* Carey Scott's daugh
ter quotes Freud and analyzes her mother's need to remarry; in *Rebel witho*
a Cause Officer Ray tells Jim that "kids sometimes need someone to talk t
other than their parents"; the teens in *Bernardine* (1957) use therapeutic ja
gon in explaining Sanford's problem with girls. The need for psychiatric hel
underscores the severity of the mental anguish at the same time as it pe
sonifies the hyperbolic itself, via the white coat of professional help. Cha
acters typically resist the need for aid, claiming a stability obviously unde
cut by their own unbalanced state.

Hyperbole on the television programs' registers in the characters' exagge
ated and often inappropriate response to seemingly trivial problems. Betty
need to earn money for a prom dress results in humiliation and deceit whe
the only job she can find is that of a scantily dressed sample-server at a loc
market;[33] Donna's call for respect for homemakers culminates in public cele
bration (from women) and castigation (from men), and ultimately in sel
reproach; Beaver's belief in his father's advice to "help people" leads him t
invite a homeless man to use the Cleaver residence; Robbie's simple urge t
express himself musically is read as hedonistic lunacy by his disapprovi
family; bride June Nelson's habitual tardiness spurs a series of events th
both exaggerates her irresponsibility and punishes her for it.

Television problems may be less extreme than the alcoholism, teen preg
nancy, or infidelity found in film, but characters' reactions to any imbro
glio or complication are identical—tears, confusion, accusation, humili
tion, guilt, and ultimate reunification catalyzed by a patriarchal or outsic
authority figure. While television usually ignores the psychological profe
sions so favored by its cinematic counterpart, it relies heavily on other so
cializing authority figures: schoolteachers and principals, government off
cials, and wise old mentors.

In addition to its reliance upon the stylistic conventions of hyperbole ar
gesture, there are a number of aural and visual conventions peculiar to th
genre. Interestingly, the texts' obsession with the hyperreal in terms of emc
tion and narrative is contradicted by a near obsession for "realistic" mise-er
scène. Both the films and the television programs utilize an obsessive atter
tion to detail and deep-focus photography which reveals that detail. Thu
representations of food, clothes, bathroom accessories, home decor, and fu

nishings that are usually obscured in the shadowy world of film noir, absent in the sparse settings of westerns, and exaggerated in the world of musicals are omnipresent in 1950's melodrama: homes are crowded claustrophobic locales, cluttered with knickknacks and pictures, or structurally distorted by geometric wallpaper, hanging dividing lamps, and low ceilings. The excessive adornment and plethora of patterns and movement that mark Sirk films allow the visual complications within the film frame to mirror the emotional problems of the characters. In *All That Heaven Allows* a room divider separates Carey Scott and her son as he says, "I don't want this [your affair with Ron] to come between us." In *There's Always Tomorrow* Cliff talks about being trapped in his life as the camera focuses on a new toy, "Rex, the walkie-talkie robot man," which is perpetually walking up and down the demonstration table and finally goes over the edge. Characters interact with their environment in a destructive manner—Deanie throws a teddy bear, Jim Stark kicks his grandmother's portrait, Cal throws chairs, Brick destroys old football posters of himself, Clint breaks Berry Berry's picture, and so on.

Television programs in particular evidenced an extreme attention to detail; like their filmic counterparts, television homes were cluttered with an assortment of knickknacks and appliances whose metaphoric signification extends beyond domestic anxiety into the realm of consumptive entrapment. Studio sets boasted functioning kitchens where well-paid propmen prepared real pot roasts and mashed potatoes for fictional families.

As Elsaesser has explained, the 1950's family melodrama stylistic exaggeration results largely from its temporal condensation. Condensation is a complex concept to apply to television because of the episode's limited form and the series' extended form. Amplification and ambiguity become even more potent in the extremely short (and commercially interrupted) television versions of family problems in which the largest of crises must be explicated and resolved in twenty-four to twenty-six minutes. However, despite the fact that these series did suffer from episodic amnesia and rampant narrative inconsistency (dogs came and went, guest stars played different characters on different episodes), the course of a series allowed a slowly unfolding character development unavailable in film. The issue of series television will be addressed more particularly in Chapter 2, on production and reception practices; here it is important to recognize that for television's family melodrama, the stylistic condensation *within* each episode and the character elaboration *between* episodes allowed for a sort of presentational shorthand which helps delineate these texts as family melodrama. The very problems these programs attempted to resolve and the predictably unstable responses the characters had to these problems, coupled with a viewer's uneasy feeling that these individuals never matured or changed, marked them with an excess missing from the sanguine sitcoms like *Make Room for Daddy*.[34]

Metaphor became more versatile and pronounced a device for the 1950's texts than it was at the turn of the century. With its more expansive vocabulary of lighting, sound, and camera movement and angles, as well as its recuperation of music and theatrical mise-en-scène, film was able to emphasize interior states in a much more extensive manner than its stage-bound ancestor. What distinguished family melodrama from other 1950's genres was its thematically inappropriate reliance upon seemingly incompatible technological tools and its overuse of visual and aural tropes which were used with more moderation in other genres. For example, 1950's melodrama relied overwhelmingly on the wide-screen format, garish color, and high-fidelity sound. *Giant, East of Eden, Tea and Sympathy* (1956), and *all* post-1954, 20th Century–Fox family-problem films were filmed in CinemaScope. Although the wide-screen format complemented the western's open plains and vistas and created visual space for elaborate production numbers in musicals, it resulted in unnaturally distanced family shots in the closed world of family melodrama. The sight of family members dispersed around the frame worked ironically to emphasize the emotional distance among them. Unable to capitalize on the wide-screen format, however, television relied upon an overabundance of close-ups and extreme close-ups as its stylistic emotional cue, the uncomfortable proximity of furrowed brows and clenched teeth giving added potency to confrontations between family members. This near-obsession with the face is another factor that separates the family melodrama from other television programs of the day, which generally favored two-shots or less constrictive close-ups.

But it is music that defines melodrama in its most *literal* sense. As David Thorburn notes:

> *Melo* is the Greek word for music. The term *melodrama* is said to have originated as a neutral designation for a spoken dramatic text with a musical accompaniment or background, an offshoot or spin-off of opera. The term came into widespread use in England during the nineteenth century, when it was appropriated by theatrical entrepreneurs as a legal device to circumvent statutes that restricted the performances of legitimate drama to certain theaters.[35]

As both emotional punctuation and structural cue, music is used to underscore the melodramatic ambience of the films and television programs. The stylistic underpinning of the texts herein explored, music serves as a quintessential point of the texts' categorization as melodrama. The use of music in the films is crucial to create emotional empathy in the spectator. In *Giant* each character has an individual theme which heralds his or her narrative introduction. The over-loud score of *Rebel without a Cause* emphasizes the torment and anxiety of the characters. The theme from *A Summer Place* undergoes twelve arrangement adaptations designed to cue the audience to the moods of the characters (seductive, matrimonial, funereal, etc.).

But while music serves film as a thematic emphasis, its function in the television programs is twofold. As Elsaesser notes, music is "both functional (i.e. of structural significance) and thematic (i.e. belonging to the expressive content) because it is used to formulate certain moods."[36] In *Father Knows Best*, the opening theme song is played intermittently throughout the program to signal both narrative resolution (structural significance) and emotional trauma (expressive content). Toward the end of every program, a sentimental scene consisting of a lecture by Father, a confession by a child, or a realization by Mother is accompanied by a slower, minor-key arrangement of the opening theme song. This convention both emphasizes the poignancy of the moment and signals to the spectator that the end of the program has been reached; the scene is thus highlighted as narrative conclusion and moral resolution. On *Leave It to Beaver,* music comes into play only during moralizing moments or scenes of sentimentality—in this way the spectator is cued to exit the realm of humor and enter the "reality" of emotion. Musically accompanied scenes are played not for laughter but for emotional catharsis and spiritual guidance. The same holds true for *My Three Sons* and *The Donna Reed Show*. Although *The Adventures of Ozzie and Harriet*, interestingly, omits a moralizing theme song, it relies on music more than any other television program, from pop star Ricky's renditions "in concert" at the end of each episode, to dream sequences or fantasies in which various cast members give voice to their feelings in song and dance.[37]

The generic constraints of 1950's family melodrama were established at the beginning of the nineteenth century when the larger generic category was defined. Over time, as narrative patterns were refined and transformed to reflect current social concerns, melodrama evolved to mirror society's new emphasis upon the family's omnipotence. Solutions continued to rest in a peripetous series of events. Characters came and went as the virtuous maiden gave way to the petulant teenager and the martyred mother relinquished her centrality to the omniscient father. The family itself operated as a character unit, revealing itself as essential for society's goals. The 1950's domestic melodrama is further distinguished by a number of thematic consistencies such

as valuation of the family, the importance of gender-ascribed roles and func-
tions, and a moral preference for capitalism and the work ethic, all circumscribed within a stylistic leitmotif of hyperbole, metaphor, and self-conscious acting. The next chapter analyzes the institutional impetus for these representational products—how the material reality of two competing institutions complemented and influenced their separate fictional outputs.

Corporate Soul-Mates: Production and Reception Practices

"Television is actually just another form of motion picture exhibition and the film industry should move aggressively and actively acquire interests in TV stations." — Ellis Arnall, president of the Society of Independent Motion Picture Producers[1]

"Balderdash! . . . Let the motion picture industry keep its cotton-pickin' entertainment philosophy off television programming. TV is far from another way to exhibit movies. It is, at its best, a completely unique medium of information and entertainment." — The Editors of *TV Guide*[2]

As early as 1944, when the president of RKO[3] issued a directive regarding distinct subject matter for each medium, the film and television industries were embroiled in a struggle over narrative territory and structural purpose. While members of the two industries failed to agree explicitly on whether, how, and for what purpose the film and television viewing processes differed, film and television's dissimilar representations of family melodrama offer implicit evidence not only that the structures of cinema and visual broadcasting were profoundly different, but that this difference contributed to each medium's narrative substance. The bulk of this chapter provides an overview of structural components of the film and television industries in the 1950's, explaining how such structural factors determined narrative representation. The different visual formats of the two media (large screen vs. small screen, color vs. black and white, collective viewing in a dark theater vs. family viewing in a well-lit living room) impacted the thematic emphases favored in the industries' individual approaches to the family melodrama, forming connections between technology and the creative product.

The film and television media differ in two areas—namely, program format and mode of technology. "Program format" encompasses those elements intrinsic to the presentation of the text. Some elements, such as length, continuity, fragmentation, and site of reception, are common to both media. Particular to television in the 1950's were such factors as influence of a sponsor—whose scheduling preferences and commercials directly affected the genre's reception—and the creation of laugh tracks—which resulted in an ambiguity regarding the programs' generic identity.[4] The mode of technology also differs significantly from one medium to the next. Television's black-and-white programs were restricted to two-shots and close-ups on the small screen, with viewer control over choice of channel. Film was larger than life, wide-screen, location-bound, in color, and controlled by an unseen force.

SECTION ONE
Program Format
Continuity versus Finality

One of the most significant structural differences between film and television texts is that a film operates as a distinct entity, while a television episode is part of an ongoing series. With the exception of sequels, each film text constructs a new set of characters, narrative expectations, conflicts and resolutions. At the same time, however, a film does not emerge from a tabula rasa, nor does it exist in a fictional vacuum. As John Ellis has pointed out, each film is bound by certain generic and stylistic expectations and each film is marketed as a specific type of viewing experience.[5] But while the film industry puts considerable energy into preparing the spectator for the cinematic experience, the television viewer is expected to possess an adequate foreknowledge of the program so as to need no guidelines for comprehension. Indeed, as David Marc and Richard Adler have noted, any given episode of a continuing series is almost inconsequential; the pleasure in watching a series emanates from the notion of continuity, the fact that a problem solved today will nevertheless rear its convoluted head the following week.[6] These marked differences in narrative closure significantly influenced the way each medium's domestic dramas solved their various crises. While the film families' resolutions rise from decisive confrontations, permanent reunions (and unions) and even death, the television programs must delay continually the inevitable, particularly with those plot elements essential for the premise of the series. For television, no resolution can be conclusive lest it undermine the very continuation of the series. Consider, for example, one of melodrama's favorite narrative conventions: the widower-with-children. In the film *The Courtship of Eddie's Father* (1963),[7] the son's preoccupation with

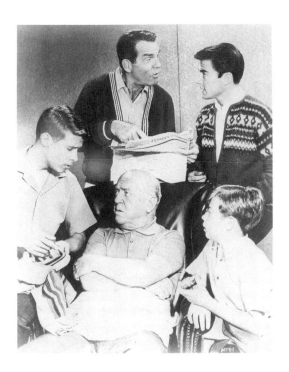

6. *My Three Sons* is the quintessential example of the widower-with-children variation of family melodrama favored by television since the early 1960's. (Copyright Viacom.)

finding his father a spouse results in the ultimate payoff of a union between his father and the divorcée across the hall. In the television series *My Three Sons* not only do the children regard their father's widowed status as unalterable, they actively discourage any matrimonial intentions.[8] For television, the underlying domestic problem (here, widowerhood) provides the very basis for the series itself and thus cannot be resolved; the single parent is prevented from marrying, sometimes indefinitely, or if the series has a long enough run, at a much later date in the series stretch. Other typical domestic melodrama plots undergo similar transformation from film to television. In film, Jim Stark (*Rebel without a Cause*) grows toward new maturity, Ted Carlson (*Man on Fire* [1957]) learns to accept his divorcée mother, and Hal Ditmore (*The Young Stranger* [1957]) decides to become a model teen. In contrast, adolescents in television's family melodrama learn a lesson each week only to forget it by the start of the following episode. As Jerry Mathers commented in reminiscing about *Leave It to Beaver,* "Luckily, we had June and Ward, the best mom and dad in the whole world, close by to teach us a lesson. Not that we ever retained those lessons for too long, but then we would never have had six seasons worth of shows if we'd always behaved like angels."[9] As John Ellis has noted:

The TV series proposes a problematic that is not resolved; narrative resolution takes place at a less fundamental level, at the level of the particular incidents. . . .

This marks a basic difference between the cinema narrative and the TV series narrative. The film text aims for a final coherent totalising vision, which sets everything back into order. [10]

A need for continuity also determined television's bias toward less severe problems than those that film explored. Because the family was seen week after week, any extreme example of anxiety or discord had to be resolved quickly, lest the television audience carry it with them into the following week's episode. "My Three Strikers," for example, a 1960–1961 episode from *My Three Sons*, shows a father-son argument over family chores and allowances. Although a fight between Steve and Mike is heavily laden with the "adolescent weepy scene codes" [11] of cinematic family melodrama (discordant music, aural hallucinations, tears, and escape), the conflict is resolved quickly and invisibly during a commercial break. [12] By the end of the program the two are happily reconciled, so that the following week, in an episode called "The Elopement," Steve can worry over a new problem. As is typical of television's domestic melodramas, this episode restructures a rather severe emotional conflict into a more manageable economic discussion. The reason, perhaps, that Mike and Steve argue about finances rather than focusing on their very obvious feelings of betrayal and disappointment is that the financial workings of the Douglas family are more readily and concretely resolved. Resistant to finality, television melodramas center their problems in areas where the solutions are on a smaller level; Mike knows his father loves him; it's just that he wants more money.

The cinematic families are permitted the double luxury of both a final solution and emotional spillover, in which the viewer can be left with a nagging ache that successful family life is hard work. Because of this, in film, the stakes of the father-son conflicts are more explicit and more elaborate. Crises arise out of a need for love and a refusal to express it, whereby the fathers and sons battle each other physically and/or verbally for mutual acceptance. The solutions to the dilemmas are often catastrophic, involving the human sacrifice of another youth or the patriarch himself in a brutal and final solution which allows no possibility for continuation. Desperate appeals for paternal affection are expressed only when the patriarch is dying (*Cat on a Hot Tin Roof*) or when the son has been irreparably hurt in some related crisis (*Blue Denim* [1959], *Splendor in the Grass*, *East of Eden*) or is in a state of emotional/physical instability (*Fear Strikes Out*, *A Hatful of Rain*). The anver to familial dysfunction is death or escape—Big Daddy (*Cat on a Hot in Roof*), Wil Stamper (*Splendor in the Grass*), and Adam Trask (*East of den*) are dead or dying; Jim Piersall (*Fear Strikes Out*) is in a mental insti- ttion; Johnny (*A Hatful of Rain*) is on his way to a drug clinic.

While the episodic nature of television demands softer confrontations, owever, it also allows a freedom of elasticity and breadth missing from the nematic versions of family life. Character becomes predominant over nar- itive, as viewers invest emotionally in pseudofamilial relationships with ieir televisual counterparts. As Ozzie Nelson noted:

> I think the main reason our show has lasted so long is that our stories have followed the boys through the various phases of growing up. This has enabled us to have a slightly different approach each year but with the same basic characters. . . . Being a family in real life, our relation- ships are honest and the viewers are able to believe what they see and associate our problems and activities with their own lives.[13]

iradoxically, the television programs based their appeal on this continuity the same time as they ignored it. While arguments and dilemmas had to ? erased so that they might not interfere with the following week's epi- ode, other, more positive (or just innocuous) events were neither moni- red nor emphasized from week to week. Thus, there are a startling number ' inconsistencies within the television programs, readily discernible by a gular viewer. For example, the Cleavers and Stones each have dogs for one iisode only; the Stones and the Andersons each own a cat for one episode ily; Donna Stone—who graduated from college after four years, during hich time she had a roommate and wanted to be an actress—is supposed have married Alex at 18 and to have been a nurse (just two years out of igh school) at the time of their marriage, but didn't work after the marriage; ie gave birth to Mary when she was 19; and although Bud Anderson's grades ere such that he was only eligible for Springfield Junior College, he is seen tending the same school as his sister (Springfield College), where he de- :lops a crush on a graduate student. Ambiguous locales and the plethora different guest-stars enlisted to play a single character add to the cross- iisode confusion. In addition, although the programs entered into a tacit ;reement with viewers that the central characters would remain (basically) ichanged, the structural reality of writers-for-hire dictated otherwise, re- ilting in a fluctuating perspective on the central family. Only on *The Adven- res of Ozzie and Harriet*, where Ozzie Nelson was the supervising writer id script consultant for every episode, was there narrative continuity. Pro- icers of the other programs allowed different groups of writers a free hand in drafting story lines. As *Father Knows Best* head writer Roswell Rogers remembers, whenever he watched an episode that was scripted by another writer, the family looked different to him—as if they were some other Anderson family.[14] His colleague Paul West concurs: "Roz Rogers is right that each writer views the stet characters in a series differently. It has been said, and truthfully, I think, that everything we write is autobiographical. Each writer will see the characters in the light of his or her own experience."[15] Dorothy Cooper Foote, another writer for the program, agrees: "Each writer has his or her own interpretation of anything. It's like two artists drawing a picture of a particular tree. Both drawings would certainly be different. But it still would be a tree."[16] As one watches from week to week, part of the pleasure of episodic television is catching those inconsistencies generated by either a laissez-faire continuity staff or the varying perspectives held by the different writers.

Program Length

Another structural consideration concerns time restrictions placed upon the two media. While feature films are hardly free from time limits and their accompanying economic imperatives (the impetus toward shortening a feature just enough to allow for one extra screening a day, for example), there is still an elasticity granted to cinema that is missing from the stop-watch mentality of episodic television. The television texts discussed here, for example, ranged in time from twenty-three minutes and forty seconds up to twenty-six minutes; the writers interviewed tailored their scripts and story ideas to measure. Dorothy Cooper Foote, who also wrote for *My Three Sons,* recalls the differences in writing for film and television:

> One learns quickly in television that time is of the essence. Trying to set up characters—plot—development—etc. is not easy to do in 26 minutes. If an actor takes five minutes to park his car and walk to his front door, there jolly well better be a story point involved. Otherwise the scene will land on the well-known cutting room floor. It's like a horse race. You get off to a running start and don't stop until you reach the finish line. There isn't time to munch the grass on the way.
>
> I must say, coming from motion pictures to television was frustrating for me. It took quite a bit of discipline on my part to realize I couldn't allow myself the luxury of overwriting. But I learned—and in the long run, found I enjoyed bringing a story into focus quickly. . . .
>
> I never attempted to write a story that I knew wouldn't fit into the twenty-six-minute structure.[17]

Because of this limited time frame, television family melodrama suffered a condensation of emotion greater even than that of its cinematic counterpart, a pressure that often dictated both the type of material to be covered and the story's resolution. So crucial was the time factor that episodes often had to be arbitrarily cut in order to fit the allotted time frame or to allow the requisite number of commercials. For example, the first twenty-two minutes of Roswell Rogers' "Betty, Girl Engineer" (1955–1956) sympathize with the Anderson girl's unusual career selection. Abruptly, however, the last minutes undercut Betty's determination as she suddenly acquiesces to traditional values. Rogers says he was never happy with that ending, feeling that the conclusion "did not ring true"; he explained that he was forced to resolve the conflict in the required length of time.[18] *The Adventures of Ozzie and Harriet* regularly tacked on one or two of Ricky's singing numbers if an episode ran too short. Toward the end of the 1950's Ricky's singing career allowed the program a flexibility the other programs did not possess, resulting in story lines with less extreme consequences, plots which revolved around a set piece or montage, or prolonged discussions about a singular event that occurred in the program. The opposite problem complicated *My Three Sons,* in which strict adherence to time restrictions was complicated by Fred MacMurray's frequent unavailability for shooting.[19]

A comparison of film and television's treatment of similar subject matter illustrates, first, how time restrictions determined a different narrative approach, and second, how they fostered television's structural preference for parallel stories. *Giant* is concerned with (among other things) the rift between Bick and his son Jordy over the fact that Jordy prefers medicine to ranching. The length of the film (197 minutes) allows the story to develop over the course of twenty-five years, during which the spectator witnesses both the repeated abortive attempts at father-son communication and their ultimate reconciliation. Although *Father Knows Best* ran for 154 episodes (approximately 3,850 minutes of viewing time), it lacked the protraction of time allowed the cinematic melodrama. Because each episode was self-contained, any conflict between Jim and Bud Anderson had to be resolved in that twenty-five-minute period. The first episode of the second season of *Father Knows Best,* "The Art of Salesmanship," shows a conflict in which Jim wants Bud to follow in his own career footsteps. But the argument is short-lived; Jim is shown the error of his ways rather rapidly. In an attempt to best utilize its limited time, television often contained two parallel story lines with the minor story line providing the solution for the major one; in this episode of *Father Knows Best,* Bud fails to live up to Jim's good selling example, while Jim fails at writing a speech for an upcoming banquet and learns that no person is suited to every occupation. In another episode of *Father Knows Best,* an abandoned teenager sponges off the Andersons at the same time th the Millers have confessed to Jim and Margaret they would like to adopt child. In *The Adventures of Ozzie and Harriet,* David's boy's club needs a civ project to fulfil a merit-badge requirement and Harriet's women's clubhou needs a new coat of paint; in *My Three Sons* Chip's embarrassment with But extroversion coincides with his school's need for a talent-show directo Writer John McGreevey recalls: "The Plot A, Plot B system which I used c that show [*My Three Sons*] and many others worked well. The main pl would feature Robbie, say. Steve might have one important moment in th plot. Plot B would be a Chip story or an Ernie story or an Uncle Charlie [*si* story and Steve would have most of his scenes in that."[20]

Thus, television's time restrictions contributed to a causal schism betwee familial problem and character response. While the film texts develope narrative complication concurrently with character reaction, the televisio programs had the disparate tasks of focusing on less explosive issues whi investing each scene with an extreme character reverberation. The two co tradictory approaches worked to make the television texts even more cha acteristically melodramatic, because the emotional responses were so at ode with the problems which catalyzed them. In addition, the televisual relian on parallel stories to overcome time restrictions heightened the sense melodramatic peripety, the double coincidences resolving two seeming unrelated problems.

The Blueprint Mentality

While some films were created by a fairly consistent group of collaborato (the so-called Sirk, Wald, Kazan, and Minnelli units), the fact that a varie of studios, actors, and technical personnel were used avoided a homog neous look. Indeed, the appeal and success of individual films depended c an exploitation of both familiar and novel features, so that the filmgoir audience would be encouraged to spend time and money on a complete "new" experience which would nevertheless meet their generic expectation Thus, even within the strong generic parameters of family melodrama, the is tremendous variation between a feudal family melodrama such as *Cat c a Hot Tin Roof* and an adolescent remarriage scenario such as *The Courtsh of Eddie's Father.* In an article on the writing of *Rebel without a Cause,* dire tor Nicholas Ray describes the creational differences between film ar television:

There is a traditional writer-director hostility in Hollywood. . . . If writers were able to work more closely with directors from the beginning of a film's conception, the results and the mutual understanding would improve. Most directors when they start making films are handed complete (though often impracticable) scripts a few days before shooting is due to start. Later, they still have to fight to work with a writer of their own choice. (Often the difficulty is that a studio likes to use one of its own contract writers, for obvious economic reasons.)[21]

While it is impossible to identify which collective difficulties and resolutions created which particular narrative twists and turns, it is feasible to posit that the volatile film narratives owed their genesis, in part, to the argumentative atmosphere which created them. Certainly, the distinct writers, producers, and directors were directly responsible for the wide variety of family types and family problems explored within the genre. In television, in contrast, writers worked within a pre-established framework of characters, usually for a program-defining producer, and in conjunction with other writers' interpretations of the central family. This resulted in a sameness, both among episodes of a particular series and between individual series themselves.

The most tightly controlled program was *The Adventures of Ozzie and Harriet,* a program created, written, produced, and directed by Ozzie Nelson. While Nelson did employ other writers (including his younger brother Don), he approved all script outlines prior to their completion, did the final rewrite, and, of course, had ultimate power on the soundstage or in the cutting room. In addition, while most television producers were at least accountable to sponsor or network control, Nelson's power was such that he was virtually immune from the whimsy of network bigwigs. In negotiating for his series, Ozzie Nelson managed to obtain the first "noncancellable ten-year contract in the history of show business."[22] Signed with ABC in August of 1949, after the show's successful five-year radio run, the contract guaranteed a basic salary for ten years, whether the Nelsons worked or not. Nelson recalls: "This proved to be invaluable in that it insulated me from any interference on the part of sponsors, advertising agencies, or network executives."[23] Joe Connelly and Bob Mosher were the producers and co-writers of *Leave it to Beaver.* While they did contract out to other writers occasionally (notably Roland MacLane and Dick Conway), they still contributed all story ideas or were credited as co-writers, fostering a singular perspective over the program's six-year run. *Father Knows Best* was conceived by Eugene Rodney and co-produced by Rodney and the show's star, Robert Young. While Young was a full partner financially and nominally, he had little impact on the program's management. (He did conceive of a flashback fantasy episode called "Stage to Yuma," which depicted the Andersons on a western adventure; it was ill-received and Young never attempted to push his ideas again.) According to all reports, Rodney was the heart and soul of the program, involved in story conception, editing, coordinating the directors, and casting all guest-stars. As director Peter Tewksbury recalls:

> With Gene Rodney, it was very different [from *My Three Sons*]. I learned how to produce films from him. . . . For four years, I met Gene at his modest bungalow in the unfashionable part of Beverly Hills for a simple lunch and for three hours on each Saturday, he would go over every item in the episode we were scheduled to film the next week. He would, in fact, read it aloud for me, stopping to discuss anything that he might consider important. Then I would not see him again until the following Saturday. He did all the casting, all the work with the writers, all the work with the editing, the props, the sets, the set dressing, the wardrobe and the make-up. He was meticulous, thorough, indefatigable and ran his company with a gentle iron hand. Nothing, but nothing, not the smallest detail of each production, escaped his attention or took place without his approval. He also did all the music, the dubbing, and the post-production.[24]

Like *Father Knows Best, The Donna Reed Show* and *My Three Sons* were also co-produced by the central actor. While Donna Reed was not confrontational in her approach, her program nevertheless followed her guidelines specifically: she was involved in all the casting, made copious notes on all scripts and story outlines, made suggestions to directors (particularly regarding the angle from which she should be shot), and had a remarkable sense of story, situation, and dialogue.[25] *My Three Sons'* executive producers Fred MacMurry and Don Fedderson exercised less control, with the result that the tenor of individual episodes was more or less serious depending on the program's producer. The show was produced and directed in its first season by *Father Knows Best* alumnus Peter Tewksbury. These initial episodes are the series' darkest, dealing with the adjustment to a motherless household and the importance of family togetherness. For the second season, Tewksbury was replaced by *Leave It to Beaver* alumnus George Tibbles; the show began to tend toward situation comedy more than domestic family melodrama. In the third and subsequent seasons Ed Hartmann produced, and the episodes—while lighter than the Tewksbury years—again emphasized familial togetherness, morals, and tenderness. (Ed Hartmann's association with the Asian community was the impetus for specific episodes dealing with Japanese and Chinese friends of the Douglas family.) Over its first three years, then, the narrative focus of *My Three Sons* changed significantly with the changes of producer, violating the continuous experience at the heart of television series.

All five programs examined in this study were produced in much the same way: contract or freelance writers pitched story ideas to the controlling producer; episodes were rehearsed and shot according to a predetermined schedule, regardless of the story line. Writers for the series were selected for their familiarity with the domestic comedy format in general and working knowledge of the program in particular. Sometimes a series of representative episodes were screened for a new writer; alternatively, the writer was given character sketches to follow. The result was a consistency of outlook both within and between programs and the occasional duplication of specific narratives. Phil Davis, writer for *My Three Sons, The Donna Reed Show,* and *Father Knows Best,* recalls that often he found himself writing the same sort of story for two different programs.[26] And Robert Fisher, writer for *The Donna Reed Show, Dennis the Menace,* and scores of other series, recalls that he had a single favorite episode—"in which the little kid is accused of stealing when he is innocent"—which he used for *seven* different family programs.[27]

Four of the five television programs followed a similar pattern of shooting—rehearsing on Monday and Tuesday and shooting on Wednesday, Thursday, and Friday. The following week's script would arrive on Friday.[28] This fast-paced schedule, coupled with the enormous quantity of episodes (thirty-nine shows per season was the norm in those days), ensured that story lines would be kept fairly simplistic in terms of both physical action and emotional preparation. James Dean was allowed the luxury of a weekend cry after his rehearsals for *East of Eden,* but the time strictures of 1950's episodic television prevented such release and, most likely, the emotional range of acting which required it. So strenuous was the work schedule that it engendered a new method of television production, "The MacMurray Method," which, in turn, influenced the look of series television still further. Before embarking on *My Three Sons,* Fred MacMurray called Robert Young, who warned MacMurray about the enormous investment of time series television required. Young's description of the long hours prompted MacMurray to shoot his series in a more star-friendly fashion.[29] The MacMurray Method ensured that Fred MacMurray's scenes were all shot in sixty-five days,[30] with the other actors completing the fill-in shots while MacMurray was on vacation. In practice this meant that all of Steve Douglas' scenes with his sons were shot first, followed by MacMurray's close-ups, usually done in an empty soundstage with a scriptgirl reading the other parts. Scenes from eight or nine episodes often were shot in one day, to better use the various sets; because of this, *My Three Sons* began each season with a stockpile of sixteen completed scripts.[31] This method affected other aspects of production as well: the boys had to have their hair cut weekly to maintain a single length and guest-stars had to be filmed in shot–reverse-shot in case contractual obligation (or death!)[32] prevented their return for pickup shots. The Mac-Murray Method had a number of narrative repercussions. To explain the actor's protracted absences, MacMurray's character was often "out of town on business." This narrative necessity encouraged other textual restrictions, such as the need to specify Steve Douglas' type of business (aerospace consultant) and to explore the degree to which Steve's absence caused consternation for his sons. In addition, the traditional screenplay- and teleplay-writing taboo against telephone-booth sequences, which were considered visually tedious and uninteresting, was rescinded and writers were instructed to create numerous scenes in which Steve Douglas talked on the telephone. These sequences were shot all in one day at one sitting, with MacMurray delivering lines for situations and dilemmas from as many as a dozen episodes.[33] Directors, writers, and actors have all noted the complexities of shooting to accommodate the star. Peter Tewksbury recalls that concessions were continually made,

> because MacMurray was available for shooting only 13 weeks of the year and during that time we had to complete his portion of all 39 episodes. We necessarily had to concentrate on the scenes he was in and save all other scenes for later shooting. This in turn required that all 39 scripts be complete in written form before Mr. MacMurray left. In practice this never happened. So, near the end of the 13 weeks we were reduced to writing scenes for Mr. MacMurray without having the least idea of what the story might turn out to be. . . . [H]e was very generous about staying an extra week if needed (probably because he got paid an extra and perhaps large amount). After he left, we then decided what story line might accommodate the scenes that had already been shot. Lots of shows with Mr. MacMurray on the telephone, calling in from out of town, etc.[;] shows in which he had little or nothing to do with the plot. . . . Because of the weird MacMurray deal, it was the hardest job in town to bring off.[34]

Writer John McGreevey notes:

> The MacMurray Method conditioned the writing of the show from day one. The producers agreed on the number of shows in which he would be "the star." In the rest of the shows, he had carefully placed scenes so that he could register strongly without actually being too involved in the story.[35]

Program temporality and production procedures thus influenced family melodrama in a number of profound ways. Narratives were constructed by writers adhering to predetermined conflicts and characters, and restricted to interior shooting. While television's family dilemmas were thus more immediately resolvable than those in film, the characters themselves were more resistant to growth or change because series' continuity depended on a perpetual pattern of error and correction. Television families did not mirror or act upon a fictional society, they *were* society, hermetic units bound by the studio-restricted space and an assembly-line approach to production. This is in stark contrast to film, which—although constrained by the realities of production costs, time standards (ninety minutes at minimum), and the strictures of genre expectations—practiced a greater freedom of expression and diversity in the representation of American family life. In film, the American family, at the mercy of larger institutions and the environment, explores social dilemmas, and finds their resolution in mortality or marriage.

Site of Reception

The difference between watching a family melodrama in a crowded public place and watching the same genre within the privacy of one's living room, alone or in the presence of family members only, had a serious impact on familial representation. John Ellis notes that "the experience of watching a film in an empty cinema is seriously disturbing. The presence of the crowd in the cinema is vital to the operation of the regime of cinematic representation. It enables a voyeuristic activity to take place that is necessary to produce the individual spectator as a point of intelligibility of the film."[36] In contrast, David Nelson recalls that one of the main reasons television family dramas trod so lightly was that they were intruders into the home:

> The big difference was that most television producers, or networks I guess, really seemed to sense a feeling of responsibility because their entertainment was going directly into the home. It was almost as if it were unsolicited, so they felt responsible for what was presented in

someone's home. Features felt, well, "if you don't want to see the picture, you don't get your wallet out and pay for a ticket" if it seems a little off-color, or whatever. So they had a lot more latitude and could be a little more realistic, or dramatic.[37]

Producers, as well as various pressure groups and the industry press, felt that television was a guest in the home; like a guest, it was expected to behave politely and inoffensively. A key point of difference between the families depicted in cinema and television relates to the treatment of controversial material. While much of television's hesitancy in exploiting sensational issues was catalyzed by sponsorship or regulatory concerns, these concerns seemed governed as well by the reality that television came, uninvited, into a person's home.

With its mass-viewing situation outside the home, film encouraged a different approach. First, because it was necessary to woo people out of the comforts of their home, filmic narratives were designed to encourage group catharsis. The reliance upon spectacle (car races, dances, image-laden love scenes) might have been inspired by the fact that a captive audience would actively participate in the filmic activities (urge the hero on, snap their fingers, neck in the back row). The darkness that enveloped the film spectator provided an anonymity denied the television viewer, thereby allowing the presentation of potentially embarrassing material. The at-home setting of television viewing generated a negative impetus for purity; no adolescent wanted to watch a love scene in the light-filled living room with Mom and Dad. In addition, the parallel domestic setting of the television medium and its viewing experience worked to emphasize the family melodrama's intimacy. Attention to decor and narrative minutiae was emphasized because the at-home viewing structure allowed the audience to interact more dynamically with the characters—to comment on their crises, to discuss their various options. Still, although television viewers were closer to both the text and fellow audience members, they were also perpetually distracted by commercials, ringing telephones and doorbells, household responsibilities, and the needs of children, necessitating redundancy, as characters discussed the same issues over and over. This viewing dynamic encouraged television's melodramas to focus on a limited number of characters and simple story lines which were emphasized by constant verbal discussion. Film's implicit contract with filmgoers, in contrast, necessitated a plot of sufficient complication to ensure that they would sit willingly for two hours. The filmic families are thus often extended families, with problems that befall multiple generations and embroil the community at large in decades-long struggles.

The Sponsored Context

Television family melodramas also differed from their filmic counterparts because of the presence of the sponsor. The advertising context of the television programs subjected them to a continual interruption by commercials as well as an intrusive participation by sponsors and their advertising agencies. It is important to note here that I am not discussing the actual censorship role the sponsor played in creating a sanitized familial enclave,[38] but rather the overall effect the fact of commercial broadcasting had on the texts themselves, and the actual capitulation by writers to the interrupted status of broadcast teleplays.

In the late 1950's and early 1960's sponsor participation in programming was not limited to commercial interruption during a telecast. Sponsors were often the co-creators, producers, or financial backers of specific programs, and thus had enormous influence on episodic series. (See Table 2.) Because sponsors required that commercials be surrounded by an environment appropriate for their message, they encouraged a blandness among programming. This ensured, first, that a mass audience would not be offended, and second, that a home audience would not be so excited by a program's impact as to ignore the commercial messages. Hubbell Robinson, former president of CBS, is quoted as saying: "Producers are there to service sponsors. They give them what they want. They give them what they think they can sell. One of the reasons we have so many formula shows today is that they're salable. If sponsors encourage originality, that's what they'll get. If they encourage formula, that's what they'll get."[39] Bob Shanks, ABC vice-president for programming, supports the idea that television programming ought to remain relatively innocuous, in light of the fact that a provoked spectator is an inattentive commercial viewer.

> Program makers are supposed to devise and produce shows that will attract mass audiences without unduly offending these audiences or too deeply moving them emotionally. Such ruffling, it is thought, will interfere with their ability to receive, recall, and respond to the commercial message. This programming reality is the unwritten, unspoken *gemeinschaft* of all professional members of the television fraternity.[40]

In addition, sponsors were very often singularly responsible for the genesis of a program idea, the program's position in the television schedule, and its consequent success or failure. Before the early 1960's broadcast television was structured so that advertisers (or their agencies) purchased blocks of time from the networks (a "time franchise") and then filled that time with a

Table 2   Sponsors and Agencies

Year	Sponsor	Advertising Agency
Father Knows Best		
1954–1955	Raleigh Cigarettes	Young and Rubicam
1955–1960	Scott Paper & Lipton Tea	J. Walter Thompson
The Donna Reed Show		
1958–1963	Campbell's Soup, Nabisco, Johnson & Johnson	Batten, Barton, Durstine & Osborn
Leave It to Beaver[a]		
1957–1959	Remington Rand	Doyle Dane Bernbach
1958–1959	Polaroid	Doyle Dane Bernbach
1959–1963	Ralston Purina	Gardner Advertising
1959–1963	Bristol-Myers	Doyle Dane Bernbach
The Adventures of Ozzie and Harriet		
1952–1956	Hotpoint and Listerine	J. Walter Thompson
1956–1966	Kodak, sole sponsor for a while, was later joined by Coke and Aunt Jemimah	J. Walter Thompson
1963–1964	American Dairy Association	J. Walter Thompson
My Three Sons		
1960–1963	Chevrolet	Campbell-Ewald
1963–1965	Chevrolet and Pontiac	Campbell-Ewald
(and beyond)	Quaker Oats	J. Walter Thompson
	Hunts	Young and Rubicam

[a] Although *Leave It to Beaver* had no "agency of record," the agency for three of the four sponsors was Doyle Dane Bernbach.

combination of entertainment and commercial programming. Writing in 1956, Lawrence Laurent noted:

> In some ways, commercial sponsorship is directly responsible for the kinds of programs which are seen on television. If the sponsor is trying to win 100 percent acceptance of his product, he is likely to prefer a program which will appeal to 100 percent of the audience. This fact accounts, in large part, for the plethora of "family situation comedies" which fill the TV schedules. The idea is to have a TV family which closely approximates the family of the viewer. Having identified itself

with the television family, the viewing family is similarly expected to identify itself with the sponsor of the TV family.[41]

The broadcasting sagas of the domestic comedies analyzed here offer ample proof for Erik Barnouw's assertion that "sponsors were helping create a dramaturgy reflecting the demographics of the supermarket."[42] For example, it was Harry Ackerman, then an advertising liaison with J. Walter Thompson, who first approached Ozzie Nelson about a program. Don Fedderson recalls that *My Three Sons* was conceptualized with mass sponsorship in mind, and that he was approached by Chevrolet for a show that was "representative of America." Mistakes by the sponsor and confidence in the program were singularly responsible for the change in network schedule for *Father Knows Best*. In 1954, Young and Rubicam managed a time franchise—Sunday at 10:00 p.m.—for Lorillard, manufacturers of Kent cigarettes. Young and Rubicam bought *Father Knows Best* from Columbia's Screen Gems for Kent, but the late time slot proved inimical; the program faltered in the ratings and was canceled by Young and Rubicam.[43] At the same time, sales representatives at NBC had been wooing the Scott Paper account. Thomas McCabe, president of Scott, finally agreed to buy a half-hour time-slot, but worried network executives by selecting *Father Knows Best* (a canceled program from another network) for his sponsored program. McCabe's personal affection for the program, coupled with an extensive letter-writing campaign from viewers irate over the show's cancellation, revived *Father Knows Best,* placing it at 8:30 p.m., where it aired successfully on NBC for the next three years. A benevolent sponsor also rescued the initially unsuccessful *Donna Reed Show* from oblivion; the president of Campbell's Soup declared he didn't care about the program's poor ratings; *he* liked it, and was willing to support its eventually very successful eight-year run.

If the sponsors could determine the very life of a program, they also influenced the sort of life its characters might lead. Writers and producers were acutely aware of the prescribed commercial breaks, and structured their story lines accordingly, so that narratives were created in segments, each with its own artificial crisis and resolution designed around the systematic advertising interruptions. This phenomenon was of such disturbing influence that it provoked critic Lawrence Laurent to write in 1956:

> In the theater, the writer can pick the time which best suits the drama and here he inserts an intermission. The television writer must arrange his characters, conflict, and plot to accommodate the commercial schedule. All creative writers work under limitations imposed by the creative

form itself, but one must doubt that any writer has quite so many handicaps as the television writer.[44]

An interesting example of this is illustrated by the problems encountered when *Father Knows Best* changed its structural format in its second season, adding an introductory scene which preceded the opening credits.[45] When Eugene Rodney wanted to rerun the 1954 Christmas and Thanksgiving programs during the 1955 season, he was presented with a problem because the first year's program lacked the pre-credit teaser sequence.[46] An 18 July 1955 letter from Fred Brisken (Screen Gems executive production assistant) to Ralph Cohn (Screen Gems advertising liaison) reads in part:

> Please be advised that under this year's format, we have an opening one and a half minute scene which does not exist on last year's two programs, and as far as we can see, it would be impossible to break into those programs at that time to adhere to this year's format. Therefore, to accommodate the first commercial we are asking you to suggest (and have approved from the sponsor) inserting the first commercial immediately after the opening bill board rather than after the one and one half minute scene because of the fact that it does not now exist.[47]

In the end, no fewer than five letters were exchanged between the program producer, the Screen Gems production chief, the Screen Gems advertising liaison, and the advertising agency to accommodate a mere twenty-second time difference.

In addition to narrative restrictions created by interruptions, the sponsor directly determined the length of the program itself, which, in turn, determined the types of story matter considered. The original script for the 1954 *Father Knows Best* Christmas program was initially considered too long. Rather than cut into the story's logical flow, Eugene Rodney requested that Kent omit some of its advertisements. He was immediately rebuked by the advertising liaison:

> Dear Gene:
> This letter is a confirmation of our phone call this morning. I have been advised by New York via teletype that due to our requests the whole problem of cutting a minute from the Christmas commercials was again reviewed and has been thoroughly discussed. All agency personnel involved are firmly opposed to cutting the commercials. I have also been asked to pass on to you the fact that Ralph Cohn also called New York and made a similar request.[48]

Writer Roswell Rogers ultimately revised the episode.[49]

Finally, the influence of sponsors was also evident in the way in which the sponsored context supported the consumerist ideology with television's family melodrama narrative. These were programs which were embedded with consumer items, the notion of purchase, and the quality of American commodities. CBS president Frank Stanton described the importance of a fictional program upholding the very real ideology of American capitalism:

> Since we are advertiser-supported we must take into account the general objectives and general desires of advertising as a whole. An advertiser has very specific practical objectives in mind. . . . So . . . we broadcasters must approach this . . . with a realization that we have no monopoly on wisdom or judgement in programming. . . . [I]t seems perfectly obvious that advertisers cannot and should not be forced into programs incompatible with their objectives.[50]

While feature-film melodrama focused upon families from all economic brackets (though all possessed a "middle-class mentality"), television centered the domestic comedies of the late 1950's explicitly in the suburban middle class. Moreover, stories about status, consumerism, economic opportunity, and the advantages of industrial capitalism made up nearly one-third of the episodes. The moral lesson always upheld the valuation of hard work, praised American opportunity and self-reliance, and preached the importance of moderation and pragmatism. The matter-of-fact use and accumulation of consumer items in conjunction with the implication that such luxuries are not extravagant but the norm served as a reiteration of the purchasing practices necessary to ensure understated comfort. Commercial-supported television with its consumerist ideology, together with the intrusive interruption of advertisements and length restrictions imposed by uncompromising sponsors, dictated family narratives which not only did not threaten the hegemonic position of postwar industrial capitalism, but continually underscored capitalistic superiority in stories designed specifically to promote sensible consumerism.

The Laugh Track

Laugh tracks originated as a means of boosting the response on programs which were filmed in front of studio audiences. Writer-producer Paul West recalls:

> The laugh-track has always been a bone of contention. It came to be used when a young engineer came up with a black box which produced

chuckles, giggles, and guffaws on command. The engineer was Charlie Douglas and his device was first used to "sweeten" natural audience response to comedy shows. Eventually, of course, the natural audience disappeared. Producers insist that viewers want to feel they are part of a live audience. [51]

The producers of all the television programs analyzed here felt some ambivalence about laugh tracks, justifying their placement by their parallel to "real" laughter. Eugene Rodney was by all accounts opposed to the inclusion of a laugh track. Robert Young recalls: "Rodney always wanted to do it without a laugh track. He stood over the laugh track man and hit him if the laugh was too loud. He was always unhappy about it." [52] In a memo dated 19 January 1954, Rodney instructs postproduction coordinator Joe Henrie to listen to the radio records from *Father Knows Best* in order to acquaint himself with the patterns of laughs:

> Herewith attached is the recording of the radio show 'BUD TAKES UP THE DANCE.' As explained to you, this will probably give you the best idea of the number and volume of laughs in the average show. After you and Dick have listened to these we could then have another short meeting to discuss laugh track policy further. [53]

In another memo to Henrie dated 21 January 1954, Rodney shows his concern that the laughs be in the appropriate spots and of the appropriate volume:

> Herewith attached is the script marked for laughs. You will note that I have extended a red line ending in a circle with our prearranged code numbers for the kind of laughs.
>
> I have determined the extent and places of laughs on three bases: (1) by referral to the original radio transcription, (2) to the laughs we received in the projection room from the people watching the dailies and first cut, and (3) my own judgment. I might say that as to number (3), I used very little of it. I have tried also to remember how these laughs will be placed in the cut scenes and doubtlessly some of them will be out of sync, but we can determine that when you cut the track. Incidentally, only for you would I stay up to 1:00 yesterday morning (and at my age) to do this. [54]

Even in a program where the producer seemed unconcerned about the presence of canned laughter, he was adamant about its verisimilitude. Ozzie Nelson rented theaters and screened two or three back-to-back episodes of *The Adventures of Ozzie and Harriet* for audiences, marking the position and volume of laughter, and then duplicating it with artificial chuckles during post-production. Tony Owen, titular producer of *The Donna Reed Show,* sat next to the laugh-track operator and urged "more laughter, louder" etc. And an early article about *Leave It to Beaver* notes:

> Beaver is one of those shows with a now-banned-at-CBS laugh track. But Connelly sees no reason for eliminating their methods of being 'unobtrusive' with laughter as gentle as Beaver's jokes. He explains: "We run each show to an audience of 18 people and then put in our laugh track to their cues. We don't believe in pumping laughter into the show. We put our laughs only where our audience cues them and we keep them at a low level."[55]

The laugh track was perhaps the most influential technological factor affecting television's family melodrama, protecting the humorous guise these serious programs wore. The most readily identifiable technical difference between the film and television texts, its ubiquity clearly steered the television programs toward different narrative conventions and resolutions from those of their filmic counterparts. Consider the generic predisposition toward maternal loss in the two media. In film, maternal loss provides a focal point of conflict between the fathers and sons in their long journey toward emotional reconciliation. In *East of Eden* Cal lambasts Adam for driving Kate away; in *Home From the Hill* (1960), *Cat on a Hot Tin Roof,* and *The Long Hot Summer* (1958) sons berate fathers for their philandering. Some films, usually those with a young protagonist, involve the child's attempt to adjust to the loss of his mother and his attempts at urging the father either to maintain the primacy of the father-son coupling (*Man on Fire*) or to remarry and replace the mother (*The Courtship of Eddie's Father*). But for television, no such castigation or commiseration is available. The theme of parent as suitor was particularly popular on television, and variations abounded during the 1960's and early 1970's (*Family Affair, Bachelor Father, The Courtship of Eddie's Father,* and *The Farmer's Daughter*). But while the theatrical versions dealt quite explicitly with the child's grief over the missing parent, emotional angst was glaringly absent from the television programs, which consistently trivialized the child's grief and repressed the father's sense of loss. The film *The Courtship of Eddie's Father* has a scene in which the father and son embrace and weep over the loss of the mother together, reassuring one another that they will always be honest about their emotions. In contrast, the television version of maternal loss negates the grief via laughter and mockery. In "Mother Bub" (*My Three Sons,* 1960–1961) young Chip breaks down over the loss of his mother. Steve comforts his son by showing him a series of old photos of his grandfather Bub[56] in a number of maternal roles—giving Chip his first birthday cake, taking him to school, and so forth, so that the boy will realize his good fortune in having a grandfather as his primary caregiver. The pictures are genuinely sentimental, as are the boy's comments about them, but underneath the dialogue we hear the perpetual sound of chuckles and titters, effectively defusing the melodramatic moment. Even those television scripts which focused on explicitly tragic material were structurally affected by an irreverent and irrelevant laugh track. Thus stories dealing with homeless youths or runaways, divorce, adolescent insecurity and doubt, and neglectful or abusive fathers—all of which were explored in a significant number of the television episodes—come across as spoof or mockery, because the viewer was continually reminded to receive these themes *as humor*. Television's laugh track thus serves as a persuasive signifier designed to dissuade the spectator from authentic feelings of grief or misery, even when the characters are experiencing such feelings, inviting the viewer to assume a cynical stance of superiority and scorn or frivolity and flippancy.

The format of the film and television texts—time constraints, the sponsored or unsponsored context, and the presence or absence of a laugh track—influenced film and television familial representations. The television families' hyperbolic responses to relatively insignificant problems were necessitated by the fact that these dilemmas had to be resolved within twenty-six minutes but have no lasting impact on family members' psyches. Perceptions of familial anxiety were further weakened by the repetitive story lines exchanged by writers' groups and by an inappropriate use of a laugh track. Sponsor participation ensured that the television families were middle-class materialists, who defined themselves and their world by their homes, cars, and consumer items. Film, unhampered by sponsors or laugh tracks, indulged its narratives with large-scale and sensationalized dilemmas as both cause for familial crises and opportunity for familial reinforcement. Film families could experience larger problems than those of television, with more definitive resolutions and greater involvement with society at large.

SECTION TWO
Mode of Technology

At the beginning of the commercial television era the motion picture and television industries went to great lengths to establish themselves as technically distinct from one another. Douglas Gomery and Dennis Dombkowski, among others, have written extensively about the mechanical approaches that the two industries used to accomplish this.[57] The technological differences between television and film—small screen versus large, black and white versus color—had a major effect on depictions of the family and family life. First, the small screen's low resolution restricted the production (or broadcast) of television programs which emphasized action, grandeur, or extensive exterior locales. (Indeed, as William Boddy has noted, one of the reasons that feature films were initially withheld from television broadcast—years after their first-run theatrical release—was that the structure of the medium, in terms of both its time and its space restrictions, would ruin the drama.)[58] Limited to a nineteen-inch frame, television emphasized the intimate, a type of programming most readily realized in the small-scale family melodramas. As early as 1956 Lawrence Laurent credited the proliferation of the family melodrama on television to its suitability for the small screen.[59] Horace Newcomb writes:

> The smallness of the television screen has always been its most noticeable physical feature. . . . Such smallness suits television for intimacy; its presence brings people into the viewer's home to act out dramas. . . . Television is at its best when it offers us faces, reactions, explorations of emotions registered by human beings. The importance is not placed on action, though that is certainly vital as stimulus. Rather it is on the reaction to the action, to the human response.[60]

The problems of the Anderson, Nelson, Cleaver, Stone, and Douglas families rarely occur outside the home; the arenas for problem exposition and solving are limited to the living rooms, kitchens, porches, schoolrooms, and offices of the central characters. Heart-to-heart talks on the open highway or during a trip to the amusement park were prohibited by scale. Problems related to action (such as camping-trip catastrophes or school athletic events) were rarely depicted, and most often were rendered in the form of post- or pre-problem discussions which could take place in the usual confines of the home. One program that attempted to circumvent its interior restrictions was *The Adventures of Ozzie and Harriet* which, in its later years, began to favor outdoor shoots. It is difficult to say, however, whether this was as much a function of narrative growth as it was one of sponsorship demands. According to Ozzie Nelson, for instance,

> The early spring of 1958 found us shooting almost as many shows outdoor as we did on the set, with Griffith Park being our favorite location spot. . . .
>   The outdoors shows served several purposes. They relieved the boredom of continually shooting in the studio, they gave us a great deal of

variety in our programming, and of course they made the Eastman Ko-
dak people very happy, since we always had our cameras with us.[61]

Ozzie Nelson prided himself on his location shooting, but even in the exterior environment each scene—after a single master shot—was composed of
nothing but close-ups and medium close-ups. This was in vivid contrast to
film's tendency to "open up" family problems. While film melodramas' central narrative concerns remained familial, the families interacted with society
at large; juvenile delinquency, corrupt schools, drugs, and abortion were
family problems discussed within the home, but visually depicted in a variety of locations.

Television's limited scale influenced not only the types of family problem
it tackled but the rendering of family life itself. The small screen emphasized
the insulation and claustrophobia characteristic of the already tight-knit
world of family melodrama. Television families seem even more isolated and
self-enclosed than their filmic counterparts, entrapped in a sameness of decor and a tightness of lens work week after week. This sense of confinement
is, again, in direct contrast to film families, whose crises were often depicted
in the most expansive of landscapes. When Bick and Leslie argued in *Giant,*
they did so on the open range of Reatta; Deanie and Bud found romantic
splendor in the open grasses off the reservoir, at a high-school dance, and
on the dusty farmlands of Kansas; Eddie and his father interacted as they
walked along a carnival midway or through a campground forest. This frame
configuration has serious ideological implications: families in films are at the
mercy of the great outdoors, their narrow personal visions at odds with the
distractions of nature, their hermetic psychological world contrasting with
the vastness of the physical world. Television families, on the other hand,
created and contained themselves in a microcosm relevant to their problems.
Problems of the home were discussed in the home; problems of the family
were discussed in an exclusively nuclear setting. Film families thus seem
victims of society and its pressures, while television families seem to create
their problems themselves. This might account for film's narrative tendency
toward social problems such as street crime and overcrowding, as well as
television's narrative inclination toward problems circumscribed by school
and the family.

Films reinforced and exaggerated their perceptual vastness through a preoccupation with the wide-screen. The CinemaScope process, invented in
France and purchased by 20th Century–Fox, was utilized in every Fox feature after 1954, and other studios employed various wide-screen processes
with increasing frequency.[62] This wide frame exaggerated the characters' im-

potency or helplessness in the face of unresolvable issues. Characters who were at odds with one another faced off across a vast open space; in *East of Eden,* Cal Trask is dwarfed by the bean field in which he lies, as if he were a product of his own farming. Even a film such as *A Hatful of Rain,* which takes place in the supposedly claustrophobic environment of a middle-class apartment, shows a seemingly endless vista, its drug-addict protagonist stretched and distorted by the wide angle process; Cecilia and Johnny are not only separated by the paradoxical width of their cloistered home, but the home itself offers the spectator a shared vision of illusion and bizarre perspective.

Sound provides another technological factor influencing the representation of family life. Rick Altman argues that television's obsession with sound tracks and its constant use of theme music to signal alterations in mood may be accounted for by its need to cue an inattentive viewer:

> [T]here is a growing body of data suggesting that intermittent attention is in fact the dominant mode of television viewing. . . .
>
> The sound track thus begins to take on an active role. In order to keep those sets operating while all viewers are either out of the room or paying little attention, the sound track must perform some quite specific functions. . . .
>
> There must be a sense that *anything really important* will be cued by the sound track. . . .
>
> The sound itself must provide desired information, events, or emotions from time to time during the flow.[63]

This obsession with the aural might account for television's emphasis on the paternal lecture as solution, a quick speech by Dad at the end of the program neatly resolving all conflicts and crises. This lecture forms the conclusion for each episode, underlined by a poignant variation on the program's musical theme and followed by a tag-line joke and a few seconds of the laugh track. Typically, each program had various "incidental" musical themes, used to indicate stasis, trouble, secrecy, the passage of time, or humor. The music of television's family melodramas performs thematic and structural duty in that it metaphorically reinforces the narrative event (sad music for a sad occasion) at the same time as it summons back a viewer's wayward attention by signaling a plot complication or resolution. It is quite possible that the moral lesson that ends the story occurs partly so that the theme music might be replayed, thereby retrieving an inattentive viewer; at the same time, the moral itself demands the musical theme for narrative emphasis. In films, sound operates more to enhance the image than to replace it; the captive movie audience attends simultaneously to visual and aural cues. This allows for both a subtlety of representation and an ambiguity regarding resolution, as an image and its accompanying music may support or undercut each other. The clarity of film sound also allows actors the luxury of vocal interpretation. The inarticulate mumblings of Cal Trask, Berry Berry, or Alfred Eaton would have been incomprehensible in the 1950's on television because of its technological inadequacies, but film's higher sound fidelity and clearer picture made these expressions of deep emotion readily understandable.[64]

The representation of the family was further influenced by the types of film stock preferred by the two different media: for the most part, feature films were produced in color, while their television counterparts were restricted to black and white.[65] It was only when dealing with "serious" social problems that the feature films favored a monochromatic outlook; at that time, the film industry considered black and white to be the more "serious" hue. Thus, subjects such as drugs (*A Hatful of Rain*), mental illness (*All Fall Down, Fear Strikes Out, The Three Faces of Eve*), abortion (*Blue Denim, Love with the Proper Stranger* [1963]), and alcoholism (*The Days of Wine and Roses, The Bottom of the Bottle* [1956]) were all filmed in black and white. The narrative or ideological implications of monochromatic versus polychromatic photography reside most crucially in the realm of the "reality effect." Films which tended toward sensationalized sex or violence gravitated toward the brilliant and exaggerated hues of vibrant Technicolor; films self-described as socially-conscious (evidenced by their marketing strategies, various reviews, and audience reception) aspired to an atmosphere of sobriety created and enhanced by the choice of black-and-white photography.

If this trained association can be assumed to be transinstitutional, television's structural reliance upon black-and-white photography (regardless of its narrative intentions or the financial costs that determined the choice) gained its programs the status of "realistic" representation. As with program length, this structural component provides a tension between form and content. While television's familial crises were less severe than those of film, the characters' hyperbolic reactions to such events, coupled with the black-and-white photography, rendered them more "serious" and imbued them with a sense of the pain of everyday activities.[66]

A final area of technological distinction stems from each medium's narrative preference for illusion or reality. As John Ellis has written,

> The cinematic regime of visual and aural representation is spectacular in its effects, because its effects are sure to be noticed. . . . It produces ambiguity in the image, more than one area of attention. . . .

> This is particularly marked in relation to TV, where the image has a very different quality . . . TV appears to be live; the film appears to be recorded.[67]

Film's attention to the spectacular is predicated in part on the larger-than-life quality of its image and the publicity attending any given film. Even in those films purportedly dealing with "real" problems, the problems selected were not those of the everyday, but those embedded in a world of sensationalism. The film industry's routine promotional materials advertised sensationalistic appeal, star quality, and directorial credentials, all of which contributed to the idea that the families on film were constructed representations—illusions carefully created by talented artists. Film promoted a sense of distance: because there were so many film actors, many of whom portrayed a number of characters, and because (with the exception of sequels) these characters appeared only once, conflation of character and star was unlikely. But television programs and stars seemed more "everyday," as John Ellis notes, lacking what he calls a "photographic effect."

> Centrally lacking in television is the photographic effect. . . . The television performer appears in subsidiary forms of circulation (newspapers, magazines) mostly during the time that the series of performances is being broadcast. The result is a drastic reduction in the distance between the circulated image and the performance.[68]

Television's marketing and production stance supports Ellis' argument. These television programs based both their appeal and the design of their narratives on their supposed "realism." This preoccupation revealed itself in a number of promotional strategies designed to underscore the verisimilitude of the television families. First, the popular press was encouraged to conflate the real-life actors and their fiction families. Barbara Billingsley (*Leave It to Beaver*) was the focus of a November *Western Family* magazine feature on "The Western Family Kitchen of the Year," an exhibit at Farmers' market in Los Angeles, in 1958. The following year, Shelley Fabares and Elinor Donahue (of *The Donna Reed Show* and *Father Knows Best*, respectively) modeled "co-ed" collectables although neither ever attended a regular public school. Mother's Day and Father's Day issues of *TV Guide* featured cover stories on Donna Reed, Jane Wyatt and Robert Young (*Father Knows Best*), Fred MacMurray (*My Three Sons*), and the Nelsons. "Private Life of a Perfect Papa," an article in the *Saturday Evening Post*, noted that *Father Knows Best* writers Roswell Rogers and Paul West went home to their children for story ideas.[69]

7. Parallels between Barbara Billingsley's "real life" sons and her television sons (Tony Dow and Jerry Mathers, pictured) were continually emphasized in 1950's publicity campaigns for *Leave It to Beaver*. (Copyright Universal.)

Actresses by profession, Jane Wyatt and Barbara Billingsley were featured in *TV Guide* housewife fashion spreads.[70] *TV Guide* quoted Jane Wyatt as bragging, "I'm gratified that I was hired for the part on the basis of the necessary acting background plus the private qualifications." The article continued: "Among the latter, are her experiences as a wife and mother."[71] The magazine gushed over Barbara Billingsley's maternal credentials as "An Expert on the Male":

> Barbara Lillian Combes Billingsley Kellino Mortensen, who as plain Barbara Billingsley has been playing the mother of two sons on ABC's *Leave It to Beaver*, . . . has been herself the mother of 2 sons, Drew, 18 and Brud, 16. "At Beaver's age in the series," she says, "both of them were very much like Beaver." "Barbara," says co producer Joseph Connelly, "gives us only one problem. In scenes where she's mad at the boys, she's always coming to us with the script and objecting. 'I don't see why June is so mad over what Beaver's done. I certainly wouldn't be.' As a result," Connelly says, "many of Beaver's crimes have been rewritten into something really heinous like lying about them, in order to give his mother a strong motive for blowing her lady-like stack."[72]

The programs also received numerous awards from civic and business organizations for their contributions toward the positive images of family life
and the professions and for an adherence to a "wholesome American life-
style." *The Donna Reed Show* won an award from the American Medical Association; *Leave It to Beaver* received accolades from the Automobile Association of America for an episode dealing with getting a driver's license; and
Sylvania presented awards to both *Father Knows Best* and *My Three Sons* for
positive portrayals of family life. Indeed, *Father Knows Best* received at least
eight national awards in its first three years for "wholesome portrayal" of the
family.[73] Robert Young made over twenty-two personal appearances during
1958, collecting prizes such as the Mt. Sinai Father of the Year Award and the
Safety Council Award.

TV Guide constantly emphasized the programs' connections with the
stars' actual families. In an article on Robert Young, for instance, it proclaimed: "Thoroughly indoctrinated with 'family spirit' at home, [Young]
constantly strives to instill that quality in *Father Knows Best*," and added that
the impetus for the program was Young's inspiration from real-life daughter
Kathy.[74] Articles occasionally mention the difficulties actors experienced in
trying to measure up to their "perfect" characters: "When grilled by his
daughter for not knowing all the answers, 'Jim Anderson,' Young replied, not
without a trace of quiet bitterness, 'has two writers. Bob Young doesn't have
any.' "[75] An article on *The Donna Reed Show*, speaking of Reed and her producer husband Tony Owen, notes: "The Owens are a double standard of
behavior, drawing a line between life as it really is and life as it is acceptable
on the TV screen. They are dead serious about keeping their viewers on the
straight-and-narrow."[76]

Such comments served to underscore the "perfection" of the television
family—a perfection so palpable as to cause envy among even its sophisticated stars. Further exploitation of the factual-fanciful connection was encouraged by the blood relations populating the programs. Paul and Patty
Petersen of *The Donna Reed Show* enjoyed enormous publicity about their
true sibling rivalries and affections, and how they crept into the fictional
characters they portrayed;[77] Stanley and Barry Livingston, who began their
careers as friends on both *The Adventures of Ozzie and Harriet* and *My Three
Sons*, eventually portrayed the real-life brothers they were. *TV Guide* critic
Cleveland Amory wrote about the Nelsons: "The fact is, it is not only a
wholesome show for the whole family, it *is* the whole family."[78] The Nelsons
are pictured on the cover of the 24 December 1954 cover of *TV Guide* because
they are "everything a family should be [and] represent all that is fine about
family life." *TV Guide* ran a number of other articles such as "The Youngest

Comic" and "Like Ozzie, Like Son," also about the real-life parallels with the Nelson family.

In another marketing variation on the theme of family, the popular press underscored the familial nature of the acting company itself, citing the fatherly concern Robert Young had for Lauren Chapin, or how Shelley Fabares and Elinor Donahue looked up to Donna Reed and Jane Wyatt, respectively. Only decades later did actors' recollections reveal these warm claims to have been somewhat exaggerated for publicity purposes.[79]

To further encourage audiences' connection between the shows and reality, the writers and producers often credited factual occurrences as the impetus behind various episode ideas. This not only underscored the supposed verisimilitude of the shows' representations of family life, it gave producers an excuse to placate critics who found the story lines mundane. For example, Ozzie Nelson justified his program's supposed "blandness" by citing its adherence to reality: "We continued to use our personal experiences as the basis for many of [the episodes]."[80] Jane Wyatt claimed, in a 1950's article, "Every bit of mischief, every trial and triumph we've portrayed, has been determined by what [the children] were actually going through in real life." Discussing his work as a writer for *The Donna Reed Show,* Nate Monaster recalls that he got ideas for the show from his own family, especially for "female stuff." "The Punishment," he recalled, in which Donna struggles with her role as disciplinarian, came right out of Monaster's marriage.[81] In this way, the "reality-effect" of television allowed the producers of family melodrama to defend all its perceived shortcomings with the explanation that they were "being realistic." Or if not exactly realistic, the families on television were at least idealized versions of what they wished family life to be.

Feature-film and television melodrama thus differed significantly in the scope of the issues they tackled. One motivation for this might have arisen from the two industries' approach to verisimilitude. With its extensive repertoire of visual and aural technological tools, feature film favored an expansive approach to the depiction of family life, an exaggeration of the everyday through Technicolor, wide-screen presentation, and high-fidelity sound. Television, bound by the restrictions of a small screen, poor sound and image quality, and black-and-white photography, was limited to more intimate depictions. Because of the conventional association of black-and-white photography with serious issues, audiences expected the television series to present less fanciful and flamboyant programs; television producers sought to exploit this limitation as an asset. Black and white meant true-to-life families, like the actors who played the characters, like the characters' relationships with one another, and like the stories upon which the episodes were based.

While there were numerous elements responsible for the distinctions between feature-film family melodrama and the genre on television, structural differences had a major effect. The feature-film family melodrama was dependent upon collective and uninterrupted viewing of a lengthy yet closed text, presented on a large and often wide screen. This resulted in cinematic families which were explosive, alienated from one another as well as their environment, and ripped apart by large issues demanding final solutions. Problems in feature film tended more toward social exposés because films were able to go on location and depict urban unrest, racial strife, or the brutality of big business. But family members were isolated from one another across vast CinemaScope plains or visually distorted apartments. Even when eventually reconciled, the hug of unification was undermined by a wide-screen close-up of grotesquely stretched faces and bodies. The environment plays a role in the feature-film melodrama, a metaphor for the societal pressures weighing upon family life and threatening to crush it with ceaseless expansion, conformity, or violence. Larger-than-life issues were favored to entice viewers into a darkened theater, which in turn encouraged a more substantial suspension of disbelief; the peripetous crises and resolutions could be expanded because the audience had abandoned its "reality check" at the box office.

Television's family dramas, in contrast, offered years-long acquaintances with familiar characters, yet the actual episodes were limited by periodic interruptions, a stopwatch attention to timing, an intrusive and often contradictory laugh track, black-and-white photography, and a small screen. Viewed by at-home families distracted by ringing telephones, crying babies, and cluttered living rooms, television families' problems were simplified so that they could be resolved in twenty-six minutes and followed by a fairly unobservant viewer. Feudal families with their myriad relations and complex social sagas were deemed unsuitable for a medium in which clarity of image was a problem and viewer attentiveness was limited. Unlike their filmic counterparts, these television programs were set in a cultural and social vacuum; current political figures or problems were not mentioned, popular music was not played, rock-and-roll images did not decorate the children's walls. Restrictive two-shots and close-ups, bound by the smaller-than-life boundaries of the television screen, reduced the home to a glimpse of consumer products mired in detail, but with no real sense of relational space. Each room existed by itself as a distinctive setting for various gender-related discussions and duties, betraying a spatial and social claustrophobia engendered by the very real technological limitations of the television industry. The small screen simply did not have the means to depict the exotic locations and expansive scenes which would have established a stronger familial-social connection. What resulted were domestic melodramas which emphasized the family as an alienated phenomenon, an isolated unit whose problems were internally created and internally resolved.

But while television families might have experienced smaller or more personalized problems than the film families, the two suffered in equally hyperbolic a fashion. Film relied on its technological achievements—bright colors, method acting, exaggerated music and sound—to transmit the melodramatic requirements of hysteria. Television utilized music doubly, as both a structural and a thematic device. The episodic nature of the medium foregrounded repetition as a means of intensifying emotional resonance, reiterating story lines between episodes and among the various shows. Even the opening credits of the programs served as a ritualistic device, foregrounding the supposed stability of the characters and their sense of familial permanence. Television's structural redundancy, coupled with the incongruous laugh track, helped to encourage contemporaneous views of these series as benign and funny and the families as secure and happy. The next chapter explores how marketing preferences and strategies operated equally to underscore film families as alienated and anxious and television families as idealized models for contemporary life.

3 What the People Want

During the 1950's the film and television industries differed markedly in their perceptions of audience composition; these disparate interpretations greatly influenced the industries' fictional constructions of family life. This chapter analyzes audience—or more exactly, the institutions' conceptions of their audiences—as a means of understanding how demographically informed ideas of audience specificity motivated complementary depictions of family life.[1] While I cannot make a definitive link between the industry's preconceived notion of a target audience and the effect—conscious or otherwise—of such a conception on the actual film and television texts, a strong and suggestive convergence of institutional concerns and thematic emphases exists. In brief, the industries' separate predilections for specialized product (film) or mass product (television) functioned concurrently with their separate predilections for certain types of story lines. The younger, more segmented audience attending feature films witnessed disturbances in family life restored by paternal-filial bonding, while the family unit viewed televisual ideals engaged in generational dispute and reconciliation. To best understand the enormous emphasis which each industry placed on audience makeup, it is necessary to review their marketing strategies.

SECTION 1: FILM
Polls and Surveys

When the film industry operated hegemonically as a truly mass medium, it was not preoccupied with specifically demographic surveys. Certain genres may very well have been designed for particular audiences (the 1940's "women's weepies," for example); for the most part, however, the industry targeted an audience of everyone between six and sixty, and produced mainstream moviegoing fare consistent with that broad audience. The film industry first began general audience surveys in the early 1940's.[2] With the postwar decline in film attendance, the industry became increasingly concerned with discovering the demographic statistics of its fans, who were still devoted. As Susan Ohmer notes:

> The advent of television in the late 1940's, however, increased competition for leisure spending. . . . The noticeable drop in box office revenues during this period served as a further impetus for the industry to adopt audience research.[3]

Audience Research Inc., the film division of the Gallup Poll organization, conducted many title tests, polls, and other public surveys for the Hollywood studios. The bulk of its work in the 1940's consisted of title-testing, previewing different versions of particular films to test the popularity of alternate endings, and inventorying the "marquee value" of individual stars. Audience Research's preview system gave a rating dial to audience members of all ages and backgrounds to evaluate the film according to various factors. From the mid-1950's, such general assessments were replaced by focused demographic inquiries conducted by Gallup and other independent companies or magazines such as *Seventeen Magazine*. Surveys habitually emphasized parallels between the film industry and the survey sponsor's own market or cited statistics to support the sponsoring organization's own ideological bent. *Seventeen Magazine,* for example, reported that teenagers comprised the bulk of the filmgoing audience.[4] A Catholic monthly, *Extension Magazine,* argued that teenagers were offended by romantic displays of affection, particularly by "older" stars.[5] As the external organizations were busily calculating audiences and audience impact, the film industry itself struggled to redefine its position as a specialized form of entertainment. In an effort to gauge its success with youth-targeted films and take statistical control over its own marketplace, in 1957 the Motion Picture Association of America (MPAA) commissioned the Opinion Research Corporation to conduct its first full-scale demographic survey. On the basis of interviews with 5,021 people in June and July of 1957, the company presented its results privately to members of the MPAA, including its president, Eric Johnston, and then to the heads of the major studios. One of the company's findings was that 72 percent of the filmgoing audience was under the age of thirty (the same group constituted 50 percent of the population as a whole). In January 1958 the results were published in the various trade journals, as well as in major daily newspapers such as the *New York Times*. The most heralded finding and the one on which the film industry focused was that the bulk of the filmgoing audience was under thirty. The *Hollywood Reporter,* for example, came out with an article titled "Opinion Youth." After 1957 the trade journals, *Film Daily Year Book,* and various position papers increasingly focused on stratification of the audience. For example, a 1962 MPAA report on increasing audience attendance asserted:

> [O]ur Product is different. Our audiences are different. While we still dominate the screens of the world, we no longer produce films strictly on the basis of mass appeal. We are a selective medium, and we must cater to special audiences with special tastes; we must gear our pictures to the diverse and ever-changing types of audience.[6]

And, as MPAA president Eric Johnston wrote in 1961:

> [T]he fact remains that more American films are being made with a direct appeal to more mature audiences. . . .
>
> From surveys conducted by the MPAA we know that there is not one audience, but many audiences. In terms of age groups—we have a teenage audience from 12 to 17; a young adult audience from 18 to 30; an adult audience up to 60; and we have a new and growing audience of retired persons.[7]

On the basis of its first refined surveys, combined with youth-oriented hype from the teen magazines, the film industry gravitated toward more specialized product, designed to attract dating teenagers and young adults. Family melodrama, with its focus on young stars, controversial subject matter, and domestic strife, was the chosen genre for exploiting the younger market. Indeed, the increase in the number of family melodramas produced in that period is directly associated with the introduction of demographic surveys.

The Industry Reaction

During the late 1950's and early 1960's the film industry was enamored of its newly available statistics and obsessed with publicizing its commitment to the notion of distinct audience tastes. Much of this self-aggrandizement was designed to boost the status of the film industry in general—not as a "mass medium," but as a popular art designed to appeal to those with more refined and idiosyncratic appetites. Thus, along with the usual reports about specific films and their target audiences, the industry issued a plethora of statements claiming that film had become a more cultivated form of entertainment.[8]

Dore Schary, production chief at MGM, stated, for example: "[W]e're competing with TV, and when the picture is good enough and big enough we know we can fill the theatres with the more discriminating people."[9] *Variety,* the *Hollywood Reporter,* and other trade journals, always ready with advice on exhibition and target audiences, became even more enthusiastic over the marketability of the "new," more stratified fare, and took special care to praise films which catered to the burgeoning teen or young-adult audience. A *Variety* review of *Blue Denim* states: "Since [the film] has the ability to attract the blue denim set, rated as the most frequent film-goers, as well as a substantial number of adults who will be interested in the theme, the picture rates as a strong [box-office] contender."[10] And a *Motion Picture Daily* review of *No Down Payment* claims: "These are the issues much in the minds of young adult movie goers, who should be absorbed in this drama and recognize that it deals with some things that are part of everyday living."[11] This identification angle was the most common approach for capitalizing on the stratified audience. A concentration on teenage stars was designed to attract a teenage audience, while other films whose central characters were middle-aged women (*There's Always Tomorrow, All That Heaven Allows, Magnificent Obsession*) were seen as tailor-made for housewives.[12] The trades also noted how a preoccupation with the teen audience influenced the filmmakers toward more sensational subjects. A *Hollywood Reporter* review of *A Summer Place* states: "A curtailing of the youthful love scenes would have brought about a more compact dramatic unity. But with half the movie audience made up of youngsters, this may be box office insurance."[13] The attention toward specific audience needs created a feedback loop in which young-adult films were made to please young-adult spectators who consequently increased their numbers as filmgoers.

The preoccupation with sensationalized themes placed the Production Code Administration (PCA) censors right in the midst of a marketing quagmire of moral obligation on the one hand and economic stability on the other. PCA director Geoffrey Shurlock noted how the nonrated code system had not yet caught up to the stratified marketing agenda: "We have a code that is intended to provide movies for an entire family. Obviously, some pictures are not for the entire family. So the code bends and twists."[14] Perhaps as a compromise, many of the films that promised sensationalism often couched their hot topics within a framework of conservativism or traditional family values. A *Variety* piece on the drug-addiction film *A Hatful of Rain* noted that it was the first film to explore "dope addiction with the approval of the Production Code. More than the story of a junkie. It touches knowingly and sensitively on a family relationship and, as such, may be more within the scope of average audiences who may find the subject of dope addiction completely foreign."[15]

While the demographic statistics were compelling in and of themselves, more crucial was the way in which the industry disseminated this information as a means of distinguishing film fare both from its mass-oriented past and from its mass-oriented competitor. The emphasis the industry moguls and trade papers put on these numbers shows demographics to have been a motivating factor in films' treatment of sensationalized subjects in the form of coming-of-age sagas and parental-teen conflicts.

The Narrative Reaction

The discovery that the filmgoing audience was composed primarily of teens and young adults determined in part the filmic family melodrama's predilection for youth-oriented stories in which teens or young adults were not only the central protagonists but also the voices of wisdom, tradition, and propriety. In an effort to continue young people's allegiance to the cinema, filmmakers created images of youth which were at once invigorating and moralistic, presenting, for example, the issue of parental-offspring trust from the teenage point of view, portraying the teen as catalyst for positive change and growth and the parents as nonunderstanding outsiders. In *A Summer Place* the central couples engage in parallel affairs. Ken, married to a frigid snob, and Sylvia, married to a lazy alcoholic, rekindle a twenty-year-old romance at the same time that their teenage children, Mollie and Johnny, fall in love. During the course of the film, the couples are continually compared. Mollie and Johnny's love, while prematurely demonstrative, is seen as "pure" and unabashedly honest. They are simply young, in love, and unable to control their ardor. Their parents, however, are depicted as liars (the adulterous Ken and Sylvia had never told their children of their previous relationship), hypocrites (the parents preach decorum while practicing adultery, alcoholism, and malevolent surveillance), and morally inept (Ken and Sylvia didn't marry twenty years earlier because of unresolved class differences). This same configuration exists in *Peyton Place,* in which teenagers Alison and Norman are innocent friends while their suspicious parents are adulterers, unwed mothers, liars, shrews, and hypocrites. In *Rebel without a Cause,* young Jim Stark wants to explain Buzz's chickie-run death to the police, while his cowardly parents urge denial and escape. The youthfulness of the protagonists served as a point of identification for the primary audience members. But while these characters seemed rebellious (due to their dress or association with popular music), they were in fact arguing for the main-

8. Teenagers were often the voice of reason and morals in film's domestic melodramas. Here, Mollie (Sandra Dee) in 1959's *A Summer Place* accuses her mother Helen (Constance Ford) of a repressive frigidity, appealing to the more liberal ideas of her father (Richard Egan). (Copyright Warner Bros.)

tenance of (or a return to) traditional values. Filmgoers thus got the double satisfaction of both seeing themselves so structurally dominant and recognizing their desires as socially correct and laudable.

In addition to the teenage appeal, the film industry also focused its family films specifically on the young-adult audience—a related but distinct group of filmgoers. Here, the sensationalistic attitudes continued to predominate, but were altered to relate more directly to the world of the post-teenager. Predominant themes were infidelity, divorce, child custody, drug and alcohol abuse, and the uneasy (or impossible) alliance between a successful career and a happy home life. Thus, *No Down Payment* centers on suburban angst, *The Man in the Gray Flannel Suit* and *Executive Suite* deal with job/home conflicts, and *The Days of Wine and Roses* focuses upon alcoholism as the result of job pressures. It is important to recognize that while the family melodramas targeted toward teens and young adults were distinct from one another, their common dependence upon sensationalized material ensured a fairly reliable crossover audience.

It seems no small coincidence that the industry's first demographic survey coincided exactly with the proliferation of the film family melodrama. The generic conventions of familial anxiety, confusion, and despair were themes which appealed to the targeted audience of dating teenagers and young adults anxious to get out of the house. The incongruous moralizing common at the ends of these films in no way negated the sensationalized topics that served to attract the filmgoer in the first place. Indeed, the voice of reason was located in those very characters with whom the target audience could identify, and so feel flattered by the implication of its own moral superiority.

SECTION 2: TELEVISION
Polls and Surveys

While the film industry was busy carving its mass audience into targeted demographic units, television overtook the motion picture as the dominant form of mass entertainment. Television was marketed as the "family" medium, to be received in the home by the entire nuclear unit. Consequently, it too chose to focus on the family as ideal subject matter. Thus, the concern with audience on the part of both the film and the television industries resulted in a generic preference for domestic family melodrama, but the demographic components of these audiences resulted in different forms of the genre—the splintered family of film for the splintered film audience, the unified television family for the mass television audience. For, unlike film, television sought *unified* families who would watch in the home, together. This resulted in a portrayal of television families as seemingly more intact than their film counterparts.

The primary sources for audience information for television were the A. C. Nielsen and Arbitron ratings companies, both of which had their origins in radio. Although it was possible for Nielsen to calculate extremely detailed demographic information, the television industry did not become interested in these specifics until late 1962. As with film, a startling consistency emerges between the number of family melodramas and the institution's use of demographic research.

Initially, during the family melodrama's most popular era, the networks favored a large, undifferentiated audience, as a means of charging substantial advertising fees. Tom Watson, manager of television research, west coast, from 1970 to 1986 for CBS (the original network for *Leave It to Beaver*) recalls that family programs "were all going after the type of family that was represented on the show—the whole family . . . without actually putting that notion into words."[16] And Arnold Becker, vice-president of television research for CBS, concurs, noting that the networks preferred to cite to advertisers large general numbers rather than to break the numbers down into groups, each with its potentially limited sponsorship appeal. Speaking of the late 1950's and early 1960's, Becker said:

> People weren't so fussy about audiences, and what CBS was looking for were shows which would attract as many households as possible. And given the social mores of the time, with a minimum of controversy. They wanted a show everybody could sit down and watch together in the living-room. There was very little emphasis on [audience] composition.[17]

Indeed, not only did the television industry perceive its audience as an amorphous whole, this generalized appeal was an important early marketing strategy. As John Ellis has noted, the specialized targets of the film industry, together with the television industry's concept of its own amorphous audience, resulted in a functional symbiosis designed to maximize each medium's potential viewership.[18] Becker takes the equation one step further, asserting that the characteristics each medium assigned to its targeted audience in turn influenced its programming, which in turn solidified the distinct audiences: "It became circular, to the degree that the adults who would have returned to the movie theaters were driven away."[19]

In the mid-1950's, although they had yet to succumb to the more refined techniques favored by their advertisers, the networks began to test-market potential programs through their in-house research departments before assigning them to the network schedule. *Leave It to Beaver,* with its cast of relative unknowns, provides an interesting example of the logistical preparations involved in the journey from pilot to series. An August 1957 report from the Program Analysis Division of CBS's Television Research Department states: "LEAVE IT TO BEAVER has the earmarks of a successful series. It was well received by all subdivisions of the audience and seems capable of acquiring and retaining a large general audience."[20] The report indicates that its sample audience was composed of eighty people, of whom 41 percent were men and 59 percent were women. It further divides the audience by age group, marital status, education, and "housewife" versus "other" occupations. Additional categories specified television ownership and geographical location (those living in the New York metropolitan area versus those in other parts of the U.S.). These categories are interesting because they emphasize the relationship between the fictional Cleaver family and the family watching at home, with the most important point of identification designated as one's status as homemaker. Research subjects participated in a program analyzer test in which they watched the pilot, "It's a Small World," and

9. In audience testing *Leave It to Beaver* was received as a "typical, and down-to-earth" depiction of family life. (Copyright Universal.)

were monitored for sensory skin responses. Interviews were conducted and questionnaires were administered after the program was finished. The report included a viewer-reactions chart showing approval and disapproval by percentage and rating along a continuum of time, a minute-by-minute account of how the show fared with the audience. The section of the report devoted to viewer comments is particularly interesting for the importance granted to the question of the show's "reality."

> About half the viewers described LEAVE IT TO BEAVER as realistic, typical, and down-to-earth. Approximately one-third thought it was a family type show—one a whole family can enjoy. . . .
> The Characters—Almost 90 per cent of the viewers commented favorably on Beaver. Approximately two-thirds of them described him as a typical American youngster, typically mischievous, wholesome, and "all boy." . . . He was thought to be an "eager" child from a "good home" who was brought up properly—one who would set a desirable example for other youngsters. . . .
> Wally, although not as well received as his younger brother, was

commented on favorably by some 75 per cent of the viewers. The majority of this group thought that, like Beaver, he was realistic, natural, typical of a boy that age, and an average American boy. . . . On the negative side, a strong minority thought that for a boy his age he was too unaggressive, mild, and quiet. He did not "boss Beaver around" as much as a "real older brother" would. Beaver seemed to be the leader and Wally the "follower." Generally, these viewers seemed to feel that Beaver overshadowed his older brother too much.

Relatively few commented on Mrs. Cleaver. The comments were mostly favorable. She was felt to portray successfully an average mother.

Still fewer viewers commented on Mr. Cleaver. Some thought he was natural and good; others thought he did not appear and act as a real father should.[21]

Viewer comments on *Leave It to Beaver* are intriguing for a number of reasons. First, they provide evidence to support the claim that the television industry was still very much concerned with equating and promoting family programs for family viewers. Second, the test audience is seen as integral to the creative process, determining how future stories might be better rendered (Wally having a stronger role, for example). And, finally, they indicate the regard with which the producers held any negative comments. Both Paul Sullivan (Wally) and Casey Adams (Ward) were replaced in their roles because of the test results. Tony Dow, the replacement Wally, was thought to be superior to Paul Sullivan not only because of his slightly more aggressive acting style but also because his shorter stature made him appear younger. Hugh Beaumont's aura of kindness and morality (he was a preacher in addition to being an actor) made his Ward a positive correction to the giddier and more emotional Casey Adams.[22]

The years 1954–1963 represent television at its most universally appealing. During its early experimental years, as William Boddy has noted, television's position as an expensive technological novelty allowed it to restrict its appeal to the "high culture" of live anthology programs or to live coverage of current affairs. By the mid-1950's through the mid-1960's, television receivers had become affordable and television programming had become more structured, with the television schedule printed in daily newspapers. Television was now firmly entrenched in most American homes; in order to solidify its status as a common household entertainment item, it had to broaden its appeal. For just about ten years, until 1963, the television industry used a variety of women's magazines, surveys, in-home demonstrations, and programming formats to encourage the purchase and use of television by middle-class nuclear families.

This concern with general audience appeal was relatively short-lived, however, and began to change in the 1960's when, given the increasing costs of advertising, sponsors began to seek proof that they were reaching their most probable consumers,[23] and pushed the networks toward more defined audience ratings. Because television programming was produced solely to encourage viewers to watch commercials and buy sponsors' products, the networks complied.

According to network executive Tom Watson, there was an additional impetus toward specificity as a means of rationalizing poor ratings.[24] ABC, the third-placed network, had entered the broadcasting field handicapped by affiliates poorly placed in smaller cities than its network rivals. To attract advertising support, the network needed to rework its small numbers so that they appeared a favorable alternative to the larger CBS and NBC audiences. So ABC conducted demographic surveys that allowed it to claim that even with fewer broadcasting outlets than its competitors, ABC attracted viewers who were more likely to be potential customers and who were thus superior. In 1962, pressured by their advertisers, NBC and CBS followed ABC in the quest for more specific information.

The A. C. Nielsen company was a prime beneficiary of this move. In a "Nielsen Newscast" from August 1963, for example, the company heralds its "new improvements" scheduled for fall 1963: "Total TV usage and program audiences reported every two months on 11 sets of demographic breaks, including three new ones (Age of Child, Children within Income Group, and Occupation of Head of House)."[25] And a 1963 Nielsen report shows how far the art of distinct demographics had come, with studies such as "Planning a TV Schedule to Reach the Light-Viewing Homes," "A Higher Rating May not Mean More Adult Viewers," "Reaching the Lady of the House," "Averages Can Be Misleading," and "When Do Working Women Watch TV?" Each of these studies boasts that further demographic studies are both possible and important for advertising purposes. The inference of a causal relationship between demographics and fictional product is supported by the fact that after the television industry solicited and responded to these refined demographic surveys, television's family melodramas underwent a significant transformation. Representations of nuclear-family life all but ceased, replaced by single-parent households, blended families, and multigenerational units.

Television's audience, then, underwent three distinct measurement phases in conjunction with television's development. In its developmental years, TV

was relatively unconcerned with actual ratings and more interested in ha-
bituating the American public to television consumption in general, offering
an abundance of distinct and often controversial material. During its highest
period of growth and penetration (from 1954 to 1963), it maximized its newly
won mass appeal by constructing the bulk of its programming for the family
viewers it wished to woo. The push toward refined statistics after 1962 fostered another change in television's program composition, toward specific
consumers within the family. It was now understood that the family no
longer sat down together to watch television, but consumed it individually.
Remarkably—and probably not coincidentally—television's fictional families mirrored the demographic specifics. No longer depicted as an amorphous nuclear enclave, TV families were splintered and resolidified into a
hodgepodge of witches, Martians, widowers, widows, combined families,
adoptive families, and extended families.

The Industry Reaction

Television's attitude toward its audience was different from that of the film
industry. While the film industry analyzed its audience, then targeted narratives at it, the television industry decided who it wanted to reach at the
outset, and designed its programming to appeal to a pre-determined group
of desirable consumers. Even in its most mass-oriented days, television was
somewhat discriminating, concerned most with attracting potential customers for sponsors' merchandise. During the period from 1954 to 1963, the primary target was the American homemaker buying for her middle-class family. A *Forbes* magazine article, for example, quotes ABC's chair, Leonard
Goldenson, and its president, Oliver Treyz, as saying: "We're after a specific
audience, . . . the young housewife—one cut above the teenager—with two
to four kids, who has to buy the clothing, the food, the soaps, the home
remedies."[26] And Marvin Mord, vice-president of ABC marketing and research, reported: "Theory was that the woman controlled the dial in the evening, so others in the family who might not have made a sitcom their first
choice came along for the ride."[27] But as Muriel Cantor argues, the television
industry does not so much appeal to the female consumer as create her:

> [T]o sell to women, corporate interests must respond to changes in
> women's position in society. This formulation differs from the demand
> mode . . . in one important respect: Women viewers are not getting the
> content they necessarily want, but the content is determined by others
> who try to keep women as consumers.[28]

The institutional response to the various audience studies is best understood by examining each point of television's formative triangle separately—the production concerns, the sponsors' desires, and the explicit critical input of audience members. Institutional conditions—the tensions between an advertising coalition which wanted to appeal to specific demographics and a network desire to reach large numbers—influenced the creative forces behind television's family melodramas. While film producers and writers might have written a screenplay for creative self-satisfaction, television's writers and producers were acutely aware of their target audience and composed their scripts accordingly. For example, on *Father Knows Best,* both Jane Wyatt and Robert Young felt the show appealed to "the whole family." Young explained further that while the advertising agencies were urging a more rigid stratification, Eugene Rodney was convinced that the program's strength lay in its general attraction: "Gene Rodney said the show was appealing because audiences see themselves in it. The ad agency constantly told us to do shows that appealed to certain groups, but we said 'If we ever do this, we'll lose the audience, we'll become too self conscious.' If you try to appeal to a gender or age, you lose the reality of it."[29]

During the 1950's sponsors were most concerned with reaching the largest consuming group possible—the middle-class family. In a sense, the television industry was proactive rather than reactive; sponsors were not so much responding to various audience surveys as directing their programming money toward specific groups, then measuring the success of their marketing strategies. The predilection toward homogeneous programming, scheduled in consistent blocks of time and appealing to an equally homogeneous consumer audience, was the cornerstone of the advertising strategy in television. As Jeff Greenfield notes:

> A typical prime-time network schedule is deliberately designed so as not to produce radical shifts in audience. Networks do not want audiences moving to switch the dial. As one successful television producer has put it, "We're a medicine show. We're here to deliver the audience to the next commercial. So the basic network policy is to set in motion, from the beginning of prime time to the end of prime time, programs to maintain and deliver those audiences to the commercial."[30]

In addition to the sponsor- and network-commissioned surveys by Nielsen and Arbitron and the explicit response by producers, networks, and agencies to the various results, there was a final awareness of audience desires, most evident in public tributes and testimonies and the fan-letter system.[31] Fans and communities paid homage to family television stars in an idiosyncratic blend of adoration and camaraderie, praising the families for being at once "just like us" and better. In June 1957, Ozzie Nelson received an honorary doctorate from Rutgers. Its citation read: "One of the most famous families in America, you and Harriet—and David and Ricky—have won the affection of millions and have brought to television entertainment rare standards of good taste and high quality. Neither time nor custom have staled your infinite variety."[32] Shelley Fabares and Tony Dow were co-winners of the Youth Foundation's Awards in 1962; the Catholic magazine *Progress* raved that Dow, despite his respectful demeanor, still managed to impress the girls, who wrote over 95 percent of his fan mail: "Elvis and Ricky may have their hoards of loyal and loud fans, but the quiet, well-mannered boy who doesn't do anything more exciting than stand on his head is apparently just as strong as ever in the swoon department."[33]

Often the relationship between the audience and the television families was more direct; fans sent the TV families questions and praise, revealing a conviction that the Andersons, Stones, et al., were "real" families.[34] Robert Young received twenty or more letters a day delivered directly to his home, with themes such as this:

> We just happened to be together when the program [*Father Knows Best*] came on, like an answer to all of us. After it was over, we decided then and there to live as a family, each person taking an interest in the others. Our home has been a better one since. Family living and sharing is the secret. That's what Father Knows Best.[35]

A letter to Barbara Billingsley strikes the same tone:

> Our family, consisting of our eight children, my wife, and myself consistently watch this interesting and thought stimulating program. As you may well know, there are fewer programs each season that are suitable fare for under-teens and young teenage families. Your "Leave It to Beaver" program is not only suitable for family viewing, but it is refreshingly pleasant to watch. . . . [You] are to be congratulated . . . in helping continue the high moral tone that can be accomplished in telecasting.[36]

Jane Wyatt recalls that she was continually approached in person and via the mail by female fans, who would complain or criticize her various homemaking skills.[37]

In addition to their letters to the creators of the programs, members of the television audience expressed their critical acclaim or disdain for various series directly to their sponsors, advertising agencies, and most often, networks. For example, the motivating factor for the Scott Paper Company's rescue of *Father Knows Best* after its early cancellation was a massive letter-writing campaign in which thousands of irate viewers expressed their anger. While it was the sponsor's imprimatur which assured the return of the series, the popular press wasted no time in exploiting the notion that television's audience had determined its fate:

> Ratings or no ratings, it's still Mr. and Mrs. Average viewer who dictate what they're to see on T.V. . . .
>
> In dropping a program in favor of one with a lower rating [*Father Knows Best* replaced *My Little Margie*], sponsors reportedly had in mind the many viewer requests for *Father*. They knew that *Father,* a show with all-family audience appeal, was telecast too late to get many children viewers.
>
> The sponsor was influenced by viewers who said they liked the show because it represents American family life as it really is and not as some TV scriptwriter thinks it is—or should be.[38]

The Narrative Reaction

While it is difficult to explicate specific correlations between articulated audience appeal and various plot points, it is possible to chart some general patterns. First and foremost the preoccupation with the positive presentation of the nuclear family itself seems motivated by a need to target that audience. As John Ellis has noted:

> The institution of broadcast TV assumes its audience to be the family; it massively centres its fictional representations around the question of family. Hence TV produces its effect of immediacy even within dramas of historically remote periods by reproducing the audience's view of itself within its fictions.[39]

Thus, television's portrayal of the seemingly secure[40] nuclear enclaves of the Stones, Nelsons, Andersons, Cleavers, and Douglases was motivated by a need to appeal to upper-middle-class families themselves. The families in these domestic comedies (unlike their filmic counterparts) spend the majority of their time at home, dining, talking, and perhaps most important, watching television. On *The Adventures of Ozzie and Harriet* and *My Three Sons* in particular, the family is often gathered around the television set, discussing its content, enjoying the camaraderie of family viewing. Indeed, there are a number of episodes within the two series that deal explicitly with television viewing. In "The Built-In Television Set" (1960–1961) and "The

Closed Circuit" (1957–1958), the Nelson family actively constructs a television and also appears on the screen. In "Almost the Sound of Music," the Douglas family sings on a television rock-and-roll program, while in "Here Comes Charley," housekeeper Fedocia's unorthodox viewing habits pit her against the program selections of Chip and Robbie.

In *The Donna Reed Show* episode "Nothing Like a Good Book" (1959–1960) Donna lectures Mary and Jeff about neglecting books in favor of the TV screen, but by the end of the episode she has recognized the futility of forced reading and the seduction of a good western. In *Father Knows Best* television becomes the unifying device between the ailing Jim and Bud Anderson in "Father Delivers the Papers" (1954–1955), as well as the catalyst for a night of togetherness in "The Great Anderson Mystery" (1958–1959). These programs indicate a preoccupation with upper-middle-class family life for its own sake as well as for its ideal environment for television watching and the togetherness it promotes. Through watching its ego-ideal actively involved in a shared familial adventure, the family at home presumably is reinforced in its own behavior.[41]

In addition to the proliferation of these supposed "mirror-images," the television narratives often focused on familial dilemmas of the time (juvenile delinquency, adoption, divorce, teen marriage, teen independence, housewife/career-woman antagonisms), and, in the process, made them more palatable to a home audience. The strategy of appropriating marginal teenage behavior such as motorcycle racing into socially correct consumerism—fathers Ozzie and Jim also ride motorbikes—may have been instigated by the need to appeal to a wide audience, piquing the viewer's interest with the depiction of current social problems but diffusing these problems with humor and/or their transformation into consumable items or laughable fads.

Finally, the television programs often dealt directly with issues raised by their audience members in fan letters or phone calls. Because the episodic series depended for its success on habitual viewing, it was afforded the luxury (or liability) of interactivity between viewers and the program. Viewer suggestions were often adopted, because producers felt that doing so both gave them a means of tapping into explicit audience desires and allowed them to use such capitulation as a promotional device in and of itself ("We listen to our viewers!"). By far the most explicit response to audience input occurred in December 1959, when a young, self-described juvenile delinquent wrote the following to Robert Young of *Father Knows Best*:

> I guest [sic] you must get hundreds of letters from all your fans, especially letters like this one. But I don't care. I know that you probably

won't even read this letter. I'm going to write it anyway. I'm what all you nice people call a J.D. I stand on a corner with a gang, wear tight slacks, a lot of make-up and have long hair. I stay out til all hours, neck in cars and answer back the cops. But every Mon. night at 8:30, I'm watching "Father Knows Best." I'm really watching you Mr. Young. And sometimes I'm pretending that your [sic] my father. Something I've always wanted, but could never even talk about.

I'm 16, have a real neat Mother, drinks all day. My "Father" is still in jail serving a 20 yr sentence. . . .

If it wasn't for you Mr. Young, and your T.V. series I'd probably shoot myself or something. To me you'll always be a father that I could dream about. I wish I could give you my address so that I'd have a small hope that maybe you'd send me a small letter, but nobody's going to make a fool of me. I don't know what kind of a person you are really. I only know you as Betty, Bud, and Cathy's father and mine.

Right now I'm crying cause I love you so much. Maybe that's why I go for older guys instead of the kids I hang out with. I don't know. I only know that I'll always be

Yours,
Terri[42]

Seeing a great promotional opportunity, the writers and producers of *Father Knows Best* immediately began work on an episode revolving around the search for Terri. Publicity proposals and script outlines show that the plan was to script a sixty-minute drama around the idea of a delinquent girl who happened to be a fan of Robert Young. Attendant publicity would underscore the real-world origins of the letter; the program would end with a direct address plea by Young to "help us find this girl." But, according to Roswell Rogers, the script's author, the story was never produced. While everyone was enthusiastic about the project, no practical work was accomplished and it was "one of those cases where things took so long they never happened."[43] Despite its unproduced status, however, "The Letter" epitomizes the extent to which television producers felt an allegiance toward their fans, and an equal obsession with publicizing that allegiance.

Just as structural imperatives dictated distinctive representations of family life, so the needs of each industry to carve out a separate audience resulted in different areas of narrative emphasis. Initially, the concentration on the family melodrama in both media was catalyzed by the growing interest in the family itself. Presidential commissions, the baby boom, the publication of Dr. Spock's advice book, the professionalization of motherhood, the growth of the teenage culture, and the developing suburbs moved the family to the center of discussion in the media, in schools, at cocktail parties, and in church. Both industries capitalized on the social currency of family life by making the family the focal point of a vast number of narratives. This pre-occupation developed into two different viewpoints of family life. In film, the industry's sudden interest in the fragmented audience produced a pre-occupation with fragmented families. In an attempt to relate to the disen-franchised youth it was courting as spectators, the film industry produced narratives glorifying young love, promoting rebels (who were only rebelling for a return to more traditional society), and attempting to show the cracks in the foundations of American family life. Such narratives appealed to the bulk of filmgoers, most of whom were either alienated teenagers or young adults grappling with their own issues of sexuality, women's rights, and the pressures of the job market.

During this period, the television industry quite literally supplanted the film industry as the truly mass medium, preferring to measure its success in large, undifferentiated numbers by appealing to the family as a whole consuming body. The networks' dual responsibility to service sponsorship needs and solidify their large mass audiences influenced TV producers to-ward a different sort of family image from that of film. On the surface, at least, the television families were created as ego-ideals, secure and perfect consumers who based that security on the purchase of essential consumer goods to support their life-style choices. Thus, the television families were marketed as secure enclaves, open to advice from their fans, tenacious in their togetherness, and unquestioningly devoted to television and the prod-ucts it marketed. The television viewer of the 1950's would ideally read these images as the road to a happy way of life and as a means of controlling any sort of marginal or questionable behavior. The two industries' concerns in producing narratives relevant to audience experience resulted in different assessments of the security of the nuclear family; the upcoming chapter ex-plores the ways in which concerns in producing narratives that were inoffen-sive to audience members resulted in a different accounting of the problems threatening that security.

4 Rules and Regulations

While film and television family melodramas shared a strong generic similarity, particularly in regard to both the hegemony of family itself and the metaphoric expression of it, they were distinct in their choice of subject matter, their methods of resolving controversial issues, and their treatment of delicate topics. These distinctions can best be understood as motivated by the various regulations operating on the texts. First, the family itself can be understood as a regulatory construct. Underlying the threats and arguments which abounded in the filmic melodramas and the incidental crises and emotional traumas which beset television characters, was the unambiguous presumption that the family was the forum for social control and systematic conformity. The successful family was portrayed as a group which understood the importance of gender-proscribed behaviors and practices, which saw itself as a self-operating unit, and which mirrored societal norms and promoted pro-social behavior.

In a way, then, the entire construct of 1950's domestic melodrama functioned as a regulatory ideal. Within the text the family represented the ultimate in rule-making and legitimate expectations of obedience. Outside the text, the regulatory elements of the film and television industries developed and reinforced rules which ensured that the fictional constructs of American life supported the capitalist status quo. This chapter provides a historical overview of the explicit and implicit influences upon the film and television media to explain how these rules were inculcated by the narratives and transmitted to the audience. While film had recently been freed from the fear of governmental censorship as a result of the free-speech ruling in the *Miracle* case,[1] it nonetheless fretted over offending state obscenity boards, the Catholic Legion of Decency, and potential filmgoers. From 1954 to 1964 *The Film Daily Year Book* dedicated no fewer than four pages per issue to the trials and tribulations of the MPAA and its various censorship dilemmas. Similarly, television had to contend with its own institutionalized restrictions set forth by the National Association of Broadcasters (NAB); it was, in addition, at the mercy of sponsor and FCC pressures. To show more clearly the impact that regulations had upon content, I present a series of case studies that show how specific regulatory considerations influence the production of specific works. These regulations played havoc with the preproduction, shooting, and even marketing stages of the film and television texts.

THE FOUNDATIONS OF CENSORSHIP
Film

The Motion Picture Production Code[2] was first drafted in 1929 by Father Daniel A. Lord, S. J., in association with Martin Quigley and Father F. J. Dineen, S. J. In March 1930 the code was accepted by the Motion Picture Producers and Distributors Association of America (MPPDA; known colloquially as the Hays office).[3] In 1933, after a trial period, the MPPDA set up the Production Code Administration (PCA) under Joseph J. Breen, a Roman Catholic, who would administer it until his retirement in 1954. By 1934, after a year of organization, the PCA was formally operative. The Motion Picture Production Code was eight pages long, and according to Roger Manvell, listed "every kind of offence conceivable which could be committed in a film against the moral susceptibilities of society."[4] A 1944 introduction to the code reiterated that producers were not under any *obligation* to abide by its restrictions, but implicit pressures were such that any film which did not conform would forgo any chance of a first run in the premier, studio-controlled exhibition houses. The PCA functioned as both censor and respondent to various pressure groups during all stages of film production. Often the PCA was involved before a script was even written, advising on the cinematic suitability of novels or unpublished stories. After a final view of the finished film, a seal of approval was awarded, along with a five-page "analysis of film content." The latter document summarized the various facets of the film, such as setting, locale, period, and genre, and gave a brief overview of content, divided into "Portrayal of Professions," "Portrayal of Races and Nationals," "Liquor," "Crime," and "Sociological Factors." Until 1961, the summary provided a space for ending ("happy," "unhappy," "moral," or "other") and "economic class." After 1961, the form included a notation for "wide screen."

The mid-1950's was a time of enormous change within the PCA. In 1954 Breen retired and was succeeded by Geoffrey Shurlock, a British national and long-employed staff member of the PCA. The most active censors during the late fifties and early sixties were Geoffrey Shurlock, Albert Van Schmuss, Jr., and John (J. A.) Vizzard. Gordon S. White occasionally made comments from the New York office. In 1956, with much fanfare in the trades and much pomp on the part of the film industry, the Motion Picture Production Code was revised, the first major revision since its development in the 1930's. The change was motivated by two major factors: the extraordinary box-office success of Otto Preminger's 1953 *The Moon is Blue*, which the producer-director successfully released without the PCA seal of approval; and the public's new and ardent concern with the effects of television, a concern which redirected public censorship activities toward the small screen.[5] According to the MPAA's president at that time, Eric Johnston, the changes made the code "simpler and more precise" and "up to date."[6] The revisions, in brief, freed motion pictures to deal with drugs, kidnaping, and abortion while instituting specific new bans on brutality, sexual behavior, bigotry, and blasphemy. Miscegenation was eliminated as an explicit taboo in the code, permitting its use as subject matter as long as it was handled like other sexually oriented material—that is, in good taste. Taboos retained included "obscene dances, blasphemy and profanity" ("hell" and "damn" could be used in moderation), and bans on nudity, exposure, and disrespect toward religion. Previously forbidden scenes such as childbirth, excessive consumption of alcohol, and sexual activity in bedrooms, were now allowed as "special subjects," as long as they were "treated with discretion, restraint or within careful limits of good taste."[7]

Although the 1956 changes provided the film industry with additional resources for subject matter as well as additional freedom in presenting that subject matter, pressures from external watchdogs coupled with more controversially minded producers added to a late-1950's debate over a new rating system, that would indicate which films could be seen by children under sixteen if accompanied by an adult.[8] A *Show Business* article noted, however, that exhibitors were vastly opposed to any system which might further stratify their rapidly decreasing audience:

> The competition of television, which since 1946 has drawn some 45 million moviegoers weekly away from the theaters, forced studios to make better films. This inevitably involved the use of controversial themes. . . . Classification may be a long way off, nevertheless, because Hollywood trembles at the thought of cutting into the teenage audience, which represents nearly 50% of those going to the movies.[9]

The continuing furor over the rating system catalyzed further revisions in 1961, allowing "homosexuality and other sexual aberrations" to be used as subjects as long as "treated with care, discretion, and restraint."[10]

During the time of the family melodrama's highest popularity, then, the MPAA code underwent its most significant changes, allowing depictions of abortion, sexual situations and "perversions," and drug abuse and alcoholism on the screen. Along with greater representation of daring material came an increased debate about rating systems, studio/PCA alliances, and pre-screenings.

Films were also subject to various other pressures, mainly from religious organizations, which had their own well-defined system of ratings which they passed along to the members of their clergy. One active group was the Protestant Motion Picture Council, which had the following rating system: A = Adult (beyond high school); MY = Mature Young People (high-school students); Y = Young People.

Ten organizations provided board members for the Green Sheet, a monthly evaluator of current films: the American Jewish Committee, the American Library Association, the Daughters of the American Revolution, the Federation of Motion Picture Councils, the Federation of Women's Clubs, the National Congress of Parents and Teachers, the National Council of Women of the USA, the National Freedom of Music Clubs, the Protestant Motion Picture Council, and the Schools Motion Picture Committee. With the exception of the library group, all representatives from these groups were women.

The most powerful of the extra-industry regulatory groups was the Legion of Decency.[11] Established in 1934 "out of exasperation with the American film industry," the Legion of Decency was responsible to the five bishops that composed the Episcopal Committee for Motion Picture, Radio and Television.[12] The office's greatest influence was with MPAA member studios, which often screened films for the office before they were released, in order to accommodate their complaints before a movie's release. The Legion of Decency made the following types of ratings: "A-1" ("morally unobjectionable for general patronage"); "A-2" ("morally unobjectionable for adults and adolescents"); "B" ("morally unobjectionable in part for all"); and "C" ("Condemned"). According to Richard S. Randall, a film could be hurt by a "C" or "B" rating and often was changed to avoid a negative rating. In 1958, the Legion of Decency added two other categories. "A-3" ("morally unobjectionable for adults"); and an untitled category for films considered "morally unobjectionable for adults, with reservations." In 1963, the latter category was named "A-4."

While film had been granted First-Amendment protection, federal, state, and local governments nonetheless exerted a subtle but potent pressure. Mark Thomas McGee and R. J. Robertson note, for example, that film hesitated to exploit the more violent aspects of juvenile delinquency mainly due to the Kefauver hearings, which in 1954, were investigating the causes of juvenile delinquency and arguing that a correlation existed between violent films and antisocial behavior.[13] In addition, the United States Information Agency (USIA) regulated films for foreign export. Interestingly, many of the films banned by the USIA were family melodramas, including *A Hatful of Rain* and *The Bottom of the Bottle* (which dealt, respectively with drug and alcohol addiction). Further governmental restraint was felt after the *Times Film Corporation v. Chicago* decision in 1961, which allowed ordinances providing for local review of films that might be considered questionable and the subsequent prohibition of their exhibition if found to be obscene.[14] The new freedom encouraged by the PCA was consequently bound by court rulings upholding the principle of community rejection of "obscene material." Four states with active censorship boards (New York, Kansas, Maryland, and Virginia) and over fifty cities capitalized on court rulings regarding local clearances. The boards were usually comprised of so-called average Americans, generally women who were usually not college graduates. These boards screened films in three ways: compulsory prescreenings, voluntary prescreenings, or "show cause" screenings in which certain films were summoned for specific reasons.

The establishment of so many rule-making bodies and their interference in the creative process had particular impact upon 1950's domestic melodramas. One means by which the film industry sought to differentiate itself from television and to continue to attract the teenage viewer was to produce domestic melodramas dealing with highly charged subject matter. The relaxation of the code in the mid-1950's, which allowed the domestic melodrama to exploit its generic tendency toward extreme situations, was thus partly responsible for the changing face of cinematic melodrama during the 1950's. Family melodrama of the 1940's, bound as it was by strict code prohibitions, could only hint at infidelity, could never mention abortion, and could depict divorce as an option only for sinful or ignorant women. Thus, almost of necessity, tales centered upon maternal devotion, adolescent coming of age, or the surmounting of economic hardship. Audience demand for teen-centered stories, coupled with the code revision, catalyzed the 1950's domestic melodrama's obsession with juvenile dilemmas, sexuality, and violence. Within the treatment of such issues, however, the code still insisted upon a moral didacticism that explicitly castigated social transgressions or implicitly showed them to be responsible for a character's misery. A film might depict abortion but it could not approve of it; it might linger on a couple's passion but it had to punish them for it. The representation of the family in film inhabited a space between a desire for audience titillation and the need for moral justification and placation. This heightened need for a moralizing solution intensified another of the genre's traditional elements, namely, peripety. In order to resolve youthful-passion films in a manner consistent with code requirements, narratives continually relied upon fate and chance to turn the tale into a social lesson. For 1950's family melodrama, then, two generic components—a tendency to depict extreme events and to resolve them through peripety—were intensified by regulatory guidelines. Two family melodramas from the late 1950's serve as examples of the kind of interaction between the PCA and the films' producers, and provide evidence for the impact such discussions had on the film texts.

In 1956 the code had been revised to allow the subject of abortion in film as long as abortion was clearly condemned.[15] This revision, along with the industry's search for youth-oriented material, encouraged the production of teen sex stories, including many which focused upon abortion as a central or marginal story element (*Splendor in the Grass, Love with the Proper Stranger, A Summer Place, Peyton Place,* and *Blue Denim*). *Blue Denim* was a top-twenty box-office hit which catapulted its teen actors, Carol Lynley and Brandon de Wilde, toward instant celebrity status. The movie attracted controversy even before shooting began. Based on the stage play by James Leo Herlihy and William Noble, it told the story of a young couple whose initiation into intimacy resulted in pregnancy. The stage play featured an illegal abortion. In the process of *Blue Demin's* transformation from play to film the abortion became a pending teen wedding, an excellent example of the machinations required by the PCA. Additional script revisions were demanded in a number of potentially "dangerous" areas, including expressions of economic and political opinions, depictions of sexual activity, and use of generally frank dialogue. Most crucially, PCA demands altered the movie's narrative emphasis to focus on the reconciliation between a strict father and his sensitive son, a new emphasis quite different from the social criticism in the play, but which placed the film squarely within the favored 1950's generic pattern.

One of the main themes of the play concerns the unbridled passion of teen youth—Art and Janet discover mutual affection and sex the same night. In the film, the young couple, imitating Art's older sister and her fiancé, fall into temptation more from curiosity and an attempt to gain peer acceptance than because of their own ardor. Because the film version emphasizes Art and Janet's thwarted attempts to marry (an option immediately discarded in the play), the social discussion of government-sanctioned reproductive control is replaced by a criticism of societal/parental objections to teenage marriage. The play's treatment of abortion is a quite explicit argument for the liberalization of abortion laws, for the advancement of women's education, and for the castigation of outmoded societal dictates. The film uses Janet's proposed abortion as a dramatic vehicle through which Art and his father prove their own senses of responsibility and love; it culminates in heroic actions designed to underscore the patriarchal code of male authority and physical/economic superiority.

Blue Denim's production battles make explicit the ways in which censorship influenced film's representations of family away from maternal/female bonding and toward a male-centered society of responsibility and authority. In 1958, Robert Vogel, in charge of censorship for MGM, had inquired about the possibility of producing the play, only to be turned down by PCA head Geoffrey Shurlock.[16] When rewrite attempts failed, the play was eventually optioned by 20th Century–Fox. Like their MGM counterparts, the producers at Fox were also at pains to rewrite the story to fall within code require-

10. In the 1959 smash hit *Blue Denim*, this seemingly chaste kiss leads to illicit sex, unwanted pregnancy, and an attempted illegal abortion. (Copyright 20th Century–Fox.)

ments. By April 1958 the following outline by producer Charles Brackett won PCA approval:

> The girl gets pregnant, decides on an abortion. The boy's conscience moves him, he tells the father. They get to the abortionist before anything happens.
>
> The parents decide that the young people must marry and preparations are made. At the last moment, the girl decides it is not fair to burden the boy with a family. She wants to take the responsibility for the child on her own shoulders. Later on, when they are more mature they can talk about marriage.[17]

During the course of filmmaking the script was revised so that the story ends with Janet attempting to escape to have the baby on her own and Art rescuing her yet again, with a smile and a promise of marriage. To circumvent public criticism—while still basing their marketing on the sensational aspects of the story—the PCA orchestrated a massive public relations effort, accompanying release of the film by a series of panel discussions by various social authorities. One guest audience included members of Congress, two representatives of the White House Conference on Children and Youth, the secretary of President Eisenhower's cabinet, the chief of the Children's Bureau of the U.S. Department of Labor, a representative of a juvenile-delinquent project, an executive of the Florence Crittendon Home for Un-Wed Mothers, the director of the National Training School for Boys, an attorney from the Department of Justice, a Juvenile Court judge, and film reporters for industry journals and daily papers.[18] Despite these efforts, the film received criticism, some from those who were offended that the sinning youth were not punished enough for their immoral behavior. *Variety* quoted New York critics angry with the "happy" marriage that ended the film:

> The "tactful" handling of the abortion theme in Twentieth Century-Fox's "Blue Denim," and the "happy ending" type of solution . . . riled several of the N.Y. Critics last week. It also dramatized Hollywood's problem in handling social problems while trying not to step on sensitive toes. . . . "Blue Denim" demonstrates Hollywood's great difficulty in coping with adult themes while appealing quite consciously to an audience which, to a very large extent, does not consist of adults. It also reflects what by now appears to have become an almost subconscious reflex, i.e. the desire to placate groups before they even start pressuring.[19]

The same *Variety* article noted that religious groups were equally distressed by the film's conclusion:

> Yet even while still in script form, some already voiced their concern on two grounds: (1) That marriage at the end would rob the whole issue of illegitimacy and proposed abortion of its severity, and (2) That it seemed like an unsound and unintelligent solution to the problem.
>
> A Catholic priest last week said that if he were approached by a young girl finding herself in such a predicament, he would never suggest marriage. "It would be wrong on both human and religious grounds," he emphasized. His solution: Don't get married. Have the child, and then either place it in a foundling home, or else keep it at home and enlist the aid of the parents in bringing it up. After a few years, when both parties reach a more responsible age, marriage would still be possible.
>
> While the Code prevented the film from following the play in that the abortion couldn't be performed, it would not have in any way dictated marriage as a final solution.[20]

And as a *Variety* review noted:

> Undoubtedly due to production code restrictions, the Edith Summer and Philip Dunne screenplay has been considerably watered down. The picture is tied up neatly in a blue ribbon to conform with code standards. The word "abortion" is never mentioned although it is obvious what is taking place. Moreover, the ending deteriorates into cliché melodrama.[21]

This last statement underscores the impact restrictions had upon generic codification and formulation. What the magazine disparagingly calls "cliché melodrama" is indeed the course of action the narrative must follow in order to appease the vocal moralists, but it is this very course of action (the nick-of-time rescue, the resolution of a social problem on familial terms, the reiteration that the family and its survival are of greatest importance) which marks the film as a typical 1950's family melodrama. And, indeed, the filmmakers based their defense of the film's ending on the fact that the marriage was a suitable resolution within the generic convention. *Variety* reported that "Scripter Dunne said last week that, while Catholic objections had been considered, the film's ending was formulated 'under no pressure at all,' and simply because it seemed dramatically most valid."[22] Another *Variety* article blasting the film's critics quotes Brackett's recourse to the melodramatic convention of reactive protagonists who adjust and respond to circumstances over which they have no control: "In arriving at an ending for 'Blue Denim' we [he includes screenwriters Philip Dunne and Edith Summer] chose a much more conventional and old-fashioned method; we went to our characters and found out to the best of our ability what they would do." [23] PCA files indicate that Brackett's and Dunne's generic arguments were somewhat disingenuous in that filmmakers continually battled the PCA both to allow the abortion to proceed and to avoid teenage marriage. The film's ultimate text and the two men's assertions emphasize both how regulations determined generic convention and how these generic conventions functioned as a safety valve in the depiction of socially prohibited behavior.

Transforming the drug-addiction play *A Hatful of Rain* into an acceptable film involved abandoning the play's social critique of military medical practices and the urban problem of street crime for a melodramatic saga of the effects of paternal neglect. As with *Blue Denim,* another studio attempted to produce *A Hatful of Rain* before 20th Century–Fox took over from independent producer Hal Wallis. This was a significant event for the film because its familiar themes of alienation and isolation would be magnified by filming in CinemaScope, the shooting method mandated by 20th Century–Fox for all its post-1954 features. In opting for the big studio, the PCA unintentionally determined that the film would stretch and distort a small two-room apartment. The PCA's restrictions on the representation of drugs and drug addiction further propelled the narrative toward the world of family melodrama. The new rules allowed drugs as subject matter as long as they were in no way shown as desirable. Thus, although the movie's plot revolved around Johnny's drug addiction, he is never shown taking drugs himself, nor experiencing any pleasure from them. The play's moving scenes of drug-induced euphoria were replaced with family melodrama's staple scenes of a young male weeping, screaming, shivering, and moaning. While some of Johnny's hysterics are because of his need for the needle, the majority of his breakdowns are incomprehensible pleas for love and understanding—the generically prescribed text of the moral occult. The only moment of actual drug-taking occurs when Johnny has gone over the edge and needs the drug merely to stabilize his behavior. The scene makes no small effort at equating drug-taking with torture; Johnny hallucinates that he is back in Korea and that the pushers are his guards. His drug-induced respite occurs offscreen and results not in any sort of euphoria or "high," but only in his declaration that he'll give up drugs. Importantly, his rantings castigate the Koreans as the source for his pain, not the army medics who got him hooked on painkillers to begin with. Thus the narrative fulfils another criterion of the family melodrama, preaching a sort of xenophobia and upholding America at the expense of other cultures. Ultimately, of course, Johnny doesn't blame the government, the war, or his injury for his drug addiction; he blames his aloof father, whose frequent absences and blindness toward the emotional needs of his two sons resulted in their individual weaknesses for drugs and for gambling. By the end of the film, Johnny's drug addiction has proven to be the breakthrough event for father and son, as Johnny's wife Cecilia (the mediator) propels the two toward newfound communication and understanding.

With their focus on sensationalized problems of abortion or drug abuse, "controversial films" were already typical family melodrama; often the strictures of the code propelled them toward more melodramatic conclusions or treatment. Every family-melodrama film of this time period dealt with some combination of sexual indiscretion, marital infidelity, juvenile delinquency, and substance abuse. The revised code permitted such subject matter, but only within the boundaries of ever-changing, self-imposed standards of acceptability—if such transgressions were duly punished. Thus the relaxation of the code encouraged the genre's predilection toward extreme events, and the strictures of the code determined that these events be treated hyperbolically and resolved through peripety and paternal intervention. The PCA's rules tacitly encouraged titillating subject matter as the means by which a moral lesson could be illustrated. Because the family melodrama upheld the moral rectitude of the family unit, it became the ideal forum for the presentation of such issues. Thus a cycle was established: controversial issues only seemed to be family problems because of the generic requirements of family melodrama; these relocated social problems then became the basis for domestic trauma—becoming increasingly distanced from the social world and increasingly regarded as native to the nuclear family. Thus, the teenage pregnancy of *A Summer Place* provides the occasion not for an abortion debate, but for a parallel series of affairs engaged in by the teenagers and their parents. Mollie and Johnny's premature sexuality results only in problems completely absolved by their marriage and reunification with the family.

In dealing with matters other than the sensationalistic, the code's conservativism resulted in the omission or softening of socially progressive narratives. For example, *No Down Payment*'s suburban dwellers are concerned when a Japanese-American wants to move into their neighborhood, Sunrise Estates. While the film makes a good case for racial tolerance, the power of the original screenplay (in which the potential neighbors were an African-American family) has been watered down considerably. The stakes of the argument are changed so that it is not the Japanese-Americans arguing with city officials for suburban inclusion, but an Anglo-American husband and wife arguing with one another over their separate claims of moral superiority. The most important part of this integration story is not that Iko gets to move to Sunrise Estates, but that Herm and his wife reconcile and that Herm resumes going to church.

On other occasions, the PCA's obsessive attention to detail allowed larger issues of social liberalism to penetrate the film text. With the elimination of the ban on what it called "miscegenation," Hollywood explored the possibilities of interracial romance and marriage, submerging problems of racial tension into familial dilemmas solved by pronouncements of love and physical embraces. For films such as *Night of the Quarter Moon* and *All the Fine Young Cannibals,* the PCA officials worried more about the word "nigger" than about the films' more controversial sanction of interracial marriage. In these cases the regulatory codes served to distract the Hollywood establishment from more radical messages of racial blending, while the melodramatic texts, forced to rely on their own generic conventions of family as panacea, ultimately promoted an otherwise-missing message of color-blindness, a message likely to be stricken from films which dealt with such issues on a social level.[24]

Because of periodic changes in code requirements during the 1950's, then, family melodramas were caught between two opposing mandates. First, in order to entice their younger audience into the theaters, the dramas were compelled to include or focus upon controversial and titillating subject matter. Indeed, the loosening of code restrictions no longer allowed the filmmakers any excuse in avoiding hot topics. Thus, family melodrama included among its favorite subject matter teen sexuality, illegitimacy, unwanted pregnancy, abortion, rape, interracial romance, drug and alcohol addiction, and, of course, juvenile delinquency. But the PCA's new determination to allow such subject matter was restricted by the moral conservativism it was sworn to uphold and by the frequent criticism aimed at it by religious groups and the popular press. The result of these two forces was an amplification of the defining generic terms of family melodrama. The genre had always been characterized by a conflation of the everyday and the extreme, by the depiction of hyperbolic behavior, by over-use of peripety, and by a calculated interpolation of the societal into the familial. With the new freedoms of the revised code, the family's problems became that much more expansive— teens were no longer thwarted by misplaced love, they were sexually active and ultimately pregnant; young men were not just shouting their anger at their reserved parents, they were boozing or shooting it up, playing death games with cars and switchblades, and raping their teachers. Because of this, the 1950's film melodramas have more in common with their uncensored nineteenth-century literary predecessors than with any film melodramas of the code-controlled 1930's and 1940's: events had to be resolved within the confines of generic expectation—fate, peripety, and familial love. The larger scale of these films' problems made them more improbable; there seemed to be no social problem so huge it could not be fixed within the confines of the family. Solution through matrimony—however unlikely and unstable—was continually represented as the optimal solution to grave social ills.

But if the newly revised film regulations suited family melodrama, it was television regulations which gave new potency to the generic imperative of hyperbole. Television replaced film as social scapegoat, and with the bulk of regulatory energy focused upon the small screen, television's family melodramas were forced to choose from a small pool of acceptable story lines. Ultimately, the insignificance of television's domestic problems in the face of the characters' incongruously exaggerated reactions to the problems further marks these texts as melodrama, in which hyperbolic response is the ultimate underlying emotional paradigm.

Television

In 1951, after increasing pressure from the government and from civic and religious groups concerned with televised sex and violence, the television industry decided to adopt its own code, the "Television Code of Good Practices." The National Association of Radio and Television Broadcasters (NARTB; later, NAB) issued its own seal, the "Seal of Good Practices," but the public was quite unaware of its existence or importance.[25] The NARTB's code was approximately four times longer than the MPAA code instructing broadcasters about their various "duties" toward the "advancement of education and culture" and cautioning them about a variety of taboos. Part of the preamble to the Television Code of Good Practices states:

> It is the responsibility of television to bear constantly in mind that the audience is primarily a home audience, and consequently that television's relationship to the viewers is that between guest and host. . . .
>
> Television and all who participate in it are jointly accountable to the American public for respect for the special needs of children, for community responsibility, for the advancement of education and culture, for the acceptability of the program materials chosen, for decency and decorum in production, and for propriety in advertising. This responsibility cannot be discharged by any given group of programs, but can

be discharged only through the highest standards of respect for the American home, applied to every moment of every program presented by television.[26]

The 1952 code underwent constant revision, but no major changes took place until 1962, when the code admitted kidnaping as subject matter and permitted "justified" divorce as long as it was not treated "casually." A new awareness of minorities was evidenced by the statement "racial or nationality types shall not be shown on television in such a manner as to ridicule the race or nationality."[27] Of course, although the code was periodically publicized and publicly proclaimed as a guard against "offensive material," it was relatively unenforceable, employing no mechanism for formal monitoring and no systematic method of punishment.[28]

While the formalized pressures of the NAB code might have been less than threatening, John Ellis has noted that the nature of television production itself necessitates strong internal control:

> Self-censorship is in most states a far more restricting form in TV than it is in cinema: the judgements that are habitually made about what "will be OK" for TV are notoriously more conservative. This is partly the result of TV's self-definition as a *mass* medium, . . . partly because of the close relationship that national TV institutions have with the controlling political elite, and partly because of the industrialized production form and the consequent difficulty of working in adventurous ways.[29]

Television's assembly-line mode of production thus provides many avenues for network, sponsor, government, and audience interference. Live television dramas might escape censorship complaints, but continuing episodic television invited systematic scrutiny on a weekly basis.

The structured nature of episodic television and the small pool of television writers worked in the code's favor; more than aware of the code, these writers internalized it, as any employee accepts and then operates under corporate dictates. As John Whedon, who wrote for both *The Donna Reed Show* and *Leave It to Beaver,* noted: "Everybody was pretty much aware of what they could do on TV."[30] Henry Sharp, another writer for *The Donna Reed Show,* concurred: "Since we knew all the prohibitions, we never ran afoul of them."[31] John McGreevey, who wrote for *My Three Sons,* recalled: "I think we accepted the limitations of the genre and pretty much pre-censored ourselves."[32] The writers recall that there were no post-production arguments over censorship because they were so careful before the fact. As Paul West notes: "I never saw a case of Code or Censorship. The family show writers all knew where the boundary lines were and we never stepped over—to my knowledge."[33]

While the television code represented a powerful force of regulation, the networks also regulated their own mores through internal departments with names such as "Broadcast Standards," "Continuity Acceptance," and "Standards and Practices." Such action was deemed necessary to keep sponsors happy, the FCC (Federal Communications Commission) away, and the public morality-mongers appeased. According to Ed Dewey, who was with NBC's Continuity Acceptance department in 1960, the NBC regulations were almost "verbatim the Blue Book [the NAB code]. The whole job [of in-house censor] was a matter of value judgments and you based your feeling on a reading of the characters. [These were] very subjective judgements." Scripts were circulated to Standards and Practices personnel, who penciled in their objections and suggestions. Such orders were adhered to by the network brass who pressured independent-minded producers to toe the line.

The third and most important regulatory factor upon television content was the presence of the sponsor. Sponsors were involved in every step of production, often financing a program's creation in the first place. A sponsor's agent, on the set at all times, met with the show's producers, communicated with the network brass, and monitored audience response to particular episodes. Networks did not frown on this close relationship; indeed, in a 1960 address to the FCC, CBS president Frank Stanton noted the beneficence of the advertising industry, remarking that "the objectives of an advertiser and the objectives of the broadcaster are the same—to make [programs] as entertaining and attractive as possible."[34] The industry's self-proclaimed determination to please the sponsor did not go unchallenged. Two FCC reports on the industry noted with displeasure the negative effect that such sponsor appeasement had on programming: "As a general proposition, sponsor aversion to controversy, thought-provoking material, 'downbeat' material, etc., permeates and shapes the production of 'formula type' program series from start to finish."[35] In addition to sexual content, many sponsors were loath to become involved in anything deemed "controversial." This usually translated into an aversion toward ethnically diverse, economically challenging, or politically idiosyncratic programming. As a sponsor noted in 1957,

> In the matter of segregation, it would be difficult to present a dramatization dealing with some aspects of this problem on a sponsored program, particularly at a time when the subject is considered highly inflammatory. At these times, certain material can best be handled

through public affairs programming. . . . It would be impossible to maintain any balance of dramatizations highlighting one side of such a currently explosive issue as segregation in a sponsored *entertainment* program.[36]

Thus, because of their debt to commercial sponsorship, many of television's family melodramas were toned down not only in terms of sexual content, but in terms of any sort of social issue, resulting in both bland heroes and fanciful villains. Especially during the era in which television programs were wholly sponsored by one company or one agency representing a variety of companies, sponsorship interference was as great an influence on television content as its own self-regulatory bodies.

While the FCC was excluded from an explicit censorship role, it nonetheless exerted tremendous influence upon program content, holding hearings on excessive violence, sexual content, and the presentation of alcohol,[37] thereby encouraging a consistent and banal presentation of subject matter on television.[38] The establishment of the networks in the 1920's and their orderly entry into television in the 1940's provided them with bureaucratic operating procedures that were most comfortable with rules and regulations and the FCC's mandate, under the broad language of the Federal Communications Act, to challenge those stations who failed to operate in the "public interest, convenience and necessity."[39]

Less formalized than the industry's self-controls, and less potent than other outside forces, the popular press and various special-interest groups also exerted control over television content. Just as the debate over ratings in the film industry was waged in the industry journals of *Variety* and the *Hollywood Reporter*, so *TV Guide* provided a forum for arguments over the merits or liabilities of various television programming.[40] The ultimate strategy was to redirect the burden of television's societal responsibility away from programmers and toward viewers, resulting in a mass proliferation of pressure groups.[41]

Because of their commercially sponsored structure, the networks owed a debt to large corporations for their genesis, technology, and dissemination as well as for their membership in the corporate "club". This provided a set of operating procedures that had the effect of upholding monopoly capitalism, pushing consumption, and maintaining the status quo, a representative agenda distinct from that of film. First and most pronounced was the ubiquitous and "happy" consuming family with its up-to-date home appliances and leisure toys. A near-obsession of the story lines was the superiority of the middle class and the importance of "things." While film's melodramas might have made passing reference to a desired commodity (a new bike, a mink coat, etc.), the only prolonged discussions of purchasable goods were usually (and not accidentally) arguments about television sets. In the television melodramas, consumer items are the narrative focus of at least one of eight episodes. Donna must have that beaded bag, Margaret wants a mink coat, Beaver needs that new jacket or sweater, Ozzie covets a new fishing reel, Chip wants a toy car, while his brother wants the real automobile. This positive portrayal of consumerism neatly fulfilled the needs of sponsors, advertising agencies, and, indirectly, the talent agencies and production companies they financed.

Second, and less obviously, the programs also continually reiterated the fairness of American capitalism and the ease with which one could achieve financial success. Over one-fifth of the episodes argue that with hard work, a good education, thrift, and foresight, one can achieve anything in America. This message is notably absent or even contradicted in the film texts.[42]

Finally, sponsors and networks were insistent that the programs associated with the products be "moral and upstanding." The obsession with single beds, chaste kisses, and solemn discussions of morality, combined with the virtual exclusion of teenage rebellion, can be traced quite consistently to specific memos from networks' censorship departments or to the internalization of such rules by the writing staff. (Eugene Rodney, for one, was usually able to fight off such heavy-handed content control, but his success in thwarting the network was based on his ability to barter one line for another, or one situation for another, thereby appeasing network qualms while maintaining some of the original ideas.) In addition to trepidation about "offensive" materials, the networks worried about future liability, so that lines and behavior were monitored by Broadcast Standards departments for content that might be "dangerous and imitable."[43] Such scrutiny frequently prevented the television texts from delving into controversial subject matter or even from sufficiently disguising it as something less threatening. And so, bound by constraints on subject matter from regulatory bodies but pressured by the conventions of its genre to invest its characters with strong emotions television texts reveal a strange incongruity between trivial event and supercharged response. Teenage girls in film scream at their mothers for not allowing them to be sexual, to be passionate, to be mature. Their hysteria, motivated by the genre's text of muteness, is somewhat understandable in relation to their repressive and frigid mothers' denial of their true physical urges. But teenage girls on television respond with this same frenzy when their mothers deprive them of such insignificant events as a country-club dance, a trip to a tennis tournament, or permission to redecorate the house with ostentatious luxury items. While these emotional tirades seem out of proportion (and indeed many critics mocked them for exactly that), they are, in essence, the hallmark of melodrama: their hyperbolic incongruity, their text of the moral occult, and their text of muteness render the television texts even more melodramatic than their filmic counterparts.

In addition to corporate pressure upon general story lines, producers were often expected to make specific changes in individual scripts to comply with sponsor demands.[44] Here, the sponsor and the producer walked a thin line between illegal product placement and preferential treatment of the sponsors' merchandise. Former Young and Rubicam vice-president David Levy recalled that he read every script of *Father Knows Best* and would discuss it by telephone from New York with producer Eugene Rodney.[45] According to writer Henry Sharp, producers had to guard continually against payoffs by sponsors to writers, so producers policed scripts to make sure writers did not mention product names. At the same time, the constant and vocal presence of the sponsor's or agency's representative on the set steered programs toward the sponsor's perspective. The look of a program was often altered after a script was written as the sponsor and the producer cooperated to portray the product (nameless but visible) in the best possible light. So, for example, when *Father Knows Best* was sponsored by Lipton's Tea, Margaret continued to serve coffee, but it had to be poured from a teapot.[46] Or, as Ozzie Nelson recalls:

> One of the big advantages of being the only sponsor or of being co-sponsor was that it was possible for us, perfectly legitimately, to give them a great deal of subliminal advertising in addition to their paid commercial blurbs. For example, while we were sponsored by Hotpoint, they furnished the kitchen with all the latest Hotpoint appliances, and if we had a choice of where to play a scene we'd move it into the kitchen where Harriet could be cooking dinner or putting dishes in the dishwasher or taking clothes out of the dryer. Or even if we were eating dinner in the dining room the Hotpoint appliances could still be seen in the background. The Listerine people, of course, were not so lucky. We weren't quite ready to write in any gargling scenes—not that they didn't try to coax us (in a nice way, of course).[47]

An examination of Eugene Rodney's files reveals the intricacy of the relationship between the sponsor and the producer. For an episode called "Time to Retire," Tony Stanford, representative for the J. Walter Thompson advertising agency, sent an urgent memo to Sonny Chalif, Screen Gems advertising liaison:

Unfortunately, I notice there is a very grievous error on Page 2, namely, the business where Margaret wipes the paint off the refrigerator. The author has boldly written, "She gets a *cloth* and wipes off the paint." Were Mr. Elliotte a new and untried author I would not have been so shocked. Surely this young man has been most derelict in failing to watch the Scott commercials. Else, he could not possibly have failed to realize that no material performs the disagreeable task of absorbing paint so well as a Scott Paper Towel.

From past experience I am sure that when this scene is shot Margaret will instinctively use a Scott Paper Towel. Correct? If so, you may consider this letter to constitute client approval.[48]

The revised script states that "she tears a Scott Paper towel from the holder and wipes off the paint."[49] For the five years during which the program was sponsored by Scott Paper, the Anderson home contained two paper-towel

11. Advertising imperatives required television programs to feature up-to-the-minute appliances and decor. Even this publicity still from *My Three Sons* seems to feature the cooking properties of the oven over the familial relationship between Uncle Charley (William Demarest) and Steve (Fred MacMurray). (Copyright Viacom.)

dispensers readily visible in all kitchen encounters; as Robert Young recalls, cast members were encouraged to use a lot of paper products.[50] *The Donna Reed Show* also reflects various sponsor interests in the background presence of Campbell's soup cans or, more blatantly, in various promotional tie-ins. For example, director Gene Nelson recalls an instance when Duncun Yo-Yo gave all members of the cast and crew large embossed yo-yo's during the filming of an episode in which Jeff does a variety of Duncun yo-yo tricks;[51] and writer Phil Davis remembers that he once wrote a one-hour episode dealing with a boat at the behest of Donna Reed and Tony Owen, who would get to keep it.[52]

Moralistic and conformist pressures upon the television family melodrama ensured that the narrative foundation for the television text would be rigidly confined to the creative depiction of innocuous dilemmas. Ultimately, however, melodramatic conventions allowed the television text to circumvent regulatory guidelines. While television melodramas could not explicitly deal with teenage pregnancy or abortion, they could and did explore youthful misconduct, parental castigation, and the anxieties of family life. Because the institutionalized conservativism demanded by networks and sponsors and internalized by writers and producers reduced television productions to superficial crises and explosive responses, the conclusion one might well draw from watching the television melodrama is that these families are even more troubled than their filmic counterparts who, after all, are dealing with the real miseries of sexual chaos and social anarchy. That television characters break down over admittance into school clubs, choices between duty and dating, and too much housework underscores the truly dysfunctional status of these families and the hyperbolic tendencies of their members.

Regulation—whether self-imposed or government mandated, whether determined by sponsorship marketing needs, or designed to appease religious organizations—had an enormous impact on the representation of family life in film and television's family melodramas. Bound much more tightly in a world of both prohibition and prescription, television families were compelled both to ignore sexuality, bodily functions, and socially controversial or progressive attitudes and to promote morality, consumerism, and patriotism. Films were encouraged by the changing standards of the PCA code to explore new transmutations of family life and relationships as they encountered homosexuality, substance abuse, illegitimate pregnancy, and abortion, but only with virtuous didacticism.

Both sets of restrictions served melodrama by encouraging it to base its narrative structure on even more extreme events (film), or to strengthen its system of representation (particularly hyperbole) through increasing disjunction between causal events and characters' responses (television). Ultimately, both the film and television texts created a sui generis system of regulation—that of the family and its values. As potent as the external restrictions were, internal, generic conventions compelled the domestic melodrama to repeatedly propose successful family life as the means to fulfillment and social harmony. And family life is articulated through an operative mode of power, gender, and economics in which the characters' purposes and participation shift according to narrative emphasis. Part 2 explores the consistency with which both media explored the same underlying issues, each from its own distinct perspective and each with its own method of resolution.

PART TWO

Textual Implications

5 Power Plays

Leonard Benson writes in *Fatherhood: A Sociological Perspective:*

> Organization within the family revolves around two axes: age, upon which an authority structure is established, and sex, according to which responsibilities are divided. Authority automatically falls to the older members of the household as long as they can remain active, and responsibilities are always divided between the sexes. In the overwhelming majority of societies for which there are adequate data, the roles of father and mother are functionally different; father is primarily responsible for instrumental and executive tasks that relate the family to its larger social environment, while women specialize in meeting expressive needs and routine tasks within the family.[1]

Benson's 1968 paradigm for family life in society serves as an appropriate model, with modification, for the dynamics of power in familial representation in late 1950's film and television. Both the film and television texts are concerned with the delineation of power—implicitly in terms of narrative structure and visual and aural stylistics, and explicitly in narratives whose focus is on generational, gender, and societal conflicts. A key difference between the two media, however, rests in the fact that on the television programs, the power structures are "correctly" aligned, while in the films, the family needs to resubscribe to the patriarchal values inherent in the definition of the successful nuclear family.

The assessment and analysis of power relationships is an enormous undertaking. Are we exploring the ideological constructs which uphold basic capitalist creeds, or the notions of world dominance, or even brute strength? In this context, the paradigm comes from the genre itself, a paradigm that explores those power relationships which are represented most consistently within the plots and themes of the texts themselves. These power relation-

ships fall into three main arenas: intrafamily relationships, interfamily relationships, and relationships between the family and society. This is not to
say that there were no dramatizations of imperialism, politics, or spirituality
within the family melodrama, but such depictions were always subordinate
to the compelling thematic and narrative emphasis upon familial power in
its various incarnations. This chapter isolates and analyzes the prevalence of
the three major configurations of power-relationships within the domestic
melodrama, and examines how such configurations were determined by the
film and television media.

Intrafamily Relations

Benson's sex-determined responsibilities—in the fictional world—are exaggerated toward an ideological maintenance of patriarchal hegemony. In the
realm of the cinematic and television family melodrama, the woman is
stripped of her domain over "expressive needs" in favor of the patriarch, who
now presides over not only "instrumental and executive tasks," but is also
the primary caregiver, object and transmitter of love, and locus of discipline
and vindication. Patriarchal hegemony is even more exaggerated along the
age continuum, where the family melodrama subscribes only partly to the
notion of generational authority. While Dad rules the roost, Mom can act
only as his moral backup; male children (as future fathers) assert more
power than their mothers or sisters. This domination by Dad is accomplished via a number of textual strategies discernible in the way in which
implicit power is established, characterized, and rendered stylistically, as
well as in its explicit narrative demarcation.

Dad's implicit power is rendered in the flow and content of familial conversation, in his omnipresence for both disciplinary and praise-giving occasions, in his frequent position at the center of the narrative, and in his visual
and aural dominance. A quick overview of the five television texts and relevant examples from a selected list of feature films demonstrate that father is
the crucial figure in family dialogues. For example, every episode of the television programs features at least one meal (usually dinner) around the
family dining room table. During the meal an issue of prominent importance
is broached: Can Wally go away to military school? Can David buy a motorcycle? Can Bud buy a motorcycle? While both parents participate in the
discussion, the boys address all their answers and questions specifically to
Ward, or Ozzie, or Jim. June, Harriet, and Margaret, meanwhile, are passive
observers, or find their questions either ignored or reacted to via a gender-
relay system, in which Mom asks a question and the children direct their

answers to Dad. When the discussion is concluded, the children shift their attention to Mom and her domestic realm: "May we be excused, Mom?" "Is there any more dessert, Mom?" "We'll do the dishes, Mom."

Because of the star-persona and production duties of Donna Reed, *The Donna Reed Show* is a bit more complex in its power-related discussions. Issues involving money, science projects, history, and math are directed toward Alex, while questions concerning dating, clothes, and social activities are usually conducted in a closed circuit of female knowledge-sharing between Donna and daughter Mary. Unlike in the other programs, Donna is the person initially addressed in the area of consumer affairs. If Jeff wants a new toy or Mary needs a new dress, they direct the question at Donna as manager of the household budget. Donna then defers to Alex as the *supplier* of that budget, and the discussion ensues. On occasion, the establishment of Donna's perceived domestic power is questioned by Alex, who insists on being the man of the house.[2]

In *My Three Sons,* Steve Douglas is the sole source of power, but in the all-male enclave, the question of the domestic versus the professional sphere is not clear-cut. The sons' questions revolve around dating, school, jobs, and

12. In the all-male sphere of *My Three Sons,* the hierarchy was based not on gender but on age, the older and younger generations vying for the affections and approval of the ultimate patriarch, Steve Douglas. (Copyright Viacom.)

moral dilemmas and Steve is the authoritative scholar on *all* issues. Grandfather (and surrogate-mom) Bub's opinion is volunteered (though never asked for) and provides a "traditional" counterpoint to the "modern" wisdom. In *My Three Sons*, ultimate power is held by middle-aged men, and the younger and older generations vie for Steve's affection and validation of their point of view.

In feature films, discussions again place the father at the center of the dialogue. In *Rebel without a Cause*, for example, Judy wants her father to give her a kiss and to listen to her school problems. Judy's nameless mother hovers on the periphery, powerless. In *Blue Denim*, mother is the authority on sister Lillian's wedding plans, but Major Malcolm Bartley is the one who activates all narrative complication and resolution, and the person to whom his son eventually turns for help.

In addition to its role in family discussions, Dad's power is made patent by the fathers' availability in times of crisis or celebration. For example, all the fathers keep employment hours that favor their involvement in the domestic scene. Jim Anderson and Ward Cleaver arrive home well before dark, and often before their children get out of school; Ozzie Nelson chose to locate his program solely on weekends[3] and Steve Douglas is a consultant whose career independence allows him both flexibility of hours and the ability to work at home. For the first four years of *The Donna Reed Show*, Alex Stone had his pediatrics practice off his foyer. Because of their remarkable proximity, the fathers are made privy to all of their children's dilemmas and delights, usurping mother's traditional position as the in-home boss. Indeed, the fathers are often home *more* frequently than the mothers; Harriet Nelson and Margaret Anderson, in particular, are often depicted as running off to go shopping, or to a women's club meeting.[4]

While Donna Stone and Margaret Anderson are often the first ones told of their children's achievements and disappointments, Alex and Jim dominate as the more authoritative parent. If the child is sharing positive news, Donna and Margaret exclaim over how "proud" father will be. If the child has been discovered in a serious breach of obedience, father is threatened as the ultimate arbiter. In the patriarchally centered world of *Leave It to Beaver, Father Knows Best*, and *The Donna Reed Show*, the children are instructed to "help your mother" but to "make your father proud." In *My Three Sons*, Steve Douglas' relationship to his family is one of extremes, in which he is either always home or always out of town. When present he is, like the other fathers, the principal distributor of praise and guilt, but even when absent, he is invoked as the ultimate authority.

In the films, paternal involvement and authority are upheld equally as the most crucial components of familial success. But the film families are depicted as more flawed than the television ones in that such paternal mastery is absent. In television programs the operation of paternal authority provides the rest of the family with a narrative solution; in the films it is the achievement of an authoritative stance in and of itself which rescues the family. Thus, the film texts also continually center fathers and fathering as the most important element for familial happiness, neglecting detailed depiction of the workplace to focus on Dad and his relationship to the home. Because of this, many of the narratives revolve around family-run businesses, in effect conflating the work world with the domestic one, thus allowing the father a physical availability that would be logically impossible if he worked for a huge corporation. Even in those family melodramas which purportedly center midlife and/or career crisis, and which explicitly criticize the workplace, there are a disproportionate number of scenes at home, for which the most important aspect of the work world is the alienating effect it has on Dad's domestic availability. For example, in *No Down Payment* Jerry Flagg is a failing car salesman, whose drinking and insecurity are costing him financial stability. While the film depicts one instance of Jerry at the car lot forcing a morally wrong purchase, there are numerous domestic scenes underscoring how Jerry's economic failure bleeds into his status as a father. He is deemed irresponsible because he buys an exorbitantly priced bicycle in a love-bribe for his son, and he is egotistical because he refuses to understand that a blandly conformist job is his best bet for supporting his family. In *There's Always Tomorrow* Clifford Groves is castigated for putting his successful business ahead of the needs of his family; his constant absences make him unaware of his son's needs, surprised by his teenage daughter's maturity, caught off-guard by his younger daughter's dancing recital, and, importantly, equally oblivious to his wife's interdependency with the children. The film underscores Cliff's separation from his family, and the implication seems to be that Dad is unhappy in his home life because he is so divorced from it.[5]

The presence of the father in the day-to-day activities of his children serves to underscore not only his involvement in disciplinary activities, but to validate liberal child-rearing policies. It is the mothers who have sets of rules—"wash your hands," "set the table," "ask to be excused"—and the fathers who assume the more trusting position of inspiring good moral behavior in their youngsters via example and trial and error. This is true for both the film and the television texts where the successful fathers understand the importance of a lengthy lecture delivered in the study. The ideological dictate is that fathers are crucial for disciplining their children and that the proper means of discipline is to talk and listen, not scream and hit. Thus,

13. The emotional separation of Cliff (Fred MacMurray) from his son (William Reynolds) is made visually literal in this scene from the 1956 film *There's Always Tomorrow*. (Copyright Universal.)

Wally and Beaver suffer the power of Dad's wrath in pedantic, didactic orations held in his study. Jim confronts the three Anderson children individually in their bedrooms, but more often confronts the clan as a whole, gathered together in the living room for a lecture on wrongdoings. Steve Douglas and Alex Stone operate in much the same way, puffing on pipes and shaming their children into confessions and self-recriminations, while the affable Ozzie Nelson adopts a nearly laissez-faire attitude toward discipline—tiptoeing around his sons' very minor transgressions, and holding family conferences to discuss what little troubles crop up. In film, the cloyingly understanding Ken in *A Summer Place* propels his daughter toward sexual maturity, Wil Stamper attempts two heart-to-heart discussions with Bud in *Splendor in the Grass,* and Tom Corbett serves up moral imperatives with fast food to little Eddie in *The Courtship of Eddie's Father.* Importantly, mothers are shut out of this disciplinary paradigm, practicing instead either the old-fashioned and condemned method of simple directives ("go wash your hands"), or the equally castigated use of screaming and brute force.

There are a number of episodes that focus upon the issue of discipline itself and serve to underscore both the liberal methods and the dominance of the father. For example, on *The Donna Reed Show*, in a 1959–1960 episode titled "The Punishment," Donna has grounded Jeff and Mary for a weekend and is feeling nervous over the severity of the punishment. When Alex arrives home from work, Donna requests that he back her up in her action. In addition to her lack of authority, Donna feels undermined by the relationship between her husband and her children. Alex is regarded as "special," the parent who loves, while Donna's day-to-day involvement with her children relegates her to the position of disciplinarian. The next day, Donna offers her husband a trade: "You can be the parent who does the disciplining and I'll be the one who's loved." Donna has made explicit a television family melodrama common denominator—that no matter how involved mothers are in the detailed upbringing of their children (and this ranges from the absence of Harriet, the subservience of June, and the inadequacies of Margaret, to the omnipresence of Donna), it is the fathers who have the final authority and respect. Donna is clearly superior to Alex in her knowledge of the children's misbehavior: she gives him a list of their wrongdoings; she notices their sloppiness and transgressions when Alex is oblivious to such things. But her knowledge is impotent against Alex's male essence. Not only is the father unaware of any wrongdoing, he fails to discipline the children even when informed. Without Donna in her rightful position as disciplinarian, the children become anxious, equating parental apathy with a lack of love, and present their parents with a surprise dinner in hopes of winning them back. Ultimately, racked by guilt, Donna recants her harsh punishment only to have Alex reprimand her for her inconsistency and then take the credit with the children himself when he issues a pardon. "The Punishment" is a microcosm of the power-relationships in the television family melodrama. Mothers are the executors of a mocked and unenforceable discipline, while fathers are rational and blessed with an acute understanding of their children's needs.

But while Steve Douglas, Jim Anderson, Ward Cleaver, and Alex Stone all practiced, to a greater or lesser degree, the liberal parenting paradigm of the "talking punishment," the power each held over his household varied. Steve Douglas, for example, was by far the most omnipotent patriarch. The title of the program, *My Three Sons*, immediately evokes associations of ownership and command. Steve's concerns are that his children be honest, responsible, and cooperative, and he encourages that behavior by a camaraderie not available in the programs with female cast members. In the Douglas clan, the "men" must stick together to ensure the irrelevance of the female, which means helping out with domestic chores. However, the lack of the feminine model means that there is a lot of leeway as to cleanliness, calm, and quiet. Thus, while Steve Douglas' *form* of control is the toughest of the TV dads, his requirements of his children are ultimately less stringent, resulting in fewer transgressions and opportunities for discipline.

Jim Anderson possesses nearly as much power as Steve Douglas, but the fact that he must share disciplinary duties with his wife results in a slight loss of potency. While the title of the program, *Father Knows Best,*[6] serves to remind the viewer of Dad's superiority, Margaret's very existence and her activities as the enforcer of courtesy and cleanliness excuse Jim from continual watchdog duty. She acts as the herald of misbehavior, while Jim is the executioner. The daughters, Betty (Princess) and Kathy (Kitten), are expected to live up to their nicknames, with regal self-control or rambunctious innocence. Consequently, while Jim's *form* of discipline (recrimination by shame and manipulation) may conform to a liberal mode of thinking, the impetus behind the punishments is often severely conservative. Jim and Margaret are strict traditionalists, requiring their children to act like miniature adults and choose the self-sacrificing model over the pleasurable option. Consequently, this is a house without music (rock and roll or otherwise), where a goodnight kiss takes center stage for an entire episode ("Crisis Over

14. In a typical scene from the oh-so-serious *Father Knows Best,* Jim carefully manipulates Betty to choose the moral path over the fun one. (Copyright Columbia.)

a Kiss" [1958–1959]), and where social events are offered as a carrot, only to be withdrawn when a crisis requires the presence of the family member ("Family Dines Out" [1955–1956], "The Promised Playhouse" [1954–1955], and "Second Best" [1959–1960]). Unlike the occasionally carefree or romantic Steve Douglas, Jim Anderson *never* has any fun, and neither does his family.

Ward Cleaver's power is not as potent as Steve Douglas' or Jim Anderson's. Because of Ward's own behavior and his wife's reaction to him, his power lacks the potency of the other TV dads. First, his reminiscences about his youth undercut his authority, constantly reminding the viewer that Ward, too, was once a mischievous little boy himself. In addition, June Cleaver does not revere her husband in the same way that Margaret Anderson does. She is much more territorial about her domestic sphere, insisting that Ward "stay out of my clean kitchen," and "don't mess up my nice new drapes"; often she is even sarcastic with Ward. Consequently, Ward must rely on his study for patriarchal emphasis, wielding his ultimate authority in a book-lined room tailored to masculine prerogative.[7]

In order to countermand Donna's star persona and strong household authority, Alex Stone also must resort to a separate male space, as well as to his stature in the medical profession. Alex Stone's authority gains its visual credibility from the mise-en-scène, and he delivers his most serious diatribes from his downstairs examining room or in the living room. Alex's domination is underscored by his physician's white coat—a costume he wears frequently around the house, in order to remind both viewer and children of his clout in the outside world.

If Dad and Dad's blessings are thematically stressed, his power in both the film and television texts is emphasized further by the father's narrative centrality. *Leave It to Beaver* may center on a youthful perspective, but Wally and Beaver, as males, are still more closely aligned with Ward than with June. They share their father's childhood experiences as Ward (and never June) reminisces about growing up. Ward is also granted offscreen status away from the home, in his identity as both working man and social entity (we see him in the club locker room after a game of golf; he is alternately happy and disgusted with his friend/nemesis Fred Rutherford). June, however, exists only in conjunction with her sons. Although she is a stay-at-home mom in a suburban neighborhood, we never see her interact with her neighborhood counterparts; she does no grocery shopping, errand running, or chauffeuring. The only evidence of June's outside life is the rare occasion when she is seen scrambling to get dinner together after a late PTA meeting—a meeting which is elided, and which gains import only as a reason for her dereliction of household chores. Finally, while there are no actual episodes about Ward's adventures, he is often the focus of the boys' attentions. Seventeen of the 100 episodes screened deal explicitly with the father-and-son relationship, in which the boys want to buy a gift for their father, or wish to join his old fraternity or to brag about his exploits. June is the subject of only one episode (an indirect reference to her as the recipient of a gaudy blouse Beaver has purchased), and, indeed, in some episodes is completely absent.

In *Father Knows Best* numerous episodes revolve around Jim's adventures or tribulations *outside* the family: his difficulty in presiding at a "roast," his insurance business, the forced retirement of one of his employees, his volunteer position as a basketball coach, a feud with a family friend. Margaret, on the other hand, gains the spotlight only when she is in a crisis over her housewife status. In the Emmy-winning "A Medal for Margaret" (1957–1958), the parasitic position of the wife and mother is made patent as the Andersons build a trophy case for their various awards and discover that Margaret has never won anything.[8]

My Three Sons, with its combination of all-male enclave and superstar father, frequently focuses on Steve Douglas as the narrative center. Often there are episodes involving his role as aerospace consultant, ignoring his offspring completely (as he struggles with a work problem, dates a "lady engineer," and gets involved in a situation-comedy burlesque of mistaken identity or bad timing). The boys aspire to be like their father, and when Steve is away on one of his frequent business trips, they remind each other of what he would say or do in response to the various crises and events. The father gains near-mythic proportions, as one whose absence underscores his importance to both the outside world and his family. Indeed, it is crucial to remember here that Steve Douglas works as an aerospace consultant during the time when America was first embarking on "manned" space travel, and his omniscience seems an anthropomorphism of satellite technology. Steve Douglas, like ComSat, hovers over the periphery of his family, beaming down messages, and alighting occasionally to remind them of his tangible and transcendental authority.

Ozzie Nelson's implicit power is reinforced, continually, by his omnipresence. Ozzie is always around, is always featured as an integral member of the story events, and frequently possesses the central position in the narrative: of the 104 episodes screened, Ozzie figures as the center of the story in 42. Even the titles reveal a patriarchal sensibility while simultaneously pointing out the multifaceted persona of father: "Ozzie's Night Out" (1953–1954); "The

Volunteer Fireman" (1955–1956); "Ozzie's Triple Banana Surprise" (1957–1958); "Ozzie, the Boatkeeper" (1960–1961); "Ozzie's Hidden Trophy" (1963–1964); "Ozzie the Treasurer" (1956–1957); "An Honor for Oz" (1965–1966); "Ozzie, the Sitter" (1965–1966). Episodes that center around Harriet are rare and always revolve around her housewife status. In "Harriet's Hairdo" (1952–1953), for example, the issue is not so much Harriet's coiffure as it is a war between the sexes concerning predictability.

Even in *The Donna Reed Show,* in which Donna figures as the central character in a multitude of episodes, the narrative direction points to a valuation of patriarchy. Out of the 102 episodes screened, 9 feature Donna in an attempt to circumvent her role as "just a housewife," only to learn the hard way that this is the best of worlds for her.[9] In another 18 episodes, Donna dominates the narrative, only to be so strongly undercut in the end that these episodes serve as moral lessons to those women pushing for some sort of equality. In each episode she is prompted to remind herself or her family of the importance of Alex, and how the Stone family needs to continually recognize and applaud Dad's contribution. In addition, there are a surprisingly large number of episodes in which Donna goes away to a reunion, or home to Iowa. Alex is never missing from an episode.

In feature films, paternal power is rendered quite differently from that of the television dads, but it is always understood as the crucial operative construct in ensuring familial success. In other words, the film fathers, too, are depicted as the key to familial love, the most important parent, the one whose opinion matters most. But the film fathers have yet to learn the proper means of controlling their families. Thus, while the television episodes depict good fathers practicing their good liberal parenting techniques, the films depict faulty fathers whose eventual mastery of these techniques provides the films with their ultimate resolution. Some of these are men who attempt to run their families on the basis of financial or physical superiority over their wives and children. Big Daddy (*Cat on a Hot Tin Roof*), Wil Varner (*The Long Hot Summer*), and Ace Stamper (*Splendor in the Grass*) make continual reference to their struggle for wealth and the consummate importance it wins for them. Ultimately these men face their own mortality, leaving it to their sons to become compassionate caretakers. Other fathers view their strength as emanating from their corporeal abilities. The fathers in *Blue Denim, Tea and Sympathy, The Unguarded Moment,* and *Five Finger Exercise,* challenge their sons to a literal physical battle, mistakenly assuming that a test of muscle will prove their relative potency. They too learn from their sensitive sons that loving communication is the panacea for familial ills and that only with the empathetic father at its head can the family survive. As in the television texts, the centrality of the father depends on a mother (or surrogate mother) who serves as a channel of information. Because many of the film fathers still must learn the successful practices of the television dads, these women also serve to remind the father to soften his approach. The fact that mother bears this knowledge is inconsequential to her own power, because it is the father's assumption of this knowledge that is the crux of the parental-child relations. Thus, in *Houseboat*, Cynzia, the Italian "maid," is the voice of the suburban middle class and must instruct the American widower on proper modern parenting techniques, but she bears no real power of her own and her emotional import to the children is immediately subordinated to Tom's once he begins to relate to his children properly. In *The Courtship of Eddie's Father,* neighbor and volunteer nurse Elizabeth must instruct the patriarch on the importance of allowing Eddie to grieve for his dead mother. Tom's positive response to her advice works, ironically, to

15. In the 1963 film *The Courtship of Eddie's Father* Elizabeth (Shirley Jones) advises Tom (Glenn Ford) to allow Eddie (Ronny Howard) to grieve over the loss of his mother, resulting in her own marginalization as the two males unite in an exclusive pact barring women. (Copyright MGM.)

minimize Elizabeth's importance to the boy, as the father and son embrace and swear to a pact of mutual secrecy.

The structural potency granted the television fathers is even more pronounced in the films. Of the eighty-nine family melodramas screened, 58 percent feature father as the dominant character, focusing upon his business success or failure, his struggle to maintain a balance between work and home life, his capitulation to societal pressures (drugs, alcohol, conformity), and, most typically, his struggle to ensure familial love and respect. Mother is the focus of only 21 percent of the films, all of them dealing with the issue of feminine power as an explicit narrative concern.[10] In those films which owed their genesis to female-oriented stage plays or novels, the narrative is carefully reworked so that male characters gain narrative supremacy.[11] The potency granted to father-son bonding over any other narrative issue is made especially patent in *Blue Denim,* a film whose story line begs to be told from the young girl's point of view. The narrative structure, however, operates to exclude Janet from the center of her story, though it is she who gets pregnant, risks an illegal abortion, and runs off to live with her aunt. The purpose of Janet's pregnancy, in ideological terms, is to force Art to come to terms with his father, to learn to accept responsibility, to confront his fast-talking friend Ernie, to ascend to manhood. The pregnancy and the abortion are merely the narrative catalyst for the climactic split and concomitant reconciliation between father and son.[12]

A final means of underscoring the patriarch's implicit power is evident in the various stylistic strategies of the texts. The large quantity of programs and films examined herein precludes an indepth textual analysis, but some generalizations can be advanced. While the television programs boast large homes with a multitude of rooms, familial interaction is limited to the following, in descending order of importance: the living room, the kitchen, the dining room, the children's bedrooms, the parents' bedroom. These rooms are coded in terms of the family members' territory: the kitchen is (provisionally) the mother's domain; the children's rooms belong to the individual offspring; all other rooms are the domain of the father. Thus, even the placement of individual scenes has an impact upon the power relations in the program.

At first glance, it would seem that the kitchen (the second-most filmed room in the home) would privilege the mother, and, indeed, dad never delivers a lecture there (except in the all-male Douglas household). But, ironically, it is her very culinary duties that cause mother's familial exclusion. During the ubiquitous dinner and breakfast scenes, the women are usually up and about serving, rather than sitting at the table. In both *The Adventures*

16. Mother's potential narrative and emotional dominance in the kitchen is undercut by the fact that she is always standing and serving, and thus too active to participate in familial discussions, as in this frame enlargement from "The Big Test," an episode from the 1955–1956 season of *Father Knows Best.*

of Ozzie and Harriet and *Father Knows Best* the set is configured so that Mom's downstage chair is usually replaced by the camera, and Mom circles upstage, coffeepot in hand, while the camera cuts from a master-shot of the other family members to two-shots and close-ups. There are even specific references to Mother's omission from discussions, as she can be heard calling from the stove, "Wait a minute, I can't hear what you're saying." In *The Donna Reed Show,* Mother's exclusion registers in her shared frame space. The Stone kitchen dinette is constructed so that Alex sits alone at the head of the table, with Jeff alone at his left; Donna and Mary sit side by side to Alex's right, quite literally crammed in front of the stove. Though each of the men is regularly accorded a close-up, Donna generally shares the frame with daughter Mary. On *Leave It to Beaver,* June is most often in the kitchen and, like Harriet, often misses conversations because of it. Ward and the boys will be having a serious discussion in the living room or study, and June will come scurrying out to inquire about the proceedings. But by the time she arrives on the scene the discussion is over, and she feebly reminds the family to "wash up for dinner" before retreating to her domestic domain. She is allowed to sit at the head of the table, but the camerawork continually emphasizes Ward's authority. The most severe negation of the mother occurs during dining-table conversation, when, in answer to a question from June, the boys turn and respond directly to their father. While the camera privileges Ward with a close-up, or a two-shot with his sons, June's on-camera solos consist of silent reaction shots or unanswered questions.

The lack of a female presence in *My Three Sons* means the kitchen is a gender-neutral location for family meals; like the Stones, the family rarely eats in the dining room. The round table and lazy Susan give an aura of democracy (nobody needs to pass any food, all partake equally) and encourages discussion. Bub, like his female counterparts, hovers around the periphery, serving food, but unlike the mothers of the other programs, the configuration of the Douglas kitchen functions to *privilege* the cook's activities rather than minimize them. The dinner table is in the rear, and often the

17. Harriet's downstage chair remains perpetually empty as she hovers in the background of this frame enlargement from "The Day After Thanksgiving," from the 1953–1954 season of *The Adventures of Ozzie and Harriet*.

18. A frame enlargement from "Spring Will Be a Little Late," an episode from the
1960–1961 season of *My Three Sons*, illustrates the kitchen camaraderie of the Douglas
clan granted by the lazy Susan on the table and the visual prominence given Bub.
Bub, like the mothers on the other programs, rarely sits down, but unlike the mothers, his activities as he travels from table to stove to sink are followed by the camera.

dinner-table discussions are secondary to Bub's hustle and bustle at the sink
or stove, in the left and right foreground, respectively.

In addition to Father's placement in the room, his activities, coupled with
Mother's immobility, work to underscore his power. When Jim Anderson
and Ward Cleaver lecture their children, their actions are blocked so as to
lecture the entire family. In the Anderson household the clan sits on the
living room sofa while Jim paces about the room, the camera following his
movements. While Margaret supposedly shares authority with him, the fact
that she sits side by side with the children, silent, with hands clasped in her
lap makes her appear equally guilty. June Cleaver also sits meekly by, appearing at best a mere appendage and at worst one of the culpable. Harriet
Nelson is consistently absent from any scene of punishment (if indeed, any
truly occur), and Donna Stone, while privileged in activity, is still photo-
graphed in a medium, level shot, while Alex is privileged by low angles and
close-ups.

The importance of visual prowess in ensuring patriarchal potency is like-wise emphasized in the feature family melodramas. For example, in *Rebel without a Cause* the need Jim Stark has for his father "to stand up" is directly associated with his desire that his father assume the reins of authority. As in other issues of familial representation, the fact that Frank Stark is unwilling to rise up (and, indeed, is caught, *kneeling* behind the stairway bannister) is a central problem of the film. At the end of the film, when Frank urges Jim to "stand up with me," the spectator realizes that a significant bridge has been crossed, and Mother, out of the frame, dwarfed by her menfolk, has seen the error of her domineering ways.

In *All Fall Down*, the weak-willed Ralph spends his time playing games in the basement until he gets the courage to confront his domineering wife, when he rises literally to the main floor of the house and takes command of his family. In *Cat on a Hot Tin Roof*, both Brick and Big Daddy retreat to the basement and arise cleansed from the Oedipal catharsis, strengthened with patriarchal prerogative. Dinner scenes in films like *Splendor in the Grass, The Young Stranger, Rebel without a Cause,* and *Blue Denim* feature a father com-manding discussions from the head of the table, with Mother most often out of frame or skirting behind him with serving platters.

Father is granted power most explicitly via dialogue and plot. In conver-sation, various family members reiterate the importance of his love and af-fection and his superiority over other family members. This is evident in *Leave It to Beaver,* in which June is forever asking Ward to explain the boys to her. June, as a woman, is not privy to the secrets little boys share, or to the feelings that fathers have. For example, when Ward makes comments such as, "That's just something that happens between fathers and sons," June responds with, "I guess that's something I'll never know." The boys say con-stantly what a "swell dad" they've got, and how they want to be just like Ward when they grow up. On *Father Knows Best,* the youngest daughter, Kathy, is thrown into wild bursts of enthusiasm concerning her father: "My daddy can fix anything," "I have the best daddy in the world," and so forth.

In an episode from *Ozzie and Harriet* titled "The Motorcycle" (1958–1959), David's desire to buy a motorcycle motivates a scene of patriarchal-filial bonding as Ozzie and David explicitly recognize their value to one another:

OZZIE: Gee, you know I guess it's true. Dave doesn't need me to help him make his decisions anymore. He seems to have figured this thing out pretty well all by himself.

HARRIET: You're forgetting.

OZZIE: Forgetting what?

HARRIET: All the talks you've had with him since he's been old enough to understand. That's why he's able to make his own decisions now.

Both *The Donna Reed Show* and *My Three Sons* are less pedantic in their praise of Father. The centrality of the mother figure means that Donna shares some of the praise in the program. There is an equal number of statements delivered by the children emphasizing "the best mom in the world" as there are comments about Alex being a wonderful dad. In *My Three Sons* Bub indirectly lauds Steve by reprimanding the boys to help him out and make him proud.

The family in the feature-film melodramas is usually suffering a crisis of patriarchy, and, therefore, the comments about how "good" a dad is are uncommon or charged with ambivalence. They are the negative side of television's positive view; but even though the dialogue may turn on how Dad has been negligent in his familial duties, the expression of need, even the existence of the debate, puts Dad in the center of the family and the position of power. The children don't worry about mother love; they are concerned that father make explicit his affection and loyalty. In *The Young Stranger* Hal has his mother's support throughout the film, but he is depicted as a borderline juvenile delinquent because of the neglect of his father. In *Rebel without a Cause* both Judy and Jim reject their mothers and focus their emotional dependencies on the patriarch. In *East of Eden* Cal is curious and angry over the maternal abandonment of his childhood, but he seeks his father's love in a variety of business schemes and tributes. In films in which Dad is not portrayed as a "bad guy" the praiseworthy comments are as frequent as they are on television, especially in those films which feature a younger child protagonist. In *The Courtship of Eddie's Father,* for example, young Eddie makes Tom swear to a pact in which they will always tell each other "everything." In *Man on Fire,* the ex-wife Gwen, a woman much maligned by her heartless husband, nevertheless refrains from criticizing him to their son: "I won't cut you down to him. He's proud of you and that's how it should be."

Masculine centering through dialogue occurs in a variety of different narrative strategies; even greater patriarchal dominance is represented in those texts in which the narrative itself focuses specifically upon the child-father bond or upon the importance of the father to his family. In the television programs the bond is evident in narratives which work to praise the father, while in the films it is expressed as an unfulfilled desire, whereby the children clamor and cry out for paternal love and recognition.

In *Leave It to Beaver* Beaver writes an essay about his father as "the most interesting character [he] ever met," and he and Wally quarrel over who "gets Dad" for a fishing trip and who gets him for a father-son picnic. In "The Bank Account" (1957–1958) the boys expend all their effort and most of their savings in buying their father a new hunting jacket. June sits by passively and misty-eyed while the boys proclaim their love for their father and Ward opens the gift. On *The Donna Reed Show,* in a 1958–1959 episode titled "The Male Ego," Donna institutes a birthday "tribute" dinner for the patriarch, complete with gifts, speeches, tears, and music. "Ozzie's Night Out" (1953–1954) focuses on the importance of the father in *all* domestic areas: when Harriet's friend Helen reminds her that husbands as wonderful as Ozzie are in demand, and that she and Harriet must be careful to give the provider an occasional respite from familial duties to keep him happy. Naturally, when Harriet insists on Ozzie's recreational evening out, the domestic equilibrium falls apart, and she calls him back soon thereafter to help balance a checkbook and assist the boys with their homework.

In *My Three Sons,* because of the literal absence of his wife, Steve Douglas rarely receives the accolades of other dads—he is dominant merely by virtue of her absence. Additionally, the program is quick to assert masculine superiority in general, with Bub winning numerous prizes for performing domestic tasks so much better than a woman would. Episodes such as "What's Cookin'?" (1962–1963), "Mother Bub" (1962–1963), "The Lostling" (1960–1961), "The People House" (1963–1964), and "Other People's Houses" (1960–1961) show Bub's superiority over other neighborhood "housewives" in the areas of cooking, sensitivity to children's needs, and home decorating.

The program most concerned with tangible awards for parenting is *Father Knows Best.* Out of the 116 episodes screened, 13 are about what a wonderful father Jim Anderson is (see Appendix C). In these episodes, either Springfield is having a contest in which the children enter their father (who always wins) or Jim doubts his worth in the business world and is made to recognize that being a father is the most important job he can do.

This explicit narrative focus on superior fathers is usually reflected negatively in the theatrical films. There, the assurance of the power of the patriarch is exemplified by narratives in which the father has *failed* in his parental duties and thereby created familial crises. Mothers are either completely absent from such dynamics (they are not mentioned during the moment of bonding, they're dead, or they have deserted the family) or their evil nature is what predicates the father-son breakdown to begin with.[13] Familial restitution depends upon a father-child reconciliation and takes the form of a delayed resolution of the Oedipal crisis. The potency of these scenes is underscored by their ubiquity in the genre. And, indeed, it is worth noting that this sort of pattern also formed the basis of much Victorian melodrama. Martha Vicinis writes that in 1914 a book called *The Ragged Trousered Philanthropists* focused on the patriarchal prerogative: "Women appear only rarely in the book but those who do are faultless. . . . Much more is made of the men's love for their children, who in all significant cases are boys."[14] In 49 of the 89 family melodramas analyzed, the major point of narrative conflict stems from some sort of aberration in the father-child relationship. The child, usually male,[15] confronts his father about the latter's incompetency as a father. Usually, but not always, the point of resolution occurs during what I call the "adolescent weepy scene." In these moments, the son (aged anywhere from 16 to 30) expresses his heartfelt need for the father's love and recognition. This, in turn, triggers a reconciliation between the patriarch and his progeny. Most often, the resolution is delayed and inspired by a disaster or crisis in which father or son becomes dependent upon the other for his life.[16] The films conclude with a new patriarchal-filial understanding in which true love has been expressed and each has taken his appropriate place in the Oedipal hierarchy. The films reiterate the notion that fathers should be moral, upstanding leaders, not their sons' equals.

Though all the theatrical releases consistently center on parental-filial confrontation and revelation, and thus explicitly underline the father's familial dominance, the terms of the conflict are often distinctive and unique. It is useful, therefore, to review briefly the distinct types of paternal-filial strife and their concomitant resolutions.

Variation No. 1: Materialism versus Love

Films: *Blue Denim, Cat on a Hot Tin Roof, The Long Hot Summer, Executive Suite, A Hatful of Rain.*

One of the most common sources of divisiveness between fathers and sons is the father's substitution of material items or wealth for time and the expression of love. The fathers are guilty of ignoring their sons and/or of giving them material possessions without benefit of their time. In *Blue Denim,* for example, Major Bartley's laissez-faire attitude about his son results in Art's seeking an illegal abortion for his girlfriend, Janet. The father is so preoccupied with his daughter's wedding (the frivolous feminine sphere) that he ignores the real-world needs of his troubled son. The resolution is catalyzed by Art's eventual confession to his father as they come to physical blows over a forged check. Major Bartley becomes the exemplary intrusive parent and aids his son in preventing Janet's abortion. In *Cat on a Hot Tin Roof* (1958)

19. The ubiquitous male, adolescent, weepy scene is exemplified in this exchange between Brick (Paul Newman) and Big Daddy (Burl Ives) in the 1958 film *Cat on a Hot Tin Roof.* (Copyright MGM.)

Brick yells at his father for trying to buy the family's love instead of showing honest affection, and Mr. Pope's neglect of his sons in *A Hatful of Rain* results in Johnny's spiral into drug addiction and his older brother's accompanying plummet into debt. In both films a life-threatening disease motivates the confession and mutual support of father and son.

Variation No. 2: The Son as Prize

Films: *Fear Strikes Out, Giant, Peyton Place* (Rodney Harrington), *Splendor in the Grass* (Bud Stamper), *Five Finger Exercise.*

An equally viable form of conflict surfaces in those relationships in which the father sees the son as some sort of super-progeny—mirroring the father's success, and regards him only as a tangible expression of his own work. These fathers don't love their sons but push them toward some sort of goal, ignoring their sons' need for unconditional love.

In *Fear Strikes Out,* Mr. Piersall is not so much in admiration of Jim's baseball abilities as he is obsessed by them, eventually pushing his son to a

nervous breakdown. The father sees in his son a chance to achieve vicari-
ously the honor of the professional athlete. All lectures about Jim's playing
strategies are couched in the first-person plural: "We'll show them we can't
be beat." In his confrontation with his father in the asylum, Jim makes explicit the problem with fathers who demand too much of their sons, telling
his father that he "wants too much," that Jim has given everything he can,
and has "got nothing left to give." In *Giant*, Bick Benedict is determined that
his son, bound for medical school, will become a professional rancher. As in
Fear Strikes Out, it is only in the face of his son's anger that the father recognizes his failings and the healing process can begin. In both cases the son's
anger is released within the safe zone of socialized acceptability: Jim loses
his temper in an institution, a place reserved for the release of "true feelings";
Jordy confronts his father after his Mexican-American wife is targeted by
racial slurs. In these films a moment of social crisis (the sons' provoked attack on others as a screened-out projection of their animosity toward their
fathers) motivates the ultimate paternal shame and filial pardon.

Variation No. 3: The Father as Negative Moral Influence

Films: *Home from the Hill* (1959), *Bernardine*, *Rebel without a Cause*, *A Sum-
mer Place*, *April Love* (1957), *The Man in the Gray Flannel Suit* (1956), *The
Tarnished Angels* (1957), *The Remarkable Mr. Pennypacker* (1959), *The Last
Time I Saw Paris* (1954; daughter), *No Down Payment* (1957), *Splendor in the
Grass* (Deanie Loomis), *The Unguarded Moment*, *Peyton Place* (Selena Cross),
God's Little Acre (1958), *All Fall Down*, *The Pleasure of His Company* (1961;
daughter).

In this case, the father has failed in his paternal duties not so much by neglect as by error or evil. The father is either derelict in his masculine prose-
lytizing (*Rebel without a Cause*, *All Fall Down*, *Splendor in the Grass*, etc.) or
overly greedy, macho, and scornful of women (*The Unguarded Moment*,
Home from the Hill, *God's Little Acre*). While rare, this category would also
include the narrative configuration of deceased fathers, whose influential
absence is made potent by the son's reference to the missing role model (*Bernardine*). Here the resolution rests not in a declaration of parental love, but
in the son's re-education of the father (if alive) or reevaluation of the father
(if deceased), coupled with a re-education of himself, learning about his
proper role in patriarchal society by correcting his father's deviant behavior.[17] It is crucial to note that within these films, the mother plays an equally

pivotal role, for it is usually by her misappropriation of the father's duties (discipline, authority, decision making) that she, in effect, undercuts his power (*Rebel without a Cause, Splendor in the Grass, All Fall Down, No Down Payment*) or so infuriates/demoralizes him that he strays off the proven path of fidelity (*Home from the Hill, The Last Time I Saw Paris, The Man in the Gray Flannel Suit*). Thus, the resolution in these films rests on the coupled factors of a reinvigoration of the father—whereby he is forced to recognize his moral responsibilities—and an elimination of the mother, either by her death or her passive resignation. However, re-education works only for those fathers who are too weak, not for those who are morally reprehensible (*Home from the Hill, The Unguarded Moment, A Summer Place, Peyton Place, God's-Little Acre*). The solution for these sinners is almost always their death.

Variation No. 4: Father is Too Strict

Films: *Tea and Sympathy, East of Eden, The Young Stranger, David and Lisa, Autumn Leaves* (1956), *Some Came Running* (1958; displaced onto older brother), *The Days of Wine and Roses* (daughter), *Gidget Goes Hawaiian* (1961; daughter).

In this configuration the problem rests in a father who is resistant to the affectionate demands of his son. There is some overlap in this category with Variation No. 1 (often the father who is too strict defends his position with the material possessions that he bestows upon his son), but I note this distinction because there is a vast difference between such fathers as Adam Trask of *East of Eden* or Thomas Ditmore of *The Young Stranger*, both of whom are undeniably harsh with their offspring, and Big Daddy of *Cat on a Hot Tin Roof*, who is (merely) guilty of replacing love with money.

For example, Adam Trask's obstinate refusal to respond positively to Cal's ingenuity with the coal-chute device for loading lettuce and his rejection of Cal's bean earnings on his birthday, coupled with his blind affection for his son Aron, result in the adolescent weepy scene in which Cal berates his father for his harshness: "You didn't really love her any more than you do me. . . . Because we weren't good like you . . . I've been jealous all my life. Tonight I even tried to buy your love, but now I don't want it anymore . . . I don't want any kind of love anymore. It doesn't pay off." In *The Young Stranger* the father doesn't trust his son, assumes immediately that his son has broken the law, and takes the side of a malevolent theater manager who wrongly accuses Hal of defacing a movie theater. Again, there is the confrontation scene, in which Hal screams out: "Can't you ever say anything to me that isn't a speech? . . . I never did know [what you really think of me]. I don't know why I ever expected you to believe me; you don't even know me. How could you ever possibly know whether I was lying or telling the truth?"

The roadblocks to reconciliation are too high to be bridged by a mere articulation of the problem, requiring instead a life-threatening disaster and a third-party intervention (by Abra in *East of Eden* and the police lieutenant in *The Young Stranger*, who reassure the father and son of their mutual innocence and interdependency).

Variation No. 5: Father Needs a Wife

Films: *Houseboat* (1958), *Man on Fire, The Courtship of Eddie's Father, The Parent Trap* (1961).

Though generally less common, an extraordinarily potent narrative in films in which the child is under sixteen is that in which an unmarried father must come to terms with his singlehood and workaholism, and, with the son's help, move toward resolidifying the family unit with a wife.

In *Houseboat* it is David's need for his father's attention which catalyzes the boy's kleptomania and thus convinces Tom of the need to remarry and reconstruct a secure nuclear family for his child. Eddie is the matchmaker between his father and their next-door neighbor in *The Courtship of Eddie's Father*, and twins Susan and Sharon successfully break up their father's disreputable affair with a money-hungry sexpot and steer him toward remarrying their mother in *The Parent Trap*.

While the origins of the father-son crisis might differ, the resolution to the problem is almost always the same. Some mortal crisis, usually threatening the life of the son, the father, or another family member, causes the two of them to come to terms in a life-saving effort. They break the melodramatic "text of muteness" and, by giving voice to the problem (a lack of expressed love), solve it. Thus, in *East of Eden*, Adam Trask's stroke allows Cal to be the nurturing son he'd always aspired to be; in *Cat on a Hot Tin Roof* Brick is also allowed to lavish tender loving care on the now cancer-ridden Big Daddy; Jim Piersall's mental breakdown and his consequent sanctuary in a mental ward allow him, in *Fear Strikes Out*, to finally tell his father off, as does Johnny's withdrawal from drugs in *A Hatful of Rain*; Eddie, David, and Ted, respectively, run away in *The Courtship of Eddie's Father, Houseboat,* and *Man on Fire,* causing the fathers to come to grips with their marital shortcomings;

and death, or the threat of it, unites the patriarch and his offspring in a new-found camaraderie in *Rebel without a Cause, All Fall Down,* and *Blue Denim.*

Occasionally, the fatal blow is carried to its logical conclusion, with either the patriarch (*Written on the Wind, Splendor in the Grass, The Tarnished Angels, Home from the Hill*) or his heir (*Written on the Wind, All Fall Down*) dying or leaving before complete reconciliation has taken place. However, in each of these films there is either a surrogate son, a brother, or a son of a son to learn the lesson of past mistakes and to construct a healthy family unit. In *Splendor in the Grass,* Ace Stamper's suicide coupled with the birth of Bud's own child ensure that Bud will not make the same mistakes as his father. In *Written on the Wind* the death of the incompetent natural son, Kyle Hadley, allows the surrogate, Mitch Wayne, to assume the place of both the dead father, Jasper Hadley, and the son, and to ensure a correct family upbringing.

If power issues are carefully delineated in terms of gender, they are emphasized equally clearly in terms of age. While the father possesses the greatest proportion of narrative power, his ideological potency varies depending on the medium. Indeed, it is in this area of generational authority that some of the starkest contrasts between television and film exist. In the film versions of family life the voice of the status quo, tradition, and morality originates in the younger generation. This is not to say that the youth in the films have any sort of actual power; I suggest merely that they provide a point of spectator identification and sympathy, in that theirs is the ideologically approved point of view. The notion that the children are the repositories of tradition and conservativism has been discussed most thoroughly in critical literature on *Rebel without a Cause.* Jim, Judy, and Plato are described as a "surrogate family," in which the unmet Oedipal needs of the three angst-ridden youths are answered by one another.[18]

Numerous other cinematic family melodramas uphold the notion that it is the younger generation that is the voice of tradition and morality. In *Home from the Hill* Rafe and Libby provide the happy communicative marriage at the end of the film designed to balance (and even cancel out) the bickering matrimonial facade of the captain (Rafe's father) and his wife. In *Peyton Place* Constance MacKenzie is the dirty-minded former sinner who gave birth to her illegitimate daughter and then lied to her about her "dead" father; Lucas Cross is the evil stepfather who browbeats his simpering wife and rapes his virginal stepdaughter, Selena. The children, on the other hand, are proponents of morality and decency: Betty wants only to marry Rodney Harrington, and Selena and Ted are also altar-bound; Alison MacKenzie has aspira-

20.   In the 1962 film *All Fall Down* Clint (Brandon de Wilde) is the introspective voice of love and reason, while his parents (Karl Malden and Angela Lansbury) are vile misanthropes. (Copyright MGM.)

tions toward a writing career and is involved in a morally upstanding friendship with her friend Norman, based on mutual trust. In *A Summer Place* Mollie and Johnny want only to wed, and it is their philandering, drinking, and intolerant parents who are at odds with the desired matrimonial pathway. In *Giant* Jordy is the proponent of racial equality while father Bick is closed-minded and bigoted. In *All Fall Down* Clint is a writer and a young man filled with insight, introspection, and diligence, but his parents are misanthropes. While all suspicion in *The Unguarded Moment* is directed toward Leonard, the real rapist turns out to be his father, Mr. Bennett, whose misogynistic diatribes had infected (but not quite overwhelmed) his only son.

But while the underlying emphasis is on the greater sagacity of youth in comparison with their elders, there are some slight variations in the manner in which this is expressed. First, if the children are too young to voice a moral superiority, an outside adult speaks for them, reminding the spectator of the discernment of youth and the obstinacy of adulthood. In *The Court-*

ship of Eddie's Father, the next-door neighbor, Elizabeth, must remind Tom Corbett of his son's acumen. In *Houseboat,* Cynzia instructs the children to be patient with their father and tells them that "sometimes it's very difficult to be a grown-up."

Sometimes, as in *Blue Denim* (and *Rebel without a Cause,* for that matter), it is readily acknowledged that adults have the actual power to assist their children;[19] they lack the insights, knowledge, or morality to do so, however, and must be assisted in carrying out their appropriate duties. Here, the adults are in a position to help the troubled teens, but the latter bear the burden of seeking out that assistance, of not only directing their parents toward their proper duties, but taking the initiative in confronting them about it as well.

On television, it is the elders who understand the importance of ritual, monogamy, monotony, and stability, and who impart this knowledge week after week to their children. As in *Rebel without a Cause,* this moral guidance most often takes the manipulative rather than the directive approach. In *Father Knows Best,* for example, the children usually err twice, first, in committing the initial transgression, and second, in lying about it. In "Dilemma for Margaret" (1955–1956), Betty becomes involved in a high-school club initiation rite which involves dressing up in ghost costumes. Betty's offense is, on the surface, a mild form of juvenile delinquency—she sneaks out of the house at night, deceiving her parents. But ideologically, her crime is readable on a much deeper level. First, she is guilty of elitism: joining an exclusive social coterie is frowned upon by the inhabitants of the mythological democratic flatlands of America. Second, the donning of the sheet evokes images of the Ku Klux Klan, further associating Betty's malfeasance with greater criminality. Finally, in covering her tracks, she is discovered by her younger brother and sister and solicits their cooperation in her deception, so she is guilty of conspiracy and moral corruption. When their daughter's offense is viewed in this way, Jim and Margaret's overwhelmingly disproportionate anger at her disobedience doesn't seem so exaggerated. As the representatives of traditional American values they are extolling equality, tolerance, and morality. Rather than confront Betty directly with a prohibition, however, her parents manipulate the teenager, through shame and guilt, into recanting her club membership, confessing to the principal, and suffering public humiliation. Jim provokes Betty with a reminder that her participation in such antics compromises her mother's impending lecture on proper child-rearing techniques, and Margaret strengthens this perspective by claiming she will now have to resign her commission as a child authority. There are numerous

21. The Anderson family stand as judge of the offscreen Bud in this episode from the 1954–1955 season of *Father Knows Best,* "Lesson in Citizenship." (Copyright Columbia.)

other examples of this technique, and the bulk of the episodes of *Father Knows Best* are constructed around moral choices and dilemmas facing the children, who must decide between pleasurable (childish) enticements and morally upstanding courses of action. In all of these cases the scenario follows a pattern of euphoria, conflict, parental lecture, shame, and self-recrimination followed by acquiescence to the parental conservative agenda and resulting pride that one has done the "right thing."

While not enforced with the conservative rigidity of *Father Knows Best,* *Leave It to Beaver* and *My Three Sons* also practice this type of moral manipulation in which, in order to learn a lesson, the children must suffer humiliation, agony, and guilt, with the conclusion resting on the verbal assessment, "You were right, Dad." In the more progressive series, *The Adventures of Ozzie and Harriet* and *The Donna Reed Show,* the children also have to toe the line, but are usually instructed quite directly by their parents as to what constitutes inappropriate behavior. Not only are the programs less demanding of the children in terms of decorum and self-sacrifice, but the children are not humiliated into learning a lesson; the parents, in either a mild directive or a completely laissez-faire approach, allow the children to make the right decision. Because the behavioral restrictions are not as potent on these programs, the children are less apt to make a mistake in the first place.

Intrafamily power relations are thus configured along a continuum of gender and age. On television, middle-aged males rank highest and women and girls are at the lower end of the scale, while the adults are the voices of American consensus concerning morality, tolerance, and tradition. In film, the males continue to dominate in terms of narrative importance, power over the family, and valuation in the eyes of the children, but when generational conflicts are at issue, the adolescents are the voices of convention, propelling their elders toward the correct actions.

Interfamily Relations

Family melodrama is predicated on the ideological hegemony of the family. While the film and television texts operate to ensure familial stability in the face of intrarelational conflict, they also validate the importance of a particular family unit in contradistinction to other clans. Family feuds serve to underscore the moral superiority of one group over another, to provide a solution to alienated families, and to eliminate troubled enclaves either by absorbing them or destroying them. Additionally, the ideological foundation upon which the central family rests serves as a point of distinction between the film and television versions of the genre; in film it is the family-protagonist who is usually troubled, while in television the family-protagonist is (arguably) idealized. By analyzing the stakes of the debate and the various victories between the dueling families, the subtle differences between the film and television texts and their similar moralizing rationales can be understood.

Most simply, in the film versions of the genre, the central nuclear unit is severely disturbed and dysfunctional. The typical narrative progression depicts the necessary maturation of the family unit into a cohesive and stable whole. Often, this growth is achieved by the family in and of itself, usually with the help of an external mediator who guides the characters toward the mandatory paternal-filial confrontation and consequent healing. Sometimes, however, the family unit is so weakened as to be unable to exist independently. Here the story focuses on one of two possible narratives, the first of which concerns the animosity between, and the eventual merging of, two separate families, the assets of one group complementing the liabilities of the other; the alternative story line focuses on extended families in which the younger generation instructs and/or eventually replaces the older, maladjusted family unit. In the first narrative two distinct family units are thus depicted as being, in some way, incomplete, and this incompleteness both causes and is complicated by familial strife. In *Houseboat*, for example, Tom Winters is divorced and then widowed, and consequently becomes the reluctant guardian for his three maladjusted children. Cynzia is a spoiled and unhappy daughter of a widower father, and is a cheat, liar, and mocker of authority. Tom is in need of a wife and a mother for his three children, while Cynzia must become a mother in order to properly reconcile her own maternal loss. The marriage of the two results in the demise of the splintered, negative families and the creation of a new, extended nuclear unit (Cynzia's father is now the happy grandpa).

In *The Parent Trap* twin sisters Sharon and Susan McKendrick (a dual role played by Hayley Mills) were separated as babies when their parents, Maggie and Mitch, divorced. The film is adamant in its ideological dictates that broken homes can be neatly sewn back together and thereby form the ideal nuclear unit. While the film is played as comedy, the situation is quite horrible; Sharon and Susan grow up not only fatherless and motherless, respectively, but without any knowledge of one another. When they meet at summer camp and deduce their connection, they agree to change places and work to unite the parents. Sharon muses: "It's scary the way nobody stays together anymore; pretty soon there will be more divorces than marriages."[20] The resolution to the conflict is to relocate businesswoman Maggie to Mitch's ranch where, barefoot and aproned, she assumes her proper role behind the kitchen stove. Other films which locate the solution for familial strife in a unification of two separate and disturbed entities are *Magnificent Obsession* (the wealthy blind widow and the irresponsible scion turned genius surgeon), *Imitation of Life* (the single career woman/mother, her daughter, the newly orphaned mulatto, and the matrimonially determined bachelor), *A Summer Place* (the reunion of childhood sweethearts via their respective divorces from an alcoholic ne'er-do-well and a frigid disciplinarian, doubled with the coupling of their children), *Man on Fire* (in which divorced father Earl Carlton relinquishes son Ted to his now infertile ex-wife and her new husband, while Earl will presumably begin a new nuclear unit with girlfriend, Nina).

Films following the other favored filmic story line—that of extended families—are often called feudal family melodramas. In them, in addition, a sacrificing of the most marginally desirable is often, but not always, imperative to the family's survival. Here the solution to the splintered family rests not in unification, but in the corrective life-styles of the children, and, typically, in a concurrent elimination of the guilty parents. In *Cat on a Hot Tin Roof, The Long Hot Summer, Splendor in the Grass,* and *Home from the Hill* the central family is both internally divided and at odds with another, equally miserable family. In *Cat on a Hot Tin Roof* Big Daddy and Big Mama suffer a loveless marriage, as the tyrannical father browbeats his son Groper and his wife, flirts with his daughter-in-law Maggie, and abuses his son Brick. The matrimonial split between the patriarch and his weak-willed wife is too severe to offer any future hope. Consequently, the solution is to render Big Daddy impotent, via his life-threatening disease, and invest all hope in the future generation of Brick and the now possibly pregnant Maggie.

The warring factions of the working-class Loomis family and the nouveau-riche Stampers of *Splendor in the Grass* are united by a squelching of passion and the creation of two distinct and distinctly middle-class family units. Bud is the disillusioned son of the unhappily married Stampers, while Deanie is the mentally off-balance romantic daughter of the henpecked Loomis and his wife, Freda. The usual course of action would be to find the solution to these two diseased families in the unification of the children, but Bud and Deanie are too infected by their familial upbringing—Bud has become physically ill and Deanie has had a nervous breakdown. Instead, the film puts its hopes in the future of the family by merging classes, ethnicities, and geographical origins, ideologically underscoring the progressive romanticism of the égalité of the American melting pot. Bud realizes his life-long dream of farming, and his marriage to the earthy Angelina produces a happy, carefree little boy (with another child on the way). No longer wealthy, he has gravitated toward the agrarian middle class. Deanie, too, is headed toward the middle of the road, engaged to a doctor and moving to a city (not to a dangerous urban environment, but to the safer surroundings of a midwest metropolis). The valuation is placed upon both compromise and a future generation that understands the importance of egalitarian unification. The troubling entities (the bombastic Wil Stamper, the promiscuous Ginny Stamper) have been sacrificed as too threatening for the continuation of the nuclear unit.

In film, then, the featured family is often split, divorced, and miserable, and the solution lies either in the unification of two contrary families, each of which fulfills the other's needs, or in the younger members' regeneration of American ideals. These are conclusive solutions, in which the guilty parties are eliminated by death (Plato as the sacrifice which unites the Stark family, Big Daddy and his impending demise, Kyle Hadley along with his misguided father) or ostracism (MaryLee left alone with her oil well, Helen and Bart missing from the end of *A Summer Place*), and their place taken by their better-adjusted or more mainstream counterparts (Jim and Judy, Mitch and Lucy, Ken and Sylvia). For film, therefore, successful family life is posited as a goal, and its realization usually indicates the conclusion to a narrative trajectory in which alienated individuals struggle to find a secure haven.

On television, the successful operation of family life forms the foundation for all other narrative complications; the security of the television clans is taken as a given from the start of the narrative. The structure of each individual episode then reveals a threat to that foundation which must be overcome through the efforts of familial confrontation and restitution. Here, interfamilial conflict functions to underscore the moral supremacy of the family-protagonist of the television series and to demonstrate how a positive family image can influence and impact a negative one. Indeed, given the marketing stance of the networks, it is probable that the viewing family, like the guest star, was to understand its familial inferiority to the Nelsons or Cleavers and then learn from their upstanding example. On television, the solution for the dysfunctional family rests not in the elimination of the guilty party, but in his or her reappropriation into a nuclear family and/or a reeducation about the importance of traditional family units, always under the guidance of the series' family-protagonist. In this way, the power of the nuclear unit is doubly assured: first, the featured families serve as an example of the "right" kind of family; and second, they often act as mediators in unifying disparate groups into a homogeneous carbon copy of their own familial structure. This is quite different from the filmic families, disparate units that are both the problem and its solution, struggling within themselves for a self-reliant "cure."

A cogent example from *Father Knows Best,* an episode called "The Persistent Guest" (1955–1956), involves a young teen, Fred, whose divorced parents have deserted him. He lives on his own in the junkyards of Springfield, sponging off unsuspecting families until they get fed up with his dependence and kick him out. The Andersons, however, function as moral judges toward less-understanding families and rehabilitate Fred as they unite him with the Millers, a childless couple aching to have a son. Here the solution, like the filmic ones, rests in joining two dysfunctional families and showing tolerance toward Fred, who is verging on delinquency. In his insecurities, his quest for a family, and his bitterness toward his parents, Fred is much like Plato in *Rebel without a Cause.* But television does not take the harsh tack of his death, nor does it require Fred or the Millers to resolve the crisis themselves. Instead, through the intervention of the Anderson clan, who provide Fred with new clothes, new manners, and a new haircut, the two distinct units are joined together. The Andersons beam proudly as young Fred shakes hands with Mr. Miller, who joyously welcomes him with "Hello, son."

"Guest in the House," a 1958–1959 episode from *The Donna Reed Show,* also deals with a splintered family and an abandoned child. David Barker is the son of a career air-force man who has placed him in military school because his wife left him. David runs away to the Stones in search of the nuclear family (much like Plato turns to Judy and Jim, and Fred to the Andersons). Again, the television version resolves David's situation by naming the episodic family as surrogate family and demonstrating how mother love can turn a child tyrant into an angel. Interestingly, the David Barker story is never fully resolved. David makes subsequent guest appearances on three more episodes of the program, each time exhibiting some sort of antisocial behavior that must be corrected through the tender care of the Stone family. In each case, the Stones intervene and communicate David's needs to his father, who then apologizes to his son and promises to change his behavior.[21]

The most common cause for the cinematic families being splintered was divorce. The episodic nature of television, production-code restrictions, and sponsor demands precluded the protagonist-family from ever experiencing legal separation, but the fear of divorce and its ramifications permeate the programs. In "Divorce, Bryant Park Style" (1964–1965) the Douglas clan must reconcile a young married couple whose new baby is causing much strife. Mike's best friend, Howard, turns to Mike (twenty years old and still living at home) for advice. The shame, guilt, and horror of divorce are made explicit in this episode, and as a result both of the efforts of Mike, Sally (Mike's fiancée), Steve Douglas, and an ineffectual (female) marriage counselor, as well as of a scary session in a divorce court, Howard and Francine renounce their intention to split up. Other television programs deal equally harshly with the notion of divorce. In the aforementioned "Persistent Guest" episode of *Father Knows Best,* Fred is abandoned because his parents are divorced (a word mentioned in hushed and horrified tones). *The Donna Reed Show* features two episodes from the first two seasons of the program dealing with the fear of divorce.[22]

It is crucial to note that while television dealt with interfamily strife, the way it was rendered was quite different from that of feature film. Rather than pitting two evil families against each other in the hope that a third, harmonious unit would emerge, the TV programs pit a dysfunctional unit against the Andersons, Stones, Cleavers, Douglases, and Nelsons, who then, as a family, act as the model for improvement, the catalyst for change, or the initiator of solutions. Much like the wild-west hero, who enters the society only to better it and leave, television's nuclear families welcome the intrusion of society's more troublesome situations in order to resolve them and restore the patriarchal conservative order. On television, the presence of the featured family allows continual comparison with any guest-starring enclaves and represents both ideological goal and active mediator in the healing process. Here, interfamilial power is possessed by the family that is most illustrative of the American bourgeois nuclear unit, and this power is constantly wielded to reunify less complete configurations. The film families, conversely, operate as the site of both problem and solution, but they must bear witness to the total destruction of either an *outsider* (Plato) or an aging family member (Wil Stamper, Adam Trask, Big Daddy) in order to accomplish their self-instigated metamorphoses.

Family and Society

The relationship established between the nuclear unit and society is a final area in which to assess familial power. For better management of such an amorphous term as "society," it can be divided up into two workable categories. First and foremost is Louis Althusser's notion of the "Ideological State Apparatus," (ISA)[23] whereby certain social institutions (the church, the education system, the legal system, the family) are identified as the impetus and retainer of ideological precepts. In the family melodrama the ISA of the family is much more potent than any other ISA, interacting with these social institutions yet continually establishing itself as more important to the formation of the individual and as the supplier of solutions. Thus, first, the position of family qua family—its status in relation to that of the other social institutions—is examined, followed by an analysis of the position of the family in society in terms of ethnicity and integration. Here, power relations between the predominantly white central families of the melodramas and their interactions with other races and ethnicities become a means for understanding the potency of familial power in articulating and resolving social dilemmas.

It might be said that family melodrama is less a morality play and more a power play. One of the key power plays in the family melodrama concerns the importance of the family itself. This is rendered in two distinct ways—as narrative focal point, and through dialogue. Structurally, the family is underscored as both cause and solution to any narrative dilemma. Crises ranging from juvenile delinquency to drug addiction to teen pregnancy are traced as both originating with and being resolved by the family situation. As Biskind notes:

> By the fifties . . . [delinquents] were no longer criminals—good or bad—they were sick, like young sex maniac John Saxon, who stalks

teacher Esther Williams in *The Unguarded Moment* (1956). . . . The new cause was bad families, not bad neighborhoods. In *The Unguarded Moment* the problem is Saxon's misogynist dad, Edward Andrews, who believes women "ought to be wiped off the face of the earth."[24]

And, as Horace Newcomb notes about the television counterparts:

> These values [of peace, love, and laughter] are grounded in the belief in the family as a supportive group. Within the family, strength abides. The strength grows out of the mutual support that each of the family members is willing to offer and for which he or she receives like support in return. Many episodes are built on the minor ways in which family members hurt one another, sometimes consciously, sometimes not. With each resolution of such a problem, however, the family unit is strengthened. The group is the sheltering unit, particularly when we are made aware of the difficulties of the world surrounding the family.[25]

An analysis of the origins and resolutions of social problems is useful in ascertaining both the power of the family against other institutions and the distinctions between the film and television texts in underscoring this potency.

In the filmic renditions of family life the various crises of communication within the nuclear unit engender a series of catastrophes. In *Rebel without a Cause* Judy, Jim, and Plato become teenage misanthropes because they don't get love and understanding at home. In *A Hatful of Rain* Johnny's drug addiction begins as a result of a war injury, but his continual dependence and, indeed, his development as an "addictive personality" are firmly rooted in his need for, and denial of, paternal love. Kirsten's addiction to first chocolate and then booze is implicitly credited to her desperate need for paternal attention in *The Days of Wine and Roses*. *Fear Strikes Out* argues that Jim Piersall's mental breakdown is caused not so much by the pressures of Big League baseball, where he is quite successful, but by his father's relentless pushiness. Crucially, however, the solutions to these problems also rest within the family unit. Within each of these family melodramas, the family is assisted by a social agent—a juvenile officer, a drug rehabilitation clinic, a member of Alcoholics Anonymous, or a psychiatrist—in discovering the proper course of action to take. The social forces do not assume the mantle of control as much as suggest, explicate, and prod the nuclear unit into a newfound model of self-sufficiency. Thus, *Rebel without a Cause* ends with Frank taking charge of his family the way Officer Ray has instructed; Johnny's father and wife in *A Hatful of Rain* are instrumental in contacting the drug center and will presumably accompany him there for his cure; Kirsten's inability to accept Joe's new sobriety in *The Days of Wine and Roses* causes the end of the marriage; and in *Fear Strikes Out* Jim Piersall plays catch with his father on a newly discovered equal basis. Such films as *Rebel without a Cause, Crime in the Streets, Dino, Splendor in the Grass, The Days of Wine and Roses, Fear Strikes Out,* and *David and Lisa* continually evoke socially sanctioned institutions as imperative to the successful functioning of the hermetically sealed nuclear enclave, but these institutions merely *instruct* the family members to reconvene as a unit to resolve their issues through love and understanding.[26] In addition, the film texts usually predicate the "cure" on some sort of explosive solution or expulsion. Buzz and Plato, as the unsavory "rebels," must be killed off; Kirsten, as the intractable alcoholic, is expelled from her family; and a gang member in *Dino* is sacrificed. The assumption in the film texts is that there is both moral behavior and dangerous behavior, and the way to deal with dangerous behavior is to eliminate it and destroy those who are unwilling to change. The moral agenda is more acute in films, which, due in part to their limited (as opposed to episodic) running time, are able to practice highly definitive conclusions to delinquent practices.

Not only is the family itself emphasized, the filmic importance of family gains additional potency in its explicit comparison with other ISAs, most notably with the workplace. In films such as *Executive Suite* (1954), *Five Finger Exercise, From the Terrace* (1960), *Strangers When We Meet,* and *The Man in the Gray Flannel Suit* the demands of the job are seen as being at odds with a satisfying family life. These fathers are spending too many hours at the office and not enough time interacting with their family, causing delinquency on the part of the children, infidelity on the part of one or both spouses, self-doubt, and torment. The solution in all of these cases is to reprioritize, cut back on hours, acquaint oneself anew with one's loved ones, and devote more effort to the domestic sphere.[27] In each of these texts the tormented father is pitted against a workaholic boss or colleague who eventually lectures him on the mutual exclusivity of a successful family life and a high-profile career. It is important to note that here the issue for Dad is never really one of success; the films underscore that a moderate amount of capital comfort awaits the nine-to-five man. Instead, the films argue for balance, depicting those who are consumed by some artistic or industrial dream as ultimately suffering the loss of their domestic world. In film, then, the family is rendered as the structural center—the site of conflict and resolution and the arena in which the lessons of socially prescribed "cures" can be enacted.

22. A common measure of "good" fathering centered on the question of how much Father sacrificed his home life for his employment success. In *The Man in the Gray Flannel Suit* Tom Rath (Gregory Peck) learns that it's better to be a nine-to-five man and have more family time than it is to be a corporate workaholic. (Copyright 20th Century–Fox.)

On television, the families are not only the most important structural grouping, they are superior to the filmic ones in their self-sufficiency. Here professional intervention is deemed unnecessary and detrimental. The family is a self-contained entity that can solve all crises on its own. This is made patent in the following conversation quoted by Applebaum from an untitled *Leave It to Beaver* episode:

> JUNE: Maybe the Beaver will outgrow being sloppy.
>
> WARD: That's not the modern approach. You can't wait for children to outgrow things. No, you have to send them to orthodontists, psychologists—they've even got experts to teach kids how to play. No self-respecting parent would dream of relying on nature anymore.[28]

Television mocks the interference of "outsiders." In *My Three Sons*, a marriage counselor's advice is inferior to that of Steve Douglas. And even though Mike Douglas is studying psychology at the university, his chosen field provides his family with numerous opportunities for derision, underscoring yet again television's preference for familial autonomy. In *The Donna Reed Show,* the military and the boarding-school atmosphere are harmful to David Barker, and the only thing necessary for the boy's happiness is a "real family." The Andersons bypass the institutionalized environs of adoption agencies and foster homes and conduct their own child-couple match with Fred and the Millers.

More important, and in direct contrast to film, however, is the means by which television deals with delinquent and socially unacceptable behavior. Interestingly, in not one interview with the writers of the television programs did an author remember writing a story of any real sociological significance. They, like the popular press, recalled the programs as dealing with issues involving prom dresses or book reports rather than with the myriad of potent issues actually covered in the television programs focusing consistently on social dilemmas such as divorce and abandonment (analyzed above), professional demands, and juvenile delinquency. The last of these issues proves the most intriguing because of the distinct manner in which television dealt with socially inappropriate behavior. In a two-pronged strategy designed to underscore the consumptive imperatives of commercial television, the programs first recognize the untoward activity and then appropriate it into mainstream culture and the province of parental authority. By assuming the mantle of authority, the parents in the television family melodramas confiscate the very rebellions of youth. While there are many examples of this strategy, it is put to its most potent use in episodes dealing with rock and roll and juvenile delinquency (manifested by fighting and joyriding).[29]

In "Almost the Sound of Music" (*My Three Sons,* 1962–1963) a nonsense rock-and-roll song written for a talent show by Robbie Douglas becomes the province of the entire Douglas clan when they perform *en famille* for a talent show. Rather than being the expression of a separate identity, extolled in theatrical films such as *Rock Rock Rock* and *The Explosive Generation,* rock and roll is rendered impotent, a mere melodic exercise uniting the generations in song. In another example from *My Three Sons,* "The Coffeehouse Set" (1964–1965), Robbie becomes involved with a beatnik-type crowd (itself an anachronism by the mid 1960's), and his family sets out to prove the preposterousness of folk music, poetry, abstract art, and long hair.

The Adventures of Ozzie and Harriet and *The Donna Reed Show,* with their examples of more liberal parents, take another, equally potent tack in disarming rock-and-roll music as a generational weapon. Here, rock and roll has the overwhelming approval of the parents, who see it as the beneficent province of young people, but something which can be appreciated by the elders. The most obvious illustration of this is Ozzie Nelson's direct involvement with son Ricky's musical career.[30] In addition to Ozzie's real-life role as his son's producer, arranger, promoter and manager, the narratives of episodes such as "The Old Band Pavilion" (1957–1958) demonstrate that rock and roll is the province of everyone. There are numerous concerts and performances in which Ozzie and Harriet cheer on their son; the two often perform duets at Ricky's parties and events; and, in two episodes, there is explicit validation of rock and roll as a viable outlet for youthful enthusiasm.

"Ozzie, the Treasurer" (1956–1957) ran three weeks after "Ricky, the Drummer" had produced a tremendous hue and cry from conservative parents, upset that the "wholesome" Nelsons were tainting the program with rock-and-roll music. This was the only time Ozzie attempted to answer viewer mail on the air, and the conversation between Ricky and his mother serves to counter those adults who might be closed-minded as far as Ricky's singing was concerned:

RICKY: Hey, Mom, what's your honest opinion of rock and roll?

HARRIET: Well, I'm not a good one to ask; your father and I have been pretty well brainwashed by now, so I can at least stay in the same room with it.

RICKY: I know you like some of it.

HARRIET: Well, I must admit there's a lot of excitement to it. I guess it's the musical expression of the modern teenager's enthusiasm or something. I'm not gonna knock it; I'll tell you that much.

RICKY: I think teenagers like to feel they're just people with normal, average reactions, and rhythm and blues records usually tell a story or express an emotion.

HARRIET: Oh, I agree with that. In fact, it leads right into your song. Here, I'll give you a downbeat.

[She raises her arms and Ricky sings.]

This attitude of approval is echoed in the equally harmonious *Donna Reed Show* when Mary, Jeff, and one of Mary's friends all embark on their singular musical successes.

The television programs also devote a number of episodes to the depiction of a (broadly defined) juvenile delinquency, either directly or, more commonly, by constructing episodes around relevant delinquent activities (fist-fighting, joyriding, motorcycle riding). In all cases, the rebellious behavior of the film delinquents is reconstituted for the television characters. Here, the television families choose to appropriate and legitimize socially questionable behavior, by motivating such activities with justifiable cause and softening them within the traditional values of "fair play," or by deeming the actions not generationally exclusive, but gender allocated and a normal part of masculine rites of passage.

My Three Sons, Leave It to Beaver, Father Knows Best, and *The Donna Reed Show* feature episodes in which the teen son is encouraged to fight. Unlike *Rebel without a Cause,* where life-threatening teen scuffles are castigated by authority figures, the television programs appropriate fighting into the mainstream, defusing it, de-marginalizing it, and incorporating adult authority figures into its success. In a 1955–1956 episode of *Father Knows Best,* "Bud, the Boxer," Jim urges Bud to take boxing lessons to defend himself against a high-school bully. In contrast to *Rebel without a Cause,* in which Frank Stark is perplexed by the cause of his son's wounds, the television father is the instigator behind his son's pugilism:

> JIM: Bud, remember what I've always told you. Never start a fight, but never run away from one either. . . . You can't hide from these things, Bud. You've got to meet the problem squarely. You're going to have to face him sooner or later. You can't avoid it. But remember this, there's to be no bare-fist fighting. . . . Go down to the YMCA this afternoon. . . . get in the ring down there and have it out. . . . When it's over, shake hands and forget it.

He takes Bud to the YMCA, enrolls him in boxing lessons, and sees to it that he becomes a champ. In this program, fighting is seen not as the domain of youth, but as the domain of *men,* and Bud and Jim are pitted against the chagrined Margaret and Betty, who scold the men for their "prehistoric" behavior. This same sort of attitude prevails on *Leave It to Beaver* when, in "Beaver and Gilbert" (1958–1959), Ward instructs Beaver to take care of a bully himself, resulting in a fistfight that meets with Ward's approval and June's concern. In the *My Three Sons* episode "The Bully" (1960–1961), Steve advises Chip to defend himself in a speech that is almost a carbon copy of the one Jim gave to Bud.

> CHIP: I thought you didn't believe in fighting, Dad.
> STEVE: I don't. I certainly don't believe in *starting* a fight. But there comes a time when a man has to defend himself. . . . You might as well grit your teeth and throw a few punches.

And a 1958–1959 episode of *The Donna Reed Show,* "Pardon My Gloves," reiterates the theme that boxing is the appropriate way to do battle and that parents are the first to offer their support to their beaten-up offspring.[31]

Another element of juvenile delinquency concerns the activity of joyriding. In *Rebel without a Cause,* the "chickie-run" results in the death of a teen and the ambiguous promise of a lesson learned. In *April Love,* Nicky's hotrodding ends in an accident, almost in a jail sentence, and in complications and anxiety for his family. In *Magnificent Obsession* and *Bernardine,* respectively, Bob Merrick and Sanford Wilson do their speeding in boats, causing a near-fatal accident for the former and a racing disqualification and humiliation for the latter. On television, the notion of joyriding is personified by motorcycles and a preoccupation with speed. These television depictions again turn a generational dispute into a gender one and applaud motorcycles as an aspect of masculine adventure. In an episode of *The Adventures of Ozzie and Harriet* ("The Motorcycle," 1958–1959), as well as in a *Father Knows Best* episode ("The Motor Scooter," 1954–1955), the fathers argue with the mothers over the relative safety of the bikes and the importance of allowing the sons some freedom and responsibility. In both programs the motorcycle becomes an emblem of adulthood, not delinquency, and an opportunity for the fathers to reap the reward of their good parenting. Interestingly, both programs end with Margaret and Harriet riding the motorbikes and demonstrating their innocuousness, while diffusing any danger with humorous spectacle.

Other episodes that deal explicitly with teenage rebellion and that defuse it through mockery are "Guest in the House" (*My Three Sons,* 1963–1964) and "Wally's Haircomb" (*Leave It to Beaver,* 1958–1959). In the former, Tony Dow guest-stars as a hayfever-stricken youth sent to the Douglases' for a pollen-free environment. With Steve out of town, and because of a number of miscommunications, the three lone boys assume that Gil Thornberry[32] is a juvenile delinquent. On his arrival, Gil proves himself to be a model teenager by cooking, cleaning, and helping around the house, only to incur suspicions with his every move. While it is true that he is not really a juvenile delinquent, he is made to substitute for one, and the ultimate message is clear: delinquency is caused by broken homes and unfounded suspicions, and with trust and the delegation of responsibility, the delinquent can become a productive citizen. In "Wally's Haircomb," fifteen-year-old Wally Cleaver begins sporting the rebellious hairstyle known as a "DA" (Duck's Ass). The association with delinquency is underscored by the fact that Wally wants his jeans "pre-washed," by the non-diegetic mock-rock music played every time he enters the scene, and by his reference to his parents as "squares." The reaction of the parents is gender split; June is horrified with Wally's appearance and keeps urging Ward to "do something," while Ward, possessed of a more cogent memory of his own youth, advises against interference. The program works to associate delinquency with a tangible, ridiculous icon—the DA—and to dismiss it as a teenager's need to conform. In the only explicit reference to delinquency, Ward assures Fred Rutherford that "it's a lot better than a lot of other things he could be doing."

For television, like film, socially unacceptable behavior becomes the realm of family intervention. Film's family solutions are the expulsion of the miscreants and a concomitant expression by family members of love and responsibility, as guided by the advice of psychosocial institutions. Television scoffs at the interference of professionals and cites the family as a singular problem-solving body. Issues of delinquency are weakened and appropriated into mainstream consumer behavior in accordance with television's advertising purposes. Previously forbidden teenage activities become an opportunity for purchase and familial bonding, grounded in normative guidelines for safety and consumption. Most crucial, perhaps, is the discovery that the television families were just as affected by delinquent trends as their filmic counterparts. The Nelsons, Cleavers, et al., were not insulated from 1950's social problems, and their dilemmas were not the innocuous problems of picking a date or a prom dress—a belief that, as incorrect as it is, is widely circulated. Instead, the television families dealt with issues quite similar to those of their filmic parallels, but found their solutions in appropriation and dilution rather than in expulsion and reformation.

The importance of the family as social institution is emphasized in both film and television texts by dialogue in which explicit comments function to underscore the structural potency of the family unit. Marriage, childrearing, motherhood, fatherhood, and the security of the home serve as conversation topics in both the film and television texts. Often, the comfort of hearth and home is initially denigrated and the story then functions to correct this inappropriate assumption with specific remarks highlighting the glory of family life. In *Bon Voyage* (1962) a teenage boy praises his sweetheart's father: "After 22 years, you're still in love with your wife. I wouldn't have thought that was possible. Why couldn't I have had an old man like you?" In *Boys' Night Out* (1962), the family situation is depicted first as dull, stifling, and unimaginative, only to be celebrated at the end of the film when the male bastion of a "boys' night out" has been transfigured into a "couple's night out." In *Five Finger Exercise* Walter is accused of having "a crush" on his family of employment; Sharon and Susan McKendrick continually extol the virtues of family life in *The Parent Trap*; and in *The Pleasure of His Company* playboy Pogo suffers endless lectures on the good family life he has missed.

The television narratives are rife with comments about the importance of family. Sometimes these center on specific issues, such as genealogy ("The Historical Andersons" [*Father Knows Best,* 1955–1956]), the extended family ("Family Reunion" [*Father Knows Best,* 1955–1956]), and the maternal heritage ("Beaver's Freckles" [*Leave It to Beaver,* 1960–1961], "Beaver's Short Pants" [*Leave It to Beaver,* 1957–1958]). In "Family Reunion" Margaret lectures her cynical family on the importance of scheduled get-togethers, and her cousin Ione reminds them that family reunions are "the one tie we have; the main root." In "Beaver's Short Pants," June defends her old-fashioned Aunt Martha to her family: "She was practically the only mother I ever knew." As the various youngsters bring home deprived and maladjusted friends, the family-protagonists also become the target of envy and admiration for outsiders. Typically, the central families of the television series are so secure that they don't discuss the importance of family life among themselves; it is up to the guest stars to comment on such "lovely families" and their "fine homes."

Power registers as a significant narrative theme in 1950's family melodrama. In both film and television stories are common that are centered upon power struggles within or between families, or in which the strength of the family is pitted against other social institutions. Obviously, there are numerous other power constructs which beg further examination and analysis, and the next two chapters address the issues of gender battles and economic contests. Before concluding this chapter, though, the construct of WASP hegemony and the way in which racial and ethnic power is understood within the genre of family melodrama will be explored. This avenue is of particular importance given that the period was one in which the public perception of civil rights was expanding and Hollywood was capitalizing on fictionalizing social changes and events. While so-called social-problem films depicted racial and ethnic themes in a more didactic and explicit way, the 1950's family melodramas used the notion of racial tension to register yet again the problem-solving potency of the family unit.[33] Here, too, is yet another example of a preference for thematic material by both the film and the television texts, texts in which the articulation of the subject matter varies according to the marketing needs of each medium.

Even though in 1950's feature films the difficulties of minority acceptance and identity took a backseat to the favored topics of delayed Oedipal crises and juvenile delinquency, a few films revolved around racism and/or ethnic identity. But while consciously marketing themselves as confronting prejudice and preaching racial harmony, these films were in fact operating to obliterate cultural distinction and its concomitant threat. The message in all of the films seems to be that America works as a melting pot if, and only if, one relinquishes all connections to heritage. This ideological agenda was constructed around two parallel but distinct narrative strategies: ethnic denial and ethnic repression.

Ethnic Denial

The most common depiction of the ethnic "other" (and the most traditional by Hollywood standards) is that in which the ethnic character attempts to hide racial identity. This disavowal can register as self-hatred or self-preservation, but always finds its moral restitution through the denial or realization of romantic love. With the newly lifted PCA ban on "miscegenation," such interracial liaisons multiplied; *Night of the Quarter Moon* (1959), *Imitation of Life,* and *Kings Go Forth* (1958), stand as three potent examples. In all three of these films the minority character is placed in a defensive position, minimizing, hiding, or accused of hiding ethnic identity, only to be rescued by a benevolent white figure who recognizes the minority status and grants acceptance. Ethnic denial in both films began preproduction when three Caucasian actresses—Julie London, Susan Kohner, and Natalie Wood—were cast to play the ethnic-minority roles. It is unclear whether the PCA relaxation on "miscegenation" referred to characters or to actors, but the very real marketing concerns of the film industry (particularly in the South) postponed "true" interracial romance until very recently.

Ethnicity is denied also through a variety of semantic and visual tropes designed to distance the characters from the "real-world" figures in the nascent civil rights movement. In *Night of the Quarter Moon* Ginny is one-quarter Portuguese-Angolan, a romantic variation on the perhaps more common African descent. As played by Julie London, Ginny's Anglo hair and features render her little more than a very tan Irish lass (a paternal line of which she is more vehemently proud). Natalie Wood's pale-skinned Monique lives in France, far from American racial unrest. Sara Jane is also a barely bronzed white girl, whose pre-diegetic father is described as very light, and who is continually mistaken (and who deliberately attempts to "pass") for white.

Ethnic denial is evident also in the way all three films center racial denial and its relationship to love (heterosexual or maternal) as the primary conflict and resolve the narrative tensions through a paradoxical reiteration of that denial. In *Kings Go Forth,* for example, Monique is both proud of and anxious about her racial heritage. Her mother is an American expatriate living in France, her father a black soldier, now deceased, and when she meets an American soldier, Sam Loggins (stationed in France after the end of World

War II), she temporarily conceals her heritage. Supposedly, Monique's deception is based not on shame, but on pragmatism: she recognizes that the equanimity with which the French treat mixed marriages doesn't work in America, and she doesn't want Sam to have to compromise his life-style. In *Night of the Quarter Moon* Ginny, too, is ambivalent about her heritage; while she is proud of her ethnicity, she recognizes the "impossibility" of a union with a white man and runs away from her suitor, Chick, who consequently proposes. After their marriage, familial and social opposition continually question the validity of heterosexual romance as a solution to racial strife. Chick's wealthy family castigates Ginny for both her working-class status and her mixed heritage and attempts to annul the marriage on the basis of Chick's mental incapacity (he was a shell-shocked POW) and Ginny's supposed racial deception. Ultimately, the race issue becomes a dramatic device by which Chick must reach his long-delayed adulthood and confront his overbearing mother. In *Imitation of Life* romantic love figures strongly, but Frankie's affection for Sara Jane is not potent enough to compensatefor his prejudice. The message is the same as in *Night of the Quarter Moon*—that heterosexual love is the means to racial assimilation—but here

23. In *Imitation of Life* Sara Jane (Susan Kohner) is ultimately beaten by boyfriend Frankie (Troy Donahue) for attempting to hide her African-American heritage. (Copyright Universal.)

it is rendered negatively, with Frankie's castigation resulting in Sara Jane's isolation.

Finally, in all three films racial heritage must be publicly recognized before it can be assimilated and ignored. It is as if the characters need only name their "affliction" ("Hi, I'm Ginny and I'm a Portuguese-Angolan") in order to be subsumed into the hegemonic order. In *Kings Go Forth* Monique's pride in her father compels her to tell the truth, and she dramatically reveals it to the disconcerted Sam. Her revelation catalyzes Sam's desertion, his buddy Britt's affections, Britt's desertion, and Sam's ultimate return when he loses a limb in battle. The film argues, in effect, that Sam and Monique's reunion depends on her admitting her ethnic liability, him admitting his physical liability, and the two then operating as if neither liability exists.

In *Night of the Quarter Moon*, the narrative dilemma centers on a premarital skinny-dipping escapade in which Ginny argues there was no doubt about her mixed heritage. The film culminates in a bizarre courtroom sequence in which Ginny is ordered to disrobe in order to demonstrate that she had not duped her mentally deficient husband into thinking he was marrying a pure Caucasian. When her lawyer rips off her dress, heterosexual chivalry overcomes sociological bigotry and Chick leaps to her rescue; the two then drive off into completely blended harmony.

In *Imitation of Life* Sara Jane is, like Ginny, concerned that her racial heritage will prevent her assimilation into American culture. But unlike Ginny (who is merely apologetic), she is *ashamed* of her heritage, and resorts to "passing for white," lying about her background, and otherwise attempting to hide the truth.[34] The film's resolution rests on Sara Jane's recognition of her heritage and subsequent dismissal of it. Her public acknowledgment of her mother reveals her blackness and could be read as a statement of racial pride (or at least acceptance). But the film does not end there; instead, Sara Jane, hysterically mourning her dead mother, is simultaneously comforted and absorbed by the all-white Meredith-Archer family, ultimately achieving the white absolution she has long desired. At the film's end the errant daughter runs into the crowd of funeral participants, screaming, "It's my mother!" A police officer blocks her way but she pushes him aside, finally embracing her mother's coffin and weeping her apologies. It is up to Lora to pull Sara Jane away, sweeping her into her arms and propelling her into a limousine along with Steve and Suzy. It is particularly interesting that in this scene the first person to whom Sara Jane declares her status represents the law, thus granting ideological weight to both her statement and its repercussions. In juxtaposition to the staring, strange, and very dark crowd, the next series of embraces and comforting and the final moment when, in effect, Lora cuddles

Sara Jane instead of her natural daughter place Sara Jane in the world of the Anglos—encased from without by the black limousine, but very much white inside it.

Ethnic Repression

In *No Down Payment* minority conflict is represented by Iko, a Japanese American hardware-store employee, and his family. They are by no means the central family in this film, which focuses on the trials and tribulations of four other households in the suburban utopia of Sunrise Estates. Indeed, just as Iko's character represses his ethnicity, so the narrative structurally represses his presence; he is marginal to the story line, and exists only to mobilize Herm, a central character, into politically correct behavior. Unlike these characters exhibiting the previous form of denial, Iko does not pretend to belong to a different race, nor does he apologize for his culture. Instead, he functions to minimize the differences between the occidental and Asian societies. He is presented as a fellow worker, a homeowner, a family man; his dress, his minimal accent, and his attitude are all Western. Even more important, Iko self-consciously underscores his Americanism as he mentions his G.I. status and, most intriguingly, the fact that his economic level grants him parity with his WASP boss. His citizenship is particularly relevant here, for the animosity toward Iko is represented as being directly related to World War II and the veterans' resentment about a former enemy. Because the hatred toward the Japanese is depicted as temporary (they were fairly well accepted before the war), it is more easily defused and forgotten than the anger toward other ethnic minorities only just beginning to demand equal rights. The key scene showing Iko's attempt at racial fusion occurs at the hardware store, where a confrontation between Iko and his boss, Herm, deliberately follows an angrily pensive moment when G.I. Troy is in his garage, surrounded by Japanese trophies. In this scene Iko argues that the long commute to work is compromising his family life and that his attempts to move into the restricted neighborhood of Sunrise Estates have been thwarted at every turn. Herm is his last resort, and Iko argues that with Herm's influence on the city council, he should be able to secure housing for him. Pressing his case, Iko notes that he is a G.I., that he makes good money ("I should be able to buy a home where I can afford one"), and that he has a wife and children depending on him. It is crucial to note the difference here between Iko and Sara Jane. Sara Jane seeks equality through deception and denial; Iko prefers his ethnicity to be treated as irrelevant and ignored. In each case, however, ethnicity is deemed as an unattractive "other" characteristic—at odds with the norm, and impossible to absorb for its own value. Ultimately, the minority characters gain access to the pleasures of American capitalism not through their own efforts but via the intervention of a benevolent white protector who, in effect, erases their cultural heritage by assimilating them into white culture.

While issues of race were centered in the filmic texts less frequently than were other "controversial" topics, the television programs were surprisingly attracted to them. Of over 500 episodes analyzed, at least one-tenth deal with the threatened infiltration of ethnic minorities into the hermetic world of the white upper-middle class. Curiously, all of the television programs examined neglect entirely the presentation of Afro-Americans. Marketing concerns (particularly regarding southern affiliates) prevented an explicit mention of integration or civil rights, and the subtle (and not-so-subtle) prejudices in casting offices contributed to a complete dismissal of black characters in domestic comedies. For example, writer Barbara Hammer scripted a telling episode of *The Donna Reed Show* ("Jeff Stands Alone," 1962–1963) in which Jeff runs away, angered at being mocked by a telephone repairman who thinks that he is pampered. In the original teleplay the re-pairman was black, strengthening the privileged position of the Stone family. On the first day of shooting, however, Hammer discovered that a white ac-tor, James Stacey, was playing the role.[35] Another writer for the program, Nate Monaster, recalls how, in 1962, he stormed into producer Tony Owen's office and complained that there hadn't been a black character on the show: "They don't have to become your neighbors, but for heaven's sake, get them on the show." With the sponsor's approval, he wrote one in as an extra. He didn't, however, pursue that agenda any further.

The television programs present more of a salad bowl than a melting pot. When minorities are featured on these programs, their ethnic heritage is made patent and quite unchangeable. Prior to 1962, television and advertis-ing executives focused on a large, undifferentiated mass of viewers, with the intent of reaching and enticing as many potential shoppers as possible. Thus, in terms of their impact on ethnic minorities, television's family melodramas of this period functioned in two ways. First, they were forced to acknowl-edge the discernible and visible ethnic minorities infiltrating America's com-munities, and such acknowledgment functioned to entice these same mi-norities to view the programs which, themselves, underscored the common goals of all Americans—namely to purchase consumer goods as the answer to complex problems of identity and self-esteem. Second, the programs had then to undercut any potential power of the ethnic groups, and did so by indicating that the true America is one in which all strive toward the ultimate goal of the neo-Puritan way of life: honesty and thrift bounded by hard work and the continuous acquisition of material products.

The programs exhibited two cooperative but distinct means by which to account for ethnic difference and then to relegate such difference to its proper marginal position. The first, which can be termed "ethnic inferiority," positions the minority character as in some way deficient and reliant upon the central WASP family for corrective guidelines. The second, which I will call "ethnic exotica," glamorizes the heritage of the ethnic "other" as a means of reminding the WASP family of its own cultural traditions, and then incorporates these traditions into the WASP way of life, denying their Asian or European origins.

Ethnic Inferiority

A number of distinct ways are used to portray ethnic inferiority within the television text. First, the minority characters are rendered physically separate from the program's central families. The Anderson's Hispanic gardener lives in a never-seen neighborhood on "the other side of town"; Tony Ferruci, the Stone's Italian milkman, lives in the city in an apartment; the Chinese and Chinese-Americans who appear on *My Three Sons* live in Chinatown. It is extremely rare to find an ethnic family living in any neighborhood similar or connected to that of the program's central family, and if they do (such as the East Indians in an episode of *My Three Sons*), it is a rental situation only, indicating that the permanent place of such minorities is away from the neatly trimmed suburban streets.

As well as implicitly demarcating the ethnic world outside the world of the central family, the programs erect a set of hierarchically inscribed values which the ethnic group fails to measure up to. Such values include, but are not limited to, intelligence (as evidenced by proper grammar, accents, literacy, scientific knowledge, and awareness of American culture); common sense (as measured by pragmatism and responsibility toward children); and truth (whereby the ethnic groups are uncovered as continual prevaricators, while the Anglos bear the standard of honesty and forthrightness).

Father Knows Best was one of the few television domestic melodramas with a recurrent ethnic character, the gardener Frank (pronounced Franque) Smith. Frank Smith first appeared on the program in a 1956–1957 episode, "Margaret Hires a Gardener." In a subsequent episode, Frank's deceptive name is revealed to have been the result of a concerted effort on the gardener's part to choose "the most American" name when he came to the United States. The implication is that a move to the United States warrants a wholesale dismissal of one's ethnic roots, beginning with the most salient of ethnic ties—one's name.

Frank's relationship with the Andersons is one of happy servant to benevolent master, and the Andersons are involved continually in Frank's private affairs, assisting him in courtship, in public speaking, and in finding other employment. Frank bears all the marks of an ethnic "inferior": he speaks broken English with a heavy Spanish accent; he dresses in grubby workclothes; his truck is noisy and barely functioning; and his hair is dirty and unkempt. His refusal to assimilate—to don a coat and tie, to correct his grammar—serves as further proof of his lack of intelligence. It is up to the Anderson family to painstakingly teach him the American way—only to see his temporary achievement collapse in a moment of crisis. For example, in "The Gardener's Big Day," (1959–1960), the governor of the state is due to visit Springfield to receive the key to the city. Frank wins an essay contest on why Springfield is the "best town in the USA," resulting in his selection as the presenter. Because of his name, the contest organizers have no idea of his ethnic background and are horrified to discover his broken English, his workclothes, and his general "unsuitability." Indeed, upon hearing Frank's noisy truck arrive in the parking lot, a city official remarks: "We've got to keep those workers from parking here; it's beginning to look like *The Grapes of Wrath*." Because he had suggested Frank for the contest, Jim Anderson is held directly responsible for Frank's involvement, and the town official, Charley (denying the gardener even the power of self-retreat), tells Jim to withdraw Frank. But the Andersons find an alternate solution: they buy him a suit and conduct, in Margaret's words, a "My Fair Lady" on him. He stays with the Andersons (sleeping outside in a tent, despite the fact that the Andersons have a guest room), and he naively informs them of the attempts by the city officials to bribe him to withdraw. When he overhears the racist remarks of Charley,[36] Frank runs away. The Anderson children discover his whereabouts and drag him to the ceremony; but by then, Frank no longer bears the mark of Anglicization. Instead, he enters cowering, hair disheveled, covered in dirt, and clutching a seedling he had been in the process of planting. When shoved on stage as presenter, he deviates from the prearranged speech, launching instead into an accent-loaded sentimental monologue concerning the diverse compatibility of nature: "No tree says to another you can't live here . . . they bow to one another and say 'hello, amigo.'"

The episode contains a number of the ideological strategies necessary for the recognition and retention of the WASP as the ruling elite. First, it underscores Frank's physical difference from the Anderson norm—his style of dress and his preference to sleep out of doors, for instance—thus relegating him to the uncivilized world of nature. Second, Frank's speech about different trees growing side by side in arboreal harmony makes explicit the message of racial tolerance at the same time as it denies the ethnic group any hope of achieving the status (read "appearance") of the white ruling class. This message of racial tolerance is unidirectional; Frank, as the only member of the Hispanic community, is pleading with the Anglos to tolerate *him* (his nontraditional appearance, his faulty English, his eco-priorities); it is not a question of him tolerating the Anglos. This patronization is made patent by the fact that his speech is greeted by stunned silence until the benevolent governor reiterates the message in proper English and congratulates Frank on his insight.

The ethnic other on *Father Knows Best* is characterized additionally by a tendency toward cowardice and prevarication. Frank's lack of intelligence and common sense often result in a series of misunderstandings perpetuated by his refusal to admit the truth. For example, in "Frank's Family Tree" (1958–1959) young Kathy continually pesters Frank about his family. Frank's lie is revealed when it can do the most damage to the Andersons' community standing: Jim, in desperate need of an insurance-banquet entertainer, compels Frank to ask his flamenco-dancing "family" to perform. Unable to avoid the determined Anderson forces, Frank is forced to confess at the last minute that he has no family, so that Jim will be forced to disgrace himself in front of his colleagues. The music intensifies and Frank bows his head, chagrined at his deception: "I have let down my best friend in the whole world, Señor Anderson." At the last minute, Frank appears on stage with the Anderson children in appropriate Mexican attire and regales the Springfield audience with song and dance. The message is complex. First, although it is the Anderson's stubborn tunnel vision that creates the problem (Kathy's preoccupation with Frank's family, Jim's determination not to hear Frank's refusal to entertain), it is Frank who bears the guilt. Second, the scene in which Frank and the children solve the entertainment dilemma is elided, leaving it to the audience to speculate as to whether the idea was Frank's or one of the Anderson children's. At the end of the program he is credited with teaching them the musical numbers, but the recognition for the last-minute ingenuity is deliberately and explicitly avoided. Third, the success of the program rests as much on the Anderson children mocking Frank's ethnic heritage as it does on Frank's authentic performance of Hispanic song and dance, demonstrating how easily WASP culture can appropriate ethnic creativity at the same time as it erects the barriers to a concomitant exchange of power.

In *The Donna Reed Show* the ethnic other is revealed not so much as intellectually lacking, as bereft of common sense and economically inferior. In "The Foundling" (1958–1959) a recently widowed Italian-American milkman leaves his 10-month-old son on the Stones' doorstep. Donna tracks him down to his tenement apartment for the appropriate reprimand. The mise-en-scène emphasizes the distinctions between the WASP world of Hilldale's suburbia and Tony's wrong-side-of-the-tracks existence. The disheveled apartment, the unlocked door, the crucifix on the wall, the laundry draped over lines inside the crowded living room, and the cluttered furnishings all function to emphasize the ethnic other as inhabiting an unpleasant and aesthetically bereft place.

It is crucial to note that the resolution for Tony rests in finding someone of his own religion and class as a helpmate. The Stones' housekeeper, Kathleen, is Irish-Catholic, working class, and indebted to the Stones' for her economic well-being. Her common sense also is brought into question when, in caring for baby Willie, she begins neglecting her housekeeping duties. Donna must remind her about her cleaning chores, just as she had to remind Tony about his parental responsibilities.

Ethnic inferiority is thus articulated in a number of distinct approaches. The WASP family is continually upheld as superior to a group of ethnic misfits who lack the refinement, honesty, cleanliness, and common sense of the dominant class. In addition, these ethnic others recognize their inferiority through a number of explicit self-recriminating statements which indicate both their regret over their unseemly behavior and their determination to overcome their unique identities and merge into the hegemonic whole. Finally, it is made patent that no matter how determined they are, they will never completely blend into the WASP world—a world that merely establishes the standards to which the ethnic groups can never measure up.

Ethnic Exotica

In addition to occupying a position that is intellectually and sensibly inferior, television's ethnic representatives operate concurrently as the receptacles of tradition, spirituality, and culture. Interestingly, appreciation for other cultures is restricted to ethnic minorities of Asian heritage, who are rendered as being spiritually superior to their Anglo counterparts and traditionally rich in areas neglected in the puritanical push for progress.

As George Lipsitz has noted about ethnically centered programs such as *The Goldbergs,*

> Through indirect but powerful demonstrations, all of these shows arbitrated complex tensions caused by economic and social change in postwar America. They evoked the experiences of the past to lend legitimacy to the dominant ideology of the present. In the process they served important social and cultural functions, not just in returning profits to investors or attracting audiences for advertisers, but most significantly as a means of ideological legitimation for a fundamental revolution in economic, social and cultural life.[37]

Owing to producer Ed Hartmann's close friendship with actor Benson Fong, *My Three Sons* presents a multitude of episodes dealing with Asian culture, specifically Chinese, Japanese, and East Indian. There are moments of interracial romance, in, for example, "Weekend in Tokyo" (1961–1962), "The Lotus Blossom" (1964–1965), and "Cherry Blossoms in Bryant Park" (1963–1964). In other episodes ("The Stone Frog," 1963–1964, "Honorable Grandfather," 1962–1963, "Charley and the Kid," 1964–1965, and "The Guys and the Dolls," 1963–1964) there is validation of other customs and cultures, in the form of icons, ritual meals, and treatment of the elderly. In addition, Steve has a semi-regular business associate named Ray Wong, whose wife, Alice, and daughter, Sally, make frequent appearances. The regular presence of the Asian culture and the respect with which it is treated work both to underscore racial tolerance and to uphold the hegemony of the white middle class—who are seen as the norm, while the Asians are seen as the exotic other. In all cases, however, the Eastern spiritualism is put in service of pragmatic American ideals—success, progress, and familial unity.

In "The Stone Frog," for example, East Indian mythology and magic are utilized to further the good grades of Chip, the dating success of Robbie, and Douglas family harmony. Indeed, by the end of the program, Siranee, the possessor of the mystical icon, uses it to gain the quintessential feminine achievement—a date with an eligible man (Steve). Interwoven with the text's moral agenda of recognizing spirituality's dangerous position, however, is the admonition that non-American cultures are bizarre, threatening, and ultimately laughable. These customs are particularly jarring when located in the sterile and incongruous environment of a suburban tract home. When Steve visits Siranee, what looks like a nondescript tract home on the outside turns out to house a beaded and curtained chamber, replete with incense, a yoga master practicing various contortionist poses, and Nehrujacketed elders spouting sayings from 400-year-old gurus. The program emphasizes that while such practices are at best exotic and at worst corrupting, ultimately they are incompatible with American practice. Whenever there is an attempt to bridge a cultural chasm through exchange, trouble ensues: Siranee's candy—an exotic ginger concoction—is an obviously tasteless affront to Chip and Ernie; Chip fails an exam when relying on the frog—purported by Siranee to possess magical qualities—instead of studying; the frog causes a rift between Chip and Ernie.

Ethnic exotics thus function doubly. First, they reinforce the notion that the melting pot is a myth and that ethnic heritage is too distinct to be subsumed into WASP culture. Second, the spiritual quality of Eastern cultures, while appreciated from the same safe distance that a tourist would appreciate it from, is held accountable for a multitude of complications and strife when adapted for WASP living situations.

In both the film and television texts the racial tensions are blurred into class distinctions: it is not because of race that the gardener Frank and the milkman Tony would never—could never—live in the Anderson neighborhood, but because of poverty, and Iko argues for equality on the basis of his financial status. The goals for the two texts are thus subtly different; while film reads as a directive toward racial *equality* predicated on an absence of difference, television argues instead for racial *harmony* among explicitly distinct groups.

The latter stance is exemplified by narrative strategies in which, first, the ethnic other must learn not only the rudiments of the American language, but the basic principles of American decorum. The milkman in *The Donna Reed Show* must learn to be a responsible father; the gardener in *Father Knows Best* must learn not to lie about his family and also to show proper respect for political figures; and Siranee in *My Three Sons* must learn that magic icons are no replacement for hard work. Second, the episodes function to solidify the consumptive consciousness of the television viewer, as Lipsitz has noted: "Television provided a locus, redefining American ethnic, class and family identities into consumer identities. . . . [E]thnics attain a false unity [with whites] through consumption of commodities."[38] Thus, Siranee uses the East Indian totem to secure a dinner date with an eligible man, Tony Ferruci uses his baby as an opportunity to shill for a new milk product, and Frank's success is predicated on creating government-sanctioned parklands. The way to be an American and to best obliterate ethnic distinction is to participate in consumptive activities.

The film and television texts, with their diminution of racial variety, present a de facto superiority of the white middle class. Even when they appear in *Imitation of Life* or on programs such as *Father Knows Best* and *My Three Sons*, the minority races are treated as "other"—dissatisfied, bumbling, or exotic, and always needful of the white family's approval or admiration. For film, the generic preoccupation with heterosexual coupling and familial reconciliation rendered ethnic identity one more obstacle in the course of romantic love or personal growth; while underscored thematically, such identity was diluted schematically and visually, and was ultimately denied and absorbed. For television, the regulatory factors of internal and external censorship, coupled with the implicit ideological imperative that television promote a homogeneous consuming society, resulted in contradictory representations of ethnic others. Minorities were to be depicted as either intellectually inferior or spiritually superior to the WASP majority, but however they were depicted, all ethnic groups were reassured that proper consuming habits and esteem for puritanical ethics would situate them along an axis of potential (although ultimately unattainable) assimilation.

24. The moral precepts of television's domestic melodrama are embodied in this frame enlargement from the opening credits of *The Donna Reed Show*. In one brief moment, notions of stability, monogamy, prosperity, and domesticity are foregrounded and applauded.

To summarize one way of understanding and relating the film and television depictions of American family life is to explore their various power dynamics. In both the film and television domestic melodramas, the family is the chosen arena for struggle, operating as the site of both struggle and resolution, within itself and toward other families and institutions. In both, too, the moral precepts are the same: patriarchy, tradition, ritual, and familial love are good, while chaos, the workplace, teenage trends, and ethnic diversity are threats to stable family life and must be destroyed or harnessed within the confines of the nuclear family. The road to resolution, however, differs somewhat for each medium. The film families most frequently begin the narrative splintered and unsure, and ultimately reach knowledge and unity with the film's conclusion. For television, each weekly episode opens with the family seemingly at peace but immediately troubled by an internal or external threat; the elimination of the threat provides characters and viewers with an opportunity for moral instruction, and positions the TV family in a temporarily secure (until next week) household. A number of narrative patterns are common to both media, and their constant reiteration strengthens their ideological import. Within the family, fathers are the most valued members, their sentimentalized discipline and moralizing a belabored fact on television and an ascribed goal in film. Children are either the voice of tradition and tolerance (film) or the target of lectures dealing with the same issues (television). Disputes between families are resolved via the integration of two dysfunctional units or by an investment in future generations, while social institutions are important only for the guidance they give the family in resolving their crises. The status quo is maintained, supposedly allowing enough flexibility for individuality; at the same time, the themes underscore the need for ritual and team play. Ethnic harmony is achieved by assimilation in the films, and by a patronizing distance in the television programs. What remains unchallenged in both depictions of family life is the unquestioning allegiance to patriarchal capitalism—an allegiance that is sometimes tested in the tiny fissures of discontent voiced by the rebels, but then quickly defused through familial reconciliation, love, or the seemingly adaptable nature of the system.

6 Boys and Girls Together

The bulk of all domestic melodrama's themes and narratives focus on gender. The generic terminology "domestic melodrama" (or "family melodrama") foregrounds issues of matriarchy and patriarchy, of femininity and masculinity, in describing a genre that centers the home and familial issues as its narrative terrain. The preceding chapter analyzed the family unit as a whole in terms of its power relations both within itself and in contrast to others. The purpose of this chapter is to examine the individuals who comprise the family unit in terms of gender, in an attempt at understanding the means by which the domestic melodrama shaped expectations regarding specific behaviors and functions. Obviously, this will once again entail exploring the notion of power and control, especially in the section on matriarchy and patriarchy. In that sense, this chapter functions as a deeper exploration of the issues raised previously, and attempts to answer the following questions: How is power within the family, that has been shown to be predicated on a construct of patriarchal hegemony, portrayed in narrative terms? How are mothers, traditionally regarded as the protectors of the domestic realm, depicted instead as detrimental or irrelevant to its successful functioning? To what end do the film and television texts underscore the potency of fathering? And how are the terms "strong" and "weak" redefined so as to ensure the continued domination of men in the workplace while at the same time allowing them to oversee the domestic world? These issues are explored within the film and television texts which function remarkably well as detailed treatises on gender-ascribed duties and responsibilities. While the previous chapter addressed the issues of who has power and what the narrative obstacles were to achieving that power, this chapter seeks out the underlying stakes of that power, the means to maintaining that power, and the ideological ramifications of that power in a domestic world that is masculinized (or a masculine world that is domesticated) and in which women are no longer the center of their familial world.

Sex, Sexuality, and Stereotypes

Both the film and television representations of family life tend toward producing and maintaining sex stereotyping. On the whole, this means adhering to a strict oppositional construct in which men and boys are associated ideally with strength, intelligence, logic, consistency, and humor, while women and girls are rendered intuitive, dependent, flighty, sentimental, and self-sacrificing. By the same token, characters who shun these traits, or who adopt those belonging to the opposite sex, are deemed dysfunctional (if they are men) or evil (if they are women). Such adopted traits include, for men, domesticity, refinement, and emotionality, and for women, ambition, assertiveness, and independence.

The preoccupation with appropriate sex-determined behavior is especially evident in dialogue. Both the film and television texts contain minilectures concerning the proper roles of men and women. For the most part, the films privilege the male point of view in the way they articulate the proper role for both sexes and define stereotypical behavior. They do this, first, by reminding men and boys to "act like men," and second, by reiterating the inadequate traits of women and girls. For example, in those films that feature teenage protagonists, there is a plethora of comments regarding the strategies of dating, invariably positioning the women as silly and unaware and the men as knowledgeable and in command.[1]

The dialogue commands that women and girls marry and that men and boys take responsibility for their actions. The preference for domestic bliss is readily apparent in a number of family melodramas. The protagonist in *Hilda Crane* is a sexually active and career-oriented woman who recognizes her mistakes in striving for self-reliance. "I thought I could be independent and I ended up being more dependent on a man than ever, on a series of men," says Hilda, who describes herself as a "woman, a failure" as if the two are synonymous and go hand in hand with experience. In *One Desire* (1955), successful businesswoman Tracy Cromwell echoes the notion that the experienced woman is destined for a life of isolation and despair.[2] While such films are quick to castigate a woman's independence or pursuit of sexual desire, their dialogue also reiterates the notion that a successful marriage is one in which the husband can look to his wife for sexual pleasure. In *This is My Love,* for example, Eddie chides his unmarried, prudish sister-in-law Vida, telling her: "No man wants an old maid for a wife; he wants a woman."

In *Boys' Night Out*, the need of the husbands for an in-town mistress is attributed directly to the unavailability of their apathetic wives. The implication in *There's Always Tomorrow* is that Clifford Groves' desire for Norma stems from his wife Marion's inattention to his romantic overtures.

The television programs, with their emphasis on adolescence and sibling rivalry, are even more rife than the films with comments on successful gender conditioning. In programs in which girls are absent (*The Adventures of Ozzie and Harriet, My Three Sons,* and *Leave It to Beaver*) sexual derision of women and elevation of men are more common and, indeed, often serve to bond the fathers with their male children. *Leave It to Beaver* abounds with sexist remarks in general, and specifically with jibes at June's family. The following conversation from "Beaver's I.Q." (1960–1961) illustrates a typical gender-related conversation:

BEAVER: Girls have got it lucky . . . they don't have to be smart, they don't have to get jobs or anything, all they got to do is get married.

JUNE: Well, being smart isn't exactly a drawback to marriage.

BEAVER: Yeah, but if they don't get married, they can become dressmakers, or cut people's nails in a barbershop or take care of kids and a lot of other dumb stuff.

Similarly derisive comments figure prominently in the dialogue of *My Three Sons*. For example, in "Daughter for a Day" (1962–1963) little Jeannie's interest in Africa and animals is read as being at odds with her gender. "Are you sure you're a girl?" asks an incredulous Chip, when Jeannie asks to see his frog. Other such comments ("I'll never trust a woman again," "It's amazing to live in a house without women this side of heaven") abound, and, indeed, every single episode has at least one remark putting down females as conniving, silly, over-bearing, rigid, or frivolous. While programs that feature daughters (*The Donna Reed Show, Father Knows Best*) contain occasional attempts at balance in criticizing the men, they are not immune to sexually derisive comments about women. In *Father Knows Best* Bud comments: "To get along with girls, you gotta be silly too"; Margaret herself comments on "Babbling females who take some little situation and blow it up"; and Jim is continually warning Bud about feminine wiles. In *The Donna Reed Show,* the dialogue mostly is not derisive of women so much as it is concerned with underscoring sexual distinctions. But even this program, with its charismatic producer-star, still resorts to the feminine put-down. On one occasion Donna says: "Women are only nice to other women when they feel sorry for them. When they envy them, they slander them." Alex also notes:

"When they created women, they made them beautiful, sensitive and warm-hearted, but they forgot to throw in logic." Both *Father Knows Best* and *The Donna Reed Show* depict the fathers as being in conspiracy with their sons, discussing the wiles and mysteries of women, while the mothers and daughters focus on the brutality and obstinacy of men.

In addition to its ubiquity in dialogue, specific gender behavior often operates as the central narrative issue and, as such, is divisible into a number of distinctive approaches, including male sexuality, careerism,[3] female sexuality, and the battle of the sexes.

Tea and Sympathy and *Suddenly Last Summer,* with their not-so-thinly disguised explorations of male homosexuality, are the most extreme examples of aberrant sexuality being depicted as the motivating force behind maternal-filial dysfunction. In each of these films parental error is held directly accountable for the sons' "mistaken" behavior. In *Suddenly Last Summer* a mother's incestuous love for her son results in his stunted sexual growth and consequent homosexuality.[4] In *Tea and Sympathy* it is an absent mother and a tyrannical father who are responsible for Tom's psychological problems, and he is explicit in his condemnation:

> [My mother] didn't live with us. She left when I was around five. She and my father are divorced. I was supposed to hold them together. That's how I happened to come into the world. I didn't work. That's a terrible thing, you know, to make a flop of the first job you get in the world. . . . I don't remember much about her except she was always going outside and telling me to bounce a ball.

The film is obsessed with masculine- and feminine-defined activities, and Tom's dysfunction is "proven" by his affection for the latter over the former. Tom likes to cook and sew, he's interested in classical and folk music and plays the guitar, and he enjoys quiet conversation and intellectual stimulation over the socially approved activities of hunting, sleeping with the town tramp, and fistfighting. At one point there is even a quiz ("How Masculine Are You?"), which the boys use as yet another means of putting down the hero. In addition to his prowess at all things domestic, Tom excels at tennis. This results in a paradoxical situation early on in the film. When Tom's father comes to watch him play, the boy freezes and fails at the game. But tennis can be read as a much more "feminine" sport than football or basketball (due to its grace, noncontact status, attention to fashion, etc.), so it is unclear whether Tom's failure is meant to be interpreted as a feminine failure at athletics in general or as a masculine failure at a feminine game. Tom resolves his sexual ambiguity by engaging in ultra-masculine activities: sleeping with and then ruining the reputation of a sensitive older woman; assaulting another woman and attempting a violent suicide; marrying and exposing his former friends in a tell-all novel. If his father's misogyny created Tom's sexual dilemma, Tom has paradoxically countered it by adopting a similarly scornful attitude toward women.

Another less severe variation of the theme of maternal transgression alleges that it is "merely" the mother's possessiveness and/or assertiveness that is responsible for her son's (or occasionally her daughter's) dysfunction. The possessiveness is not incestuous, and the resulting dysfunction is thus less drastic than homosexuality. In some cases, the gender balance becomes more disturbed when the father rebels against the maternal possessiveness by becoming more dominating and macho, while at the same time refusing to challenge the mother in the child-rearing domain. The resolution is catalyzed by a crisis that leads to the softening of the mother, a consequent forgiveness by the father, and successful role-modeling for the offspring. Films in this category include *Home from the Hill* (in which Theron's lack of self-confidence stems directly from his mother's possessiveness) and *Five Finger Exercise* (in which Stan lectures Louise about her hold on their son Phillip: "You're turning him into a mama's boy"). In each of these films the domain of gender traits has become harmfully exaggerated. The mothers' overnurturing has led to a schism between father and son, while the fathers inflate their own masculine aggressiveness and then abandon their sons to the cloying touch of their mothers and the questionable influence of younger male surrogates. In both films the sons then attempt to identify with the father too ardently and too late, resulting in tragedy.

Sex traits are centered equally often in an alternative narrative pattern which questions female sexuality. Just as previously the men had to cast off their "softer" side in favor of more macho pursuits, so in this case the misappropriation of gender roles is depicted as a misguided female independence, and the woman must duly be instructed on her proper maternal function. In some films the problem lies in careerism (for example, *Hilda Crane*, *Imitation of Life*, *The Thrill of it All* [1963], *Marjorie Morningstar* [1958], *The Unguarded Moment*, *Peyton Place*, and *There's Always Tomorrow*). Such films feature women who have put their careers ahead of their families and suffer the consequence of unhappy love affairs and/or ungrateful or spiteful children until they reconcile themselves to the ultimate choice of dependency and domesticity.[5] Other women are guilty of sexual aggressiveness and, unless rescued and rehabilitated by a man, are punished by isolation or even death. Such films include *Written on the Wind* (1956), *Cat on a Hot Tin Roof*,

All the Fine Young Cannibals (1960), *Splendor in the Grass, Love with the Proper Stranger, Home from the Hill, The Long Hot Summer, A Summer Place, From the Terrace, No Down Payment, Strangers When We Meet* (1960), *The Last Time I Saw Paris,* and *The Cobweb* (1955).

As David Rodowick has noted:

> As opposed to the male characters, whose conflicts devolve from the difficulty of attaining an active sexual identity in which patriarchal power can be confirmed and reproduced, the conflict of the women stems from the difficulty of subjugating and channeling feminine sexuality according to the passive functions which patriarchy has defined for it; that is, heterosexual monogamy and maternity. In this manner, feminine sexuality is always in excess of the social system which seeks to contain it.[6]

For example, in *Splendor in the Grass* the sexually active Ginny Stamper suffers first an illegal abortion and then an automobile accident. The sexually ambivalent Deanie, when finally acquiescing to her carnal desires, attempts suicide and then is committed to a sanatorium. Juanita, the high-school

25. Deanie's transformation into a vibrantly sexual woman will be punished with her nervous breakdown and near-suicide in the 1961 film *Splendor in the Grass*. (Copyright Warner Bros.)

hussy, has an affair with Bud and is consequently absent from his life. It is only through careful psychological rehabilitation that Deanie is able to come to terms with the proper repressive role of femininity, and at the end of the film she is engaged to a doctor, who is equally placid and benumbed. Meanwhile, Bud, who has been engaged in a number of sexual activities, is granted his lifelong wish (a farm of his own), and is blessed with a sweet and caring wife and a little boy.[7]

In *A Summer Place, All the Fine Young Cannibals, Blue Denim, Love with the Proper Stranger, Home from the Hill,* and *No Down Payment* teenage, unmarried sex always results in the girl's pregnancy and a series of events designed to punish her. In *Blue Denim* and *Love with the Proper Stranger* both Janet and Angie, respectively, pay the price for sexuality in visits to abortionists, only to be rescued by their men.[8] In *No Down Payment* Leola's pregnancy ten years previously led to her having to give the boy up for adoption. Eventually, she suffers the social ostracism meted out to sexually active women when she is banished from the tightly knit suburban community. In *A Summer Place, All the Fine Young Cannibals,* and *Home from the Hill* Molly, Salome, and Libby, respectively, get pregnant from their first teen tryst and are only extricated from their predicament by a man making a benevolent marriage proposal.[9] *Strangers When We Meet, The Last Time I Saw Paris,* and *From the Terrace* feature married women who have strayed into sexual liaisons and are punished harshly for their transgressions, while the men are left with the promise of domestic bliss. *Cat on a Hot Tin Roof* and *The Long Hot Summer* feature wives whose crimes are not so heinous because their sexuality is targeted toward their husbands. The solution rests in the husbands' coming to terms with their overbearing fathers and learning to take command of their wives.[10]

The sheer number of films which center the sexuality of women underscores ideological currency. Remarkably, all of these films come to the same thematic conclusions, in which passion is used as a point of demarcation between the two genders. Men are encouraged to be sexual and initiate conquests, while women are culpable of numerous transgressions originating in their desire for sexual satisfaction. Thus, a woman who has sex outside marriage is punished by isolation and death, even if her infidelity was inspired by her husband's neglect. Teenage girls who discover the physical pleasures of first love are punished with pregnancy, and women who are passionate in their marriages must learn that they are only to respond to, not initiate, sexual relations.

In addition to focusing on narratives concerned with sexual relations, the films also rely on an explicit or implicit battle of the sexes in order to underscore male superiority at the expense of female intelligence, candor, or self-reliance. In *Please Don't Eat the Daisies* Kate's mother, Miss Susie, advises her son-in-law, Larry, on how to reconcile with her daughter: "Loving her is one thing—letting her think she's intelligent is another. And look where it's got you. Into a house you don't want and a lot of ridiculous interference with your career. She's good and scared now and that's the way you ought to keep her—right under your thumb." In *Boys' Night Out* men and women are pitted against one another as warriors over sexual turf. Men are portrayed as sex-starved adolescents who prefer sexual dalliances with a mistress to their domestic responsibilities, and women are either heedless shrews or manipulative flirts. By the film's end the men have recognized their dependence on their wives for stability and the wives have realized that they must acquiesce to their husbands' demands in order to maintain a balance.

In the television programs sex-trait themes are manifested either as adolescent gender-identity crises resolved by parental intervention or as battles of the sexes. The first type mostly concern females learning to be less assertive and demanding. Such narratives are most common on *Father Knows Best,* in which Betty, and later Kathy, must learn to give in to traditional demands for femininity. Unlike the oversexualized females of the cinema, these girls must learn to be more enticing and to channel their career desires or athletic prowess into more suitable romantic strategies.

In "Betty's Career Problem" (1959–1960), while Betty's impending graduation has spurred her to seek a scholastic award and to apply for numerous jobs, she has also to deal with the attendant insecurities about her future. The episode pits her against her nemesis, Cliff, for the same job as department-store buyer, using their competition to reiterate the message that women must (and should) choose matrimony over careers, and that a woman's proper role is as a muse. Cliff credits Betty for his past victories, saying that she "keeps me on my toes." A store manager informs Betty that "training pretty girls for career jobs doesn't pay off. . . . You beautiful girls usually end up in front of the altar." Betty's parents remind her that as a man, Cliff deserves full-time employment more than she does. At the end of the episode, the two have coincidentally been recruited to model wedding attire in a store fashion show, and Betty tells Cliff that the buyer job is his: "I found something you can never do better than I can—be a bride." Other episodes, such as "Betty, Girl Engineer (1955–1956) and "Betty, the Pioneer Woman" (1958–1959), reiterate this notion that while a woman might be perfectly capable of pursuing a career, she will find her ultimate happiness in serving a husband. The episodes are startling for the fervency with which Betty initially defends her career options and the ultimate hysteria and martyrdom with which she eventually relinquishes them. Betty Friedan, spotlighted by the media in 1963 for her publication that year of *The Feminine Mystique,* wrote a two-part essay for *TV Guide* focusing on just this notion:

> It is perhaps a tribute to real male vanity, or real male contempt to [sic] the female, that television critics often complain of this silly-boob image of the husband, never noticing that the wife in these situation comedies is an even more silly boob. Evidently, in order to retain her "femininity" that wife always has to lose the battle in the end—or rather, demonstrate her true superiority by magnanimously letting the poor fool think he won it.[11]

Later episodes of the series focus on Kathy and her somewhat reluctant transition from tomboy to woman. These episodes are particularly interesting for the amnesia they exhibit concerning Betty's many past career aspirations. While Betty might assert a liberal definition of femininity when an episode concerns her own future professional plans, when her younger sister is spotlighted, she joins in wholeheartedly with her mother's conservative philosophies. In "Kathy Becomes a Girl" (1959–1960) Betty and Margaret take the youngster in hand and paint, pull, and powder her so that she might become dateable. Ultimately, it is up to Father, with his male sagacity and strength, to convince Kathy of the psychological rewards of being a woman:

JIM: We men are happiest when we can be the big male protectors. You let a man know you recognize this as his obligation and he'll go all out to prove you're right.

KATHY: Say, we girls have got it made; all we have to do is sit back and be waited on.

JIM: Well, you mustn't overdo it. It's very important for a girl to be capable and self-sufficient.

KATHY: I am self-sufficient. I can beat Errol at arm wrestling any day.

JIM: That's the worst thing you can do. Never try to beat a man at his own game. You just try to best the women at theirs.

The episode ends with Kathy in dress and high heels, faking a sprained ankle so that the young boys attending her party (arranged by her father) can appropriately wait on her. The message is clear: Being a woman is dressing up and manipulating men into doing one's bidding. Beneath the surface looms the assumption that this life on the pedestal ensures real freedom and/or leisure and is infinitely preferable to a life of self-determination and independence. Importantly, Jim, the purveyor of knowledge, fulfills his task with a mere lecture, but the true work involved in transforming the capable tomboy into the "helpless" manipulator is accomplished by the women in the family, who, rather than relaxing in Jim's promised leisurely feminine world, scurry about transforming Kathy, baking a cake, and buying shoes and ice cream.

The anxieties about gender identity during this period were evidenced in a reevaluation of gender roles and stereotypes, whereby young girls had to learn the art of feminine wiles and how to curb their business ambitions. Most often, these anxieties were voiced in arguments about the mutual exclusivity of careers and motherhood, in which the scripts were adamant that the character traits necessary for a successful career were at odds with those necessary for a successful domestic life. For example, in a memo about a script in which Mary runs for class president, Donna Reed (described by those who worked with her as a feminist)[12] notes that while it is fine that Mary assert herself, the writers should guard against offending any men: "Yes, women's rights have been established; yes, the domineering male can be a pain; but beware of being an obnoxious feminist. The two sexes do, after all, have to live together."[13] In addition, there are a number of episodes in which Donna must advise career women on how to land a man and/or achieve the preferred domestic lifestyle for womanhood,[14] or which feature Mary and Donna teaching intellectual women to hide their scholarly prowess, wear makeup, and entice the males.[15]

While gender identity and instruction form a focal point of the television programs featuring teenage girls and their beautiful and charismatic mothers, they are absent entirely from Leave It to Beaver and The Adventures of Ozzie and Harriet.[16] The message seems to be that while girls need to learn to be women, boys require no such instruction for their masculine maturation. On both programs, the male is the unequivocal norm; Ozzie, Ricky, and David and Ward, Wally, and Beaver operate in a hermetically sealed masculine world, and both Harriet and June passively revolve around their orbit. Because of its hegemony, there are no discussions of what it means to be male, or of what constitutes a boy's proper behavior or identity. At the same time, because of its invisibility, there is no discussion either of what it means to be female. Instead, woman is treated as synonymous with housewife, her behavior effortlessly naturalized by the serene June and Harriet.

Like their feature-film counterparts, the television programs also favor battle-of-the-sexes-type narratives, in which male and female behavior are seen as biologically determined, immutable, and contrary. Such episodes are those that center upon a woman's recognition of her inferiority to men, and in which characters realize the verity and wisdom of delegating tasks and traits by gender. Importantly, as will become clear in the analysis of *My Three Sons*, gender-specific behaviors are adhered to only to the extent that they serve patriarchy. The ideological bottom line is the continuation of masculine control, and sometimes such dominance is assured only through the relaxation of gender-preferred duties.

The case of *My Three Sons* is particularly intriguing, because its entire premise is founded on gender-related spheres of control. In originating the concept for *My Three Sons*, producer Don Fedderson was adamant about the humorous impetus for the program: "The notion of five men in a house is inherently funny because men are in need of a woman around the house . . . men do stupid things around the house."[17] The program is based on the notion that the men will be unable to cope in the domestic sphere without female help and that this will create confusion and chaos. While this attitude might have influenced the creation of the program initially, in actuality, the smooth function of the Douglas household is dependent on the complete elimination of women. The Douglas family not only manages without a

26. From 1960 to 1964, Bub was the perfect domestic helpmate to Steve on *My Three Sons*, even bringing him coffee in a cup and saucer, as in this frame enlargement from "Spring Will Be a Little Late," from the 1960–1961 season.

27. In 1965 William De-
marest replaced William
Frawley (Bub), as his
"brother" Uncle Charley,
seen here in a publicity
photo for *My Three Sons*.
(Copyright Viacom.)

woman, it *thrives,* and various episodes deal specifically with the problems engendered when a woman does indeed cross the Douglas threshold.
Throughout the series run Bub, and then his brother, Charley, manage all
domestic tasks successfully for the Douglas clan. The only time trouble ensues is when either of them is away.[18] In *My Three Sons,* Bryant Park is most
tenaciously a man's world, in which gender battles are fought over everything from domestic turf to school elections ("Lady President," 1964–1965),
and in which the males are always rendered superior. In "The People House"
(1963–1964) the Douglases are rewarded for their home-decorating prowess.
"What's Cookin'?" (1962–1963) showcases the cooking talents of Bub, who,
unlike his hysterical women competitors, is completely at ease cooking for
a PTA contest, winning over the *male* judges with both his charm and his
culinary skills. In "The Lostling" (1960–1961) the Douglas family nurture an
infant girl whose negligent mother left her sleeping in the car while the
family moved into a new home. In "Daughter for a Day" (1962–1963) Jeannie
Hill comes to stay with the Douglas family while her mother, Elizabeth (a

career woman), lectures on home economics.[19] When her mother comes to pick her up, Jeannie smiles gratefully at the Douglas patriarch: "Now when I play house, I'll know what a *real* family is like."[20] In "Mother Bub" (1962–1963) Steve uses some photos of Grandfather Bub in maternal poses to reassure the motherless Chip that a "real mother" isn't necessary.

The Adventures of Ozzie and Harriet features numerous episodes in which the men are pitted against the women in some sort of contest. This occurs most frequently in the later years (1959–1964), when the boys are grown and the episodes center on Ozzie and Harriet and their friends Joe and Clara Randolph. The men and women battle it out over who has more ESP, who is better at keeping secrets, who has more or less curiosity, who can hold a better fundraiser, who can work at a gas station, etc. Rick, Dave, June, and Kris are also embroiled in arguments, over who is more possessive, clinging, jealous, or trusting—fights which ultimately reveal the wives as paranoid, career women as predatory, and marriage as a continual test for a woman's domestic skills.

In *Leave It to Beaver* Beaver is continually set upon by Judy—the only female child appearing regularly in the program—who is seen by both her fellow students as well as by adults as egotistical, snobbish, and bratty. In all cases, Judy's unappealing behavior is attributed to the fact that, in Beaver's words, "she's a girl." Additionally, Judy's activities regularly catalyze Beaver's problems. Her bragging about her father's war efforts impels Beaver to lie about Ward's combat medals; when she boasts that her father is on an "important" business trip and can't make a school picnic, Beaver pretends he is in a similar position, leading to painful complications. Girls on *Leave It to Beaver* represent vanity and entrapment, and in all her battles with Beaver, Judy must forever swallow humble pie and acquiesce to the male domain.

Sex traits are represented distinctly by dialogue and as central narrative issues in both the film and television depictions of family. The films claim more serious breaches of gender contracts, in the form of sexual preference and promiscuity—issues ignored in the television programs. Both media, however, work diligently to ensure a conservative patriarchal agenda concerning proper behavior of the sexes. Women must be homemakers, adhere to the male ego, and be loving, but must not be possessive toward their children; men must be responsible, diligent, athletic, and strong. Where no women are present, men's multiple talents allow them to function successfully in the domestic sphere, but women are reminded that their talents are unwanted and ineffective in traditionally male arenas. Beyond issues revolving around household tasks and career choice, the family melodramas of

28. Boys had boy skills and girls had girl skills. In this frame enlargement from "How the Other Half Lives," an episode from the 1960–1961 season of *The Donna Reed Show,* Jeff (Paul Petersen) tries to teach guest star Gigi Perreau (Ginny) the fine art of passing a football.

both film and television focus upon the importance of the proper practice of parental duties, a misinterpretation of proper gender functioning within these roles producing crisis and misery.

Matriarchy and Patriarchy

> "You can't be our mother, you're our friend!"
> "One can be a friend and a mother too. Of course it's most unusual." [21]

In family melodrama, the family provides both the primary subject matter and the structural vehicle for all narratives. The previous chapter examined how the various narrative emphases placed men and women, mothers and fathers in differing positions of power. Here, the focus is upon the explicit delineation of maternal and paternal characteristics. The examples are those which clearly illuminate how the viewer was to regard mothers and fathers—those moments in the texts when family function was foregrounded as subject matter and vehemently discussed and analyzed. It was noted earlier that the structural positioning of the characters operates to ensure the fathers' positive force and the mothers' negative force or unnecessary existence. In both the film and the television texts the ultimate goal is to depict mothers as either implicitly silly and superfluous or explicitly evil; the resolution to familial dysfunction is Mother's figurative absence (via her narrative unimportance) or literal elimination. But how is this ideological goal accomplished? And what, beyond a simple narrative emphasis on fathers over mothers, works to completely undermine the value of the maternal and replace it with a mutually exclusive paternal love?

While the depiction of wives and mothers in film is distinct from that in television, ultimately both serve the same ideological goal. In both media there is a reiteration of two seemingly incompatible themes: the elevation of housewifery and motherhood as a career, and, paradoxically, the denigration of the mother as overly involved in her children's lives and/or overly prideful of that involvement. The wives and mothers in the films are usually in some way dysfunctional (they are careerists or evil), while in the television programs June, Harriet, Donna, and Margaret are basically happy and efficient at their domestic tasks. When conflict does arise it is either personified by a guest-star, who must be instructed by the TV mom on domestic expediency, or characterized by an idiosyncratic crisis of self-identity during which the mother must be reminded of her ideal lifestyle. One of the most common means by which both the film and television texts strip women of their power is by minimizing their importance to the outside world and insisting on their status as housewives and mothers. In a strident acquiescence to patriarchal hegemony, the texts work in either a two-tiered strategy of minimization and punishment for careerist desires or an explicit celebration of domestic activities, both of which function to render careerism an anathema for women and domesticity their salvation.

In the first level of ideological work, the mothers are told that any career is secondary to the fulfillment one achieves in the domestic sphere. In the films, such dogma is usually directed at women who have already opted for professional status and must be steered in an alternate direction. These are women who have families but are guilty of neglecting them because of outside interests. The films work to undercut the woman's contribution to the outside world and insist on her return to the familial fold. Films in this category include *Imitation of Life*, *Peyton Place*, *The Long Hot Summer*, *The Parent Trap*, and *Some Came Running*.

In *Imitation of Life* Lora Meredith (Lana Turner) is continually placing her acting career above the immediate needs of her daughter Suzie. While she showers her daughter with material possessions, she is unavailable as a confidante or companion. Although Lora is not overtly punished for her career decision (Suzie, for example, is not a juvenile delinquent, and Lora's boyfriend, Steve Archer, is still attentive), she is made to recognize the inadequacies of her life on the stage (a mere imitation) compared with the fulfillment she could experience as a wife and mother. At the end, with the departure of her daughter for college, the death of her maid, Annie, and the self-imposed alienation of Annie's daughter, Sara Jane, Lora recognizes that only by her submersion in the family unit can she rescue it. In *Peyton Place,* Constance MacKenzie (again Lana Turner) has similarly focused on her dress-shop business and financial security. While she has been a fairly attentive mother, she is also a female isolationist, and the "unnatural" familial setting of a single mother and daughter is held as inadequate. By the end of the film, Constance has remarried and reconciled with her daughter, recognizing that a career doesn't hold a candle to the most important job a woman can have—that of wife and mother.

Such narrative strategies are less apparent in the television programs, wherein the wives are solely occupied with housewifery and motherhood. However, one particularly cogent example occurs in a 1955–1956 episode of *Father Knows Best,* titled "Woman in the House." In this episode an old friend of Jim's leaves his new young bride with the Andersons while he is off on business. Jill is an intellectual who reads Kafka and scorns all of Margaret's wifely duties: "She probably even makes her own shoes." Margaret is furious at this derision and yells at Jim: "I felt like a fool. . . . How would you feel if someone were making fun of you . . . a sweet, silly, provincial wife?" Margaret's combat ploy is to become a consummate martyr, waiting on Jill the whole time, even while complaining about her laziness. But beneath Margaret's stoic superiority are deep-seated feelings of insecurity and uselessness. Betty tells her to "stop repressing," and later Margaret sobs on Jim's shoulder, saying she feels like a "repressed neurotic." The resolution to the crisis occurs when Jill reveals to Kathy her own meaningless life. She has "no kids, . . . no mommy, . . . no friends." Kathy wisely advises Margaret that Jill needs something to do, whereupon Margaret sets Jill to work. The end of the episode reveals Jill washing dishes and happily offering to sew a button on for Jim, while Margaret sips tea and reads Kafka. The message seems, at its most basic, to emphasize that women are happiest when engaged in domestic duty; Margaret had no cause for insecurity because her life was exactly what the childless/motherless Jill was longing for. An alternate reading of this episode is equally problematic for a vision of women's real liberation, in that it rests on the assumption that the only means for female relaxation is to exploit another woman; Margaret can rest only as long as Jill takes over the tedious housewifely chores.[22]

A second narrative paradigm involves the actual punishment of the career woman (rather than the mere minimization of her career), by either denying her the pleasures of familial life or revealing how her career wreaks havoc on husband and children. Films in this category include *The Unguarded Moment, Please Don't Eat the Daisies, The Thrill of it All, Executive Suite, There's Always Tomorrow*, and *The Courtship of Eddie's Father.*

In *The Unguarded Moment*, Lois Conway is punished for her devotion to her teaching career, first by being nearly raped by her student Leonard, then by being slandered as a seducer of her students, and, finally, by being attacked by Leonard's father. At the end of the film, Lois is rescued doubly by her police-officer boyfriend—first, as he officially saves her from the clutches of an assailant, and second, as his romantic intentions deliver her from spinsterhood. In *There's Always Tomorrow* Norma Veil, a successful fashion entrepreneur, is nonetheless lonely and envious of Clifford and Marian Groves: "I'd trade anything for a family like yours." Barbara Stanwyck repeats this performance in *Executive Suite,* in which, as Julia Treadway, the mistress of the company's founder, she realizes how little power she has after his death.

Rita, Tom Corbett's girlfriend in *The Courtship of Eddie's Father,* has a chance at marriage, but she also is too preoccupied with her career. Her rigidity regarding her professional life and family time (she wants Eddie sent away while the newlyweds adjust to marriage) engenders a breakup. Her stand for equality is made explicit, and it presages the couple's eventual demise:

> RITA: That old saying—behind every man there's a woman. That's not for me. I want to stand right alongside him. Is that asking too much?
>
> TOM: I'm afraid you're going to have to be satisfied with the vote right now. I don't think that'll ever become a national movement.[23]

If single career women are punished with lonely isolation, married females who seek job fulfillment are threatened with divorce and/or the loss of their children. Two film examples coincidentally star Doris Day as the wife who ventures outside the home, only to realize the trouble it causes. In one, *Please Don't Eat the Daisies,* it is Kate MacKaye's challenge to her husband's authority by asserting her own theatrical talents that results in their marital discord. In the other, *The Thrill of it All,* Beverly Boyer's explosive success as a spokeswoman for "Happy Soap" disrupts her family routine and

29. Evil career woman Rita (Dina Merrill) prefers poodles to children and equality to housewifely subordination in the 1963 film *The Courtship of Eddie's Father*. (Copyright MGM.)

angers her successful obstetrician husband. Although Beverly continually tries to fit her professional duties into her domestic world, the two spheres are depicted as horrifically incompatible. The conflict between the couple is resolved only when Beverly is given the opportunity of assisting Gerry in delivering a baby, a course of action which reiterates her helpmate status, Gerry's nobility, and the maternal bliss associated with childbirth. By the end of the film's nine-month diegesis, Beverly herself has been reborn as a "doctor's wife," good and dutiful and intent upon having another baby.

This hostile attitude toward wives is echoed in the television programs. One of the reasons this topic was so often exploited in the television series stemmed from the fact that these housewife parts were played by such incongruously strong actresses. As Robert Alley and Irby Brown note,

> The representation of women is complicated because in the early days of family series the names of women abounded—Donna Reed, Lucille Ball, Loretta Young, Eve Arden, Spring Byington, Jane Wyman. Typi-

30. In the 1963 film *The Thrill of It All* Beverly Boyer (Doris Day) faces the wrath of her husband (James Garner) and her housekeeper (Zasu Pitts) when she attempts to balance a career with her domestic duties. (Copyright Universal.)

cally, the role of women in the society was portrayed along traditional lines, but at least there were dominant personalities visible among female performers.[24]

This contradiction of strong actress/passive role resulted in a number of episodes in which the mother questions her domestic career if only to establish that even women with intelligence, fortitude, and creativity are happiest when serving their men. In "Mrs. Stone and Dr. Hyde" (1962–1963) Donna replaces Alex's nurse/receptionist while the latter is off on a honeymoon. At the office Alex becomes a brute (the "Hyde" of the title) and berates Donna for taking personal calls (when the calls were for him), yelling at her over the intercom box, criticizing her every movement. After efficiently handling the office, she tenders her resignation at the end of the day, but fate intervenes in the form of a comatose diabetic child. Suddenly, Alex and Donna work together as doctor and nurse, while dramatic music punctuates the shot–reverse-shot close-ups and Donna looks at Alex with admiration

31. Beverly's restitution depends on her subordinating herself to her husband's needs and literally reimmersing herself in the maternal when she assists her husband's patient (Arlene Francis) in childbirth. (Copyright Universal.)

and tears in her eyes. As with Beverly and *Gerry* in *The Thrill of it All,* the proper role for a doctor's wife is as a subordinate helpmate and nurse, not as an individual careerist.[25] Alex's totally unfounded objections to Donna's office prowess are nonetheless supported by her apology at the end of the episode. She will even relinquish her paycheck (using it for a gift for his permanent secretary), thereby wiping out the last residue of any sort of self-determination.

In "Pickles for Charity" (1959–1960) and "A Woman's Place" (1962–1963) Donna transgresses even further, starting her own company in the former and running for city council in the latter. In each episode a respective surplus of merchandise and work compels her to beg for her former domestic life-style. Peter Biskind notes the economic imperative in creating the domestic manager out of the stay-at-home wife and mother:

> There were a number of practical reasons for bestowing power upon housewives. One of them was that weak women made poor consumers. Hidden persuader Ernst Dichter told Betty Friedan that the passive, conservative "True Housewife" was threatened by modern, labor-saving products. . . . [W]omen were to be made to believe that they were "ex-

perts," "managers," "executives," and that the home was a business or factory. The managerial mother was a career woman after all; it's just that her career was the home and family.[26]

Women need not seek employment outside the home, then, because they already had a career. Indeed, housewifery was seen as a full-time job with a requisite model of dress and behavior. Numerous magazine articles during the late 1950's and early 1960's offered advice from the television wives and mothers on how better to excel at their domestic careers. Barbara Billingsley, especially, was the subject of a multitude of women's magazine and *TV Guide* interviews extolling the credentials of the housewife. In "Barbara Billingsley's Advice to Homemakers: Dress up to Your Role," for example, the actress notes: "There are occasions when a homemaker feels and looks better if she's dressed up. No matter how hectic things get, try to keep yourself up. We try on *Leave It to Beaver*—June Cleaver always changes her dress to look fresh when the children come home from school."[27] And in "Barbara Billingsley's fashions" she advises: "A woman managing a home has a career, just as an office worker does. And an attractive career girl gives her job more stature."[28]

32. Barbara Billingsley was promoted as the consummate fashion-plate housewife. Here, pictured with Tony Dow in a publicity photo for *Leave It to Beaver,* she is the model of tasteful dress and accessories. (Copyright Universal.)

Father Knows Best likewise featured highly forthright actresses (Jane Wyatt and Elinor Donahue), and it, too, has a multitude of episodes reminding the viewer that strong women must learn to subjugate themselves. Some of these (discussed previously) involve Betty learning her proper vocational goals ("Betty, Girl Engineer," 1955–1956, and "Betty's Career Problem, 1959–1960). Margaret's domestic dissatisfaction, however, is much more strongly punished than are Betty's transgressions, as she suffers embarrassment, humiliation, shame, and regret. While Betty is steered away from the enticement of a career toward the more pleasurable pursuit of romance, Margaret is explicitly castigated for expressing any sort of self-interest. In "Mother Goes to School" (1957–1958) Margaret enrolls in some university courses only to incur the wrath and scorn of her daughter when they get placed in the same English class. In "It's a Small World" (1958–1959) Margaret's choice to honor her commitment at a charity luncheon rather than accompany Jim on a business trip to New York is depicted as both painful and self-serving. In "Good Joke on Mom" (1959–1960) her selection by the Women's Aid League as the building "chairman" for a new children's clinic meets with familial derision and scorn (her children rib her that a "mother is good only for cooking and scrubbing"). Her attempts to create a position for herself that is more than "photogenic" result in a series of catastrophes from which only her husband and children can save her. Margaret, ridiculed by her family for being merely a housewife, is equally chastised for attempting to circumvent those restrictions and punished with public humiliation in the process. The title of the episode and the continual laugh track underscore the truly malevolent attitude toward Margaret and her attempts at self-determination.

In addition to punishing a mother for her career desires, the television texts, like their filmic counterparts, also attack those women who have opted for a career *instead* of children, but usually the conclusion is more optimistic. Here, the career woman (usually a friend of the family's) is happy in her career (if somewhat lonely) and must be convinced that marriage is the *better* way. Unlike poor Norma Veil of *There's Always Tomorrow*, Molly of "The Career Woman" (*The Donna Reed Show*, 1959–1960) gets a second chance, and, with the help of Donna and Alex, will marry her own small-town doctor and settle down to a life of domestic bliss. Other career women, such as librarians, spinster cousins, and single schoolteachers, must merely be taught the proper feminine wiles and they too can give up their less desirable professions for a domestic diploma. These women, like Norma Veil, serve to reinforce the opinion that the domestic sphere is preferable, because if they had it to do over again, they would settle down to a life of babies and baking.

In "An Extraordinary Woman" (*Father Knows Best, 1958–1959*), Dr. Mary Lou Brown, by then a famous physician working in third-world countries, says to Margaret:

> [Y]ou always seemed to know the true value of everything. You were so confident. . . . Coming back from the airport all Jim talked about was you. He said you were the most extraordinary woman he'd ever known. . . . Jim said that the one thing he always admired in anyone was the ability to do a job well, no matter what it is. He said the way you go about being a wife and mother makes it an enviable art. . . . You know, Margaret, you have the world at your feet, you have everything any woman could possibly want.

This episode, like *There's Always Tomorrow* and *Executive Suite,* reiterates the superior position of the housewife at the same time as it underscores the loneliness of the career woman. Just as Norma Veil did before her, Mary Lou Brown flies over the happy household, looking out of her airplane window wistfully and sadly.

When the films and television programs are not rechanneling careerist desires or punishing careerist activities, they work, through dialogue, to explicitly extol the virtues of being a good wife and mother. Often, these conversations occur in the careerist episodes (such as those mentioned above), but sometimes they involve a capable wife and mother training a young bride in the glories of being a housewife. All of these narratives point out that serving a man offers the ultimate in personal satisfaction, and they usually contain explicit dialogue glorifying the position of the housewife. While this configuration is rare in the films, in which the central family and supporting families are dysfunctional, one film, *No Down Payment,* does exemplify some of these strategies when the attractive and organized Jeanne tries to instruct the hapless Leola ("a good natured slob").

Again, the marginality of June Cleaver and Harriet Nelson, together with the female-less Douglas household, result in a dearth of episodes dealing with explicit praise of Mom and her work. Occasionally, June and Harriet are complimented on a meal or an outfit, but for the most part, their efforts are minimized and, consequently, praise seems unnecessary. Donna Stone and Margaret Anderson, however, operate explicitly as paragons of housewifery whose duties are narratively singled out, emulated, complained about, and complimented. In "Margaret Disowns Her Family" (1956–1957) Margaret helps a young bride not only with the practical matters of cooking and cleaning, but also in reassuring her that the rewards for housewifery are unparalleled. In "The First Child" (1959–1960) Donna hovers reassuringly

33. "Good" housewife Jeanne (Patricia Owens) gives domestic advice to the sloppy Leola (Joanne Woodward) in the 1957 film *No Down Payment*. (Copyright 20th Century–Fox.)

over a young couple, nervous about its new baby. In "Three Part Mother" (1958–1959) Donna succeeds at being in three places at once—Jeff's basketball game, Mary's girl's club meeting, and Alex's lecture—and is rewarded as her family fights over her. At the end of the episode, she tucks all her family (including her husband!) into bed and smiles sweetly, their calling voices ringing in her ears.

Sometimes, an episode will dare to question the supposedly intractable bliss of happy homemaking. In these episodes, the wives express dissatisfaction with their seemingly insignificant lot, and must be reminded by children and spouse how important they are. In "Brief Vacation" (1956–1957) Margaret, fed up with the constant and ungracious demands of her family, decides to take a day off from housewifery, strolling through the "French district" of Springfield. She has her portrait painted, buys a hat, and eats in a small café, neglecting the small, humdrum chores of the day. When the rest of the family arrive home to find her just doing the breakfast dishes, they criticize her lack of organization and worry that she's having some sort of breakdown. Jim, perplexed, must ask his secretary what the problem is, and with the imagined threat of divorce looming large in his head, races home to find Margaret placing Kathy's pet frog in a cage. She rants at Jim for exaggerating her one day off into such a dilemma: "Why am I the only one around here who can't do anything out of the ordinary? . . . [Put the frog] back in his cage where he belongs, just like me." When Betty comes home with more chores for Margaret, Jim, having seen the light, lectures his daughter, "Your mother isn't just a worker we keep in a cage." Taking Margaret to the French district for dinner, he reassures her that she is the "hub about which we all circle and depend." The show is startling for the criticism it directs toward the mundane duties of homemaking, but it also reiterates the warning that straying from the nest can cause untold aggravation and harm. The lesson is twofold: Women should recognize their value as the passive center of the home, and men must remind the women of their value, lest they venture into the real world.

While the films and programs thus work mightily to assure and reassure women of the importance of their housewifely duties (and the impossibility of outside employment), they also, paradoxically, work to undercut their sense of self-worth. Women are caught in a double bind: they are crucial to the maintenance of the home, but their duties are not so important that they should be smug or conceited. Additionally, there are those mothers who exaggerate their importance to the point of harm, and they must be carefully redirected to a voiceless marginal existence.

Although popular journals such as *Good Housekeeping* and *Ladies' Home Journal* extolled the virtues of motherhood, the importance of maintaining the home, and the necessity of being a good wife, there was another strain—that of antimaternalism—rampant in postwar America, that seemed to find its loudest expression both in the cinematic family melodrama and in television's domestic comedies. This antimaternalism was at its least vindictive in the simple marginalization of the housewife position, and at its most condemnatory in the treatment of mothers, which took on a distinct tone of vilification, echoing the 1940's writings of Philip Wylie and Edward Strecker. In 1942 Wylie wrote that the American male had become weak and unproductive due to his overwhelming sentimental attachment to his mother. She had squelched his natural "barbarianism," forcing him toward either a violent or a neurotic adulthood:

Mom is everywhere and everything and damned near everybody, and from her depends all the rest of the U.S. . . . . Her boy, having been protected by her love and care, even shudderingly shielded from his logical development through his barbaric period of childhood . . . is cushioned against any major step in his progress toward maturity.[29]

Strecker, in his 1946 book *Their Mothers' Sons,* defines seven categories of "moms"—here a deliberately derisive term[30]—and cautions that mothers can err on the side both of overprotectiveness and of overstrictness:

> A mom will take advantage of [her] natural mother urge to hold her child or children to her. The real mother fights the urge and lovingly does everything in her power to make her children stand on their own feet. She prepares them for an adult life. The mothers of men and women capable of facing life maturely are not apt to be the traditional mom type. More likely mom is sweet, doting, "self-sacrificing." But the obverse of this case, the capable, stern, self-contained, domineering mom is not uncommon.[31]

David Considine notes that while it took Hollywood a decade to respond to Strecker's and Wylie's contentions, when it finally did respond, it did so with relentless fervor:

> The long-preserved image of the mother as the heart and hub of the home, the one who interpreted life to her husband and the children, underwent a major change. . . . Shrill, vitriolic, materialistic, suspicious and predatory, she is a thoroughly anti-life character totally lacking in sensitivity and incapable of functioning as a mother.[32]

While many of the narratives worked to underscore the importance of a domestic career for women, an equal number of texts paradoxically worked to minimize her contributions, or, more vehemently, to condemn her for her overinvolvement. The negative treatment of housewives and mothers works as a crucial point of distinction between the television and film portrayals of family life. In the films, the mothers are, for the most part, either completely absent and unimportant to the family domain or evil and the cause of its dysfunction. In the television programs, however, the mothers either operate as depersonalized drones or, if they are more active in the family situation, are reminded continually that they must maintain a patina of modesty and invisibility. These patterns are evident in three major thematic paradigms: self-effacement (only in the television programs), obliteration, and denigration.

The theme of self-effacement dominates those television series in which the mother's role is most pronounced—*Father Knows Best* and *The Donna Reed Show*. Here, Mother is told to attend to her duties efficiently but modestly, to defer praise onto the father, and to minimize her contributions. *Father Knows Best* tends to punish Margaret for any attempts at self-glorification, while *The Donna Reed Show* (with the mother character the narrative center and Reed the producer) takes a more indirect route in castigating Donna for her attempts at soliciting respect. Two episodes of *Father Knows Best* illustrate the problems engendered by mothers who demand appreciation; the first deals with Margaret's attempt at self-fulfillment outside her housewife status, while the second is more directly related to her position as domestic goddess. In "A Medal for Margaret" (1957–1958) Margaret is engulfed in self-pity because she's never won any sort of award the way the rest of the family has. When the others decide to build a trophy case to house their various prizes, Margaret decides to enter the Springfield ladies fishing contest. Without telling her family, she hires a private tutor and practices daily until she becomes an expert. On the day of the contest, in her excitement at her prowess, she runs over to brag happily to neighbor Myrtle Davis and trips, spraining her arm (a case in which, quite literally, pride comes before a fall).[33] Margaret is devastated and humiliated until the rest of the family, in an effort to cheer her up, present her with various trophies for assisting them. Crucially, these awards are not for her own activities, but for Margaret's aid with *her family's* endeavors (driving Bud so he can deliver his newspapers in the rain, making Betty's costume for a play, providing Kathy with PTA bake-sale goodies). While the possibility exists to do so, no accolades are given for any of Margaret's individual accomplishments (her cooking or home-decorating skills, for example). Each award thus reiterates the parasitic nature of the housewife/mother's happiness—she has no projects of her own, and her only contribution consists of doing the physical labor for the family's creative and productive ideas. In addition, the text works to remind us that, in Marc's words, "Medals and trophies are fine, but modern homemakers (that is, modern women) are motivated by something more complex—love and the sense of duty that grows from it."[34] Mothers must learn, therefore, not to attempt any sort of self-aggrandizement, as it leads only to physical calamity, and is unnecessary anyway.

In "Big Shot Bud" (1958–1959) Margaret is once again punished, this time for merely accepting a bottle of perfume from Bud as "payment" for cleaning his girlfriend's sweater. In his zealousness, Bud decides to buy his mother a gift he can't afford, resulting in a financial calamity. Margaret, her perception fuzzy from Bud's compliments, is oblivious to her son's distress (in effect, *failing* in the very function she's just been rewarded for) and blithely plans a celebratory dinner. Jim eventually bails Bud out and, amazingly, the episode ends with a *father* and son bonding over the troubles caused in rewarding mothers.[35]

The Donna Reed Show is even more replete with episodes that remind the housewife that while her duties are crucial to the successful functioning of the family sphere, they are, in effect, valueless, and that part of her role depends on modesty and self-effacement. The most blatant example is "Just a Housewife" (1959–1960), in which Donna's innocent suggestion for a more complimentary term than "housewife" is depicted as a revolutionary cause célèbre. In "The Ideal Wife" (1958–1959) Donna is upset because her happy nature is not only taken for granted, it also labels her a "goody-goody." In "Lucky Girl" (1959–1960) Donna is angry because the townspeople are continually raving about Alex and telling her how lucky she is to be married to such a wonderful man. Immediately after her complaint, she is rendered a helpless, hysterical mother in the face of Jeff's stomach pain.[36] She calls her "acute resentment" a case of "temporary madness," undercutting the legitimacy of her earlier arguments and reminding women viewers that any complaints about their "lucky" status are ill-founded. The first lesson for mothers, then, is one of self-effacement. The dominant, capable, and charismatic women of *Father Knows Best* and *The Donna Reed Show* continually and in quite explicit terms remind the viewer that the most successful housewife is

34. In this rare scene, from a 1960–1961 episode of *The Donna Reed Show,* "How the Other Half Lives," Donna is shown doing actual hard domestic labor (sewing curtains). For the most part, the domestic chores on television's melodramas were structurally absent, rendering the mother's functions insubstantial and marginal.

35. The successful housewife was one who was modest and self-effacing, and who accepted compliments demurely. In this scene from "How the Other Half Lives," Alex praises Donna on a job well done.

one who does her duty sweetly and unheroically, that to call for or receive accolades results in pain, punishment, guilt, or self-recrimination. The second lesson for mothers is that they must continuously reward their *husbands'* achievements as breadwinners and parents (as discussed in the previous chapter). So, while women were told to be demure and self-effacing, the men were being congratulated on their "new" active roles as heads of households, peacemakers, lovers of small children, and paternal giants. Patricia Mellencamp, in her work on *I Love Lucy* and *Burns and Allen*, summarizes the transformation of the housewife that was catalyzed by the move away from the urban presentational sitcoms of the late 1940's and early 1950's to the representational domestic comedies of the late 1950's and early 1960's:

> For me, two issues are central: the importance in early 1950's comedy of idiosyncratically powerful female stars, usually in their late thirties or forties; and the gradual erosion of that power that occurred in the representation of women within comedy formats. In situation comedy, pacification of women occurred between 1950 and 1960 without a single

critical mention that the genre's terrain had altered: the housewife, although still ruling the familial roost, changed from being a humorous rebel or well-dressed, wise-cracking, naive dissenter who wanted or had a paid job . . . to being a contented, if not blissfully happy, understanding homebody.[37]

In an equally potent strategy for maternal minimization, other film and television texts worked right from the start to obliterate the mother/wife from any narrative importance. Unlike the episodes mentioned above, these are texts in which the women are completely incidental to, or missing from, the family dynamic. Darrell Hamamoto comments on this peripheral value given to the housewife profession:

> Heads of households in the television situation comedies of the fifties seemed to occupy either one of two extreme polarities. They could be either the understanding family patriarch or they could be the bumbling father. That mothers were never portrayed in an unflattering light may indicate the manner of subtle condescension American society at that time conferred upon her when she was still kept apart from the job market.[38]

In the filmic representations this obliteration is depicted in narratives in which mothers are explicitly absent or silly, while in the television programs the mothers are seen as both superfluous and subordinate. These representations either underscore Mother as narratively unimportant via her structural elimination or locate her explicit absence as cause for familial problems. For example, a multitude of the filmic families are missing mothers altogether. In some of these films the missing mother is not even a narrative factor. Except for briefly comparing the similar attributes of mother and daughter, Janet's father never mentions his dead wife in *Blue Denim*. In other films—notably *The Long Hot Summer*, *Lonelyhearts*, *Love with the Proper Stranger*, *The Cobweb*, *Tammy and the Bachelor* (1957), *The Days of Wine and Roses*, and *Some Came Running*—the missing matriarch is not discussed and never claims status as even a negative influence on the family dynamic. In other more maternally critical films such as *Tea and Sympathy* and *The Unguarded Moment* the hyper-misogyny and machismo of the father are directly related to the mother's desertion. The fathers (both played by Edward Andrews) discuss the departure of the mother in harsh terms, and the sexual behavior of their sons (homosexuality and sexual violence, respectively) is seen as resulting from the lack of the mother's influence. In *East of Eden* Kate's desertion of her family is the implicit reason for Adam Trask's obsessive strictness with his sons. While her desertion is predicated on Adam's rigid control of her, it is she who is structurally and thematically culpable for the familial chaos which ensues. Her money catalyzes Cal's abortive attempt to win his father's affections, and her reappearance in her sons' lives causes Aron to have a nervous breakdown and run to war, ultimately leading to Adam's stroke.

While not as diabolically bitter about the missing matriarch, other films do in some ways depict the mother's absence as the reason for familial dilemma. Both *Man on Fire* and *Move Over Darling* function similarly to *East of Eden*, in that they involve the reinsertion of a previously absent mother, but because the viewer is at times privy to the maternal point of view, they lack the vindictiveness of the latter. In both films, the mother has made an unexpected return and claim on her children, causing them untold confusion and grief, and eventual resignation. In *Rebel without a Cause* Plato's mother is off gallivanting in Hawaii on his birthday, and his despondency provokes him to kill some puppies. In *April Love* Nicky's mother works all day and "can't ride herd on him," which necessitates his being sent to stay with his more stable aunt and uncle. In this case, Nicky's criminality is created by the neglect of his mother, while his rehabilitation then depends on her obliteration.

Finally, there are mothers who are dead before the film begins, and whose literal absence creates a multitude of problems for the family that are resolved not so much through reinsertion of the maternal as through paternal intervention. In *Houseboat* and *The Courtship of Eddie's Father* the death of the mother catalyzes familial disorder—David's petty thievery, Robert's introspection, and Elizabeth's fear at night in *Houseboat*, and Eddie's despondency in *The Courtship of Eddie's Father*. In both films the solution to these problems is suggested by a woman (a maid and a nurse, respectively), but it must be executed singularly by the father. The survival of the family rests on the father voicing his love for his children and becoming more involved with their lives. The replacement mom is valued only for her domestic duties (cooking, cleaning, and taking temperatures).

In the films, then, absent mothers are treated in various ways. First, they may be narratively elided, not existing in any reference nor being held accountable for any turmoil or pain. Second, their absence may be blamed for the errant behavior of their children and/or the misogyny of their former spouses. Third, they may be punished twice—once for leaving the household, and then for returning to it uninvited. And finally, the death of a mother may lead to a rebonding with the father, who then searches for a replacement domestic professional.

36. Such a moment of maternal plenitude was absent from all the television programs except *The Donna Reed Show*. Even here, such depictions of mother-child
bonding were few and far between, the emphasis being upon father-child love and
reconciliation.

In the television programs, the absence of mothers is articulated through
their structural unimportance or, as in the case of *My Three Sons*, by their
literal omission. In both cases, the absence of the mothers holds disturbingly
little consequence for the familial function. In a *TV Guide* article from the
early 1960's Betty Friedan noted the malevolence with which television eliminated mothers from the family circle:

> Does the new plethora of widowers, bachelor fathers, and unmarried
> mature men on television, who pay a maid or houseboy or, perhaps, a
> robot to get the household drudgery done, signify unconscious rebel-
> lion against that [nasty, vengeful, martyr] "housewife" altogether? [39]

Television's maternal obliteration was characterized first by elimination of
the mother as an independent character, and then by dismissal of the mother
as an integral part of her child's upbringing. The preponderance of this tactic
was sufficiently pronounced to disturb even some of the programs' most ardent admirers. Jane Wyatt, for example, who otherwise has nothing but

praise for *Father Knows Best,* finds fault with the minimization of the mother's identity: "My only complaint was you never saw her reading a book, or going to the office, or playing tennis. Mom always had to be around with nothing to do . . . just to say 'wash your hands.' So I just sat around waiting to go on."[40] It is interesting to see this comment from Wyatt, who, along with Donna Reed, could be classified as a much more active participant than either June Cleaver or Harriet Nelson. In both *Leave It to Beaver* and *The Adventures of Ozzie and Harriet* the mother's presence is signified only by the meals she prepares and the neatness of the house. Diana Meehan, in her book *Ladies of the Evening,* notes that while Harriet's presence within the household is continual, it is passive and ill-defined:

> When Ozzie identified typical activities of each family member in one episode, Harriet was described as "reading a magazine" in the living room. She apparently had no outside interests other than the care and concerns of her family, and even her phone conversations involved descriptions of what Ozzie or their sons were doing.[41]

37. Even in scenes in which she appears, Harriet is marginalized. Here, she silently puts a bowl of flowers on the table (something she did in nearly every episode), while Rick and Ozzie discuss Ricky's current crisis.

And, as Mary Beth Haralovich has observed, "unlike Margaret, June is structured on the periphery of the socialization of her children, in the passive space of the home."[42] In both *The Adventures of Ozzie and Harriet* and *Leave It to Beaver* there are complete episodes in which the mothers never make an appearance. The women are seen for a moment at the program's opening in which it is explained that they are going off to "visit relatives," and are never heard from again. Sometimes this gains enough narrative importance to warrant a mini-crisis (as when June's Aunt Martha does an even less capable job of mothering than June, and Ward must intervene), but more often than not, the episode functions in a motherless stability, the sole concern being the father-son bonding.

Obliteration of the mother is part of the melodramatic tradition from which these films and programs emerged. David Grimsted has noted about eighteenth- and nineteenth-century melodrama that "the mother appeared less often than the father in the serious plays of the period. Perhaps issuing moral platitudes or forcing a daughter to wed against her will was considered man's work; whatever the reason, the mother was often dead—'an angel spirit'—or at least a less centrally important character."[43] By the early 1960's the elimination of the mother character had become quite literal, and the lack of the feminine domestic was so pronounced as to inspire a *TV Guide* article which bemoaned the "decline of strong female parts" and, for actresses, "the constant frustration of being . . . the eternal spectator rather than a participant in the main action."[44] A producer of *Bonanza* claimed that women were simply too complicated for teleplays: "Writing-wise, a woman, with all her special feminine problems, gets to be a nuisance. Many things have to be explained."[45]

One of the most successful and earliest configurations of the missing mother was, of course, *My Three Sons*. Unlike most of the theatrical films, however, in this case the absence of the matriarch was not presented as any sort of narrative problem. This is a family that functions not only beautifully without a mother, but, more importantly, better than those with mothers. In "Other People's Houses" (1960–1961), for example, Laura and George Ferguson are guilty of over-refining their son Hank. Their spotless home and their gourmet dinners are held up as deficient in comparison with the friendly and casual chaos of the Douglas household.

In addition to her literal absence, the mother is further obliterated via her ridiculous or unaware behavior. In the films the women are depicted primarily as silly or mere appendages of their more dominant husbands. When mothers are not absent from the narrative, the spectator is encouraged to believe that their presence is unnecessary, and, indeed, often detrimental to successful familial relations. For example, in *Rebel without a Cause* Judy is adamant that she wants her father to pick her up from the station; she is not interested in her mother's love or acceptance, and the fulcrum of familial crisis and resolution rests firmly with the patriarch. In *Splendor in the Grass* Bud's mother (introduced only as "my wife") is a passive observer at meals, where she voices inane non sequiturs about her son's diet when he is in an obvious state of crisis. In *Giant* Leslie's mother is ridiculous, mistakenly calling Bick "Beckwith" and Texas "Nevada," and needing the statistics about the Reatta ranch to be repeated. In *Bernardine* both Mrs. Bowman and Mrs. Wilson are unaware of their respective sons' adventures and difficulties, as is Mrs. Bartley in *Blue Denim*.

The television programs differ from their filmic counterparts in that mother is never depicted as a scatterbrained idiot. *Leave It to Beaver,* however, does continually depict June as naïve and bewildered when it comes to understanding the behavior of her two boys. She frequently asks Ward's advice, and is genuinely puzzled by Wally and Beaver's actions. As Mary Beth Haralovich has noted:

> Wondering how to approach instances of boyish behavior, June positions herself firmly at a loss. She frequently asks, mystified, "Ward, did boys do this when you were their age?" And Ward always reassures June that whatever their sons are doing (brothers fighting, for example) is a normal stage of development of boys, imparting to her his superior social and familial knowledge.[46]

By far the most important factor in distinguishing the film families from the television families is the filmic construction of the mother as enemy. While the television programs might devalue her input or highlight her misjudgment, they never depict her in any evil or malevolent manner. Any parenting mistakes that Margaret, Donna, Harriet, or June might commit are due to their naïveté or shortsightedness. In the films, however, the mothers are malevolent and harmful creatures whose attitudes and actions cause the family calamity, and whose consequent expulsion or incapacitation is often the determining factor in familial resolution.

It is important to note that at issue here is not the woman's character as a whole, but only her competency as a mother. Thus, while Lora Meredith in *Imitation of Life* is guilty of careerism and therefore maternal negligence, she is not explicitly an evil mother. Indeed, her problem is her *lack* of involvement with her child, and the film's resolution depends on her assuming her maternal role more strongly. In the examples which follow, conversely, the mothers are overinvolved and guilty of outright smothering evil, parasitic demands, or sexual promiscuity. Further, the narrative explicitly blames this malevolent behavior for the familial strife which ensues.

The more common depiction of the filmic mothers is not as marginal or superfluous, but as an evil or detrimental "(s)mother." Much has been written about the malevolence of mothers in the films of the late 1950's. Peter Biskind devotes an entire chapter to mothering gone wrong and makes the point that while in so-called liberal films mothers are guilty of neglecting their children, in conservative films they are castigated for castrating either their husbands or sons with their overpowering demands and presence.[47] Leonard Benson noted in his sociological study on fathers that

> Our expectations for husbands and wives are still influenced by the traditional concepts of patriarchy: thus, for example, obstinate husbands are almost always more socially acceptable than stubborn wives. The father who fights for his dignity through the exercise of misguided authority is likely to receive our sympathy; in a comparable plight mother seems villainous. In the "mother manipulates the father" comedies, the manipulating wife must be, above all, feminine—for all her trickery. . . . [T]he suburban shrew is probably a more common stereotype to most people than any male counterpart they can imagine.[48]

The quintessential representation of evil mothering is in *Rebel without a Cause,* in which the initial introduction to motherhood occurs in a police station, where the three deprived offspring—Jim, Judy, and Plato—are all reeling from maternal neglect. Jim's mother arrives from a dance, dressed formally, bickering with her husband, Frank, and criticizing her son. She looks nothing like the aproned homebody we associate with traditional maternal images. Jim's paternal grandmother is an older-generation version of his mother, dressed in formal attire, critical, and sharp-tongued. Throughout the course of the film, the mothers are rendered either as rotten (both Mrs. Starks) or useless/absent (Judy and Plato's mothers). The younger Mrs. Stark—Jim's mother—yells at Frank for offering cigars to Ray and is critical of her obviously unhappy son. When these women attempt to do their traditional maternal jobs, they fail; Jim's mother is criticized for the school lunch she prepares for her son, she gets ill and is unable to clean the house, she "nearly died giving birth," and she needs pills to sleep. The dialogue works diligently to ensure that the spectator recognizes these mothers as evil or unnecessary. Jim complains continually about his mother's domination of his father: "She eats him alive and he takes it. . . . If he had guts to knock Mom cold once, then maybe she'd be happy and stop pickin' on him. 'Cause they make mush out of him." Later, he yells at his father for donning an apron and tending to Mrs. Stark. "You shouldn't do that!" he cries, convincing his father and the spectator that not only should mothers not get ill, they should not be cared for when they do. While Biskind argues this film fits the liberal agenda in that Mrs. Stark is a mother who does not love enough, the resolution of the film is at odds with this assessment. If the problem were that Mrs. Stark needed to be more demonstrative with her son, the climactic scene should incorporate both parents in the son's embrace. This is not the case, however, because the issue is not love but control, and the simple narrative dilemma is that Mrs. Stark has too much of it, and Mr. Stark too little. The resolution is therefore to strip Mrs. Stark of her narrative power and to center the father-son bonding. In other words, the hero's troubles emerge from her presence, and the resolution lies in her absence. This configuration is similar to that of *Five Finger Exercise,* in which Phillip is also restored to the family unit after the sacrifice of an outsider (the tutor, Walter) and Stan asserts his patriarchal control over the now recalcitrant and apologetic Louise. Both films end with the patriarch comforting a sadder but wiser family and leading them toward a more stable family existence.

Other family melodramas offer a far grimmer picture of (s)motherhood, its consequences, and the punishments visited upon mother and child. In all of these cases, the relationship centers upon a near-incestuous devotion of a mother toward her son, for which she is profoundly punished. In *Home from the Hill* Hannah not only clings to her child, but attempts to ruin the admiration he has for his father. Her vindictive jealousy ruins the paternal-filial bond, enraging and embittering her son and pushing him toward a course of self-destruction which leads indirectly to her husband's death and her son's exile from the community. In *All Fall Down* Annabelle's blind affection for her ne'er-do-well son Berry Berry has incurred the self-pity and then the wrath of her husband, Ralph, and the cynicism of her other son, Clint. Annabelle's possessiveness results in her son's hatred as well as his womanizing, which, in turn, leads to the suicide of his pregnant girlfriend, Echo. In the end, Annabelle is left isolated in her tenacious maternal possessiveness, a victim of her own exaggerated affections. In *Hilda Crane* Mrs. Burns' insatiable need to keep her son Russell by her side and away from the desirable Hilda leads first to Russell's cynical resignation—he deserts his true love—and then to her own death when the angry Hilda confronts her with the truth about her malevolent influence.[49] In *Peyton Place* Norman Page, freed from his horrifically repressive mother, comments, "As soon as I got away from my mother, I realized how wonderful life was." In *Return to Peyton*

Place, Ted has turned on his clinging mother and publicly humiliated her, and will leave Peyton Place with his foreign bride. In *Stranger in My Arms* Burgoyne Beasely obsesses about her son even after his death, and she is castigated at the film's end by her husband and deserted by both her daughter and her daughter-in-law.

A variation on the possessive-mother theme concerns mothers who are overwhelmingly strict with their children—a configuration that concerns mothers and daughters only. In *A Summer Place, Splendor in the Grass, Peyton Place, Return to Peyton Place,* and, to a certain extent, even *Hilda Crane* and *Picnic* (1955), the mothers are guilty of, at worst, a frigid resistance to sexual behavior, and at best, a castigation of their daughters' life-styles. In the more mild case, the mothers of the grown-up daughters of *Hilda Crane* and *Picnic* are afraid not so much of their daughters' sexuality as of a recurring female pattern of "easy virtue," and resulting spinsterhood. The confrontation between these women and their daughters is minimal compared with that of the frigid females of *Peyton Place, A Summer Place,* and *Splendor in the Grass.* In *Splendor in the Grass* Deanie attempts a sexually oriented discussion with her mother, only to have her mother remind her that "no nice girl has those feelings. . . . a woman puts up with it, to have children." Mrs. Loomis' denial of Deanie's sexual feelings and her castigation of her suspected behavior ("He didn't spoil you, did he?") work to push her daughter toward a nervous breakdown. In *A Summer Place,* from the very beginning, Helen is established as a rigid, frigid disciplinarian. She dresses her daughter, Mollie, in little-girl clothes, wanting her to appear flat-chested. As the film progresses, Helen's terrorizing of her daughter continues: she has her forcibly examined by a doctor to determine her virginity, she forbids Mollie to see Johnny, and she tries to ruin the bond between father and daughter by informing Mollie of Ken's affair with Johnny's mother, Sylvia, causing Mollie to run off in a panic. The film is particularly fascinating in its dual castigation of the mothers (Helen is punished for her antisexuality, while Sylvia is punished—though eventually rescued—for being overly sexual). The resolution of the film depends on Mollie deserting her hysterical mother to stay with Ken and Sylvia, leaving Helen alone with her artificial Christmas tree and her hatred of men.[50] *Peyton Place* is a complex film in that its malevolent mother represents both the frigid and the overly sexual woman. Indeed, the entire film is about the hypocrisy of adults who preach morality but behave otherwise: Constance MacKenzie, the mother of the illegitimate Alison, lectures her daughter on staying "respectable," and the two become the focal point for the depiction of the sexual hypocrisy of mothers and the punishment they invite. At the end of the film, Connie's public humiliation is the only sufficient payment for her previous repressive behavior. *Peyton Place* has an ending that is more hopeful than that awaiting other repressive mothers, but it is dependent upon a Catholic attitude of confession and exoneration.[51]

The agenda of these films is, then, first to render Wylie's dastardly mothers in all their configurations. It depicts mothers as Wylie saw them—cruel, demonic, smothering. Next, it suggests the solution to this problem as being one of elimination. Mothers either are relegated to a position that is out of frame and lacking in narrative importance, with fathers offering both narrative closure and emotional sustenance, or they must suffer public condemnation and humiliation in order to win back their tolerant (but never loving) daughters.

A final, less extreme variant of the (s)mother consists of those women who are guilty of neglecting their husbands in favor of their children, or of being a bit too worried about the offspring, without being pathological about it. On occasion, this type of mother also appears in the television programs, where she must be instructed by the central family on proper maternal distance. In *There's Always Tomorrow,* for example, Marian Groves continually attends to the children when Clifford wants to get her alone. Her frequent preference for her children's desires over those of her husband leads to his near-affair with designer Norma Veil. It is Norma who lectures the Groves children about their misplaced affections, telling them they should stop thinking of Mother all the time, and display some affection for Dad.[52] At the end of the film, Marian, while never explicitly learning of Cliff's liaison, seems to have learned her lesson; she is romantic with her husband, suggesting they spend some time alone together, and as she and Cliff stroll around their yard, the children smile from behind the bars of security windows at what a "handsome couple" they make.[53]

In *The Donna Reed Show* a 1959–1960 episode titled "All Mothers Worry," guest-starring, as Mrs. Dorsey, Ann Doran (Jim Stark's evil mother in *Rebel without a Cause*), centers on the overprotectiveness of mothers. Here, Donna must instruct Mrs. Dorsey on the importance of letting her son experience both the thrills and rewards of little league football. In *Leave It to Beaver* the perpetual presence of Mrs. Mondello serves as an implicit reminder of the superior Mrs. Cleaver. Larry Mondello, Beaver's best friend, is an overweight, whining troublemaker, and his mother is also overweight, as well as neurotic and incapable of controlling her son. These moms, while not possessive or sexually repressive, are guilty of maternal overindulgence and overprotectiveness, and need either the threat of an affair (in the films) or the guidance of a superior mother (on the television programs) to steer them on the correct path toward separateness.

A second evil configuration depicts the mother as a leech. Here she is guilty, first, of the traditional parasitic position of the stay-at-home wife. This is usually not a problem in films of this period, in which women were being reminded it was not only preferable, but their duty, to remain at home. However, remaining at home also meant being content with one's lot and contributing to the household in the way of domestic chores, and these women are neglectful of their household duties (because of either laziness or wealth). Second, these women are greedy or discontented with their social standing. Sometimes it is a material request (such as in *The Catered Affair*); on other occasions the request is for the child itself (*Man on Fire*); and sometimes these women are guilty of pure snobbery, a mother rejecting her daughter's suitor because that person does not meet her individual standards (*From the Terrace*).

In *The Catered Affair* Aggie is so concerned with propriety and impressing others that she is prepared to sacrifice husband Tom's chance at owning his own taxicab, just so that she can put on an extravagant wedding for her daughter, Jane. Aggie is doubly vilified, first, by putting her children before her husband, and second, by using her husband's hard-earned salary for her own pleasure. In the end, Aggie must apologize for the expenditure, and she reconciles with Tom's partner so that the two men might still own a taxi. In *Man on Fire* the dialogue is explicit as to the position of the housewife and mother. Ted Carlson sees his mother as nothing but a lazy leech, a woman who expended no energy in his care and now wants to cling to him and destroy the relationship between him and his father.

The depiction of the mother as leech is not as common as that of other maternal degenerates, partly because her parasitic position is, by definition, part of her stay-at-home role. Nevertheless, these texts serve to emphasize the dire consequences awaiting those women who have extended, or who are accused of extending, domestic service into a dangerous dependency.

The final, and more common, configuration of maternal transgression resides in the explicit expression of Mom's sexuality. A multitude of cinematic family melodramas construct a narrative dilemma out of either the mother's past sordid behavior or her current dalliances. When the sexuality occurs pre-diegetically, these mothers use the memory of their tainted life-style and its concomitant guilt to manipulate and repress their daughters. Such films as *Peyton Place* and its sequel and *Picnic* function in this way, altering the sexual mother into a (s)mother. In other films the sexual behavior of the mother becomes the narrative focus, and these women are punished more for sex-trait errors than for maternal abuse (*Strangers When We Meet* and *The Last Time I Saw Paris,* discussed above). Here, the concern is mostly with mothers whose sexual appeal or practices directly interfere with the maternal function, and who consequently catalyze an explicit confrontation with either the husbands or the children over Mom's errant behavior. In these films there are two distinct types of sexual mother, the first being the woman who is *strong* and sexual, whose desire for life and general passion is ultimately channeled toward more specifically targeted ardor and/or attempts at self-fulfillment. Films in this category include *Giant, The Pleasure of His Company, East of Eden, If a Man Answers, A Summer Place,* and *The Cobweb.* The second type is the mother who is *weakened* by her sexual desires and who has punished herself even before patriarchy raises its mighty hand of discipline. Films in this category include *From the Terrace, All That Heaven Allows,* and *Period of Adjustment.*

From the beginning, *Giant* works to render Leslie at once sexually active, disobedient, and subversive. Her husband, Bick, first glimpses her as she rides her rearing stallion, Warwinds. Her hair flying, her ecstatic expression, and the traditional association between horses and sexuality all serve to depict her as a desirable and desiring woman. Leslie's sexuality and independence are explicitly interwoven, and eventually—and paradoxically—one is used to crush the other. The evening after the funeral of Luz (a woman punished during the sexually metaphoric act of riding Leslie's horse), the men sit in the cavernous living room of Reatta, while the women are in a separate conversation pit with their knitting. As the men talk politics, Leslie comes over to enter the conversation. Her valid arguments about women's ability to talk politics are squelched by Bick's ordering her up to bed, where her sexual energies can be properly channeled. With her horse killed, and her coincidental pregnancy, Leslie is redirected toward her proper maternal role and is seemingly chagrined over her earlier behavior: "You knew what a frightful girl I was when you married me." Joan Mellen offers insightful analysis of this transformation:

> *Giant* is even presciently aware of the coming demand for the liberation of women. . . . Leslie objects in stridently rebellious terms to being demeaned, befitting the fifties film's confidence in the possibility of raising

> prickly issues only to put them to sleep once and for all. . . . Her demand
> that women be treated as the equals of men vanishes like a summer
> tantrum, as if it had been solved by this one fit of anger, something a
> woman must get off her chest, but in no sense an integral part of her
> life. . . . Like the issue of racism, the problem of the equality of women
> is to be solved by the patronizing indulgence of good-natured males
> who reform themselves by lending a tolerant ear.[54]

But Leslie, while she has seemingly been stripped of her sexuality, has not yet been sufficiently punished for it, and the film works to depict her as being inadequate as a mother and ultimately marginal to the reconciliation between her son and her husband. In other words, because Leslie's independence was equated with her sexuality, when she is stripped of her passions she is also stripped of her self-confidence, and it is only in relenting to her husband's wishes that she fills her proper docile role.

In *A Summer Place* and *The Cobweb* Sylvia and Karen are both given lessons in respectability—Sylvia by her son, and Karen by the threat of her husband's desertion. The women repress their sexuality and become upstanding and helpful wives. Sylvia is no longer the sexually passionate woman of the film's beginning—she and Ken sleep in twin beds and worry about their children's morality. Karen has become a reborn mother, using the controversial draperies to nurture the mixed-up and needy Stevie. Like Leslie, these women have not been punished so harshly, for their crimes were of independence and a desperate love for a man; they have, nevertheless, been sufficiently squelched and redirected toward their maternal function.

In *East of Eden* Kate fares far worse because she has not only continued her sexual activities, she has profited by them. Kate is the catalyst for all the calamity in the film and is harshly punished for her transgressions by the physical pain of her arthritis, by the wound to her vanity caused by the public exhibition of her faded beauty, and, most importantly, by the humiliation she suffers at the encounter with her two sons. While Adam, too, suffers shame, remorse, grief, and the physical incapacitation brought about by his stroke, he is nonetheless newly reconciled with Cal and, indeed, all of these tribulations are at least partly responsible for the reunion between father and son; Kate, of course, is completely isolated.

Some of the films offer a more lighthearted look at the sexually active mother, but in these films, too, the woman is ultimately punished. In *If a Man Answers* Chantal is presented as a fickle flirt whose attempts to make her straying husband jealous backfire, resulting in ridicule and despair. In *The Pleasure of His Company* a formerly sexually active mother pays for her once-passionate life with a mundane and boring marriage.

A different filmic fate awaits those mothers who are sexually dependent. These narratives portray a mother's desires as being illustrative of her weakness; the woman is a slave to passion and love and, as a result, is derelict in her maternal duties. In *All That Heaven Allows* Carey Scott is virtually incapacitated by her attraction to Ron Kirby. Pressure from the community, her children, and her lackluster suitor convince her that her passion is unnatural and harmful. Caught between her hormones and propriety, Carey is not only incapacitated, she is triply punished. First, in expressing her desires, she alienates her children, who mock her and put her down. Second, when she relinquishes the affair for their sake, her children desert her, leaving her with the empty pleasures of a television set for company. And finally, at the end of the film, in following the course of her libido, she is punished a third time when, in running to meet her, Ron falls and lapses into unconsciousness. Though he awakens later in her arms, he is now a weak and needful man for whom Carey must now play the maternal role. In *From the Terrace* Sam's marriage to his career, coupled with his sexual philanderings, have driven his wife, Martha, to alcoholism and an extramarital affair. Likewise, Mary, Martha's daughter-in-law, is a victim of her husband Alfred's inattention and she, too, embarks on a series of affairs. Both women, while seemingly sexual aggressors, are in reality weakened by their passions: Mary is depicted as a nymphomaniac, someone who is the butt of ribald masculine derision, who pleads futilely for her husband to make love with her, and who stands screaming, deserted on a sidewalk, at the end of the film; Martha, on the other hand, is driven to alcoholism, and her fate is to disappear, isolated from her family and in the care of a nurse, her lover beaten up by Alfred and her husband dead.

Mothers, then, are depicted as malevolent in the cinematic versions of the family melodrama, and this denigration takes three distinct paths. The most heinous of crimes is possessiveness, and its punishment is isolation, loneliness, or even death. Mothers who are leeches are not as ubiquitous in the narratives, but their castigation is equally potent, centered in their publicly displayed entreaties and/or their obliteration. Mothers who are sexually active and thereby neglect their children are punished with isolation, and mothers who are intent on using their sexuality as emulative models or merely for their own self-fulfillment find their comeuppance is their self-imposed repression and indentured servitude toward their husbands.

38. Father does know best as here, in "The Big Test," from the 1955–1956 season of *Father Knows Best,* Jim lectures Bud (Billy Gray) on the importance of honesty.

Gender operates as a key thematic and defining principle of the family melodrama. Not only were both the film and television texts overwhelmingly consistent in predicating familial success on an uncontested structural valuation of paternal fatherhood and masculine dominance, but the gender-specific terms of this power were reiterated in a number of story lines common to both the film and the television texts. Both media were tremendously concerned with sex traits and stereotypes and, indeed, followed the same conservative agenda in prescribing sexually determined behavior. Girls were to be docile, domestic, and modest, while boys were to be logical, intelligent, and confident. The power struggles that were implicit in the structural centering of fathers and boys were explicated in gender-based narratives in which battles between the sexes reiterated a conservative and patriarchal ideological creed. More important for a genre constructed around the family unit, both the film and the television texts worked tenaciously to define the desired functions of parenthood, prescribing a rigid set of activities for mothers and fathers. The film versions of these ideological dictates were different from their television incarnations. In the films the family-protagonist is a troubled entity whose very crises originate in inappropriate parenting

39. In a similar staging, in "Man in a Trenchcoat," from the 1960–1961 season of *My Three Sons,* Steve is seen lecturing Robbie (Don Grady) on the same topic. In both photos the boys are downcast (Robbie with a black eye) and the fathers are busily shaming them into the "proper" behavior.

practices. Possessive and repressive mothers and weak-willed or overly macho fathers cause a series of dysfunctional dynamics and/or sexual perversion or experimentation. The restitution of the family depends on the punishment of the guilty party (typically the mother), who is castigated with death (her own or that of her child), madness, or, at the very least, social ostracism or humiliation. The films operate as pedagogical frameworks in which the displaced power positions and then the sex-determined means for regaining balance are evident.

In the television programs, the family-protagonist is depicted as an ideologically favored model, and the episodes operate to reiterate proper behavior more than to correct transgressions. Analysis of the power configurations in television reveals that women are not depicted as being important for the emotional needs of their families. Fathers are the ideological choice for all aspects of familial operation, and women's structural purpose in domestic melodrama is to center the father within the text and within the family. An exploration of gender and gender traits reveals the textual strategies for restricting women from the domestic sphere. First, women are reminded of the glory of homemaking, and of its superiority to any career alternative. Second, these wives and mothers are instructed that part of their domestic glory lies in its very invisibility. In this sense, the mothers are explicitly reminded to remove themselves from familial centrality, just as the maternal characters are implicitly relegated from narrative centrality. Television's narratives echo the filmic ones in their castigation of female careerism, but here the mothers are punished with guilt and exhaustion rather than with a husband's infidelity (or threatened infidelity). Indeed, on television, the lonely career woman is (usually) happily mated at the end of the narrative, and the married career-seeker is reminded of the preferred status of domestic servitude. In addition, while the films may punish women with a harsh obliteration, the television programs minimize a mother's importance more discretely, either by manipulating the mother to be a party to her own self-effacement or by structuring the narrative so that she only hangs about the periphery—not as stupid or ineffectual as her cinematic counterpart, but, ultimately, equally unimportant to the family's affective functioning. The domestic family melodrama returned to these themes again and again, continually reminding the viewer that the key to secure family life lay in a strict adherence to social-sexual codes and dictates. The next chapter will explore how these texts were equally adamant that familial success was also predicated on a strict allegiance to certain economic principles.

7 Family Finances

The thematic and structural consistencies within the film and television domestic melodrama emphasized a view that the successful American family was unquestioningly patriarchal, WASP, self-reliant, and conservative. Such a family was also, as this chapter will demonstrate, unfailingly middle class. Just as the family-protagonist embodied and personified a multitude of social crises and questions, reconfiguring alcoholism, drug abuse, abortion, juvenile delinquency, and teen sexuality into the tidy and resolvable dilemma of paternal-filial miscommunication, so the family was also the site of economic ideals. The domestic family melodrama thus personalizes the economic as well as the social, functioning to underscore the supremacy of a particular economic mode by inferring its organic relationship to American family life. The film and television domestic melodramas were both implicitly and explicitly concerned with exploring intrafamilial economic systems and the socioeconomic status of the family. Additionally, for the television programs especially, there is an emphasis upon consumerism, coupled with a continual appreciation of middle-class values and an invocation of and respect for the Puritan ethic.

The three most emphasized areas of intrafamilial economics were the division of labor and tasks, the financially based compensation of family members for these tasks, and the attitude toward money as evidence of a less tangible characteristic (such as honesty, greed, or selfishness). One of the main points of distinction between the film and television representations of the family concerns the varying emphasis each medium places on the day-to-day household activities of the family members. While the films' crises focus on life-shattering conflicts of teen pregnancy, divorce, or infidelity, the television problems are often constructed around the mundane domestic tasks themselves.[1] Domestic duties form a powerful but implicit subtext within the films, but they are often the subject matter of an entire episode for television. The chapters on gender and power uncovered the paternally centered motivation for successful family life and the sex-driven characteristics that were the foundation for that power. The origins of power, the maintenance of that power, and the concomitant erosion of maternal potency were often predicated on the cash value for gender-determined jobs and tasks. Within each of the television families, the members are distinguished by their responsibility for certain tasks. These jobs are divided according to age and gender, and those duties performed by the older, male members have a higher value.

The first and most obvious division of labor is between home and work. In all the television programs, the fathers are afforded respectability and comfort upon their return from the "real" working world. Their time at home, for the most part, is leisure time, and any work they do is either in response to a call for help from the wife or, more commonly, an extension of their business duties. In the first case, Ward or Jim or Alex are occasionally seen helping June or Margaret or Donna set the table or dry the dishes. The men never attempt any of the chores on their own, nor do they assist in any other type of household work; it is indeed, only the husband's participation in the relatively minor tasks of before- and after-dinner duties that allows the husband and wife to discuss family problems without the intrusion of the children, while providing a forum for the exemplary behavior of the husbands. In the second case, Ward Cleaver, Jim Anderson, Steve Douglas, and, most distinctly, Dr. Alex Stone are depicted as being engaged after hours on work projects in their homes. Because of this, they are unavailable for help with the domestic duties, and gain additional economic potency for doing wage-earning work in a traditionally wageless environment. The mothers, of course, are in charge of all domestic duties, ranging from cooking, sewing, cleaning, and decorating to involvement with civic groups and other volunteer organizations, PTA and child-rearing activities, and the social scheduling of family events.[2]

As if to emphasize the importance of gender-specific work, each program has at least one episode in which the wife (or, in the case of My Three Sons, the domestic substitute, Bub or Uncle Charley) is called away, and the father must take over the housekeeping activities. In all of these cases the father's ineptitude at performing simple domestic chores simultaneously underscores his unsuitability for such menial labor and reinforces the mother's alternative power in managing these very activities. In every example the father attempts to minimize the difficulties associated with housekeeping by applying a "scientific" method, explaining to the skeptical children that their mother could run the house much more efficiently if only she would follow a businesslike plan. Inevitably the plan is undercut by the necessity for flexibility and multiphasic attention to detail normally practiced by the mother, and the father learns a "lesson." The lesson reiterates the notion that competency at certain jobs is gender defined and restricted, and that women, with their "lack of logic," are better suited for tasks which defy scientific reason.[3] *Leave It to Beaver,* because of June's marginal position, presents gender-specific duties slightly differently. When June goes away, her Aunt Martha arrives to take over the domestic tasks, so Ward is rarely seen struggling with domestic fallout. Instead, he is given the opportunity to be even more sanctimonious than usual, criticizing Aunt Martha for her female shortcomings as well as her old-fashioned notions. June's homecoming is welcomed not because it will relieve chaos, but because it will liberate Ward from having to police the actions of an alternate domestic worker. On this program women are, at best, inconsequential (as in the case of June), and at worst, deleterious to the happy household (as in the case of Aunt Martha). This same attitude pervades *The Adventures of Ozzie and Harriet,* in which Harriet, perhaps the most passive of all wives, is never gone long enough to cause even a ripple in the Nelson household.

In addition to the distinctions between the domestic duties expected of husbands and wives, the responsibilities that the children must bear are also of a specific nature. Most obviously, the girls are expected to set the table, help prepare dinner, iron, sew, and keep their bedrooms clean. Crucially, however, they do not engage in any more elaborate housekeeping duties (vacuuming, washing the floor, making dinner alone, or washing windows), because these fall under the mother's domain and are considered part of her full-time job. The boys' duties vary, depending on whether or not they have sisters. In homes in which there are no daughters (*My Three Sons, Leave It to Beaver,* and *The Adventures of Ozzie and Harriet*) the sons are much more actively involved in domestic tasks. Wally and Beaver wash and dry dishes, are expected to keep their bathroom clean, and are shown straightening out their rooms. In *My Three Sons* the all-male household encourages a delegation of tasks, and the importance of such specialization is underscored by the frequency with which such assignments become the focus of the narrative. In "Organization Woman" (1960–1961), "My Three Strikers" (1960–1961), "Domestic Trouble" (1960–1961), "Brotherly Love" (1960–1961), "The People House" (1963–1964), "Woman's Work" (1964–1965), "Here Comes Charley" (1964–1965), "You're in My Power" (1964–1965), and many others the boys are shown quarreling about their chores, being nagged to perform their tasks, and being punished for neglecting them. The chores consist of both inside and outside duties, including washing and drying dishes, yard work, painting and other household repairs, and keeping the house neat. But, as in the other shows, only the mother figure (in this case, Bub or Uncle Charley) is responsible for meal-planning and cooking, ironing and laundry, washing the floors, vacuuming, and dusting.

In the programs which feature both sons and daughters the delegation of duties among them is as gender restrictive as it is among the adults. Both Bud and Jeff are nagged by their respective fathers to mow the lawn or clean out the garage. But, interestingly, while the girls are seen performing their tasks in each episode (Mary and Betty especially are active in the kitchen, helping to cook, setting the table, and helping with the dishes), the boys are more often seen running in and out of the house, nibbling on food, or covered with dirt or grease from an automobile or building project. In addition, the boys usually have other, "real-world" jobs, such as newspaper delivery, which become the focus of various narratives.

One way that the film and television texts thus differ in familial representation is in the explicit articulation of the delegation of household duties. While the films may indicate Mother's domestic position and Father's "real-world" employment, there are no household discussions or maternal nagging for the family to cooperate with domestic duties. In the television programs, by contrast, arguments concerning dish-washing or lawn-mowing responsibilities abound, and often form the narrative focus as the gender- and age-distinct familial functions are called into question and ultimately reinforced.

In addition to delegation of responsibilities, money itself is often featured as a central focus of the narrative of the family melodrama. In the film versions of family life money has an evaluative function wherein it is proffered continually as a substitute for love. The wealthy heirs of *Cat on a Hot Tin Roof, Written on the Wind, The Long Hot Summer,* and *From the Terrace,* among other films, berate their fathers for giving materially rather than of themselves. Money is the means by which the fathers measure their attitudes toward their children, and these parents must be taught by their lovelorn sons that the exchange of emotion is more important than the exchange of things. Thus Big Daddy and Wil Varner think they have demonstrated their affections, but in reality they have only offered empty materialism. If some filmic fathers equate the giving of money with the giving of love, other filmic parents *withhold* financial gain as a parallel to withholding love or attention. Again, the parent mistakenly invests material things with an emotional potency, and Papa Harrington and Wade Hunnicutt really think, until corrected by their sons, that they can hurt their children by withholding an inheritance. The message is twofold: first, that in their misperception of its emotional import for their children, the parents are overly obsessed with money; and second, that the children recognize the true value of emotional exchange as superior to the value of material goods.

In the television programs the love between the fathers and sons is not in question, and the fathers rely on finances as a means of manipulation. Money is held out as reward or punishment, but deliberately underscored as something quite separate from emotional ties. Here the fathers lecture their children that money shouldn't interfere, either positively or negatively, with their already-established relationships, yet at the same time they rely upon its potency as a motivator. For example, in "My Three Strikers," a 1960–1961 episode from *My Three Sons* discussed previously, the boys' need for an allowance increase and Steve's desire for their further responsibility are resolved in strictly economic terms. The entire Douglas clan has had a night of dreams and nightmares in which each son envisions the father as a tyrannical overlord. Steve awakens from a disturbing vision of his children going on strike, while he is powerless to stop them. As each awakens from his night traumas, he ventures downstairs for a snack, where, in a scene highly reminiscent of the adolescent weepy film debates, Mike tries to negotiate with Steve over a higher allowance. Mike is desperate, screaming about his expenses, whining about his embarrassment at pretending to fill his car with gas; Steve is calm and patronizing, and Mike reacts by tearfully yelling, "How can we talk if you won't even listen?" and leaving the room, while a nightmare flashback plays on the soundtrack. The two eventually come to terms, with Steve running the family like a corporation, assigning monetary value to extra chores, penalties for late completion of duties, and bonuses for jobs well done. He smiles to his sons: "Nowadays [a strike] is not so necessary because the bosses and workers can talk to each other like Mike and I did." The parallel to a corporation makes explicit the terms in which the domestic family operates: each member is expected to fulfill certain duties for financial reward or compensation. The neglect of such duties results in a dock in pay/allowance.

Money is also the means by which various characters prove their adaptability to situations, their honesty, their greed, or their patience. In the films the materialism of the parents, who regard money as the quintessential defining characteristic of superior breeding, is often pitted against their children's sense of equanimity—Rodney Harrington will marry the poorer Betty Anderson, Russell Burns doesn't care about the tainted past of Hilda Crane, Mary St. John wants Alfred Eaton, and Jordy Benedict weds the Mexican-

American Juana. Their attitude toward wealth as something "tainted" or "phoney" underscores a superiority on the part of the younger generation. In the television programs this generational wisdom is reversed, in that it is the younger generation who must be reminded continually by the older that other, less tangible qualities are more important than financial gain, that greed is a vile attribute, and that honesty is crucial in the handling of financial matters.

One of the main critical misinterpretations of the television family melodrama was that its characters were not concerned with money or life's tangibles, and that each member always recognized that honor and moral superiority were the true measures of one's worth. For example, David Marc notes in *Comic Visions* that "evil was not among the problems one encountered in Springfield"; and the Andersons, according to TV critics Harry Castleman and Walter Podrazik, "were never greedy, stupid, or mischievous, just unlucky or unwise."[4] A review of 100 episodes each from the five series studied here, however, reveals a quite different emphasis. While the ending moral might be that one should value the spiritual over the financial, that lesson came only after a good twenty-four minutes of greed or avarice. In addition, the episodic nature of the medium meant that these parables concerning the superiority of intangibles were quickly forgotten from one week to the next by the adolescents and teens bent on attaining that new dress or car, or seduced by the promise of glamour and riches. As Applebaum notes, such financial preoccupations formed a sizable proportion of the problems in television's family melodramas: "like adults—most of [Beaver's] troubles have to do with money and the lack of it."[5] The acquisition of, or responsibility for, relatively large sums of money often formed the locus of a morality tale in which the younger generation had to learn moderation or modesty. In "The Cookie Fund" (*Leave It to Beaver*, 1958–1959), for example, Beaver and his friend Larry Mondello are appointed co-treasurers of the funds raised by the class in a cookie sale. The money functions initially as a test of the boys' honesty and maturity, as they must handle the book balancing, keep the money safely locked away, and avoid any minor pilferage. It operates also to contrast the boys' good character with that of an older boy who extorts the funds from the youngsters on the pretense of "starving." When the time comes to pay the cookie manufacturer, Beaver and Larry are left without funds and confess their misdeed to the president of the cookie company. The boys must make up the difference themselves, and Beaver woefully approaches his father for a loan. The message in the story is multiple: that the guardianship of money is a tremendous responsibility; that unscrupulous con artists will take advantage of honest youngsters; and that Beaver and Larry are honest (Ward tells Beaver he "trusts" him enough to lend him the money and Miss Landers says the boys may continue as cookie monitors despite the mishap). In *Father Knows Best* Kathy Anderson's problem in "Kathy, Girl Executive" (1958–1959) lies in the intoxication of sudden wealth and power, and she must be taught, like Beaver, that when one is in a position of financial superiority, one should show deference and modesty. In "Jim's Big Surprise" (1959–1960) the Andersons are immediately made to feel remorse and shame for their materialistic desires when they misinterpret Jim's "Father of the Year" award as a luxurious prize—maybe a trip to Hawaii, a swimming pool, a new car, a maid. In the end, the children—as well as Margaret—are made to realize that Father's value as an available parent is only possible because he doesn't work the overly long hours necessary to provide them with all those luxuries.

Both "Beaver and Kenneth" (*Leave It to Beaver,* 1960–1961) and "Bad Influence" (*Father Knows Best,* 1955–1956) deal with the pitfalls awaiting those who mistakenly think they can buy friendship. "Operation Deadbeat" (1958–1959) and "The Soft Touch" (1962–1963), two episodes from *The Donna Reed Show,* center upon the unsuccessful collection of past-due accounts. In each, Donna is annoyed that Alex doesn't press his patients for the money they owe. Alex feels his patients will pay eventually, and he doesn't want to become a "bill collector." A series of crises convince Donna that preoccupation with financial recompense blinds one to the true goodness of people and that Alex, as a beneficent doctor, has the right idea.

The relationship of the characters toward money illustrates another means by which the family melodrama personalizes social concerns into familial ones. Both the film and television texts present money as a means by which the characters define love and their relationship to one another. The filmic narratives paint the parents as misguided materialists who substitute money for affection and attempt to use it as a manipulative device. In the television programs money functions as a seducer that is eventually refused, as a means by which one learns responsibility, as being inconsequential to the true value of life, and as a test of individuality and honesty. The elders (particularly the fathers) use money as a means of instructing their families on the relative superiority of intangible rewards.

Economics figures predominantly in both texts as a genre-defining term, with the bulk of family melodramas representing a middle-class position and vision. The middle class is defined within the texts as an economic stratum that views itself as hardworking and deserving of the rewards such hard work brings. Middle-class values and life-styles are implicit in the familial characterizations (the occupation of the fathers, the appearance of homes and dress), and also register in explicit comments by the characters in the context of the narrative situations (the behavior and attitudes of the characters). Quite typically, the expressed viewpoint is that the middle-class lifestyle is not only the preferred one, it is the most natural.

One of the most interesting common denominators among the paternal occupations in both film and television is the emphasis placed upon self-reliance. Whether the men are professionals or running a business, they are for the most part virtually self-employed. The only narratives in which the father is employed by a larger firm or corporation are those in which the corporation plays a central role in the narrative, usually forcing the father to choose between his home and work life. Such films, which include *From the Terrace, The Days of Wine and Roses, The Cobweb, The Man in the Gray Flannel Suit, No Down Payment,* and *Executive Suite,* will be discussed at length later, in an analysis of explicit comments on status.

For the most part, the films are populated with a multitude of either managers of small stores or factories (as in *Blue Denim, Five Finger Exercise, Man on Fire, The Catered Affair, There's Always Tomorrow, Peyton Place* [Harrington], *All That Heaven Allows,* and *Splendor in the Grass* [Loomis]), landowners and farmers or ranchers (as in *Splendor in the Grass* [Stamper], *East of Eden, Home from the Hill, Giant, Cat on a Hot Tin Roof, The Long Hot Summer, Written on the Wind, From the Terrace, Night of the Quarter Moon, State Fair,* and *April Love*), or professionals who, for all intents and purposes, function as their own superiors (as in *Magnificent Obsession, Blue Denim* [Janet's father], *Please Don't Eat the Daisies, Peyton Place* [Rossi], *Boys' Night Out, Strangers When We Meet, Houseboat, Mr. Hobbs Takes a Vacation, Take Her—She's Mine, Gidget Goes Hawaiian,* and *Tunnel of Love*). Their occupations allow these men a flexibility of time and place which encourages their interaction with their family. In the films in which the fathers own factories or shops, part of the conflict with their sons concerns the inheritance of the family business. The factory is often an extension of the home environment, providing a site for argument and reconciliation. Fathers who actually live in their work space, such as the ranchers and oilmen, are given even more opportunity for familial interaction, and the spillover between family economics and corporate economics is profound, as the den becomes the place for professional and domestic strife. Crucially, the basically self-sufficient employment of the fathers functions to underscore the hermetically rendered family unit, reiterating and emphasizing the generic necessity that the problems in the film be constructed in purely personal terms. The failures of the fathers, the future ambitions of the sons, and the conflict between generations are interwoven with work and family expectations. If Jody Varner (*The Long Hot Summer*) is a failure, it's because his father won't allow him to work the farm; if Bud Stamper (*Splendor in the Grass*) is a disappointment, it's because he won't become head of his father's oil company; and Kyle Hadley's failure and his sister Marylee's success in *Written on the Wind* are measured strictly against the expectations of their father, Jasper, concerning his children's involvement in his oil empire.

In the films the self-employment of the fathers thus encourages the expectation of professional inheritance and the concomitant failure when the sons reject the family line of work. In addition, it eliminates the social as in any way responsible for any familial problems or solutions. Even the less privileged families of *The Catered Affair* and the Loomises in *Splendor in the Grass* are self-employed, as cabbies or store owners—occupations which foster responsibility, regret, self-flagellation, or satisfaction, rather than any castigation of the outside social sphere. As Peter Biskind has noted about *All That Heaven Allows*, Ron Kirby is not the Thoreauesque individualist he professes to be, but merely a self-employed entrepreneur: "[Ron] *owns* a nursery, where he grows trees; we're relieved to discover that he's actually as middle-class as [Carey] is. Deep inside his breast there beats the heart of a small businessman."[6] The self-employment functions as a leveling agent because, despite the slight differences in financial gain, these men are all masters of their own time, destiny, and decisions; they are as responsible for their businesses as they are for their families, each of which represents a flip side of the same claustrophobic self-perpetuating environment.

In the television programs the fathers are equally self-reliant, and their businesses function to allow them the time to interact with their families. In *The Donna Reed Show,* for example, Alex is not only a physician, but a pediatrician (so his professional world revolves around children) who has his practice in his home. His office, for the first four years of the program, is right off the foyer, separated by two double sliding doors. He is thus privy to all domestic crises and conversations, and Donna and the children often wander into his office at all times of day for counsel and advice. Even when he is not involved in the conversations, the closed double doors and the spectator's knowledge combine to reinforce Alex's continued physical presence and dominance. The selection of Steve Douglas' job on *My Three Sons* was carefully calculated by producer Don Fedderson: "We wanted something he could work on at home."[7] Steve Douglas works as an aeronautical consultant. Though he is usually employed by the same engineering firm (Universal Research), he is free to come and go as he pleases, often works at a drafting table in his bedroom, and flies off for frequent business meetings. His occupation serves a dual purpose of accessibility—in that he works at home and can resolve family crises—and unavailability (in his trips abroad)—which usually catalyzes these same crises. In addition, his trips to exotic places often serve as the impetus for adventures for the entire family, as the boys and Bub accompany him to Japan, or Tahiti, or on a cruise. Jim Anderson, as a manager of his own branch of an insurance franchise, the Cavelier Insurance Company, is free to make his own hours, often coming home by four in the afternoon, and occasionally going in to work on a Saturday morning for the sake of various episodic complexities. He, too, is pictured working at his study desk or, conversely, advising his children in the confines of his private downtown office. Importantly, however, while we may hear Jim complain occasionally about a "lost account," we rarely see him actually occupied with business duties. Unlike Steve Douglas or Alex Stone, who are pictured, respectively, performing their engineering and medical tasks, most of the images of Jim Anderson at work are during moments of interruption—when he must *stop* conducting business in order to meet his family's needs. This has the immediate twofold effect of demonstrating Jim's belief that "father" is his most crucial role and, at the same time, rendering him more of an "everyman." As Mark Crispen Miller notes: "Since we almost never saw him working, we had no sense that there was any class above his own; and he had no competition in the class below him."[8] Although their jobs remain ill-defined at best, Ward Cleaver and Ozzie Nelson arrive home from "downtown" in the late afternoon, too, and mention business lunches; Ward is also depicted conducting business in his study. It is worth noting here that Ozzie Nelson's profession in the film *Here Come the Nelsons* (1951), the prototype for the television series, was that of an advertising executive. In his autobiography, however, Nelson notes that the fuzziness of his TV occupation resulted from the fusion of the variety/sitcom format of his early radio programs, on which he played a vacationing band leader. He recalls:

> [W]hen we started on radio back in 1944 I was a band leader both on the show and in real life, and . . . if I were suddenly to become a plumber or an insurance salesman it would simply not ring true . . . our scenes were almost always played as if it were a Saturday or Sunday, and . . . we were careful never to have me at home while the boys went off to school. . . . I did occasionally go downtown to an office, but I never designated the kind of work I did because by my not designating a specific job people were able to identify with me more readily.[9]

There is a good amount of homogeneity, then, in terms of paternal occupations, designed to convey a sense of seamless security. As writer-producer

Paul West (*Father Knows Best, The Donna Reed Show*) notes, "It seemed an unwritten law that we never discussed money in the shows except when it was involved as a learning experience for one of the children. Father was never rich but he never had any money problems—that we talked about."[10] These flexible professions thus ensure financial stability at the same time that they facilitate the father-family relationship via his constant availability. In the films, with their negative depictions of family life, this translates into one more arena in which the fathers can be disappointed in the sons' inadequacy.

Another implicit indicator of the status of the families in the film and television melodramas rests in the representation of the homes and property of the families. In the films the homes belong to a vast array of supposedly variant classes—farmers, oilmen, shop owners, lawyers, doctors, accountants—but are eerily alike, embedded with a middle-class sensibility in design, furnishings, and division of domestic space. For example, in *Splendor in the Grass* Bud Stamper and Deanie Loomis are of supposedly different classes—his family is wealthy, hers is middle class. Yet the houses they live in are nearly identical in layout. Deanie and Bud each have their own bedrooms, as does Bud's sister, Ginny. In a series of cross-cuttings the bedrooms are stylistically emphasized as similar to one another—smallish, with a single bed, a mirror, and clothes flung around. Both families eat formally in a dining room and have discussions in the living room or parlor. Bud and Deanie both wear casual shirts, sweaters, and other school apparel, and while Ginny's dress is more flamboyant, this is a function of her wanton personality rather than any indication of her wealthy class.

The supposedly poorer families of *The Catered Affair* (1956) and *A Hatful of Rain* live in very comfortable middle-class apartments. The homes are carefully furnished with up-to-date appliances and fabrics; the occupants have their own rooms (although in the latter, Johnny's brother Polo does live with them temporarily); their meals are sumptuous, accompanied by beer or wine; and there are books, knickknacks, radios, and other indicators of popular culture and expendable income. Interestingly, the status of the family in *A Hatful of Rain* became a point of critical appreciation. A review notes:

> The screenplay is an improvement on the play in at least one respect. The economic status of the people involved has been upped a notch, so it deals now with the middle-class, and this is important because it immeasurably broadens the base of acceptance and identification.[11]

Even in those environments which might preclude the presentation of a middle-class life-style—a Texas ranch, a Maryland houseboat—the middle-class sensibilities prevail. In *Giant* the austere Victorian mansion of the sprawling Reatta is transformed as the diegetic time period moves toward the 1950's period of production. The house interior, painted white, is sprawling ranch style; Bick and Leslie lie in twin beds; a swimming pool beckons in the backyard. In *Houseboat,* Cynzia and Tom put labor and time into altering the dusty and obviously water-worn boat into a tract home on the river, complete with wallpaper and again, a predominantly white decor, a kitchen and dinette furnished with modern appliances, and even a second-story sleeping deck that allows for the overheard conversations and subterfuge by the children who are so ubiquitous to the genre.

While the outside and surrounding scenery might vary, then, the interiors of the filmic homes are startlingly alike. The signifiers of wealth, such as candelabra, ornate furnishings, stark, empty rooms (or, conversely, sheaths of brocades and silk) are missing, even when the family wealth would encourage such decor. The supposedly lower classes do not suffer from cramped, crowded, or dirty environments, but enjoy an equal amount of space and tasteful decor. In addition, the characters wear utilitarian and practical clothing that is squarely middle class—shirtwaist dresses and skirts for the women, and casual slacks or suits for the men. Even in wealthy homes tuxedos and gowns, diamonds and furs are never evident, while in the poorer homes the women's attire is hardly outdated or in disrepair.

In the television programs all five homes are highly similar and represent unequivocally the middle class.[12] To begin with, all have nearly identical addresses, serving to underscore the suburban ubiquity which was home to the television middle class. The Andersons lived at 607 Maple, Springfield, the Cleavers at 211 Pine Street, Mayfield; the Stones lived in Hilldale, and the Douglases in Bryant Park. It is interesting to note the nominal association with trees, nature, and parks that underscores both the pastoral bliss of the suburban community as well as its separation from truly rural life. Each home is equipped with a formal dining room, a living room, a kitchen and dinette, a formal entryway, a backyard with a picnic table, a den (which serves as a TV room for the Nelsons, as Dr. Stone's office for the Stones, as Ward and Jim's studies, and as Bub or Uncle Charley's bedroom), and assorted bedrooms for the children. Interestingly, despite the size of the homes, most of the children are forced to share bedrooms. Wally and Beaver share a room although there is an unused guest room that sits idle most of the year; David and Ricky share a bedroom although the floorplan of the Nelson home indicates another bedroom; and Chip and Robbie also share.

Homes in which there are both sexes split the bedrooms up, typically according to sex, but in *Father Knows Best* (perhaps to avoid skirmishes or charges of favoritism) Betty and Kathy have their own rooms.

Horace Newcomb comments on the homogeneity of the domestic comedy homes:

> Such homes reflect prosperity but not elegance. The standard of living is based on comfort; the rule of existence is neatness. During the meal scenes there is always plenty to eat, and a teen-ager frequently opens a refrigerator to pour another glass of milk. There is shabbiness or disarray only when called for by the script, and in such circumstances care is taken to indicate that it is an arranged form of clutter; the audience is immediately cued by the laugh track and the opening shots that this episode depends on a rearranged set of physical expectations.[13]

All of the homes are filled with comfortable furniture, books, paintings, plants, and the most up-to-date modern appliances (washing machines, electric stoves, electric mixers, etc.), but family photos, television sets, and musical instruments appear only when they relate to the plot.[14] Automobiles are owned by the father, while the sons might possess a motorbike or jalopy. In most cases, the mothers do not own a car (unless, again, a particular plot makes it necessary). Although the Nelsons drive the more luxurious Chrysler Imperial, the other families own modest family cars—sedans and wagons designed for utilitarian purposes and needs.[15] Crucially, perhaps, the cars are always of the latest make and model and are in good repair. Clothes often form the focus of an episodic crisis (a new prom dress, a trendy sweatshirt), and are discussed below in relation to consumerism. It is important to mention here that, as with the films, in the television programs clothes, like the decor, are functional and not ostentatious. The women wear shirtwaist dresses, the girls are dressed in skirts or occasionally blue jeans, and the boys wear slacks or jeans. Father is always dressed in a suit or, more casually, slacks and a sweater or sports jacket.[16]

Like their appearance, the characters' behavior also implies a certain middle-class sensibility. These are people, in both media, who make and serve their own meals, who tidy their own homes (even if assisted by an occasional housekeeper), who belong to civic organizations and youth groups, who work long but not overly stressful workdays, and who enjoy vacations and weekends as times for recreational activities. Even in those feature-film families whose very words and community standing indicate their wealth, their mode of behavior is much more identifiable as middle class. For example,

40. The uniform of the good middle class: Tim Considine in a suit in an early publicity photo for *My Three Sons*. (Courtesy Viacom.)

the Benedicts of *Giant* live on the vast ranges of Reatta, raise herds of cattle, and oversee the poor Hispanic community that sharecrops on their lands. Yet Leslie arises at 5:00 A.M. to fix Bick's breakfast, the babies are cared for by family members and not nursemaids, and the family eats in roadside diners. In *The Last Time I Saw Paris* Helen bathes her daughter, feeds her, and ultimately defers these maternal practices to Charles when she goes off philandering; in *Home From the Hill* Hannah pours a late-night glass of milk for her son; in *The Parent Trap* Maggie works deftly in the kitchen, preparing a stew.

The television programs also feature numerous instances in which the behavior of the characters is emphatically middle class. For example, the family members are heavily involved in civic and community groups, participate in volunteer work, and invest and participate in home improvement. The families are wealthy enough to have their own cars, yet they usually wash them themselves; they redecorate their living rooms, but haggle over prices and pick the middle-range price of fabrics and wallpaper; the mothers are experts on the sewing machine when designing a school-play costume or altering a dress, but most of their families' clothes are purchased ready-made at department stores and bear the mark of conservative quality; all the families have memberships at country clubs, where Ozzie and Ward, in particular, might play a round of golf; and while the families might eschew habitual attendance at formal dances, Jim, Alex, and Steve all possess tuxedos. The families are financially secure enough that neither mother nor children need contribute to the family budget, but the children occasionally take on the gender-specific duties of newspaper delivery (boys) or babysitting (girls) to earn enough extra money to purchase a bike or some gadget, a dress or a sweater.

The hegemony of the middle class is not accidental. Indeed, the domestic emphasis of the genre for both media and the consumerist agenda of the television texts demanded a weltanschauung that was home centered and commodity dependent. As Molly Haskell comments:

> Central to the woman's film is the notion of middle-classness, not just as an economic status, but as a state of mind and a relatively rigid moral code. The circumscribed world of the housewife corresponds to the state of woman in general, confronted by a range of options so limited she might as well inhabit a cell.[17]

One of the key narrative issues in the family melodrama concerns the success or failure of maternal practice in terms of, for example, the completion of a number of domestic chores, including, specifically, child-care, cleaning, and cooking. The middle class provides the perfect textual arena in which the women can informally emphasize their domestic prowess in these areas, without it becoming the central narrative conflict. In a wealthy family, these household duties are performed for pay by hired women, eliminating both the need for wifely participation and the consequent patriarchal evaluation such participation demands. On the other hand, working-class women, tethered to outside employment or lacking the modern equipment necessary for efficient housekeeping, serve as inadequate domestic role models because the text must focus explicitly and exclusively on their social or financial inadequacy (rather than on the dysfunction of the family). In terms of the representation of men, middle-class behavior was crucial to the common textual theme of home-life versus professional life. The fathers in the film and television texts continually question their priorities regarding work and family, money and love, presence and absence. If the family were wealthy, this dilemma would be absent because Dad's abundance of leisure time would eliminate the need for him to grapple with family-versus-work decisions.[18] The father of a poor family, in contrast, would have no choice as to how home and work life were balanced because the extra work hours would be necessary for the family's very survival. As far as the representation of the family as a whole was concerned, the hermetically isolated unit of the family in the typical family melodrama demanded a middle-class sensibility for its very self-sufficiency. A wealthy family would be too intricately involved with a large number of dependents outside the nuclear unit (servants and employees), and a poor family would be similarly dependent upon outsiders (welfare workers and landlords). The middle-class family can be focused upon exclusively as a social unit because its only true contact with outsiders comes in the form either of paying clients or customers or of the family members being paying clients or customers themselves. Finally, for the television series, the play between material necessity and material desire is particularly crucial for supporting a consumerist economy. If the families were wealthy enough, the children would be showered with items whenever they desired them; if the families were struggling, the occasional new dress or bike would be an economic impossibility, while family members would be forced to carry on the burden of outside employment. Middle-class families, though, are comfortable enough to rely on one income for necessities and the occasional treat, and on adolescent contributions for any extra goodies. It is this middle-class status itself that creates a plethora of episodes underscoring thrift, work experience, the value of family versus the value of pretense, the pleasure in consumer items, and the inherent satisfaction in working to purchase them.

In addition to the more subtle articulations of socioeconomic status, the films and television programs are replete with dialogue and specific narrative strategies which underscore the class sensibilities of the central family. The families' middle-class status is, in this way, made explicit through a narrative problem itself or via character delineation. In *The Last Time I Saw Paris,* for example, Charles and Helen are supposedly struggling while Charles tries to establish his writing career. When a previously defunct mine begins to pay out, the family experiences an immediate rise in class. Charles and Helen comment on both their relative poverty and, later, their relative wealth, bemoaning the former and being grateful for the latter. Interestingly, however, their standard of living never seems to change. They live in the same house, dress the same way, frequent the same restaurants. The film has established that Paris is a great place to be when one is poor, and the lack of change in Charles and Helen's life-style underscores this. While money and class might be a topic of conversation, it is irrelevant to the middle-class style in which the family lives. In *The Catered Affair* Aggie complains to Tom about their supposed inferior status, and places them, through her dialogue, in the lower-middle-class stratum. However, by the end of the film, Tom owns his own cab, having become a self-sufficient businessman, much like Jim Anderson or Steve Douglas, and the status of the family is guaranteed to rise. In addition, the occupation of their daughter, Jane, as a schoolteacher, and her engagement to another teacher ensure the continued dominance of the middle-class arena, which becomes ideologically vested with the virtue inherent in the professionalism and respect afforded the occupation of teaching.

Other films discuss class explicitly not because it is problematic, but because class is a specific component of character. For example, in *No Down Payment,* a film about the specific troubles and traumas faced by a credit-buying suburban community, the characters are forthright about their class status. At one point in the film, Herm says: "Nobody in this development is allowed to have a house they can afford." Continuing the discussion, David says, "I don't think any of us are millionaires, but we're all living well . . . we were all born at the right time." Herm adds: "I guess we all have it better than our parents did." These conversations are crucial in emphasizing the economic homogeneity among the residents, while the narrative events work to underscore the anxiety and difficulties met by the characters in achieving that status. In other films various speeches applaud the middle class for its comparative camaraderie, sensibility, and closeness to nature.[19] Ron Kirby castigates Carey Scott's society comrades in *All That Heaven Allows* in a speech imbued with American individuality and praising the middle spectrum; and Mitch and Lucy are not only living exemplars of the moderate life-style, they are its vocal proponents when they discuss the wealthy and much conflicted Hadley family in *Written on the Wind.*

In the television programs the explicit demarcation of the middle-class status of the family is typically achieved by punitive episodes directed toward the children's financial transgressions. In "Big Shot Bud" (*Father Knows Best,* 1958–1959), for example, Bud Anderson encounters a string of troublesome complexities when he buys his mother an expensive bottle of perfume. That he lies to his parents, borrows money from his sister, requests pay advancements from an employer, and works overtime in a construction company all stems from the fact that he has purchased something beyond his middle-class means. In "Bud Lives it Up" (1959–1960) he exploits a debating-team expense account to impress a girl, and winds up with the threat of expulsion and a particularly remonstrative lecture from Dad.[20] In his castigation of his son, Jim explicitly classifies the Anderson economic status as that of "a comfortable home." The other television families continually note their "comfortable life-styles," their recognition of their own hard work and its concomitant rewards, and their comparative financial equanimity.

Often, the programs and films are concerned with materialistic desires which can or (more often) cannot be met within the confines of the family's middle-class status. Mary Beth Haralovich has presented extensive work on the domestic programs as they constructed real-world consumers; here I am more concerned with the actual presentation of consumerism *within* the texts. In other words, how concerned are the characters with making purchases? How does this concern indicate a satisfaction or dissatisfaction with their middle-class status? And is there a difference in consumptive power between the feature-film families and those presented on broadcast television? In addition to their preoccupation with consumerism, both media, but especially the television programs, work diligently to ensure a superior attitude toward the middle class. Simply by dint of its ubiquity, the middle-class family gains potency, but more importantly, numerous narratives are structured around a Manichaean division between rich and middle class, or, more rarely, between poor and middle class which serves to underscore the preference for a moderate life-style. Finally, the representation of familial economics can be examined via its centering in narratives that question the priorities of careerism as opposed to those of a balanced family life.

Both the films and the television programs explicitly convey the notion that hard work produces success, a sense of well-being, and material goods. In a strange dynamic, the television programs fluctuate between advising that hard work is its own reward, that hard work produces the ability to purchase consumer goods, and that consumer goods, in and of themselves, are important only for their function as compensation for the meritorious or as instruments for self-motivation. In conveying the message that hard work is its own reward, the television programs in particular are concerned with the presentation of the Puritan work ethic, wherein hard work, thriftiness, responsibility, and selflessness are regarded as invaluable. For example, in "Bud, the Willing Worker" (*Father Knows Best,* 1959–1960), Jim urges Bud to work at a local service station without pay in an effort to prove his determination. Jim is convinced that when the station owner, Bill, witnesses Bud's energy and commitment he will reward him with a full-time job. In the mean time, Bud is expected to work for free, the good experience considered reward enough. As is typical of the television programs, there is a division across gender lines, with the pure work ethic extolled by Jim and Bill and the opposition to such "slave mentality" voiced by Betty and Margaret (particularly ironically, given their own experience of being housewives). In the end, Jim is deemed correct, Bud is rewarded with a job as an assistant manager, and the women's objections look shortsighted and foolish.

Thrift, as another component of the Puritan ethic, is equally approved. In *The Donna Reed Show* it becomes first the target and then the laudable trait in "A Penny Earned" (1959–1960). The episode works to underscore both the pragmatic and the creative benefits associated with thrifty behavior, as Donna eschews purchasing a new dress in favor of dying an old one. Alex is impressed with her ingenuity, and her thriftiness is explicitly coded as exemplary behavior for a housewife. In "Monetary System," a 1952–1953 episode of *The Adventures of Ozzie and Harriet,* the Nelson family learns through the bad example of a debt-burdened buddy that extravagance is not only wasteful, it is dangerous. The notion that paying by installments is hazardous, that lending money is foolish, and that one should live only on one's immediate income is reiterated over and over in the television programs. "The Credit Card," a 1962–1963 episode of *Leave It to Beaver,* and "Beaver Makes a Loan" from the 1959–1960 season both deal with the pitfalls of credit. In the former, Ward lectures June, the boys, and the viewer that "using a credit card is just like stealing—buying things you can't afford to pay for." In "Beaver Makes a Loan" Beaver and his best friend Larry Mondello nearly come to blows over Larry's seventy-five-cent debt. Something similar occurs in *The Adventures of Ozzie and Harriet,* "Lending Money to Wally" (1961–1962), in which Rick embezzles from the fraternity treasury in order to assist Wally in an ill-fated credit-based business venture.

The films don't center the issue of hard work as predominantly as the television programs do, but some contain moments when characters learn the rewards of physical labor and cooperative effort. In *Houseboat,* for example, Cynzia is a bored, overeducated aristocrat until she learns the pleasures of boiling an egg, swabbing a deck, and dressing and caring for children. The solution for juvenile delinquency in *Crime in the Streets* and *April Love* is hard physical labor that leaves the misguided youths too bone-tired to make any trouble.

In addition to encouraging the appreciation of hard work for its own sake, the television programs also preach that hard work can lead to very tangible rewards. In countless episodes of *Father Knows Best* Jim advises his children that to earn the spoils of a middle-class life, they need only work hard, that a new car or dress can be earned simply by dint of personal effort. In "Family Dines Out" (1955–1956), for example, he lectures Bud that anyone can be

wealthy and enjoy luxury with some "hard work, perseverance, and determination. That's the wonderful thing about living in America. Anyone who's
not afraid of hard work has the chance to be a success."

It is important to recognize here that the most desirable result of hard
work is the *ability* to purchase—it is not necessarily the commodities themselves. This attitude seems most directly related to the structural needs of
television: although the advertising industry most generally promotes the
axiom that money *does* buy happiness, due to changing sponsors, programs
can't get any more specific. Of all the programs studied here, *Leave It to
Beaver* is the most overwhelmingly concerned with commodity fetishism.
"Capt. Jack" (1957–1958), "The Pipe" (1958–1959), "Wally's Present" (1958–
1959), "Wally's New Suit" (1958–1959), "Beaver's Ring" (1958–1959), "Beaver's
Sweater" (1959–1960), "Sweatshirt Monsters" (1961–1962), "Beaver's Jacket"
(1961–1962), and "Beaver's Typewriter" (1961–1962) all deal with the purchase of much-demanded consumer items and the consequent trouble they
can cause. The episodes have an interesting cumulative effect, simultaneously reiterating the desire for consumer items and underscoring the perils
in investing emotionally in inappropriate purchases. Tellingly, the rampant
materialism that these episodes preach is a certain type of materialism, in
which specific commodities are granted superior status over others. While
the boys sometimes keep the item, at the end of most episodes the prize has
been relinquished and the youth is explicitly grateful for the moral lesson he
has learned. In this child-centered program consumerism is depicted as
adult behavior, something which requires a grown-up maturity to be practiced successfully.

The Adventures of Ozzie and Harriet equates consumption with confusion,
and while the purchaser is eventually rewarded with the commodity, the
path to satisfaction is strewn with conflict. Once again, maturity is seen as a
necessary qualification for purchasing, the childish Wally Plumbstead encountering numerous complications whenever he buys something (as in, for
example, "Wally's Television Set," 1963–1964).

The Donna Reed Show follows a slightly different path in tackling the complexities of commodity fetishism, but with a similar assertion that being a
consumer requires certain characteristics. Here, one may purchase, but only
if one is meritorious; the acquisition of commodities functions both as a test
of character for the recipient and as a reward for the successful completion
of that test. This sort of "earn a perk" attitude prevails in "The Football Uniform" (1958–1959), in which son Jeff is instructed that he must earn the
money himself for his football uniform. In *Father Knows Best,* too, consumer
items function as rewards: Bud is granted a car for his diligence, an outboard

motor for his good grades, and a motorbike for demonstrating responsibility; Margaret gets a fishing rod and reel for her persistence in proving herself; Betty receives a new prom gown for both earning the money to buy it and then giving that money to her brother to bail him out of a dilemma.

In *My Three Sons* gifts and their exchange function as an unspoken parallel to the less "masculine" exchange of emotions. In "Mother Bub" (1962–1963) Steve buys Chip a toy car as a token of his love and in an effort to compensate his son for the lack of a mother. In "A Car of His Own" (1963–1964) middle son Robbie inherits brother Mike's car, only to demonstrate his ingenuity and self-reliance as he trades it and upgrades, and ultimately profits from a series of successful automotive repairs and exchanges. The automobile in the Douglas family represents, first, the affection of one brother for another, and ultimately, the tangible demonstration of a young man's initiation into capitalism. Robbie is rewarded with a car of his own, coupled with a sense of self-satisfaction and worth at having turned a profit on his own initiative.[21]

Thus, while the implicit reinforcement of consumerism is encouraged by the materially loaded-down television homes, the explicit message is more complicated, rendering consumer products as desirable but potentially dangerous, and thereby encouraging *thoughtful* rather than impulsive buying.

The television programs were permeated with advertising and consumerist dogma. The films, since they collected their money more directly at the box office, could afford (quite literally) to castigate material goods or to ignore them completely. While the filmic youngsters might flaunt their commodities—new cars, boats, clothing—the films elide both the purchase of the goods and the economic struggle to attain them. Even in those films centering class status, commodities are an implicit component of a domestic ideal rather than something explicitly desired. For example, *The Catered Affair* centers upon the dilemma of providing an elegant wedding, but while Aggie is concerned with arranging the hall rental and supplying a buffet, music, and flowers, her focus is upon the event itself, rather than on the acquisition of things. With the exception of the daughter's wedding dress, most of the purchases in the film are at best temporary and, for the most part, intangible. In *Written on the Wind*, Kyle Hadley tries to win over the self-confident Lucy with a beautiful hotel suite, closets filled with expensive clothes, and vanity tables laden with cosmetics and perfume. While these items do represent an abundance of consumer goods, their purchase and purchase price is elided, Lucy is both mocking and nonchalant in her acceptance of them, and their carefully arranged placement in the rooms makes them seem part of the pre-existing decor rather than recent additions. In

Giant, Jett Rink initially flaunts his wealth, only to invoke the disdain of the townspeople, causing him to become a social reject and a drunken failure.

In addition to its widespread representation, the middle class is granted an explicit hegemony in both the films and the television series. Most commonly this preference for the moderate life-style is expressed as a comparative advantage, articulated in the films by their negative focus on the wealthy, and in the television programs by their positive emphasis on the middle class. In most of the films, as already discussed, the family-protagonist lives a middle-class life-style. While (by generic definition) the family is troubled, it has reached a tenable, if tenuous, accord by the film's end. For the wealthy families in these narratives, however, no such happy ending exists. Wealth is seen as an instigator of trouble and a barrier to reconciliation. In *Rebel without a Cause,* for example, Plato is depicted as the "poor little rich boy," abandoned by his mother who is continually jetting off to exotic places. Wealth is implicated in Plato's death, as he steals the gun his mother has placed under her pillow, an upper-class sign of paranoia and protectiveness regarding one's commodities. In *The Young Stranger* it is Hal's father's wealth and position as a movie producer that directly antagonize the theater owner toward Hal. In contrast, Hal's best friend, Gerry, a middle-class boy who mows the family lawn but has roast beef for dinner, is seen as calm, patient, and an exemplary youngster. The competitive back-biting of the Varners in *The Long Hot Summer,* the Hadleys in *Written on the Wind,* and Big Daddy in *Cat on a Hot Tin Roof* demonstrates that wealth causes anxiety and bitterness. Familial and business restitution is achieved by an outsider or familial black sheep who values the principles of hard work previously abandoned by the elders and their spoiled offspring.[22] This person recognizes that the family's wealth is not as important as pride in the corporation or the sheer joy of hard work, and his ascension into the familial dynasty assures the family the attainment of middle class perspectives. Richard de Cordova provides an interesting analysis of the superiority of the middle-class, noting that the more brazen members of the wealthy families have parallels with the lower classes:

> [Mary Lee's] position in [*Written on the Wind*] is very much like that of Jeanie [Ginny] in *Splendor in the Grass.* Both films represent the decadence of the feudal order by linking it in some way with the working class. It is as if class is figured on a continuum which goes full circle, allowing lower and upper class to meet as two extremes and thus casting the bourgeois order as the ideal middle ground.[23]

Carey Scott's rich but empty life in *All That Heaven Allows* and Ralph Hopkins' sprawling apartment in *The Man in the Gray Flannel Suit* are depicted as devoid of love and affection as compared, respectively, with the congenial Mick, Aleda, and Ron and the cacophonous affections of Tom and his family. Money, while important for a middle-class life-style, reaches a point of diminishing return. In *Home from the Hill* Wade Hunnicutt is the wealthiest man in town, but he is also incorrigible as a womanizer and a drunkard. Albert Holstead, a middle-class shopkeeper, is, in comparison, morally superior, stable, and compassionate. The superiority of the middle class is an explicit narrative component of *Houseboat,* in which Cynzia, a wealthy conductor's daughter, fakes her lower-class-housekeeper status to gain entry into the middle-class Winters family. Her privileged upbringing is depicted as stifling, while her fabricated lower-class homelessness is seen as physically dangerous. Eventually, Cynzia becomes the voice of the middle class, urging Tom to move out of the city because it is no place for children, insisting on familial fun in place of exotic adventure, and lauding the virtues of romantic strolls over country-club snobbery. The elite—Tom's sister-in-law Carolyn and Cynzia's father—are ultimately deserted, as the newly formed Winters family enjoys its bourgeois life-style.

In the films, then, the middle class represents the ultimate harmonizing goal. For the lower classes, it offers cleanliness, private domestic space, a respite from city life, and clear-cut gender roles and values. For the upper classes, it is an inviting alternative to their cold and empty lives, a life-style in which self-achievement coupled with familial cooperation is encouraged, and in which personal relationships are emphasized over the blind accumulation of wealth.

In the television programs the preoccupation with middle-class hegemony is most clearly expressed in the valuation of the middle-class existence in and of itself. The point of view is, in each case, that of the family-protagonist, through whose encounters with the wealthy the viewer is reminded that a comfortable life-style is highly preferable to an extravagant one. While the rich are not depicted as the miserable malcontents of the feature films, they are rendered as ultimately less happy, stable, or fulfilled than their middle-class counterparts. The twofold lesson directed in these programs toward the youngsters in the family is, first, that the rich are not too different from "us"—they are not consumed with elitism or status—and second, and perhaps somewhat paradoxically, that the rich are inferior to the middle class in their inability to relax, have fun, and really appreciate the joy of any particular commodity because of their accumulation of many meaningless purchases.

41. Mary (Shelley Fabares) wants to put on airs to impress her rich friend. Here, she rhapsodizes over a pair of candlesticks in "How the Other Half Lives," from the 1960–1961 season of *The Donna Reed Show*.

In an amazing testimony to their consistency, four of the five programs discussed here present an identical story (and *Father Knows Best* does so twice) of the mistaken snobbishness developed by the children in response to a wealthy friend. In *The Donna Reed Show* Mary befriends the wealthy Ginny in "How the Other Half Lives" (1960–1961), and then proceeds to "remake" the Stones in an effort to impress her. She runs around borrowing silver candlesticks and lace napkins, criticizing Jeff, and nagging her mother, Donna, about her housekeeping and cooking efforts. It is up to Donna to remind her daughter that what Ginny values in her is not material but emotional. Ultimately, Mary must recognize that it is the lack of something which gives it emotional currency.

> DONNA: Mary, do you remember that green cashmere sweater that you wanted so badly? It was very expensive and you could hardly bring yourself to mention it, but we got it for you. Do you remember how much you loved that green sweater?
>
> MARY: I still love it, Mother, but what has that got to do with anything?

42. The formal tone of the Stone dinner (dining room, candlesticks, Jeff in a suit) in "How the Other Half Lives" contrasts with their normal "more comfortable" kitchen-style dinners. Here, Mary's efforts to impress her rich friend Ginny (guest-star Gigi Perreau) are ultimately negated by Jeff's middle-class casualness, which Ginny seems to prefer.

> DONNA: I suppose Ginny has lots of cashmere sweaters. . . . Do you think that she loves any of her sweaters as much as you love that green one? Don't you think it's better to have a few things you care a lot about than a lot of things you don't care much about? . . . Maybe Jeff is Ginny's green cashmere sweater. . . . Ginny is a rich little girl. She has everything that she wants, but there's one thing she hasn't got—a brother.

In the *Father Knows Best* episodes "Family Dines Out" (1955–1956) and "Bud, the Debutante" (1958–1959), Betty and Bud, respectively, must learn the power of their own class and the importance of being true to one's economic status as they learn from their wealthy friends the true value of casual entertaining and close familial interaction. It is crucial to note here that the schism is never between rich and poor, but is rather between rich and middle class. Bud is not in a socioeconomic position that forces him into complete austerity; he can afford to take Molly to movies, malt shops, and bowling. The truly underprivileged, for whom Bud's ordinary night out might prove an envied adventure, are completely ignored in the narrative.

In *Leave It to Beaver* Wally must confess to a pen-pal girlfriend, in "Wally's Glamour Girl" (1960–1961), that he is not as wealthy as he made himself out to be in his letters. As with the other examples, however, Wally and Kitty are sufficiently well-off to attend a country-club dance, Kitty in a new (albeit "unglamorous") gown and Wally in a blue suit, and driven there in Wally's father's current-year car. In addition, the two had begun their correspondence at summer camp, another indication of their relatively high status.

This affirmation of the middle class as being more genuine, fun-loving, and easygoing than the rich works not only to imbue the middle group with ideological hegemony, but to elide any true class distinctions. Because in nearly every case the schism is between well-off and more-well-off, there is never an issue of real deprivation or competition. Instead, the secure suburbanites are depicted as a homogeneous whole, with the sole distinctions residing in a few prominently displayed commodities, the decor of the houses, and occupations of the fathers. Fisk and Hartley comment that the consistency with which characters view their social world results in a sort of de facto classlessness:

> Television articulates the responses of people to their class condition, not the class condition itself. Hence it is primarily a medium for the expression of classes *for themselves*. Here again, however, the expression is rarely one of oppositional solidarity of either the dominant or the subordinate class towards one another. Rather, television—along with most other commercial enterprises—exploits the competitive fragmentation among people who belong to what is objectively the same, subordinate, class. Hence social divisions on television as elsewhere emerge as a kind of sliding scale of social stratification as opposed to primary class division.[24]

Molly and Bud simply want to go out to have fun; their age group and common high-school experience are more binding than their parents' income; the issue is not whether they can afford to go out at all, but where they will go, and because they reside in the relatively hermetic town of Springfield (it has just one country club, one concert hall, etc.), there are not that many opportunities for class elitism to begin with.

In "Bud, the Speculator" (*Father Knows Best*, 1959–1960), "The Grateful Patient" (*The Donna Reed Show*, 1958–1959), and "Let's Take Stock" (*My Three Sons*, 1962–1963) the Andersons, the Stones, and the Douglases, respectively, learn the hard way that financial gambles (such as investing in stock and buying real estate) are a risky business, and it is better to be happy with one's middle-class existence. Other episodes, such as "Ward's Millions" (*Leave It to Beaver,* 1960–1961) and "The Mink Coat" (*Father Knows Best,* 1954–1955), present the enticement of wealth or extravagant items, only to conclude that the more anonymous middle-class existence is preferable.

Status politics dominate the programs, with members of the upper-middle class learning about their superior position over the wealthy. Rarely—in only one episode of the five hundred screened—is there a conflict and challenge to middle-class hegemony from the working class. In a 1958–1959 episode of *Leave It to Beaver,* "The Grass is Always Greener," Beaver and Wally's friendship with the two sons of their garbage collector teaches them to value the rewards of their suburban existence. While the episode pays brief lip-service to the ideal that material goods don't matter (Ward pontificates: "There are different ways of being poor. Some people are poor in some ways and rich in others"), the program constructs a dichotomy between the living arrangements of the two families, with obvious preference for the Cleaver clan. The Fletchers live on the other side of town, eat cheese sandwiches outside, have no real lawn or yard, and play in the dump next door. The Cleavers sit at a carefully set luncheon table and eat tuna with homemade mayonnaise, and the boys have their own tool kit and work space in the garage. Additionally, though, the episode softens the conception of working class: Henry Fletcher is not a typical garbage man; he lives in the suburban small-town environs of Mayfield; he owns his own garbage-collection business and his own home; and he drives his own automobile. Unlike an urban hourly wage earner renting a crowded apartment (such as Ralph Kramden in *The Honeymooners* [1955–1956]), Henry is, for all intents and purposes, as well off as the Cleavers; the only difference is his blue-collar employment. The ideological agenda of the episode is, first, to underscore Beaver's equanimity; second, to emphasize the universality of adolescent envy (the Fletcher boys think the Cleaver parents are wonderful; the Cleaver boys are bowled over by the Fletchers); and finally, to remind the middle class of its advantages—shady trees and lawns, fathers with tool kits, and pretty mothers who serve fairly formal lunches.

On television, then, the middle class is held to be the most easy going, happy, and principled of the various social strata—a class envied by both the wealthy (whose lives are prim and proper) and the lower classes (who are tired of dirt, junk, and cheese sandwiches). Dorothy Cooper Foote, writer for many of the financially oriented episodes of *Father Knows Best,* sums up her appreciation of middle-class values: "In retrospect, I'm sure my family background must have sparked many of these ideas. I came from a family who did represent the perfect balance between family commitment and economic comfort. I always felt secure—not because of money—but because of love." [25]

In addition to their affirmation of the middle class in and of itself, the film and television texts strive to emphasize a "classless society," in which the union between poor and rich operates as the best solution to their relative deprivation as each meets in the more stable compromise of a middle-class life-style. T. B. Bottomore noted that this attitude was prevalent in analyses of "real-world" relationships in the 1950's.

> Instead of the opposition between major classes in political struggle it was now the manifestations of the social prestige in the local community, evaluated in terms of consumption patterns and styles of life, or occupational prestige and individual mobility through the educational system, which absorbed the attention of sociologists. The underlying conception was that of America as a middle-class society in which some people were simply more middle-class than others. [26]

These sliding barriers find their expression in the heterosexual coupling of supposed class opposites. In *Peyton Place,* for example, it is the youngsters who understand the American classless society, and it is they who must teach the adults that elitism results only in schism and social breakdown. Rodney Harrington goes against the wishes of his father and marries Betty Anderson. Rodney's war-related death causes his father to accept the lower-class bride and to repent for his earlier misunderstanding, while Betty has been transformed into a noble widow. In *A Summer Place* the wealthy Mollie marries the disadvantaged Johnny; the poor Sarah (Salome) marries the rich Tony in *All the Fine Young Cannibals;* in *Giant* Jordy Benedict weds the lower-class Chicana, Juana; and society matron Carey Scott is paired off with Ron Kirby, gardener extraordinaire, in *All That Heaven Allows.* In each of these cases, extenuating complications or changes in life-style threaten the wealthy just enough to ensure that the couple will pursue a middle-class, rather than a wealthy, existence. [27]

Both the films and the television programs privilege the middle class—in its ubiquity, in the mental and moral health of its family members, and in its position as the summation of the marriage of rich and poor. The difference between the two media lies primarily in their perspectives: in the cinematic versions the emphasis is placed on the unhappiness of the wealthy, with the middle class serving as goal and solution; in the television versions the emphasis is placed on the satisfaction of the middle class itself, underscoring its naturalness, while the true economics required for its attainment are elided and the notion of class difference is suppressed.

A final means by which the middle class is implied to represent the preferred mode of life lies in the prioritization of home over office. While the films and television programs are adamant in their support of the Puritan work ethic, they are equally dogmatic that an individual should devote large amounts of time to the family unit. Families in which the parents (usually the fathers) are absent because of their constant devotion to the corporation and money-making are judged dysfunctional. Hence, both generations of Eatons in *From the Terrace* suffer when first Sam and then Alfred devote more time to the office than they do to home life. The Hadleys of *Written on the Wind* are victims of Jasper's marriage to the oil business; in *Cat on a Hot Tin Roof* Big Daddy's preoccupation with his land holdings and wealth has shut him off from a loving relationship with his son Brick and fostered a materialistic obsession on the part of his other son, Gooper; and Mr. Pennypacker's continual business trips in *The Remarkable Mr. Pennypacker* have affected his home life directly in his decision to start a second family to take care of his needs on his stays away from home.

Often, the cinematic versions of the family melodrama confront the issue of work versus home directly, explicitly criticizing those men who are married to their jobs at the expense of their family, and applauding the protagonist for opting for a better way. In *From the Terrace,* for example, Alfred's pursuit of the dollar has both resulted from and been perpetuated by his marriage to the wealthy Mary St. John. By the film's end, his encounter with the more balanced life-style of Natalie and her family has influenced him to give up the dog-eat-dog world of corporate machinations. In *The Man in the Gray Flannel Suit* Tom and his boss, Ralph Hopkins, are presented as opposites in the business-home dichotomy. Hopkins advises Tom to spend a lot of time with his family,[28] and explicitly blames his own long work hours for his daughter's elopement with an older man.[29]

On television the workaholic fathers (always guest-stars) are not so much condemned as they are pitied, while the central family functions as the paradigm for a successful balance of work and home life. Just as the women had to be reminded of their status as viable homemakers, so, too, the fathers must be reminded of their importance as fathers. This is most explicit in *Father Knows Best,* in which Jim and Margaret are constantly reassuring one another about how their family is able to share so many activities together because Jim is home more frequently than most fathers. In "The Grass is Greener" (1955–1956), for example, Jim castigates himself for lacking the extra drive to get to work early, exercise, and make pre-dawn business calls. Ultimately, when reacquainted with a highly successful college buddy, he learns that prioritizing his family's needs over those of his business has paid off in emotional satisfaction. Margaret reassures him: "You're a success as a man, as a husband and father . . . I do love you for the way you are and for what you are."[30]

In *The Donna Reed Show* Alex is more consistently conflicted in his choices between work and home life. As a pediatrician, he is often called away on emergencies, and his unavailability often becomes a narrative focal point: he can't go camping with Jeff, he has to miss a school talent show or a father-son football game. Ironically, however, these programs are constructed so as merely to demonstrate how Alex overcomes these professional obstacles to make time for his son. The absence is merely a threatened one, and the episode functions, first, to teach Alex how important he is to his family, and second, to teach the children how much Alex sacrifices to be with them.

The representation of economics in the family melodrama underscores the ideological dictates of the genre. These are texts that are circumscribed by a stylistic hyperbole in which directors, art directors, and performers flesh out fictional representation in unprecedented heights of metaphorical excess. At the same time, the successful functioning of the family unit within these texts depends upon adhering to rigidly defined norms of behavior and attitude. In brief, the family was structured as a hierarchy, with the terms of ascension dependent upon gender first and economics second. An exploration of the economic themes within the film and television texts allows us to see how gender-distinct behaviors both influenced and were influenced by family finances. Within the family unit, fathers are more valued than mothers because they are paid for their labor. The film and television families operate under the explicit strictures of gender-delegated divisions of labor, which relegate women and girls to a lower status, while arguing at the same time that family success is predicated on the completion of these domestic tasks. Money is the measure of a child's maturation, it is the foundation for demonstrations of sacrifice and greed, it is the weapon used by sons against fathers, and it is the unspoken absence in the housewives' daily duties. If men are not allowed to be emotional, they can at least be generous with material items. In the films, however, this behavior castigates the fathers as bad dads who must be trained to give time instead of money. In the television texts material goods serve as the means of diffusing social problems (via the family purchase of a motorcycle, for example) and substitute for the culturally disapproved physical affection between fathers and sons.

The generic assertion that the family is the key unit for social control, development, and achievement is further refined. Regardless of their supposed "true" economic standing, both the film and television families occupy a financial middle ground, discernible in their dress, decor, behaviors, and attitudes, and in the professional and/or self-employed status of the fathers. This economic standing allows the middle-class families a flexibility absent in the lives of the very poor or the very rich, who are dependent on the public and private sector for their daily existence. The superiority of the middle-class families is predicated on their ability to be self-contained, dependent on neither servants nor unsympathetic bosses. Further, this middle-class exclusivity ultimately serves the ideological dictate of patriarchy, in allowing the texts to explore the middle-class woman's anxieties (domestic pressures, complaints, drudgery), and then to base familial restitution in her happy assumption of her housewifely duties.

Consumerism is seen either as a threat to family harmony (in the films) or as a test by which the family members prove their emotional maturity and selflessness (on the television programs). Ironically, consumerism is not a gender-restrictive trait, whereby women might be portrayed as spendthrifts or incessant shoppers. Instead, in keeping with the masculine prerogative of the genre, consumerism is reconfigured as yet another quality allowing for (or impeding) father-son bonding.

Ultimately, the generic requirement of stylistic extremism in the family melodrama can be seen to be tempered by a financial sobriety and an emphasis upon the economic middle ground as an imperative for happiness. Indeed, the extreme severity of the events and calamities that befall the family-protagonist are resolved only once the family recognizes and accepts the strict requirements of familial hierarchy, wherein power is predicated on patriarchy and financial stability is measured by moderation.

8 Conclusion

During the 1950's American culture focused its attention upon the family and family life with a newfound intensity. The postwar integration of veterans back into the workforce, coupled with the return of women to full-time domesticity, created enormous tension and anxiety. Men questioned their place in society, the corporation, and the family. The growth of the suburbs meant that the white-collar worker was absent from home for long work hours and had to undertake long commutes, and often his financial support of his family was predicated on his physical absence from them. Women, relinquishing the economic freedom of their World War II careers, were angry and concerned with how to mesh their education and skills with the politically desired position of housewife. Teenagers, free from both the burdens of the Depression and the military duties required of previous generations, were defining themselves on the basis of music, dare-devil activities, specific consumptive habits, and a rebellious appearance, which horrified and frightened their elders. Not surprisingly, the American media was fairly bursting with advice and directives on how the new American family was to see itself. Dr. Spock published his renowned book, essentially professionalizing motherhood, so that the process of child-rearing was no longer viewed as innate and natural, but was deemed to be a learned skill, dependent on male specialists. President Eisenhower commissioned a study on family life with the purpose of issuing guidelines to the American public on producing a happy and secure family. The Kefauver panel examined the origins of and solutions for juvenile delinquency. Women's magazines offered a plethora of columns designed to encourage women's passive contentment in the home. The entertainment media, traditionally channels for social commentary and exploitation, quite naturally examined these questions within their own fictional constructs, and the family melodrama, as a long-favored genre, was a natural forum for dealing with these issues. But it was not just the social obsession with American family life that encouraged the explosion of the domestic melodrama between 1954 and 1963. As has been shown, there were a number of structural, marketing, and regulatory demands which not only encouraged this generic preference, but motivated its distinct permutations.

At the same time that the country was undergoing a reevaluation and definition of family life, the film industry was going through the same process regarding its hegemonic identity. The decline in business caused by the conflation of postwar events (the Paramount decree, the baby boom, and the cut in studio overheads and decrease in production) encouraged the film studios to redirect their money and energy into different types of films. Given the popularity of television, the most competitive films, initially, were those which were most technologically distinct from the television experience. Thus, there was a plethora of big-screen westerns, musicals, and epics. At the same time, the film studios recognized the economic viability of the small screen, and in a number of watershed business deals they became the primary suppliers of television programming, in essence making money at both ends.

For television, this period was one of solidification: television ownership rose and stabilized; production became studio-bound and filmed (rather than live from New York); the three networks carved out their schedules; advertising procedures were refined; and television replaced radio as the at-home entertainment preference.

When the film and television industries are viewed from any critical standpoint, it is crucial that they are understood ultimately as big business looking to sell their product to an audience. It was the obsession with finding and keeping that audience that perhaps determined the dominance of the domestic melodrama for both the film and television industries. As the film industry became less a mass medium and more specialized, it was necessary to assess who its most frequent customers were and then to tailor films to entice their return. The discovery that the bulk of their audience was under thirty was of crucial importance for the studios and accounts for the abundance of teen-oriented films featuring rock and roll, camp horror, and juvenile delinquency. It spurred the inclusion of young men and women in newly designed versions of traditional genres, so that westerns now co-starred the likes of Ricky Nelson and Tony Perkins and musicals featured such stars as Ann-Margret and Pat Boone. Ultimately, it motivated a profound interest in the family melodrama as the genre that was best suited for exploring the concerns of American youth.

The television industry was no stranger to marketing or audience surveys. Its genesis in radio and its connection with advertising had established certain methods of obtaining audience information. It was in 1930's soap operas that the notion of a "mail hook" was introduced, whereby listeners wrote in for a recipe, for example, and the sponsors were able quickly to glean a socio-economic profile of the typical listener. In the 1950's the networks were determined to reach as many consumers as possible—large family groups who would be interested in furnishing and feeding a household. One of the best ways to encourage consumer families to watch a program and buy the products was by example, presenting television consumer families as "typical" visions of American family life that the viewer would want to emulate.

These three factors—society's obsession with the family, the newly envisioned young adult film audience, and the newly established family television audience—were probably the most crucial reasons for the preponderance of domestic family melodramas during that period.

The family melodrama was not a newfound creation of the 1950's, but was in fact a genre that was nearly 200 years old and had undergone considerable thematic refinement during the course of its existence. Initially, family melodrama had focused upon the innocent virgin and her allegiance to God. Stories were constructed around the upholding of her virtue and her spiritual ascension. As it developed, the family melodrama abandoned these female-centered sagas for male coming-of-age tales, in which the likes of Pip or David Copperfield traversed the perilous landscape ultimately to meet with their long-lost fathers or lovers. Rags-to-riches stories gradually gave way to maternal sacrifice and, particularly with the popularity of the 1930's and 1940's films, women's magazines and radio abounded with examples of strong and valiant mothers who single-handedly protected their children.

While the reconfiguration of the family melodrama into its 1950's incarnation cannot absolutely be linked to societal pressure, it could be, perhaps, that in order to strip women of their reluctantly relinquished power, it was deemed necessary to weaken their centrality on all fronts. They were no longer at the center of film and television narratives, and they now held a questionable position as the operative force in domestic life, wherein they were expected to perform the necessary domestic duties but continually to uphold their husbands as more important. What is certain, however, is that the 1950's family melodramas did undergo a significant thematic transformation that was remarkably consistent in both the film and television texts. Most important among these new thematic tropes was the centrality of the father to the functioning of the family. While in reality men were spending more time away from home than ever before, the fictional dads were always available, and were much more desired than the mother in their ability to resolve family crises. Both the film and television texts predicated familial happiness on paternal involvement, but they approached it from different positions of stability. In the film texts, the family is in chaos because Dad is not performing his fatherly duties correctly. He is too strict (Adam Trask), or he is too busy (Big Daddy), or he is too weak (Frank Stark). Mr. Piersall is too egocentric, wanting his son's baseball success to be his own; Mr. Pope is unloving and his sons react with alcohol and drug addiction; Wil Stamper is too self-absorbed and his pride causes his suicide and his son's poverty. In case after case, the film fathers do not measure up, and because of this, their sons (and, indeed, their entire families) are a mess. The crucial narrative issue is for the sons to call attention to their fathers' failures (always in the adolescent weepy scene) and for the fathers to recognize their importance to the family unit. Teenage rebels could thus flock to the theaters and hear their creed reiterated by the central character: "You just don't understand me!" The ideological message was for fathers to be strong, loving, responsive, and accessible. If men were anxious about their role in the newly defined sub-urbanized family, these films presented them with dogmatic reassurance that they were important, that they were indeed crucial for their family's happiness, and that their position as the hub of the family was secure, despite any economic or social liberation their wives might have undergone during the war years.

Television sought a different audience—the family—and a different result—the purchase of consumer products—from film, and its paternally centered narratives were also distinct. Dad in the television series is loving and stoic, deeply involved with his children's lives, attentive to their needs, and physically available. The narrative issue here was for fathers to manipulate their children into making upstanding choices on the basis of a set of moral precepts founded on capitalism, consumerism, and quasi-religious notions of good and bad. There might be an adolescent weepy scene in the series in which a child screams, "You don't understand me!," but on television the father is quick to assert (and the viewer agrees), "Of course I do." The narrative is constructed to reveal the fallibility of the child, and each series functions as an ideological model for family viewers to emulate. On television, therefore, it is Bud who is egocentric and self-absorbed; it is Mike who is too materialistic; it is Betty who is more concerned with social appearance than familial obligation; and it is Mary who is vain, Robbie and Jeff who are weak, and Kathy and Chip who are naïve.

The centralization of fathers and the father-filial bond resulted in a consequent denigration of the status of the mother. In light of the social imperative to force women back into the home, the maliciousness or negligibility with which mothers were regarded in the texts seems particularly incongru-

ous. Maybe the message was that women are only as important as their duties, and that the successful family rested on the invisible logistics that
women provided for its survival. In the smoothly running household the
well-fed and well-clothed father and children were free to engage in their
required psychic bonding. Or maybe, as stated at the beginning of this chapter, 1950's society demanded a subjugation of women on all fronts in order
to firmly erase their World War II achievements. Regardless of the impetus
for it, however, the second most consistent theme of the 1950's melodrama
was the disparagement of motherhood.

While the media shared a disdain for motherhood, however, they accomplished its debasement differently and, most probably, as a result of their
different audiences. The maternal debasement favored by both media was
much more malevolent in the film productions, whose audience of young
adults and dating teens identified with the youth and could project their own
generational conflicts onto the screen. Here, the worst of the mothers are
guilty of aberrant sexuality, possessiveness, or careerism; they are explicitly
evil and appropriately punished with death, the loss of a child, or profound
humiliation. Violet Venable thus pays for her incestuous feelings for Sebastian with his death and her loss of sanity in *Suddenly Last Summer;* Beverly
Boyer watches her marriage crumble when she begins to do soap commercials in *The Thrill of it All;* and Leola loses her husband and Jeanne is raped
because both women are guilty of demanding a sexual or financial potency
from their husbands in *No Down Payment.* When not explicitly evil, the
filmic mothers are literally absent or narratively unimportant. Often, family
resolution results without Mom's presence; Mrs. Stamper, Big Mama, and
Mrs. Piersall are physically available for the children, and they do love them,
but their contribution to their children's psychic healing is nil—they do not
even witness the adolescent weepy reunion, remaining instead out of the
scene, above the basement, or away from the mental hospital. Then, too,
some films predicate familial healing on the very absence of the mother. In
Houseboat the death of Mrs. Winters allows the children to bond with their
father and find domestic bliss. Cal Trask's reunion with his father in *East of
Eden* is predicated on their mutual disillusionment with Kate and their allegiance against the detestable nurse—at whose expense, indeed, they also
share a joke. In *Splendor in the Grass,* Deanie is able both to confront Bud
and her past and to move toward emotional stability because her father finally stands up to her mother and effectively shuts her up.[1] And in *A Summer
Place* Mollie flees her frigid mother, Helen, and runs to the arms of her
daddy, Ken, who welcomes her and her lover, Johnny.

Television's success was predicated on family harmony, and was even marketed as a form of leisure in which the whole family could enjoy each other's company. A complete castigation of motherhood would be inappropriate in a medium which depended upon the mother-consumer for its financial success. Instead, Mother was seen as the consummate domestic worker and comfort for the husband, who bore the brunt of the emotive chores, taking charge of the family's psychological development and well-being. This does not mean that the homemakers were blissfully performing their duties; in actuality, the television programs were quite attracted to narratives which bluntly explored the very dilemmas that were then consuming so much space in women's magazines. Narratives abounded that addressed such issues as whether the life of a mother was as fulfilling as that of a career-woman, whether a mother could also work outside the home, the seeming exploitation of the mother by her family, and the position of Mom within the family hierarchy. The consistency with which the series raised these issues is matched only by the consistency with which they resolved them. In every case, the mother is reassured that to be a housewife is the "best job" she can have, that she is loved for her attention to her family's needs, and that the best status she can hope to attain is one of invisibility. Donna is told that she must be modest and understand how "lucky" she is to be married to a man like Alex; Margaret learns that her importance to her family is best defined by how she has helped them achieve their goals at the expense of her own. June and Harriet demonstrate by example how marginal their attitudes are to the running of the family (their advice is neither solicited nor necessary), but how crucial their smoothly running house is to Ward and Ozzie's parenting duties. *My Three Sons* takes the notion even further, positing an exclusively male household as perhaps a warning that women must participate in their own domestic self-effacement or be eliminated entirely. The unimportance of the television mothers was matched by their often ridiculous or superfluous activities, which again underscored their relatively meaningless position in family life. Arranging flowers, polishing silver, and filling candy dishes are almost laughably incongruous when compared with the father-to-child bonding which takes up the bulk of the narrative. Coupled with the puzzled questions of a June Cleaver or the furrowed brow of a Margaret Anderson, those activities underscore the mother's off-kilter relationship with her family.

It is certainly obvious why the television programs would not duplicate the malevolent images of the screen mothers. But if the mother's softer representation is seen as being predicated on audience appeal, the unanswerable question is raised of how and why viewer-mothers of the 1950's so happily watched these programs and identified with their own self-effacement. The answer, perhaps, lies in the programs' presentational format. Television's family melodramas, which bear just as many of the generic requirements as the film versions, have heretofore been regarded as comedies, primarily because of their laugh tracks and repetitive plots. The initial expectation on viewing these series is one of humor, and the programs are peppered with just enough jokes to convince the viewer that even the most serious of problems are laughable. A surface viewing of the programs also indicates a much stronger maternal presence than is revealed on closer examination. The 1950's mother-viewers saw June Cleaver and Donna Stone as ever-present, well-groomed, and vocal women. They *seemed* to be crucial to the emotional needs of their children, just as these series *seemed* to be comedies. Only with a closer reading and the benefit of forty years' hindsight does it become clear that visibility does not render the television mothers important any more than the laugh track renders the domestic melodrama a comedy.

Family ideology and myth traditionally claimed that with age comes wisdom and power, but in the 1950's this cultural imperative was being transformed by the emergence of a strong (and potentially dangerous) youth culture, an increase in violent crime and social anomie, and an emphasis on the United States as being the seat of future ingenuity and high-tech solutions. Consequently, although the treatment of generational ideology in the film texts is distinct from that of the television texts, both have an identical goal: to redirect any youthful transgressions toward scientific exploration and to put youthful energy in the service of preaching conservative moral dogma. Thus, the films underscore the wisdom of the young, who are rebellious in appearance only, and actually desire the most circumspect of worlds in which fathers and mothers know their proper gender roles, in which children can go to school unthreatened, and in which the young can pursue their romantic and creative visions. *The Young Stranger, Rebel without a Cause,* and *Peyton Place* are quintessential examples of films in which the teenagers are rebelling for a return to the status quo, in which the youth are much more conservative than their elders, and in which the young must ultimately convince their elders to be moral, honest, and upright. On the television series, the super-conservative parents encourage a youthful rebellion that is objectively quite benign, but that is regarded by the parents and, with their hysterical responses, by the teens as well, to be quite extreme. Since the sponsored structure of the television industry and the networks' self-policing groups prohibited any controversial teen expression (there is no mention of teen sexuality or pregnancy, and no drug use), teenage rebellion is typically watered down and represented by tangible (and purchasable) goods—a motorcycle, a hot-rod, a haircut. The terms of rebellion thus no longer foreground the ideological issue, the argument being redirected toward issues of affordability, responsibility, or family togetherness. Unlike the films, in which the youths strive to convince their parents to be moral, the television programs associate power with the elder generation, who sermonize and bring their children back to a more conservative status quo, and then appropriate the attractive symbol of the rebellion as a family purchase or event. With the purchase of motorcycles by Bud and David, the classic icon of teenage freedom is redefined into a middle-class consumable product about which Jim and Ozzie must raise the usual concerns of economic feasibility, maturity, and safety, and which they eventually share with their sons as a form of male bonding. For the Nelsons, rock-and-roll music is a family affair, with Ozzie producing Ricky's hit records or introducing him at concerts, and with Harriet "giving a downbeat" so her son can begin a song. Teenage culture on television is diluted and transfigured into a consumerist issue that the viewing parents can understand: How much does it cost, and can parents have it too?

America in the 1950's was torn apart by racial and ethnic tensions, by delinquency, and by a paradoxical attraction to and disillusionment with suburban conformity. Again, these cultural fissures found voice in the fictional narratives of the family melodrama, but because the film industry was concerned with attracting the romantic and dating youth, whereas the television industry was concerned with best exploiting demographic groups for advertising purposes, the narrative trajectories of the two media differed. In the films, the solution to racism is intermarriage and a blending of the distinct racial or ethnic characteristics, while on television, members of the minority are seen as an inferior or exotic other, as definitely being separate, and either disparaged or admired for that separateness, but ultimately comparable to the WASP family in their successful functioning as consumers.

Despite their seeming attention to the wealthy, both the film and television texts are preoccupied with middle-class family life, and one of the predominant themes of both texts posits the importance of family over wealth and power, and cautions against materialism. Filmic examples abound in which the son or son-substitute berates the patriarch for his misguided use of money to show affection. These sons—Brick in *Cat on a Hot Tin Roof,* Alfred in *From the Terrace,* and Hal in *The Young Stranger*—lambaste their fathers' misdirected material gifts and argue that what they really need is love. The films make clear in no uncertain terms that it is impossible to buy affection, and detrimental to even try. The television programs, bound by the selling demands of sponsorship on the one hand and the demands of the paternally ascribed morality of its narratives on the other, exhibited an incongruity regarding materialism. Sometimes, like the films, the programs criticize purchasing for its own sake. Several episodes revolve around Jeff, or Bud, or Beaver either attempting to befriend a boy through gift-giving or accepting such gifts in return for their friendship. Such activities always motivate the paternal lecture which reiterates the theme that one cannot buy friends. More often, however, consumer items function in the television programs as tests of character, as opportunities for a youngster to demonstrate responsibility (riding a motorbike safely), determination (working in a store to earn money for a dress), frugality (saving enough money for a set of spark plugs), generosity (buying Dad a sweater or Mom a bottle of perfume), or merit (being rewarded with an outboard motor for getting good grades). For the television programs, consumer items are a tool by which the parents can reward or punish their children in conjunction with other effective parenting strategies. The TV parents would never err like the bad fathers of film by substituting gifts for real expressions of affection, but they do demonstrate the use of material items as effective incentives or as visible tokens of less-tangible exchanges.

While the texts were lauding the value of a middle-class life-style, they were simultaneously critiquing various aspects of its existence. For film, this meant a continual hard-edged attack on television, advertising, and over-demanding businesses. In *The Man in the Gray Flannel Suit, No Down Payment, The Thrill of it All,* and, to a lesser degree, *Bigger Than Life* and *All That Heaven Allows,* there are explicit condemnations of television, centering on the medium's crass commercialism, numbing effect, and destruction of family conversation. Advertising is seen at best as a frivolous lie, and at worst as manipulative dogma designed to destroy traditional value systems. Bosses who demand more than regular hours from their employees are depicted as being bent on the ruination of family togetherness. Television, of course, could castigate neither itself nor advertising. Indeed, quite a number of television episodes feature the family-protagonist happily absorbed in watching the television and enjoying the camaraderie of the activity. There are specific episodes touting the importance of advertising, such as when Mary gives advice to an ugly-duckling girlfriend, when Kathy starts an in-home business, and when Robbie needs help with a project. But if the television programs differ from the films in their acceptance of television and advertising, they match the films frame for frame in their reiteration of the importance of home life and the fact that nine to five is a long enough workday. Both media thus neatly elide the difficulties in attaining middle-class status and indeed argue its relative achievability with story lines designed to emphasize the synergy between a moderate work life and successful family involvement. In the films the middle class is celebrated by a devaluation of the upper class, which is depicted as poisoned, troubled, and perpetually unhappy; in the television programs the hegemonic status of the middle class is guaranteed by its favorable comparison with the upper and lower classes, which are seen as less cooperative, fun-loving, relaxed, and happy than the middle class.

The film and television family melodramas of the 1950's were thus characterized by their consistent thematic emphasis on patriarchy, the devaluation of motherhood, and the reconfiguration of social problems into familial ones, and by their preference for middle-class values. The solution for the problems within the texts rested with the families themselves, with love and communication being the answers to innumerable problems and burdens. However, the structure of the two industries worked to encourage slightly different resolutions. For film, a text limited to two hours in which characters were introduced and never seen again meant that familial restitution often depended upon elimination of the problematic member. A patriarchal tyrant died or was incapacitated, a rebellious youth was killed, a frigid wife was divorced. Because the episodic nature of the television texts did not allow for such finality, the problems on television were less intense than those in film. Thus, the guest-starring family became the locus for true conflict and complication (divorce, delinquency, abandonment), while the family-protagonist served as the model and instigator for solution. Sometimes, the series incorporated a troublemaker as a semi-regular character—Eddie Haskell on *Leave It to Beaver,* Smitty on *The Donna Reed Show,* and Ernie on *My Three Sons.* These characters functioned as receptacles of risk, their behavior characterized by social inappropriateness that needed the intervention of the family-protagonist. The solution foisted upon the likes of Eddie or Ernie[2] could be (and often was) quite extreme, because they were not seen every week and their families were invisible. Thus each time he appears, a troublemaker such as Eddie, like the troublemaker Plato in *Rebel without a Cause,* ends up being eliminated for the good of the family-protagonist; in television, however, Eddie will reappear a few weeks later with a new moral dilemma.

In addition to their impact on themes and resolutions, specific structural and regulatory demands refined and elaborated the long-standing traditions of the melodramatic genre itself. The family melodrama was an entertainment staple since its literary and theatrical inception in the eighteenth century, and by the 1950's had become characterized by an ever-increasing metaphoric hyperbole and familial codependency. Melodrama moved from turn-of-the-century morality plays to personalized tales of social dilemmas to confrontational conundrums of familial anxiety. In their final transformation into films and television programs, these family melodramas retained some of their traditional features—the text of muteness, metaphor, and the figures of hyperbole and peripety. It is in these most basic of generic elements that the impact of representational practices can be seen. The melodrama was always characterized by metaphor: a red dress represented sexuality; actors gestured instead of verbalizing and wept in lieu of pontificating; music stood for certain characters and their relationships and indicated the play's progression. The varied stylistic vocabulary possible with twentieth-century film and television resulted in an elaboration of these generic elements. Metaphor registered not only in the cluttered mise-en-scène and the method-acting style, but in camera angles, distorting lenses, wide-screen technology, and stereo sound which allowed the genre an emotional intensification. Alienated families were now visually distanced across a vast CinemaScope screen; Cal Trask's conflict with his rigid father in *East of Eden* is emphasized by a canted frame, as he swings through the screen at an oblique angle; Deanie's sexual confusion in *Splendor in the Grass* is emphasized by the overhead shot of her near-literal drowning in a sea of thwarted passion; and Jim Stark's dysfunctional family in *Rebel without a Cause* is condemned by a point-of-view perspective in which we see his mother upside down. The television texts redefine family melodrama by adding to its stylistic repertoire a dependency on choker close-ups and musical exposition. On television's claustrophobic small screen the problems became more hermetic and suffocating, the black-and-white photography lending a de facto seriousness to the most inconsequential of dilemmas. While melodrama had traditionally relied upon music to convey moods and themes, it was television that truly utilized the musical soundtrack as a formal narrative device indicating story progression, character importance, trouble, and resolution. It is quite possible in the television series to listen only to the music track and to know exactly what is happening in the narrative; this is melodrama in its purest sense.

The hyperbole registered within these texts also varies according to the medium. In the films hyperbole is exemplified by the extreme nature of the problems (more than one-third of the central characters require psychiatric assistance) and by the characters' extreme reactions to these quandaries. The hyperbolic tendency of family melodrama was further intensified by structural and regulatory demands. In terms of structural demands, cinematic technology rendered the smallest of problems huge in wide-screen, garish color or with the use of cacophonous sounds. Deanie's thwarted sexuality in *Splendor in the Grass*, for example, is intensified merely by its visual and

aural extremism. The relaxation of the film code allowed the studios to explore the most controversial of issues, so that themes that were once unacceptable were given new encouragement in terms of their filmic depiction.
Cinematic family melodrama was free to move beyond the 1940's narratives
of mother love toward mother incest, and to progress from filial neglect as a
cause for anxiety to a point at which it could be blamed for everything from
drug addiction to homosexuality. The structural requirements and the regulatory guidelines of the television medium intensified the generic properties
of hyperbole and peripety on television programs still further. First, the
shorter length forced television to rely on parallel stories and extreme emotional response, from the opening moments of each episode. There was no
time to get to know a character or a situation; the twenty-four minutes meant
that the viewer was always thrust in medias res—typically, into a moment
of heightened anxiety for a central character. Additionally, because the
shortened time span prevented elaborate story-telling, the characters' extreme reactions are often provoked by the simplest of narratives (one which
can be adequately presented in an interrupted half-hour). This makes the
hyperbolic response (typical for traditional melodrama) even more pronounced on television, because such reactions truly are unmotivated. One
need only reflect on Betty Anderson to grasp the truly exaggerated reactions
of all of the family members to the seemingly inconsequential crises which
befall them. Regulations also restricted the television programs from dealing
with more sensationalized issues of teen pregnancy, abortion, and drug
abuse, although they could and did touch upon teen drinking, divorce, and
delinquency. This meant further dilution into seemingly inconsequential
problems which, nevertheless, provoked extremely charged responses and,
in effect, intensified television's melodramatic status.

The period from 1954 to 1963 was crucial for the film and television industries. During this time, the film industry assessed and targeted a diversified
audience, completely revamped its regulatory code, and developed a consistent reliance upon wide-screen formats. Television solidified its dependency
on studio-produced episodic series financed by intrusive sponsors and their
agencies, embedded itself in the American home as the predominant form of
mass entertainment, and refined its blueprint mode of production. While
their structural elements, audience goals, and regulatory limits varied sub-
stantially, the two industries were equally engrossed in producing fictional
representations of American family life. These fictional representations
shared a strong thematic and ideological foundation whose distinct articulations were predicated in the industries' material practices and in the needs
of their audiences.

The depiction of the middle-class nuclear family became far less common from 1963 onward. Both the film and television texts gravitated toward new configurations of family life or abandoned family drama altogether. During the 1960's and 1970's films were predominantly political thrillers, James Bond adventures, screen versions of Broadway musicals, romantic comedies, and corporate critiques. There were some family melodramas (particularly those with a social message, such as *Guess Who's Coming to Dinner* [1967] and *The Godfather* [1971]), but most films featuring the family tended explicitly to castigate it and call for its destruction (*Who's Afraid of Virginia Woolf?* [1966], *The Graduate* [1966], and *Harold and Maude* [1971]). The genre based on a familialization of the social, a valuation of fatherhood, and a concomitant denigration of motherhood had disappeared. Stories in which young men castigated their parents and wailed for love with stylistic excess and hyperbole were gone. On television, the traditional family melodrama disappeared, to be replaced by single-parent households, the blended Brady family, or supernatural situation comedies. Space shows, cop shows, and medical shows abounded, but the nuclear family dealing with topical problems was absent. In the 1970's the family reappeared as a troubled and satirized cartoon with producer Norman Lear's *All in the Family* and *Maude,* while the MTM production company proved that the family was replicable in the workforce with *The Mary Tyler Moore Show* and *The Bob Newhart Show.*

The demise of the nuclear family-protagonist occurred simultaneously in the film and television industries, and at a time which is generally considered to have been a turning point in American sociocultural history. In 1963 the assassination of John F. Kennedy, the publication of Betty Friedan's *The Feminine Mystique,* and the rising tide of the civil rights and free speech movements heralded the demise of the idealized perception of the nuclear family. The family was no longer the popular topic of discussion it had been in the Eisenhower administration. Instead, individuals and their roles in terms of women's rights, minority rights, teenagers, and protests became the conversational fodder at cocktail parties. Divorce and "free love" called into question the very logic of American family life and steered arguments away from how to maintain family life and toward defining the family itself. With the family as an institution in question, family melodrama ceased to function in its traditional form as the ideal locus for social discussion and reform. Instead, fictional works extended outward, toward social criticism, and avoided the tenuous job of depicting the quickly splintering nuclear unit. The film industry capitalized on the media's interest in Vietnam, civil rights, social ennui, and anarchy, or avoided these topics altogether with fanciful escapist plots. Television explored social issues through a maze of patriarchal teacher and doctor programs (*Mr. Novak, Room 222, Dr. Kildare,* and *Medical Center*), or avoided them altogether in outer space or on witches' broomsticks. The changing demographics of both industries also motivated a move away from earlier genres. The introduction of the MPAA rating system allowed the film industry to go even further in depicting so-called "adult" situations and themes—which had moved beyond the world of adolescent angst toward an examination of sexual mores and violence. In television the Nielsen company was producing detailed reports concerning which family members preferred which programs, and the two-television household was now common. Television viewers were no longer family consumers, they were individual family members, and the programming was geared toward gender- or age-specific interests (*Here Come the Brides* for girls and *The Wild Wild West* for boys).[3]

But despite its curtailment during the 1960's and 1970's, the domestic family melodrama did not altogether disappear. In fact, beginning in the late 1970's with *Kramer vs. Kramer* (1979) on film and *Family, Family Ties,* and *The Cosby Show* on television, the family melodrama experienced a resurgence that was to last throughout the 1980's. These texts are nearly identical to their 1950's predecessors, stressing the omnipotence of the father, the strength of the family unit, and the importance granted holidays, birthdays, and even simple family suppers. On television, Mother has been given a job and a more defined position in her children's emotional lives, but close analysis reveals that there is still consistently more structural and emotional power granted to the father (he has the right answer, he gets the funniest lines). On film, the women are even more vilified than their predecessors, beyond rescue from a man, and banished from family life (this is particularly true in *Kramer vs. Kramer* and *Ordinary People* [1980], and in *Terms of Endearment* [1983], Emma must *die* to assure the continuation of the family unit). This rejuvenation of the family melodrama occurred during a period of extreme American conservatism, whereby family had once again become a focal point of community discussion. Both industries were beset by corporate buy-outs and mergers, acquisition and selling of television holdings, and major technological upheaval in the form of the introduction of cable and videotape. These phenomena, together with the return to familial interest by both industries at exactly the same time, demand further investigation: What patterns are being repeated in terms of subjects and themes and the institutional imperatives for them?

The 1990's began as a decade in which "family values" moved to the forefront of electoral politics but faded as a catch-phrase following the election of President William Clinton and the advent of his less conservative administration. However, the 1994 congressional elections indicate that the country is once again following a more conservative agenda. Will the increased lip-service to traditional values result in a new spate of family melodramas? In the past, the nature of the family in the White House has seemed more of a factor than the political make-up of Congress (which was Democratic during the terms of both Presidents Eisenhower and Reagan). The Clinton household is modern in character, with a working, independent mother and an only child, and the dearth of domestic drama may be related in some way to the absence of an idealized First Family. For now, there is an ebb in the production of family melodramas by both industries, as television becomes enamored once more with the western, with superheroes, and with cop shows. The few television family melodramas of the decade (*A Year in the Life*, *Homefront*, and *I'll Fly Away*) were canceled not because they were unpopular, but because they were too expensive to produce, especially given the extraordinary gold mines of news and reality programs. In films, when the family is featured at all, it is no longer controlled by the father, but instead by mischievous sons (*Home Alone* [1990], *Home Alone 2: Lost in New York* [1992], and *Dennis the Menace* [1993]). The concern is more with social issues (the films of Spike Lee) or with friendship (*Thelma and Louise* [1991], *Fried Green Tomatoes* [1991]), romance, adventure, or fantasy.

These patterns of ebb and flow are intriguing for the questions they raise about the causal relationship between the sociocultural sphere, institutional needs, and subject matter. As the twenty-first century approaches, new critical tools are needed for understanding and explaining not only how the media's systematic ideological construction of the family impacts viewers' understanding of their own families and the relationship of those families to society, but how these representations can be manipulated toward the establishment of a more harmonious home life.

APPENDIXES

A Television Statistics

Ratings, Selected Awards, and Prizes

Ratings for the five programs studied were not overwhelmingly high by today's standards. Only *Father Knows Best* and *My Three Sons* achieved top-ten status, and then only after they were fairly well-established. But while their ratings were not at the top, these programs all earned considerable shares. (A rating is the percentage of households watching a particular program out of all the U.S. households owning a television set; a share is the percentage of households watching a particular program out of all the houses using television [HUT]—that is, out of all the television sets which are actually in use at a given time. During the mid-1950's through the early 1960's, though as many as five additional VHF channels existed, television programming and viewing was dominated by the three networks, each of which, ideally, could expect a 33 percent share of the HUT. Any program which had a share of 30 percent and above was doing well, and any program with over 33 percent was a considerable success.

More important, all of the shows studied had tremendous longevity despite somewhat mediocre ratings. While *The Adventures of Ozzie and Harriet* never ranked in the top twenty-five, it was consistently the most-watched program during its time slot, and was one of the longest-running programs in television history. *Leave It to Beaver* was also the most-watched program of its time slot, and its six-year run ended only because the production personnel decided it was time to close shop.

The Adventures of Ozzie and Harriet

While it never ranked in the top twenty-five, the show remained in first-run production for fourteen years.

Awards: "The Pajama Game" (1954–1955) won the Christopher Award, given out by the Christophers, a movement started in New York in 1945 by Father James Keller to encourage men and women to accept personal responsibility for constructive social change. The award was to "encourage good people to do their best so a standard of excellence will beckon creative minds." Ozzie got an honorary doctorate from Rutgers; Harriet was a *Los Angeles Times* woman of the year for 1959; and a "genii" award was given by the Radio and Television Women of Southern California.

Father Knows Best

Counting prime-time reruns, the show ran for eight years. It broke into the top twenty-five in 1957, with nineteen million viewers weekly.

Ratings: 1957–1958, 25th/27.7 rating; 1958–1959, 14th/28.3 rating; 1959–1960, 6th/29.7 rating.

International TV Almanac reported that *Father Knows Best* was the second-best program after *The Phil Silvers Show* in the Quigley poll for 1957, and was named best comedy film series in 1958.

Awards: Emmy Award for best actor in a dramatic series: Robert Young, 1956; Emmy Awards for best actor/actress in dramatic or comedy series: Robert Young/Jane Wyatt, 1957; Emmy Award for best actress in comedy series: Jane Wyatt, 1958–1959; Emmy Award for best director, for "A Medal for Margaret" (a portrayal of "wholesome, yet individual motherhood"): Peter Tewksbury, 1958–1959; Emmy Award for outstanding performance by an actress in a series: Jane Wyatt, 1959–1960. *Look Magazine* award for best comedy series, 1958 and 1959. Writers Guild Award for "Margaret's Old Flame," 1959, to Dorothy Cooper Foote. Mt. Sinai Father of the Year Award and the Safety Council Award to Robert Young in 1958. Sylvania TV Award, 1954, for "wholesome family entertainment," given to Dorothy Cooper Foote, who also won a TV-Radio Writer's Annual Award in 1956 for "Spirit of Youth," and an Emmy nomination for 1959–1960.

Leave It to Beaver

The show was never in the top twenty-five.

Awards: In 1957, it was runner-up for best new show in the Emmy Awards, behind *The 7 Lively Arts* anthology cultural series. It was nominated for two Emmy Awards and received over fifty-five awards (mainly from civic and church groups). It also won two Christopher Awards and, in 1961–1962, the NEA's School Bell Award. It won the latter for "Eddie Quits School," an episode written by Dick Conway and Roland MacLane, in which Wally is "instrumental in getting Eddie to go back to school without Eddie being aware of it." In 1962, Tony Dow won a Youth Foundation's Award, and two episodes from the 1962–1963 season, "Wally's License" and "Wally Buys a Car," received accolades from the Automobile Association of America.

The Donna Reed Show

Ratings: 1963–1964: 16th/24.5 rating. All other years the show was not in the top twenty-five.

Awards: The show won many youth and women's group awards, as well as one from the American Medical Association (AMA), whose president made a cameo appearance. In 1962 Donna Reed won a Golden Globe Award as best actress; Shelley Fabares won a Youth Foundation's Award the same year.

My Three Sons

On the air for twelve seasons, the show was one of the longest running domestic comedies (behind only *The Adventures of Ozzie and Harriet*).

Ratings: 1960–1961, 13th/25.8 rating/40 share; 1961–1962, 11th/24.7 rating/38 share; 1962–1963, not in top 25, 21 rating/32 share; 1963–1964, not in top 25, 21.9 rating/34 share; 1964–1965, 13th/25.5 rating/39 share.

According to Viacom, the program averaged a 22.2 rating and a 35 percent share during its twelve-year network run. Share information and averages come from Viacom research (Jean Goldberg, July 1975).

Awards: Golden Globe, 1961, for best show, and a Sylvania TV Award.

B Film Statistics

Number of family melodramas produced (percentage of total number of U.S. releases).

1954 = 8 (4%)
1955 = 11 (5%)
1956 = 22 (9%)
1957 = 28 (11%)
1958 = 37 (15%)
1959 = 21 (11%)
1960 = 22 (14%)
1961 = 17 (13%)
1962 = 17 (10%)
1963 = 18 (20%)
1964 = 3 (3%)

Percentage of family melodrama films ranking among the twenty top-grossing films.

1954 = 5%
1955 = 10%
1956 = 25%
1957 = 15%
1958 = 20%
1959 = 10%
1960 = 25%
1961 = 20%
1962 = 5%
1963 = 5%
1964 = 5%

Top-grossing films:

1954 = *Magnificent Obsession*

1955 = *East of Eden* and *The Blackboard Jungle*

1956 = *Picnic, Rebel without a Cause, The Bad Seed, The Man in the Gray Flannel Suit,* and *The Man with the Golden Arm*

1957 = *Written on the Wind, Giant,* and *April Love*

1958 = *Cat on a Hot Tin Roof, God's Little Acre, The Long Hot Summer,* and *Peyton Place*

1959 = *Imitation of Life, Some Came Running**

1960 = *Suddenly Last Summer, Portrait in Black, Please Don't Eat the Daisies, From the Terrace,* and *Home from the Hill*

1961 = *The Parent Trap, Splendor in the Grass, Where the Boys Are,* and *Parrish*

1962 = *Splendor in the Grass*

1963 = *The Thrill of it All*

1964 = *Love with the Proper Stranger*

*The Quigley list of box-office "grossers" for 1959 also includes *Blue Denim* and *This Earth is Mine. Film Daily Year Book* (1954–1965) and *Motion Picture Almanac* (1954–1965).

C Narrative Patterns

The lists below categorize the various film and television texts by subject matter. For the film texts, especially, there is some overlap. For example, a film like *Written on the Wind* fits into both the category of faulty family dynamics and that of marital strife. Consequently, the total number of films listed for all categories is greater than the eighty-nine films closely analyzed.

It is interesting to note that forty-three of these films (49 percent) have an adolescent weepy scene directed at the father. (I have designated these films with an asterisk [*].)

The totals of films from all categories (teen coming of age, faulty family dynamics, marital strife, societal ills, and remarriage/courtship) in which the father-son or the father-daughter relationship is crucial adds up to a total of forty-four films, or 51 percent. Mother-child relationships, in contrast, predominate in only sixteen of the eighty-nine films (18 percent).

Films

1. Teen point of view on coming of age

All the Fine Young Cannibals
*April Love
*Bernardine
*Blue Denim
Crime in the Streets
*David and Lisa
*Dino
*East of Eden
*Fear Strikes Out
Love with the Proper Stranger
Marjorie Morningstar
*Rebel without a Cause
Rock, Rock, Rock
*A Summer Place
*Tea and Sympathy
*The Young Stranger

1a. Teen point of view on coming of age, father-son relationship crucial

*April Love
*Bernardine
*Blue Denim
*Dino
*East of Eden
*Fear Strikes Out
*Rebel without a Cause
*Tea and Sympathy
*The Young Stranger

1b. Teen point of view on coming of age, father-daughter relationship crucial

 All the Fine Young Cannibals
 Love with the Proper Stranger
*A Summer Place

1c. Teen point of view on coming of age, mother-child relationship crucial

*Bernardine
*David and Lisa

2. Mixed point of view/Faulty family dynamics

*All Fall Down
*All the Way Home
 Bon Voyage
 The Catered Affair
*Cat on a Hot Tin Roof
*The Explosive Generation
*Five Finger Exercise
*Four Horsemen of the Apocalypse
*Giant
 Gidget Goes Hawaiian
*God's Little Acre
*Home from the Hill
*The Long Hot Summer
 Mr. Hobbs Takes a Vacation
*Peyton Place
*Return to Peyton Place
*Splendor in the Grass
 Take Her—She's Mine
*The Unguarded Moment

2a. Mixed point of view/Faulty family dynamics, father is crucial

*All Fall Down
*All the Way Home

   Bon Voyage
Cat on a Hot Tin Roof
The Explosive Generation
Five Finger Exercise
Four Horsemen of the Apocalypse
From the Terrace
Giant
   Gidget Goes Hawaiian
God's Little Acre
Home from the Hill
The Long Hot Summer
   Mr. Hobbs Takes a Vacation
Peyton Place
Return to Peyton Place
Splendor in the Grass
   Take Her—She's Mine
The Unguarded Moment
Written on the Wind

2b. Mixed point of view/Faulty family dynamics, mother is crucial

All Fall Down
   The Catered Affair
The Explosive Generation
Five Finger Exercise
Peyton Place
Return to Peyton Place
Splendor in the Grass

3. Marital strife/Conflict with work/Extra-marital affair

(Note: Some of these films feature father-child or mother-child bonding scenes crucial to the film's resolution, although these do not provide the central focus of the narrative.)

   Another Time, Another Place
Autumn Leaves
   Boys' Night Out
   A Child is Waiting
The Cobweb (weepy scene directed at psychiatrist)
   Come Next Spring
Executive Suite
From the Terrace
   A Gathering of Eagles
   Home Before Dark
   If a Man Answers
   It's a Woman's World
   The Last Time I Saw Paris

*Lonelyhearts
  The Man in the Gray Flannel Suit
*No Down Payment
  One Desire
  Period of Adjustment
  Please Don't Eat the Daisies
  The Pleasure of His Company
*The Remarkable Mr. Pennypacker
  The Shrike
*Strangers When We Meet
*The Tarnished Angels
  That Night
  There's Always Tomorrow
  This is My Love
  The Thrill of It All
  Tunnel of Love
*Written on the Wind

4. Societal strife (drugs, alcohol, racism, mental illness)

*The Bottom of the Bottle
  The Days of Wine and Roses
*A Hatful of Rain
  Kings Go Forth
*Night of the Quarter Moon
  Suddenly Last Summer
  The Three Faces of Eve

5. Remarriage/Courtship

  All That Heaven Allows
  Butterfield 8
*The Courtship of Eddie's Father
  Hilda Crane
  Houseboat
  Imitation of Life
  Magnificent Obsession
*Man on Fire
  Move Over Darling
  The Parent Trap
  Picnic
*Some Came Running (weepy scene directed at a brother)
  State Fair
*Stranger in My Arms
  Tammy and the Bachelor

Television

As with the films, there are cases of categorical overlap. In addition, I have not listed every single television text. Five hundred television episodes naturally produced a wealth of possible narrative types, some more general than others. I have created the categories below based on their prominence as plot topics, and then organized the programs accordingly. I have defined "prominence" as any topic which constituted at least ten percent of the episodes of any particular series. In addition, it should be noted that the selection was based only on those episodes actually screened. A quick perusal through the synopses available (in *TV Guide* or in Larry Gianakos' *TV Drama Series Programming*) might have contributed more examples to one category or another, but synopses are often unreliable as thorough narrative summations and therefore were not included.

As the following lists make evident, the most common narratives focused on issues concerning a housewife's role or gender identity (careerism, role-reversal). For example, on *Father Knows Best* 25 (22 percent) of the 115 episodes screened fit this category. On *The Donna Reed Show* this category represented 20 (20 percent) of 102 episodes, and on *My Three Sons* it represented 23 (23 percent) of 101 episodes.

While consumerism was not a common plot point for all the shows (it is notably absent from *Father Knows Best*), it figured so predominantly on *Leave It to Beaver* that it warranted its own category. A full 11 percent of the episodes of this show centered on the explicit purchase of consumer items, and the program's preoccupation with the work ethic (a separate category) was evident in an additional 15 percent of the programs, together making for an economic emphasis in over 26 percent of all *Leave It to Beaver* episodes.

It should be noted that the category "valuation of the father" represents only those episodes which are constructed in their entirety around the father's ego; valuation of the father occurs to some extent in nearly every episode of every program, especially in conjunction with denigration of the housewife.

1. Housewife/Gender identity

Father Knows Best

1954–1955:
Margaret Goes Dancing
1955–1956:
Advantage to Betty
Betty, Girl Engineer
Betty Hates Carter
Dilemma for Margaret
Family Reunion
No Partiality
Woman in the House
1956–1957:
Brief Vacation
1957–1958:
Big Sister
A Medal for Margaret
The Rivals

1958–1959:
Betty Makes a Choice
Betty the Pioneer Woman
Crisis over a Kiss
An Extraordinary Woman
It's a Small World
Kathy, Girl Executive
Kathy Grows Up
1959–1960:
Betty's Career Problem
Bud Hides behind a Skirt
Cupid Knows Best
Good Joke on Mom
Kathy Becomes a Girl
Kathy's Big Deception

The Donna Reed Show

1958–1959:
The Beaded Bag
The Busybody
The Hike
The Ideal Wife
Mary's Campaign
Mary's Double Date
Three Part Mother
Weekend Trip
1959–1960:
Alex Runs the House
The Career Woman
Just a Housewife
Lucky Girl
Mary's Crusade
Pickles for Charity
The Punishment
1962–1963:
Big Sixteen
Mrs. Stone and Dr. Hyde
Pioneer Woman
To Be a Boy
A Woman's Place

Leave It to Beaver

1957–1958:
Party Invitation
Wally's Girl Trouble

1958–1959:
Her Idol
1959–1960:
School Sweater
1960–1961:
The Dramatic Club
Mother's Helper

The Adventures of Ozzie and Harriet

1952–1953:
Curiosity
Harriet's Hairdo
Riviera Ballet
1953–1954:
Ozzie's Night Out
1957–1958:
A Cruise for Harriet
1960–1961:
Bowling with the Wives
1963–1964:
June Is Always Late
Rick's Wedding Ring
The Torn Dress
1964–1965:
The Exotic Housemother
1965–1966:
Ozzie, the Sitter

My Three Sons

1960–1961:
Bub Leaves Home
Domestic Trouble
Lady Engineer
The Little Ragpicker
The Lostling
Organization Woman
Other People's Houses
1962–1963:
The Beauty Contest
Daughter for a Day
Mother Bub
Pretty as a Picture
What's Cookin'?
1963–1964:
Cherry Blossoms in Bryant Park

The People House
The Substitute Teacher
The Tree
1964–1965:
Charley and the Kid
Here Comes Charley
Lady in the Air
Lady President
The Practical Shower
A Serious Girl
Women's Work

2. Middle-class superiority/Puritan work ethic

Father Knows Best

1954–1955:
Bud, the Snob
Father Delivers the Papers
Jim, the Farmer
The Mink Coat
1955–1956:
Art of Salesmanship
Bad Influence
Betty Earns a Formal
Family Dines Out
The Grass is Greener
1958–1959:
Big Shot Bud
Bud, the Carpenter
Bud, the Debutante
Hard Luck Leo
1959–1960:
Bud Lives it Up
Bud, the Speculator
Bud, the Willing Worker
Family Contest
The $500 Letter

The Donna Reed Show

1958–1959:
The Grateful Patient
It's the Principle of the Thing
Jeff's Double Life
Operation Deadbeat

1959–1960:
The Free Soul
Jeff, the Financial Genius
A Penny Earned
1960–1961:
How the Other Half Lives
The Model Daughter
1962–1963:
Jeff Stands Alone

Leave It to Beaver

1957–1958:
The Broken Window
Wally's Job
Water Anyone?
1958–1959:
The Cookie Fund
The Garage Painters
The Grass Is Always Greener
1959–1960:
Beaver Makes a Loan
Wally, the Businessman
1960–1961:
Beaver and Kenneth
Beaver Goes in Business
Wally's Glamor Girl
Ward's Millions
1962–1963:
Beaver the Caddy
The Credit Card
Wally's Dinner Date

The Adventures of Ozzie and Harriet

1952–1953:
Monetary System
1953–1954:
The Credit Reference
1960–1961:
David Gets Discouraged
1961–1962:
The Backyard Pet Show
The High Cost of Dating
Lending Money to Wally

My Three Sons

1960–1961:
My Three Strikers
1962–1963:
High on the Hog
Let's Take Stock
The System
1963–1964:
House for Sale
Tramp Goes Hollywood
Will Success Spoil Chip Douglas?
1964–1965:
A Touch of Larceny

3. Consumerism

The Donna Reed Show

1958–1959:
The Football Uniform

Leave It to Beaver

1958–1959:
Beaver's Ring
Beaver's Sweater
The Lost Watch
The Pipe
Wally's New Suit
Wally's Present
1960–1961:
Beaver's Big Contest
Chuckie's New Shoes
1961–1962:
Beaver's Jacket
Beaver's Typewriter
Sweatshirt Monsters

The Adventures of Ozzie and Harriet

1953–1954:
The Swimming Pool
1958–1959:
The Buckingham

1960–1961:
The Built-In Television Set
The Fraternity Junk Drive
A Piano for the Fraternity
Selling Ricky's Drums
Two Small Boys and a Dog
1961–1962:
The Savings Stamps
Ten for the Tigers
1963–1964:
Wally's TV Set

My Three Sons

1963–1964:
A Car of His Own
The Toupee

4. Teen rebellion/Societal strife (divorce, runaways)

Father Knows Best

1954–1955:
Live My Own Life
The Motor Scooter
1955–1956:
Bud, the Boxer
The Persistent Guest
1956–1957:
Homing Pigeon

The Donna Reed Show

1958–1959:
Boys Will Be Boys
Do You Trust Your Child?
Guest in the House
Nothing but the Truth
Pardon My Gloves
The Parting of the Ways
1959–1960:
A Difference of Opinion
The First Quarrel
A Friend Indeed
The New Mother

Leave It to Beaver

1957–1958:
Lumpy Rutherford
1958–1959:
Wally's Haircomb
1961–1962:
Beaver Takes a Drive
1962–1963:
Box Office Attraction
The Moustache
Wally's Practical Joke

The Adventures of Ozzie and Harriet

1958–1959:
The Motorcycle
The Runaways

My Three Sons

1960–1961:
The Bully
The Delinquent
1962–1963:
Chip's Last Fight
1963–1964:
Guest in the House
1964–1965:
Divorce, Bryant Park Style

5. Valuation of the father

Father Knows Best

1954–1955:
Father of the Year
Proud Father
Typical Father
1955–1956:
Father, the Naturalist
Hero Father
The House Painter
1956–1957:
Class Prophecy
1957–1958:
Father's Biography

1958–1959:
The Basketball Coach
The Grass Is Greener
The Ideal Father
A Man of Merit
1959–1960:
Jim's Big Surprise

The Donna Reed Show

1958–1959:
The Ideal Father
The Male Ego
1959–1960:
The Neighborly Gesture
1962–1963:
Man to Man

Leave It to Beaver

1957–1958:
The Bank Account
Perfect Father
1958–1959:
Beaver's Hero
Ward's Problem

The Adventures of Ozzie and Harriet

1956–1957:
Ozzie, the Treasurer
1965–1966:
An Honor for Oz

Notes

Introduction

1. Prior to 1948 the five major film studios enjoyed monopoly power resulting from the film industry's fully vertical integration at the production, distribution, and exhibition levels. For a complete account of the Paramount case, see Michael Conant, *Antitrust in the Motion-Picture Industry*.

2. For a discussion of the decrease in major-motion-picture studio output and its possible causes, see Robert W. Crandell, "The Postwar Performance of the Motion Picture Industry," *The Antitrust Bulletin* 20, no. 1 (spring 1975): 49–85. Crandell notes that "beginning in 1953, output of the major distributors was [sic] contracted steadily through the early 1960's to an annual rate of less than 50% of 1951 output" (57–58). For a discussion of the decline in motion-picture audiences, see Douglas Gomery, "The Coming of Television and the 'Lost' Motion Picture," *The Journal of Film and Video* 37, no. 3 (summer 1985): 5–11.

3. Garth Jowett, *Film, the Democratic Art*, p. 348.

4. Ibid., *Film*, p. 349.

5. Ibid., p. 375.

6. The programs—*The 20th Century–Fox Hour* and *MGM Parade*—were little more than lengthy trailers for upcoming feature-film releases.

7. Even the trade almanac *Film Daily Year Book* instituted a separate section on television beginning in 1959.

8. Of these series, only *Cheyenne* attained any sort of popularity; indeed, its success, along with that of *Gunsmoke* and *The Life and Legend of Wyatt Earp*, helped spawn what was to be a decade-long glut of television westerns.

9. See Christopher Anderson, "Negotiating the Television Text: The Transformation of *Warner Bros. Presents*," in *Making Television: Authorship and the Production Process*, ed. Robert Thompson and Gary Burns, pp. 95–116. Anderson's article is particularly enlightening in its description of product differentiation for a particular genre—the western—at a time of tremendous institutional uncertainty. No one, he argues, not even any of the program's producers, was certain of how the key players (sponsors, networks, studios, regulatory bodies) would work together and how their cooperation might affect both the industries and their products.

10. James L. Baughman, "The Weakest Chain and the Strongest Link," in *Hollywood in the Age of Television*, ed. Tino Balio, pp. 91–114.

11. See William Boddy, *Fifties Television: The Industry and Its Critics,* for an articulate analysis of the relationships between these different groups.

12. Ibid., p. 1.

13. David Marc, "Screen Gems: Prime-Time Story-Telling," in *Making Television: Authorship and the Production Process,* ed. Robert Thompson and Gary Burns, pp. 137–144.

14. As Tino Balio and others have noted, Hollywood's loss of audience had actually begun in 1947—a decade before television achieved high viewer penetration—and was caused by the baby boom, the Paramount decree, the move toward big-budget, event-type films, and other factors. See Balio, *Hollywood in the Age of Television.*

15. For information on Hollywood's use of technology for purposes of differentiation, see Dennis J. Dombkowski, "Film and Television: An Analytical History of Economic and Creative Integration," Ph.D. diss.; Allan Larson, "Integration and Attempted Integration between the Motion Picture and Television Industries through 1956," Ph.D. diss.; David Bordwell, Kristin Thompson, and Janet Staiger, *The Classical Hollywood Cinema;* and relevant chapters in Balio, *Hollywood in the Age of Television.*

16. See Dombkowski, "Film and Television"; Larson, "Integration and Attempted Integration"; and Bordwell, Thompson, and Staiger, *Classical Hollywood Cinema.*

17. See Timothy R. White, "Hollywood's Attempt at Appropriating Television: The Case of Paramount Pictures," in Balio, *Hollywood in the Age of Television,* for a good discussion of the motion picture studio investments in subscription television.

18. For film, see Thomas Elsaesser, "Tales of Sound and Fury: Observations of the Family Melodrama," *Monogram* no. 4 (1972): 12–15, and John G. Cawelti, *Adventure, Mystery, and Romance;* for television's domestic comedies see Mary Beth Haralovich, "Suburban Family Sitcoms and Consumer Product Design" (paper), and "Sitcoms and Suburbs: Positioning the 1950's Homemaker," *Quarterly Journal of Film and Video* 11, no. 1 (May 1989): 61–83; and Lynn Spigel, "Installing the Television Set: Popular Discourses on Television and Domestic Space, 1948–1955," *Camera Obscura,* no. 16 (January 1988): 11–48.

19. See, for example, *Who's Afraid of Virginia Woolf?, The Graduate,* and even *The Happiest Millionaire*—which ends with the romantic couple deserting their extended, old-moneyed family to build cars in Detroit!

20. Jon Lewis, *The Road to Romance and Ruin: Teen Films and Youth Culture,* p. 47. See also Thomas Doherty, *Teenagers and Teenpics: The Juvenilization of American Movies in the 1950s,* and David M. Considine, *The Cinema of Adolescence.*

21. This figure reflects both domestic melodramas and situation comedies. See Table 1.

22. John Ellis, *Visible Fictions: Cinema, Television, Video,* pp. 176–177.

23. From 1915 to 1952 films were regarded by the court as a business and therefore not protected by the First Amendment (*Mutual v Ohio*). In 1952 the Miracle case restored First-Amendment protection to the film industry, establishing that films were both a source of information and a medium for "the communication of ideas." Although there have been a number of books published on these legislative regulations, this scholarship neglects both the implicit regulations of sponsorship and the explicit credos of the networks' standards and practices departments. In addition, these works fail to articulate the links between the regulatory forces of film and television or to provide a full account of the effect such rulings had on the content of family melodrama. See S. M. Besen, *Misregulating Television: Network Dominance and the FCC;* Harry P. Warner, *Radio and Television Rights;* Barry Cole and Mal Oettinger, *Reluctant Regulators: The FCC and the Broadcast Audience;* Geoffrey Cowan, *See No Evil: The Backstage Battle over Sex and Violence on Television;* Ira H. Carmen, *Movies,*

Censorship, and the Law; Paul W. Facey, *The Legion of Decency: A Sociological Analysis of the Emergence and Development of a Pressure Group;* Stephen Farber, *The Movie Rating Game;* Erwin Krasnow, et al., *The Politics of Broadcast Regulation;* and Richard S. Randall, *Censorship of the Movies.*

24. Ellis, *Visible Fictions,* p. 238.

25. Textual analysis, which is distinct from content analysis, emphasizes how texts produce meanings rather than what meanings can be discovered in them. Based on the literary analyses of Roland Barthes, textual analysis is predicated on the idea that a book, film, or television program represents not a distinct object of study but an intersection of various "codes" which signify meaning. In this context, codes are those conventions that represent (or signify) distinct opportunities for understanding how texts produce meaning. Thus in film, for example, a low-angle shot of a character, coupled with other conventions such as harsh lighting, ominous music, and confining sets, might signify the character as evil and powerful. For a good presentation of close textual readings, see Roland Barthes, *Image, Music, Text* and *S/Z.* For the application of this technique to film, see Stephen Heath, *Questions of Cinema* and Stephen Heath and Patricia Mellencamp, *Cinema and Language.*

26. The ideological approach relies on the method developed most fully in the article *Young Mr. Lincoln* in *Cahiers du Cinéma,* no. 223 (1970) (reprinted in *Movies and Methods I,* ed. Bill Nichols, pp. 493–528). The operating principle in this method is that deconstructing the film and television codes—taking them apart and noting their ordering, their repetitions, and their contradictions makes it possible to ascertain certain ideological operations within the texts. "Ideology," in this model, is not a conscious choice of various worldviews but is a system of representation consistent with the dominant interests of society, that is constructed by a multitude of elements and that is unknowable to the audience member. Althusser's argument is that because we are all "inside ideology" we do not consciously choose our place; rather, we are steered toward support of ruling ideas via a predescribed placement (interpellation). See Louis Althusser, "Ideology and Ideological State Apparatuses," in his *Lenin and Philosophy,* pp. 23–70.

Recent work on film and television explains not only the depiction of women on the screen but also how this depiction can be read by a female spectator. These critics have taken Molly Haskell's study on female stereotypes, *From Reverence to Rape,* and enlarged it according to developments in semiology and contemporary film theory. No longer so interested in the types of roles women play (mother, whore), this approach examines the importance women have for narrative complication and resolution, their visual depiction, and whether viewers can "read against the grain" (the surface codes of the texts) to uncover women's repressed importance. Good treatments of the feminist critical method can be found in E. Ann Kaplan, *Women and Film, Both Sides of the Camera;* Annette Kuhn, *Women's Pictures: Feminism and Cinema;* and Mary Ann Doane, Patricia Mellencamp, and Linda Williams, eds., *Re-Vision, Essays in Feminist Film Criticism.* Also recommended is Laura Mulvey's ground-breaking piece, "Visual Pleasure and Narrative Cinema," *Screen,* 16, no. 3 (1975): 6–18.

27. Gender analysis has been the focus of previous work on melodrama. See, for example, Jackie Byars, "Gender Representation in American Family Melodramas of the 1950s" (Ph.D. diss., published as *All That Hollywood Allows: Re-Reading Gender in 1950s Melodrama).* Mary Beth Haralovich has written extensively on television programs as they construct real-world consumers (see note 18); and in my chapter on familial economics I examine the presentation of consumerism *within* the programs.

1　The Melodramatic Territory

1. See Horace Newcomb, *TV: The Most Popular Art.*
2. Peter Brooks, *The Melodramatic Imagination;* Cawelti, *Adventure, Mystery, and Romance.* See also Elsaesser, "Tales of Sound and Fury."
3. I provide only a schematic review of these terms here, and refer the reader to the original sources for a more thorough discussion.
4. Brooks, *Melodramatic Imagination,* p. xi.
5. While I would argue that Brooks' use of the term *repression* is slightly off the mark (i.e., the conscious nature of the utterances seem more a victory over *suppression*), his recognition of melodrama's exteriorization of internal feelings is crucial. Freud makes a profound distinction between the two concepts, arguing that suppression involves moral, conscious, and preconscious prohibitions, while repression is an unconscious defense mechanism of the ego. See Sigmund Freud, *The Interpretation of Dreams,* p. 645 n.
6. Brooks, *Melodramatic Imagination,* p. 56.
7. Cawelti, *Adventure, Mystery, and Romance,* p. 262.
8. Brooks and Cawelti differ in their opinions of the pertinence of religion to the traditional melodrama. Brooks, arguing that melodrama evolved simultaneously with the elimination of formalized religion in the modern world, claims that "melodrama may be born of the very anxiety created by the guilt experienced when the allegiance and ordering that pertained to a sacred system of things no longer obtain" (Brooks, *Melodramatic Imagination,* p. 200). Cawelti, on the other hand, sees religion as "the cement tying together the other social and moral ideas" and writes that "the melodramatic formula . . . dramatized the congruence between the social ideals of domesticity, romantic love, and respectable mobility and the religious faith in the divine governance of the world" (Cawelti, *Adventure, Mystery, and Romance,* p. 270).
9. David N. Rodowick, "Madness, Authority and Ideology: The Domestic Melodrama of the 1950's," in *Home is Where the Heart Is: Studies in Melodrama and the Woman's Film,* ed. Christine Gledhill, p. 276.
10. According to Cawelti, "increasing ambivalence about divine providence as the cornerstone of society was accompanied by doubts about the two other value complexes that were basic to the earlier melodramatic vision: the purity and domestic submissiveness of women and the ideal of the respectable, middle-class family" (*Adventure, Mystery, and Romance,* p. 275).
11. Elsaesser, "Tales of Sound and Fury," pp. 3–4.
12. Ibid., p. 8.
13. David Grimsted, *Melodrama Unveiled,* p. 10.
14. The term "modern" is used loosely here, referring to a period from roughly the turn of the century until after World War II.
15. See, for example, the work of Harold Robbins, in which unacquainted characters interact independently in the circumscribed universe of auto racing, the Hollywood studios, networks, corporations, etc.
16. Ellis, *Visible Fictions,* p. 69.
17. This preoccupation becomes particularly intriguing in light of the comments of television production personnel who continually defend their domestic programs as being, if not a mirror of life, at least a picture of how life "should be." This is discussed further in Chapter 2.

18. Gledhill, *Home is Where the Heart Is,* p. 21.

19. Original production ended in 1960; prime-time reruns aired thereafter.

20. *Father Knows Best* originated on radio in 1949 with Eugene Rodney and Robert Young as producers, Young as the star, and Roswell Rogers as the head writer. All three continued their association with the television series. *The Adventures of Ozzie and Harriet* began on radio as an extension of the two actors' supporting roles (providing musical entertainment) on *The Red Skelton Show.* In 1944, when Skelton was drafted into the army, the Nelsons were asked to replace the comedian, providing skits about their home life interspersed with musical numbers. Gradually the skits became the focus of the program, which evolved into an episodic format. In 1949 David and Ricky Nelson joined the program, playing themselves. In 1951 the Nelson family starred in a feature film for Universal Studios, *Here Come the Nelsons,* designed to spark and test audience interest in a visual version of the radio program.

21. Elsaesser, "Tales of Sound and Fury." Elsaesser also first suggested the genre's susceptibility to ironic readings. This characteristic is more a post hoc critical apprehension of the text than it is a mode of the text itself. Consequently, I will not attempt to locate the ironic or contradictory articulations of these films and programs, but will underscore their textual melodramatic elements. For good readings of various ironic possibilities in a number of films, see Gledhill, *Home is Where the Heart Is* and Byars, *All That Hollywood Allows.*

22. Byars, "Gender Representation," pp. 38–39.

23. See Appendix C for a list of specific film titles and the categories into which they have been placed.

24. See Appendix C for a categorization of the five hundred television episodes.

25. I do not expect the reader to be familiar with all or even most of the examples listed here and elsewhere in my text. By invoking so many titles I hope I will hit upon at least one within the reader's viewing experience.

26. In the case of *Stella Dallas,* for example, it is Stella who insists on the importance of her daughter's relationship with her wealthy father (Stella's former husband); the text works to emphasize the importance of mother love and sacrifice in determining the psychic well-being of a child.

27. What after all, is the meaning of the title *My Three Sons?* It seems to indicate that Steve Douglas independently conceived, delivered, and raised his children without the help of his recently deceased wife. The late Mrs. Douglas, according to narrative explanation, passed away with the birth of their third child, Chip, when Robbie was six and Mike was nine. Yet they demonstrate no real memory of their mother, nor any sense of personal loss.

28. Noël Carroll, "The Family Plot and *Magnificent Obsession,*" in *Melodrama,* ed. Daniel C. Gerould, p. 199. My husband has observed that, in light of the author's name ("Christmas" Carroll), it is easy to understand the bite contained within his analysis.

29. See, for example, the birthday scenes in *East of Eden* and *Cat on a Hot Tin Roof,* the Christmas and New Year scenes in *Splendor in the Grass,* and the Christmas scene in *All Fall Down* (indeed, *All Fall Down* revolves around Berry Berry's Christmas homecoming).

30. For example, a *Father Knows Best* Christmas program was rerun for three years straight although the children had aged noticeably from 1954 to 1957. Such rerunning of material grants it a pseudo-home-movie status, in which the audience relives Anderson family memories as if they were their own—commenting on how young the children look, etc.

31. It is interesting to note how many of these actors studied the method of the New York

Actor's Studio. The famed technique which relied upon the nonverbal expression of interior states (mumbles, gestures, and distorted expressions) seems ideal for a modern interpretation of nineteenth-century melodrama's exaggerated acting style.

32. Obviously, all acting relies somewhat on gesture; the distinction between melodramatic acting and less histrionic approaches is one of degree. In melodrama, actors obsessively shun the spoken word, relying almost exclusively upon gesture as their means of communication. Even when an actor chooses to verbalize, the words are often mumbled or otherwise unintelligible because of the overwhelmingly emotional tone.

33. It is Betty's *response* to this turn of events that renders it melodramatic. Had she seen the humor in this harmless part-time job or even (perhaps more realistically) been apathetic about the event, this episode would be merely situation or domestic comedy. Instead, Betty tearfully relives her shame at having to get a job, the embarrassment of wearing a uniform, and the fear that someone she knows will see her making a fool of herself. In this way, a simple after-school job becomes grounds for charges of parental abuse and an equally excessive parental response.

34. I am well aware that *I Love Lucy,* with its extraordinary narrative events as well as the character's overemotional responses, lack of learning, and predictable behavior, could perhaps be read within this definition. *I Love Lucy,* however, escapes the classification because the various dilemmas it chose to deal with were (typically) so fanciful. The proscenium presentation of the program, its fairly minimalist setting, Ricky's occupation, and the star-based focus on Lucille Ball also place the program beyond the mimetic world of domestic melodrama examined here.

35. David Thorburn, "Television Melodrama," in *Television as Cultural Force,* ed. Richard Adler, p. 78.

36. Elsaesser, "Tales of Sound and Fury," p. 5.

37. Quite often, the narrative of the program was constructed around a musical "set piece" which, much as in musical comedy, functioned as the moment of revelation, celebration, or confrontation. For more on this phenomenon, see Nina Leibman, "The Rock 'n Roller Coaster: Popular Music in 1950's Film and Television" (paper).

2   Corporate Soul-Mates

1. Excerpt from Ellis Arnall's speech at a trade luncheon, quoted in "Motion Picture Industry Should Stay Out of TV Programming," *TV Guide,* 12 January 1957, inside front cover.

2. Ibid., *TV Guide*'s reply to the Arnall remark.

3. "Movies now Active in Telefield," *Radio-Television Daily,* 15 June 1954, 5, 7, quoted in Larson, "Integration and Attempted Integration," pp. 60–61.

4. Interestingly, this ambivalence can be seen in the industry's own relation to the program. For example, *Father Knows Best* won Emmy Awards four years in a row in both the actor and actress categories. In 1956 Young was named best actor in a dramatic series, and the following year both Young and Wyatt won similar awards in the actor and actress divisions. However, in 1958 Wyatt was named best actress again, this time for comedy, and the program won a directing award, also for comedy. By 1959, when the program won again, it did so in a category merely titled "series."

5. Ellis, *Visible Fictions,* p. 30.

6. David Marc, *Demographic Vistas: Television in American Culture,* p. 12; Richard Adler, *Television as Cultural Force,* p. 8.

7. Ironically, this was remade into a highly successful television series in which Tom Corbett's promised remarriage was stalled on a weekly basis, offering the possibility of continual dating trials and errors.

8. Eventually Steve Douglas did remarry, in the 1969–1970 season, but this was after the family had already splintered: son Robbie was married and the father of triplets, and son Chip was grown and going to college.

9. Irwin Applebaum, *The World According to Beaver*, p. 2.

10. Ellis, *Visible Fictions*, pp. 154–156.

11. This pattern is discussed in Chapter 5.

12. The structural influence on "My Three Strikers" is intriguing. At the time that the episode was written, the Writers Guild of America (WGA) was on strike against the film and television industries. Because *My Three Sons* producer Don Fedderson had already agreed to a favorable contract with his writing staff, the union allowed them to continue to write for the program, despite the WGA's industry-wide prohibition. This episode was written by Arnold and Lois Peyser, with the specific approval of the WGA, as a means of publicly airing the terms of the dispute. Arnold and Lois Peyser, interview with author, 7 June 1989.

13. Sara Davidson, *Real Property*, p. 11.

14. Roswell Rogers, interview with author, 8 March 1989.

15. Paul West, letter to author, 23 March 1989.

16. Dorothy Cooper Foote, letter to author, 18 April 1989.

17. Ibid.

18. Rogers, interview. Interestingly, the thought of extending the half-hour format by means of a two-part episode was not considered during the late 1950's. Phil Davis (writer for *My Three Sons, The Donna Reed Show,* and *Father Knows Best*) and Paul West (writer-producer for *The Donna Reed Show* and *My Three Sons*) recalled that two-parters were discouraged. In the words of West, "At that time, for some unknown reason, it was believed that viewers would not remember what happened last week." Phil Davis, letter to author, 12 March 1989; West, letter.

19. The so-called MacMurray Method, which refers to the actor's idiosyncratic contractual shooting agreement, will be discussed in the following section.

20. John McGreevey, letter to author, 6 July 1989.

21. Nicholas Ray, "Story into Script," *Sight and Sound* (autumn 1956): 71.

22. Ozzie Nelson, *Ozzie*, p. 210.

23. Nelson, *Ozzie*, pp. 210–211.

24. Peter Tewksbury, letter to author, 25 June 1989.

25. Paul Petersen, interview with author, 14 March 1989; Shelley Fabares, interview with author, 29 June 1989; Barbara Hammer Avedon, interview with author, 6 March 1989; William Roberts, interview with author, 5 March 1989; Nate Monaster, telephone interview with author, 10 March 1989.

26. Davis, letter.

27. Robert Fisher, telephone interview with author, 10 February 1989.

28. The exception to this was *My Three Sons*.

29. John Stephens, interview with author, 11 July 1989; Fred MacMurray, interview with author, 17 July 1989.

30. These days were not necessarily consecutive.

31. *Father Knows Best* began its first season with all thirty-nine episodes already written ahead of shooting, but this was highly unusual and did not recur. This unusual first-season prepa-

ration was facilitated by the practice of giving many of the old radio scripts to script consultants (Barbara Hammer Avedon, for one), who rewrote them for the visual medium.

32. In the twelve years the program aired, this unfortunate happenstance occurred only once, when an elderly actor died between his initial group scene and the close-up work to be filmed later. Using a rear camera shot, focused on only the back of a double, the episode proceeded as planned. Stephens, interview; MacMurray, interview.

33. Arnold and Lois Peyser, interview.

34. Tewksbury, letter.

35. McGreevey, letter.

36. Ellis, *Visible Fictions*, p. 88.

37. David Nelson, interview with author, 8 February 1988.

38. This is discussed thoroughly in Chapter 4.

39. Hubbell Robinson, quoted in Leon Morse, "Hubbell Robinson Evaluates TV Programming Today," *Television*, December 1959, 49–50. This article is cited in William Boddy, "From the 'Golden Age' to the 'Vast Wasteland': The Struggles over Market Power and Dramatic Formats in 1950's Television," Ph.D. diss., p. 381.

40. Bob Shanks, quoted in Erik Barnouw, *The Sponsor: Notes on a Modern Potentate*, p. 114.

41. Lawrence Laurent, "Commercial Television: What are Its Educational Possibilities and Limits?" in *Television's Impact on American Culture*, ed. William Y. Elliot, p. 154.

42. Barnouw, *The Sponsor*, p. 73.

43. David Levy, telephone interview with author, 28 April 1989.

44. Laurent, "Commercial Television," p. 154.

45. This occurred in the program's transition from a CBS–Kent Cigarette program to its new identity as an NBC–Scott Paper program.

46. Importantly, Rodney needed Scott Paper's permission just to rerun the episode at all, regardless of time restrictions.

47. Fred Brisken to Ralph Cohn, 18 July 1955, Eugene Rodney Collection, Theater Arts Library, University of California at Los Angeles.

48. Jay Bottomley to Eugene Rodney, 6 November 1954, Eugene Rodney Collection.

49. Rogers, interview.

50. Frank Stanton, testimony before the Federal Communications Commission Hearings on Television, 29 January 1960, CBS Files, Theater Arts Library, UCLA, 10.

51. West, letter.

52. Robert Young, telephone interview with author, 11 March 1989.

53. Eugene Rodney to Joe Henrie, 19 January 1954, Eugene Rodney Collection.

54. Ibid.

55. Erslene Johnson, "They'll Leave it to Beaver Again for Third Year," *NEA Newsletter*, 6 November 1959.

56. It is notable, of course, that Steve shows Chip pictures not of his real mother—whose presumed importance to the Douglas family is continually unspoken or ignored—but of her substitute.

57. See Dombkowski, "Film and Television." Also see Gomery, "The Coming of Television."

58. See Boddy, "From the 'Golden Age' to the 'Vast Wasteland.'"

59. Laurent, "Commercial Television," p. 166.

60. Newcomb, *Popular Art*, pp. 245–246.

61. Nelson, *Ozzie*, p. 256.

62. For a good discussion of CinemaScope, see Larson, "Integration and Attempted Integration," p. 196. The bulk of family melodramas were produced by MGM (nineteen analyzed herein) and 20th Century–Fox (nineteen analyzed). Fox worked entirely, and MGM predominantly, in the wide-screen format. Their stylistic preferences thus work to reinforce the definition of family melodrama as one in which the small family battles the encroaching world.

63. Rick Altman, "Television Sound," in *Studies in Entertainment: Critical Approaches to Mass Culture,* ed. Tania Modleski, pp. 42–43.

64. Obviously, the technological revolution of the 1990's has changed the stakes of aural supremacy considerably, with computer discs, stereo television, HDTV, etc., but in the 1950's the differences in sound quality between the two media were quite pronounced.

65. *My Three Sons* began color production in 1965, and *The Donna Reed Show* and *The Adventures of Ozzie and Harriet* added hues in 1966.

66. These television programs prided themselves, and were heralded for, their "realism," a claim based in part, I think, on their black-and-white photography.

67. Ellis, *Visible Fictions,* pp. 58–59.

68. Ibid., pp. 105–106.

69. Bob Eddy, "Private Life of a Perfect Papa," *Saturday Evening Post,* 27 April 1957, 28–29.

70. The ordinariness of the role of "housewife" was somewhat problematized by the glamorous actresses who portrayed them. While the majority of articles continued to emphasize the "wifely" escapades of program stars, they did occasionally acknowledge their differences from the women at home. See, in particular, "Wow! All Those Beautiful TV Wives!," *Chicago American TV Pictorial,* 19 February 1961. The article notes: "How many a husband, mesmerized by his television set night after night, must have looked across the living room at his somewhat-less-attractive spouse, and wondered wistfully why true life isn't more like life as it is lived on television."

71. "Who Needs the Social Register?" *TV Guide,* 21 November 1955, 13–15.

72. "An Expert on the Male," *TV Guide,* 25 February 1961.

73. "It's Not Always Father Who 'Knows Best' for Backstage Problems," *TV Guide,* 16 February 1957, 19. This article also notes how cast members had teasing conflicts before getting to be friends and how Betty cried when criticized. The article quotes Eugene Rodney as saying that letters from fans praise the show for helping them with real problems.

74. "The Family Spirit," *TV Guide,* 24 December 1954, 17.

75. "Why Father Still has His Day," *TV Guide,* 14 June 1958, 20.

76. Marion Dern, "Sweet, Sincere and Solvent," *TV Guide,* 20 June 1964, 11.

77. See "Paul and Patty Petersen of *The Donna Reed Show,*" picture feature, *TV Guide,* 1 August 1964, 8–9.

78. Cleveland Amory, review of *The Adventures of Ozzie and Harriet, TV Guide,* 6 June 1964, 3.

79. Cast members claim never to have conflated their own identities with those of their characters; they considered themselves professionals and in no way saw their TV families as a sort of surrogate family. In fact, the truth was often that their real lives were poles apart from their onscreen family life. While the popular press bragged about congenial familial atmospheres, Elinor Donahue angered cast and crew by eloping with a sound man and becoming pregnant, Billy Gray was reprimanded for a number of petty juvenile escapades (culminating with a marijuana arrest in 1960), and Lauren Chapin faced her own substance abuse problems. Tony Dow, interview with author, 17 September 1987; Jerry Mathers, inter-

view with author, 15 September 1987; Bill Gray, interview with author, 2 February 1988; Elinor Donahue, interview with author, 1 February 1988; Paul Petersen, interview; and Shelley Fabares, interview with author, 29 June 1989.

80. Nelson, *Ozzie*, p. 282.
81. Monaster, interview.

3   What the People Want

1. My intent in examining audience is quite distinct from that of the theoretical method of "constructed spectatorship." For theoretical discussions of the constructed spectator, see the work of Laura Mulvey and Tania Modleski. For a pertinent comparison between "spectator" and "social audience," see Annette Kuhn, who states that "looking at spectators and at audiences demands different methodologies and theoretical frameworks. . . . The spectator, for example, is a subject constituted in signification. . . . A group of people seated in a single auditorium looking at a film, or . . . watching the same television programme is a social audience." Annette Kuhn, "Women's Genres: Melodrama, Soap Opera and Theory," in *Home is Where the Heart Is,* ed. Christine Gledhill, p. 343.
2. Susan Ohmer, "Like/Dislike/Like Very Much: Reception Theory and Audience Research of the 1940's" (paper).
3. Ibid.
4. "Teenage Girls Our Best Customers" was a report issued by *Seventeen Magazine* revealing that teenage girls were the best film customers in 1962. In 1962, 45.5 percent of all teen girls went to the movies once a week; in 1963, 49.8 percent of all teen girls went that often. Clipping files, "Audience," The Margaret Herrick Library, Academy of Motion Picture Arts and Sciences.
5. "Old Stars Making Love in Pix Opposed by Fans in U.S. Poll," *Hollywood Reporter,* 24 June 1957.
6. "To Improve Public Attendance Towards the American Motion Picture at Home and Abroad," MPAA report, October, 1962, 2, Clipping Files, "Audience," Margaret Herrick Library.
7. *Film Daily Year Book,* 1961, p. 65, reflecting on 1960 and the prior four years.
8. These statements were often issued as claims of relative improvement over the more "mass-oriented" (read crass) outpourings of television.
9. Milton MacKaye, "The Big Brawl: Hollywood vs. Television," part 2, *Saturday Evening Post,* 26 January 1952, p. 122.
10. Review of *Blue Denim, Variety,* 29 July 1959.
11. Richard Gertner, review of *No Down Payment, Motion Picture Daily,* 30 September 1957.
12. See review of *Magnificent Obsession, Variety,* 11 May 1954; review of *All That Heaven Allows, Variety,* 26 May 1955; review of *There's Always Tomorrow, Hollywood Reporter,* 12 January 1956.
13. Jack Moffitt, review of *A Summer Place, Hollywood Reporter,* 7 October 1959.
14. Steward Hagerty, "Censorship," *Show Business,* 28 November 1961, 72.
15. Review of *A Hatful of Rain, Variety,* 18 June 1957.
16. Tom Watson, interview with author, 23 May 1989.
17. Arnold Becker, interview with author, 5 April 1989.
18. Ellis, *Visible Fictions,* p. 249.

19. Becker, interview.

20. Tore Hallonquist, CBS-TV Research Department Program Analysis Division Report No. 20-57, August 1957.

21. Ibid.

22. Brian Levant, interview with author, 15 September 1987.

23. For example, David Levy, vice president of programming for Young and Rubicam, said the company did demographic breakdowns for the first season of *Father Knows Best,* looking for a "smoking type" audience. Levy, interview.

24. Watson, interview.

25. "Nielsen Newscast," vol. 12, no. 3, August 1963.

26. "The abc of ABC," *Forbes,* 15 June 1959, 17, quoted in Boddy, "From the 'Golden Age' to the 'Vast Wasteland,'" p. 224.

27. Marvin Mord, vice president of ABC marketing and research, quoted in Susan Horowitz, "Sitcom Domesticus: A Species Endangered by Social Change," *Channels,* September/October 1984, 22.

28. Muriel Cantor, "Audience Control," in *Television: The Critical View,* 3d ed., ed. Horace Newcomb, p. 326.

29. Young, interview.

30. Jeff Greenfield, *Television: The First Fifty Years,* p. 56.

31. A good source for evidence of the audience-program relationship consists of the various teen magazines and tabloids of the period. An exhaustive study of such materials was beyond the scope of this project, but an admittedly scant look at a few teen magazines of the period revealed a large number of articles on teen stars: their "real" home life, how they handled dating and school problems, their attitudes towards various popular fads, etc. There were frequent write-in contests asking fans' favorite stars. A 1962 issue of *16 Magazine,* for example, named Shelley Fabares as "best actress," Paul Petersen as "most promising actor," and Ricky Nelson (in a tie with Richard Chamberlain) as "best actor." See "Reader's Poll," *16 Magazine,* November 1962.

32. Nelson, *Ozzie,* pp. 253–254.

33. Lyle White, "Tony Dow—TV's Favorite Big Brother," *Progress,* December 1962.

34. No doubt, just as many fan letters were sent to film stars as to television stars, but those letters are generally unavailable as film studios did not collect them—feature-film mail was sent to agents, studios, film magazines, and the stars directly. In contrast, the networks operated as a sort of receptacle for all mail, making it more available for scholarly study.

    There is reason to believe that letters written by television fans are unique in tone and content. First, film stars acted in a number of different films, and letters to Sandra Dee or Rock Hudson focused on the star and the star's persona, not on the actor's character in a particular film. Second, while fans felt perfectly comfortable writing to the head of a network or station, few sent letters to the head of a major studio. Perhaps because television came into the home and the viewer felt she or he had a certain proprietary relationship with the product, perhaps because of the immediacy of the viewing experience and their potential to influence the coming weeks' episodes, and perhaps because of the perceived unity among network, program, star, and performer-based commercial (the endless seam that Raymond Williams describes as the television text), television viewers used fan letters as a forum for voicing complaints, suggesting story lines, or noting the personal impact of a particular episode.

35. Bob Eddy, "Private Life of a Perfect Papa," p. 176.

36. Hilary R. Skees to the "President of ABC," 15 January 1962, Barbara Billingsley personal collection.

37. Jane Wyatt, telephone interview with author, 9 May 1989. Wyatt once received a letter from a fan who was irate about the way she ironed on the program. Wyatt says she actually looked up ironing in a housekeeping book to make sure she had it right and continued to do it the same way.

38. "P.S. We Want Father!" *TV Guide*, 3 September 1955, 21.

39. Ellis, *Visible Fictions*, p. 136.

40. While the analysis herein clearly demonstrates the insecurity of these television families, I wish to stress that they were initially *marketed* and *received* by the general viewership as "happy" and "ideal." It is only with the application of a more rigorous reading that we can locate the undercurrents of despair and anxiety that plagued these familial groups.

41. The bulk of television-set ownership during this time period was by the so-called middle and lower classes. By 1959 TV was available to 90 percent of all American homes, with actual ownership levels at 70.2 percent. According to *The Film Daily Year Book,* which separated ownership by class (although it did not define specifically how much income defined each class level), the middle class owned 71 percent of all television sets in 1959. Statistics for 1960–1962 are as follows: In 1960 TV reached 85.1 percent of the total U.S. population; 11.5 percent of television owners were upper class, 71 percent were middle class, and 17.5 percent were lower class. In 1961 the ownership by class was the same as in 1960. In 1962 statistics no longer showed class ownership as a percentage of the total, but showed how much of each class owned a TV. Eighty-two percent of the lower class owned televisions, 96 percent of the middle class owned televisions, and only 25 percent of the upper class owned televisions. *The Film Daily Year Book,* 1960–1963.

These figures must be regarded with some caution; the U.S. typically defines itself as "classless." With no true income figures reported, the terms upper, middle, and lower class cannot be defined.

42. "Terri" to Robert Young, Eugene Rodney Collection.

43. Rogers, interview.

4 Rules and Regulations

1. In 1952 the U.S. Supreme Court ruled in *Burstyn v Wilson* that films were "a significant medium for the communication of ideas"; as such, they were protected as free speech under the First Amendment to the Constitution. See Richard S. Randall, "Censorship: From *The Miracle* to *Deep Throat,*" in *The American Film Industry,* ed. Tino Balio, pp. 510–536.

2. A number of thorough histories of the genesis and operation of the Motion Picture Production Code exist. See Balio, *American Film Industry;* Randall, *Censorship of the Movies;* Bordwell, Thompson, and Staiger, *Classical Hollywood Cinema.*

3. After 1945 the MPPDA formally changed its name to the MPAA (Motion Picture Association of America), dropping the word "distributor" from its organizational title.

4. Roger Manvell, "The Cinema and Society," in *Film and Society,* ed. Richard Dyer MacCann, pp. 94–95.

5. Richard Dyer MacCann, *Hollywood in Transition,* p. 29.

6. *Film Daily,* vol. 110, no. 112, 12 December 1956, pp. 1, 5, 8–9.

7. The section states: "ix. Special subjects—The following subjects must be treated with discretion, restraint or within careful limits of good taste.

    1. Bedroom scenes

    2. Hangings and electrocutions

    3. Liquor and drinking

    4. Surgical operations and childbirth

    5. Third degree methods."

Ibid.

8. In 1957 *Variety* reported that the MPAA was considering a modified rating system, to be enforced by the PCA. Quoting an unnamed source, the article stated: "The Code can no longer guarantee that each and every film will be suitable for the whole audience, young and old, narrow and broad-minded." Fred Hift, "Mull Pix Classification System," *Variety*, 1957.

9. Hagerty, "Censorship," pp. 72, 74.

10. The acceptance of homosexuality as subject matter provides an interesting example of the balance between economics and public appeasement carefully maintained by the industry. Remarking on these 1961 changes, Richard S. Randall notes that the impetus behind code relaxation was often economic: "The industry has long been charged with manipulating the code . . . to suit its own ends. For example, some critics observe that the code revision in 1961 to allow homosexuality . . . was made *after* several major companies had gone into production with large-budget films dealing, at least in part, with homosexuality." Randall, *Censorship of the Movies*, pp. 205–206.

11. Indeed, as Thomas Schatz has noted, the PCA was in many ways a response to the Legion of Decency.

12. Randall, *Censorship of the Movies*, p. 186.

13. Mark Thomas McGee and R. J. Robertson, *The J. D. Films*, pp. 46–47.

14. Carmen, *Movies, Censorship, and the Law*, 102.

15. *Film Daily*, clipping, 11 December 1956.

16. Geoffrey Shurlock, memo to "self" regarding *Blue Denim*, February 1958, Production Code Files, Margaret Herrick Library.

17. Jack Vizzard, memo to "self" regarding *Blue Denim*, April 1958, Production Code Files, Margaret Herrick Library.

18. *Film Daily*, clipping, no date.

19. "Softened Script in Abortion Theme; Pros and Cons Follow 'Blue Denim,'" *Variety*, 5 August 1959, 2, 78.

20. Ibid., p. 2.

21. Review of *Blue Denim*, *Variety*.

22. "Softened Script in Abortion Theme," p. 2.

23. "'Blue Denim' Ending Sad, Not Happy; Critics Crazy, Thinks Chas Brackett," *Variety*, 11 August 1959.

24. I am thinking here of the social dramas of *No Way Out* (1950), *To Sir with Love* (1967), and even *The Blackboard Jungle* (1955), all of which regarded the problem of racism and its solution as political and cultural rather than resolvable within the confines of matrimonial relationships.

25. In 1956 critic Lawrence Laurent noted: "[The] job of policing the content of television programming falls, almost by default, to the National Association of Radio and Television

Broadcasters. . . . The NARTB, then, is the industry's proof of self-regulation and self-policing of the industry. . . . Nearly all of the NARTB members subscribe to the Television Code of Good Practices. . . . The stations which subscribe to the Code are allowed to display the 'Seal of Good Practices.' This seal may be revoked—though none has ever been revoked at this writing—if the station refuses to desist from practices which violate the Code. The loss of the seal, however, does not appear to be particularly severe punishment, even if it were more than a theoretical possibility. . . . [F]ew members of the audience have ever heard of the [NARTB]." Laurent, "Commercial Television," pp. 148–149.

26. *International Television Almanac,* 1962, pp. 742–750. "Acceptability of Program Material" and "Decency and Decorum" were eliminated as categories in the 1962 *International Television Almanac* and condensed under the heading "General Program Standards." Included in the list as new categories were those prohibiting "deceptive program practices," added as a result of the quiz show scandals. No fewer than five rules dealing with game shows urged broadcasters to ensure that such contests were "genuine" and not "controlled by collusion." The "Continuing List" of section "a-iii" was also eliminated in the 1962 changes.

27. *International Television Almanac,* 1962, pp. 742–750.

28. For a good discussion of this, see Kathryn Montgomery, *Target: Prime Time; Advocacy Groups and the Struggle over Entertainment Television,* p. 13.

29. Ellis, *Visible Fictions,* p. 226.

30. John Whedon, telephone interview with author, 9 March 1989.

31. Henry Sharp, telephone interview with author, 19 March 1989.

32. McGreevey, letter.

33. Paul West, letter.

34. Frank Stanton, testimony before the FCC, 29 January 1960, CBS Files, Theatre Arts Library, UCLA.

35. FCC Interim Report, 1965, p. 371, quoted in Boddy, "From the 'Golden Age' to the 'Vast Wasteland,'" p. 301. See also FCC Report, 1960.

36. "Billion Dollar Whipping Boy," article by unnamed sponsor, *Television Age,* 4 November 1957, 29–31, quoted in Boddy, op. cit., p. 309.

37. Harry Castleman and Walter J. Podrazik, *Watching TV: Four Decades of American Television,* p. 130.

38. See Louis F. Jaffe, "The Scandal in TV Licensing," *Harper's,* September 1957, 79–84, which provides an excellent discussion of the FCC's practices in allocating licenses, how these practices affected owned-and-operated stations as well as affiliates, and the concomitant effect of these practices on programming.

39. In 1960, for example, the FCC issued a strong advisory on programming in its "Programming Policy Statement," which attempted to use this clause to justify its explicit suggestions regarding how broadcasters met their "public responsibility."

40. In 1961 a "conversation" between *TV Guide* and the chair of the FCC at that time, Newton Minow, focused on the industry's continuous debate over televised violence. *TV Guide* demanded that the government regulate network violence; Minow responded that the NAB was, in fact, doing an adequate job of censorship and that it was parents' duty to become more involved with their children's viewing habits. Newton H. Minow, "FCC's Reply to *TV Guide,*" in *TV Guide: The First 25 Years,* ed. J. S. Harris, p. 54.

41. Montgomery, *Target: Prime Time,* pp. 18–20. See this book for a thorough account of the development and impact of pressure groups.

42. A number of films depict the unfairness of the system or its immorality, including *East of*

Eden, All Fall Down, Splendor in the Grass, Executive Suite, The Man in the Gray Flannel Suit, and *The Catered Affair.*

43. In a line in the script for "Family Reunion" Jim says: "I remember when I was a kid, I put a little stone on a railroad track, and that little stone derailed a big freight." An undated NBC memo cautions: "[S]uggest you have Jim use some simile other than the stone on the railroad track or at least have him state it objectively, without himself as the culprit. This could be copied by a young viewer with disastrous results." In the episode as produced, Jim says, "It's a known fact that a little stone can derail a train." Undated NBC memo, Eugene Rodney Collection.

44. Interestingly, in all interviews I conducted with producers, writers, stars, and directors of these programs, individuals deny any resentment they might have had toward sponsor interference, recalling the president of Scott Paper, Campbell's Soup, Chevrolet, or Eastman-Kodak much as one would a benevolent, generous uncle. They recall no tampering with scripts and remember with fondness the end-of-the-year packages of paper goods or cans of soup that their cast and crew received from sponsors each year.

45. Levy, interview.

46. Wyatt, interview.

47. Nelson, *Ozzie,* pp. 241–242. Nelson also notes that the sponsorship of the American Dairy Association encouraged all those malt-shop scenes (p. 280).

48. Tony Stanford, memo to Sonny Chalif regarding "Time to Retire," 28 October 1959, Eugene Rodney Collection.

49. "Time to Retire," final script, Eugene Rodney Collection.

50. In its first season, *Father Knows Best* was sponsored by Raleigh/Kent cigarettes; Jim, cigarette foregrounded, debates a family problem. Perhaps because it was so contrary to his own instincts, Robert Young *does* remember this pressure: "I thought it was the dumbest act of the agency to put a cigarette sponsor on a family show. They insisted that I smoke." Young, interview.

51. Gene Nelson, personal interview with author, 22 March 1989.

52. The two had a chance to be awarded a "snazzy cabin cruiser, if we'd do a show featuring the boat, (name prominently exposed, of course). I got the assignment, but the script was never shot—something about network qualms." Davis, letter. Part of the reason *Leave It to Beaver* and *My Three Sons* reveal far fewer instances of direct sponsorship interference may have been their lack of an "agency of record." In the advertising world, an agency of record is appointed by the sponsor as an official representative of the company. For example, BBD&O was the agency of record for Campbell's Soup in their sponsorship of *The Donna Reed Show;* it was BBD&O's responsibility to be Campbell's watchdog on the set. The primary sponsors of *Leave It to Beaver*—Remington Rand and Polaroid—did not have agencies of record for the program because they sponsored a lot of other programs through "scatter buys." Rather than do a "program buy" of one thirty-minute comedy, for example, these companies (operating as most advertisers do today) purchased sixty-second spots on many different programs.

5 Power Plays

1. Leonard Benson, *Fatherhood, A Sociological Perspective,* p. 16. Inherent in this concept of power is the notion of "authority," that is, legitimized power, or the admitted right to rule and govern, make decisions, and enforce obedience. This concept of power explicitly precludes any notions held by Plato's Thrasymachus—namely, that "might is right."

2. See, for example, "The Male Ego" (1958–1959).

3. In his autobiography, Ozzie Nelson mentions that he organized the program's episodes so that each would take place on a weekend, in order to explain why Ozzie was home. See Nelson, *Ozzie*, pp. 197–198.

4. Ozzie Nelson even operates as a "neighborhood father," counseling his sons' friends as well. See, for example, "David Writes a Column" (1953–1954), "The Runaways," (1958–1959), "The Pony" (1958–1959), "The Backyard Pet Show" (1961–1962), and "Ten for the Tigers" (1961–1962).

5. Interestingly, Cliff is portrayed by actor Fred MacMurray, whose intrusive parenting techniques in the television program *My Three Sons* seem just the ticket to cure the problems of the fictional Groves family.

6. Importantly, in the radio precursor, the title was followed by a question mark, intended originally as an ironic statement.

7. In the first two years of the program, the Cleaver home did not have a study, and Ward's desk was situated in front of bookshelves in the living room.

8. See David Marc, *Comic Visions: Television Comedy and American Culture*, pp. 56–59, for a complete discussion of "A Medal for Margaret." Other episodes featuring Margaret's crisis of confidence about her status as homemaker are analyzed in Chapter 6, in which these issues are addressed comprehensively.

9. These episodes are discussed at length in Chapter 6; I cite them here as evidence that there are power gradations within the category of narrative focus.

10. See the following analysis of explicit power for a full discussion of these texts.

11. There is an explicit letter regarding this for the transformation of the novel *Peyton Place* into the film. Producer Jerry Wald notes: "[Director Mark] Robson and I are quite concerned about the Makris [Rossi] role. . . . Now that the script has been rewritten so that this role has equal importance and footage to the role of Connie, we think we should be able to attract an important star for this part." Jerry Wald to Lew Schrieber, 1957, Mark Robson Collection, Theater Arts Library, UCLA.

12. For a full discussion of this film see Nina Leibman, "The Way we Weren't: Abortion 1950's Style in *Blue Denim* and *Our Time*," *The Velvet Light Trap* no. 29 (spring 1992): 31–42.

13. The relationship between mothers and children will be thoroughly addressed in Chapter 6.

14. Martha Vicinis, *Suffer and Be Still*, p. 113.

15. Forty of the forty-nine films focus on the father-son relationship.

16. Sometimes, though rarely, the resolution is not forthcoming. In *Home From the Hill* Wade is dying; illegitimate son Rafe begs his father to finally recognize him: "I've waited my whole life to hear you say . . . 'my son,'" but Wade dies before fulfilling the request. Rafe is recognized as a Hunnicutt only after his father's death, when Wade's wife Hannah marks his grave with "father of Raphael and Theron." In *Tea and Sympathy* the reconciliation (or lack thereof) is elided, as the last filmic moment between Tom and Harold occurs with Harold's angry exit.

17. The potency of this sort of fatherly failing is noteworthy because of the "real-world" discussions it merits in sociological works. For example, Kenneth Keniston noted in 1963 that the "gentleman's agreement" between generations that neither will interfere with the other creates problems: "One of these problems appears very vividly in the *absence of paternal exemplars* in many contemporary plays, novels, and films. One of the characteristic facts about most of our modern heroes is that they have no fathers—or, when they do have

fathers, these are portrayed as inadequate or in some other way as psychologically absent. Take Augie March or Holden Caulfield, . . . or consider the leading character in a film like *Rebel without a Cause*. None of them has a father who can act as a model or for that matter as a target of overt rebellion. The same is true, though less dramatically, for a great many young people today." Kenneth Keniston, "Social Change and Youth in America," in *Youth: Change and Challenge*, ed. Erik Erikson, p. 172.

18. See Joan Mellen, *Big Bad Wolves: Masculinity in the American Film*, p. 215; and Peter Biskind, *Seeing is Believing: How Hollywood Taught Us to Stop Worrying and Love the Fifties*, p. 208.

19. Indeed, part of the teenagers' frustration stems from their knowledge that while they are the voice of convention and morality, they have no power to enforce it.

20. Interestingly, while the girls begin their relationship by feuding, they are united, in part, during a discussion of teen idols, including the ultimate "family" boy, Ricky Nelson.

21. In yet another example of the primacy of the father-child relationship, "The New Mother" reiterates that an attentive father is far preferable to Major Barker's pending remarriage to a career woman. As soon as his fiancée expresses her wish that David remain at the military academy so that the newlyweds might better adjust to marriage, the major breaks off the relationship, in essence punishing the woman for a practice he has long maintained himself.

22. See "The Parting of the Ways" (1958–1959) and "A Difference of Opinion" (1959–1960).

23. Althusser, "Ideology and Ideological State Apparatuses," pp. 23–70.

24. Biskind, *Seeing is Believing*, p. 199.

25. Newcomb, *TV: The Most Popular Art*, p. 55.

26. Indeed, heterosexual coupling is deemed more important than any institutional guidance; Bud's union with Angelina and Deanie's pending marriage to John are the true harbingers of their newfound mental health in *Splendor in the Grass*; in *David and Lisa* the central characters find their cure in one another; and Jim and Judy grow up as they grow together in *Rebel without a Cause*.

27. In "Tales of Sound and Fury" Elsaesser discusses the irony of pitting the domestic against the industrial in films which cater to upper-middle-class values. Most of the environments would be severely impoverished were it not for the fathers working just those kinds of hours which preclude familial involvement.

28. Applebaum, *The World According to Beaver*, p. 167.

29. I am using an extremely broad definition of juvenile delinquency. During this period definitions of delinquency included young people involved with crime (gangs, petty thievery, vandalism, street fights), as well as those who were merely enamored of the cultural trappings of a rebellious lifestyle (rock-and-roll music, fast cars and motorcycles, distinct hairdos and clothing).

30. Rick's first hit, a remake of Fats Domino's "I'm Walkin'," was initially performed on an April 1957 episode called "Ricky, the Drummer." For a good account of the genesis of Ricky's interest in a professional musical career, see Nelson, *Ozzie;* Sara Davidson, "A Nice Normal Family," in her *Real Property;* and the television tribute *Rick Nelson: A Brother Remembers*, produced by David Nelson, Disney Channel, 1988.

31. It is important to note here that while the television heroes engage in potentially delinquent behavior, they themselves are not the bad guys; indeed, Chip, Bud, Beaver, and Jeff function as police officers, doing battle against the real (usually offscreen) delinquents. The catalyst for fighting is similar to that in the theatrical films (a bad kid taunts the hero), but in the

films the young person joins in the battle and hides his involvement from his parents, while in the television programs, the parents and the young join together to rid society of a malcontent.

32. It is impossible to escape the intertextual references in this episode. "Gil Thornberry" sounds ironically like "Wil Thornberry," David Nelson's best friend in *The Adventures of Ozzie and Harriet,* and, of course, Tony Dow played the clean-as-a-whistle Wally Cleaver in *Leave It to Beaver.*

33. For a thorough and compelling analysis of Hollywood's social-problem films, see Peter Roffman and Jim Purdy, *The Hollywood Social Problem Film.*

34. For two interesting alternate readings of the issue of race and class in this film, see Michael E. Selig, "Contradiction and Reading: Social Class and Sex Class in *Imitation of Life,*" *Wide Angle* 10, no. 4 (1988): 13–23; and Marina Hueng, "What's the Matter with Sara Jane?: Daughters and Mothers in Douglas Sirk's *Imitation of Life,*" *Cinema Journal* 26, no. 3 (1987): 21–43.

35. Hammer Avedon, interview.

36. Interestingly, when the idealistic Kathy begs her father to defend the gardener, Jim *defends* Charley's remarks as merely ignorant rather than malevolent.

37. George Lipsitz, "The Meaning of Memory: Family, Class and Ethnicity in Early Network Television," *Camera Obscura* no. 16 (January 1988): 80–81.

38. Ibid., pp. 85, 106.

6 Boys and Girls Together

1. See, for example, *Bernardine* and *There's Always Tomorrow.*

2. Brandon French has noted a real-world impetus to such domestic emphases: "A comparable worship of domesticity arose during the nineteenth century in reaction against the movement for women's suffrage. . . . This reactionary counterforce, in both the nineteenth century and in the fifties, was merely evidence of the threat that women's emancipation posed to the collective imagination of the culture during these transitional times, and perhaps the best evidence that the emancipation was gaining ground." Brandon French, *On the Verge of Revolt: Women in American Films of the Fifties,* p. 113.

3. Because careerism is always discussed in relationship to a failed maternal function, I discuss it in the upcoming section, "Matriarchy and Patriarchy."

4. In asserting this cause-effect relationship between sexual immaturity and homosexuality I am depending upon Freud's interpretation of homosexuality as a form of narcissism. This reading of the film is predicated on both general psychoanalytic film theory and that being voiced specifically within the text of the film, in which Violet is held accountable by Dr. John Cuckorwicz. See Sigmund Freud, *Three Essays on the Theory of Sexuality,* trans. James Strachey, pp. 2–15.

5. See the upcoming section, "Matriarchy and Patriarchy."

6. Rodowick, "Madness, Authority, and Ideology," p. 272.

7. For a lengthy analysis of the various sexual encounters and their concomitant results, see Leibman, "Sexual Misdemeanor/Psychoanalytic Felony," *Cinema Journal* 26, no. 2 (1987): 26–38.

8. In *Blue Denim* Janet makes explicit her guilt, saying, "It was my fault. I liked him more than he liked me."

9. It is important to remember the fine and somewhat contradictory line walked by sexually

active wives. While they must curb their passions and never initiate sex, they must also be ardent in response to their husbands.

10. For a useful discussion of the dynamics in the southern family drama, see Thomas Schatz, *Hollywood Genres,* p. 237.

11. Betty Friedan, "Television and the Feminine Mystique," in Harris, *TV Guide: The First 25 Years,* p. 95.

12. Hammer Avedon, interview; Fabares, interview; Petersen, interview; Donna Reed's widower, Col. Grover Asmus III, interview with author, 16 March 1989; and Monaster, telephone interview.

13. Donna Reed, handwritten memo concerning "Mary for President" by Phil Leslie, 11 June 1958, personal collection Col. Grover Asmus III.

14. See "The Career Woman" (1959–1960).

15. See "Mary's Crusade" (1959–1960) and "Donna Plays Cupid" (1958–1959).

16. With its all-male cast, *My Three Sons* does, ironically and consistently, foreground issues of proper gender duties and traits. Because all of these discussions are couched in terms of the gender battles between men and women, they are analyzed in the upcoming section, "Matriarchy and Patriarchy."

17. Don Fedderson, telephone interview with author, 9 September 1987.

18. See, for example, "Woman's Work," and "Here Comes Charley," both from the 1964–1965 season.

19. It is rare in the world of television or film melodrama for a career woman to have a vocation outside of traditional "women's fields." In *Imitation of Life* and *The Thrill of it All,* for example, Lora and Beverly are actresses; in *There's Always Tomorrow* and "The Career Woman," a 1959–1960 episode of *The Donna Reed Show,* the women work in fashion; in the 1962–1963 episode "Daughter for a Day" on *My Three Sons* Elizabeth Hill is an expert on home economics. In episodes in which the woman's career falls within the "masculine" fields of medicine, engineering, or law, there is always an appropriate moment of shock as well as mistaken identity when the other characters learn of her employment—see, for example, from *My Three Sons,* "Lady Engineer" (1960–1961), "Doctor in the House" (1962–1963), and "Lady President" (1964–1965); from *Father Knows Best,* "An Extraordinary Woman" (1958–1959); and from *The Adventures of Ozzie and Harriet,* "The Lawyers' Convention" (1963–1964).

20. The child's dual assertion that the femaleless Douglas family is a "real" family and that her own upbringing (by her obviously loving and capable mother) is deficient normalizes the all-male household while simultaneously castigating divorce, single mothers, and women in general.

21. Conversation between the Winters children and Cynzia, the maid and ersatz mother of *Houseboat.*

22. I am grateful to Mimi White, who pointed out this reading to me.

23. The statement is particularly pertinent in that the film was released in 1963, the year in which Betty Friedan's *The Feminine Mystique* was published and the benchmark year for the second women's movement in America.

24. Robert S. Alley and Irby B. Brown, "The Family on Television," *The Caucus Quarterly* (August 1984): 26.

25. It is important to recognize the distinction here between Donna's general help around the office and her professional assistance as a nurse. The first job was threatening because Donna was, in effect, in charge of an entire sector of her husband's world—reorganizing

the bill-paying procedure, charting patients, and operating autonomously. In the second job she was literally at her husband's side and following his minute-by-minute orders.

26. Biskind, *Seeing is Believing,* 266.

27. "Barbara Billingsley's Advice to Homemakers," *TV Guide,* 25 February 1961, 10–11.

28. "Barbara Billingsley's Fashions," *TV Guide,* 13 May 1961, 224–225.

29. Philip Wylie, *A Generation of Vipers,* p. 50, quoted by Considine, *Cinema of Adolescence,* p. 208.

30. Strecker defines "mom" as "a convenient verbal hook upon which to hang an indictment of the woman who has failed in the elementary mother function of weaning her offspring emotionally as well as physically," and lists seven classifications of "mom": "'the common garden variety' of mom, the 'self-sacrificing' mom, the 'ailing' mom, the 'pollyanna' mom, the 'protective' mom, the 'pretty-addlepate' mom, and the 'pseudo-intellectual' mom." Edward A. Strecker, *Their Mother's Sons,* pp. 13, 54.

31. Strecker, *Their Mother's Sons,* p. 32.

32. Considine, *Cinema of Adolescence,* p. 62.

33. In his discussion of this episode, David Marc calls this "housewife hubris." *Comic Visions,* p. 58.

34. Ibid., p. 59.

35. It is crucial, of course, to remember all the episodes singing the praises of father (discussed in the previous chapter). In none of these stories do the children suffer any sort of anxiety or punishment for lauding the patriarchal function. Indeed, complications often arise because the children are not grateful enough. See, for example, "Ideal Father" (1958–1959).

36. Although Donna is a trained nurse, she is continually stymied by the most simple of medical problems, turning to Alex for help.

37. Patricia Mellencamp, "Situation Comedy, Feminism, and Freud, Discourse of Gracie and Lucy," in *Studies in Entertainment: Critical Approaches to Mass Culture,* ed. Tania Modleski, p. 81.

38. Darrell Hamamoto, "Television Situation Comedy and Post-War Liberal Ideology: 1950–1980," Ph.D. diss., pp. 70–71, since revised and published as *Nervous Laughter: Television Situation Comedy and Liberal Democratic Ideology* (New York: Praeger, 1989).

39. Friedan, "Television," p. 97.

40. Wyatt, interview.

41. Diana Meehan, *Ladies of the Evening: Women Characters of Prime-Time Television,* p. 37.

42. Haralovich, "Sitcoms and Suburbs," p. 79.

43. Grimsted, *Melodrama Unveiled,* p. 183.

44. "Television's Tight Little Band," *TV Guide* 11 January 1964: 21.

45. Ibid.

46. Haralovich, "Sitcoms and Suburbs," p. 79.

47. See Biskind, *Seeing is Believing,* particularly the chapter on mothers.

48. Benson, *Fatherhood,* p. 104.

49. This is a particularly interesting film, in which each child confronts the other's mother, Hilda yelling at Mrs. Burns and Russell criticizing Stella. Because the reunion of the couple depends on Russell's successful resolution of the Oedipal crisis, however, his mother must die (to let him transfer his affections to Hilda), while Mrs. Crane must merely be silenced, allowing her daughter to assume the maternal role.

50. It is true that Bart (Sylvia's husband and Johnny's father) is also left alone, destitute and alcoholic, but the specter of Ken as the perfect husband and father is strong enough to

cancel out the weak father image; indeed, Ken replaces him. Sylvia, on the other hand, is like Mollie, the seductress. When she says to the children "we live in a glass house, we're not throwing any stones," she reminds the spectator that it is women who accept the guilt publicly and who also do the seducing privately.

51. Strangely, in the sequel, *Return to Peyton Place,* Connie has forgotten her lessons of honest sexuality, condemning Alison's book as "cheap, dirty, and vulgar," and lecturing her daughter once again on propriety. Once again, at the end of the film, she must publicly admit her errors in order to reinstate herself into her daughter's good graces.

52. The patriarchal slant on the narrative is particularly strong here, because the mother hardly receives any affection. She does the children's bidding, follows their orders, and arranges her time around theirs, but is not recompensed with gratitude. What Norma Veil is arguing for is, first, that the children shower Dad with love and attention, and, second, that they act independently enough to allow Mom to go in that direction, too.

53. Interestingly, a film review of the period pointed out the double bind in which Marian Groves was caught: "The mother of a teenage family, if she neglects her children in order to remain a real lover and mate to her husband, may produce the tragedy of juvenile delinquency. And, if she yields to all the thoughtlessly selfish demands of her youngsters, the man she is married to must almost inevitably feel that he has been shunted into the position of being a mere provider of household comforts." Review of *There's Always Tomorrow.*

54. Mellen, *Big Bad Wolves,* pp. 236–237.

7 Family Finances

1. There are very few exceptions to this. Even in the cases of motherhood-careerism or the widowed father, film families do not suffer because of a misdivision of labor. Careerist mothers all have housekeepers to assist them, as do widowed fathers; children usually have no chores to do at all. The only film of those screened which actually targets a mother neglecting her housekeeping duties is *The Thrill of it All,* where Gerry claims the house is in chaos without his wife's supervision. The children and the home are actually functioning quite well; Gerry's anger at his wife and his jealousy of her success cause *him* to wreak havoc on the house—driving into a soap-filled swimming pool, for example.

2. Because, as discussed in the previous chapter, Mother is usually de-emphasized in the narrative, her participation in such outside activities is usually elided and referred to only after the fact, or as an indicator of her neglect of her more important stay-at-home functions: June is late making dinner because she had a PTA meeting, Donna's home is in turmoil when she runs for city council, and Margaret worries about, and then refers to, a speech on child-rearing she is never shown giving.

3. See *The Donna Reed Show,* "Alex Runs the House" (1959–1960), and *My Three Sons,* "Women's Work" (1964–1965).

4. Castleman and Podrazik, *Watching TV,* p. 119, quoted in Marc, *Comic Visions,* p. 52.

5. Applebaum, *The World According to Beaver,* p. 111.

6. Biskind, *Seeing is Believing,* p. 323.

7. Fedderson, interview.

8. Mark Crispen Miller, "Prime Time: Deride and Conquer," in *Watching Television: A Pantheon Guide to Popular Culture,* ed. Todd Gitlin, p. 197.

9. Nelson, *Ozzie,* pp. 197–198.

10. West, letter.

11. Review of *A Hatful of Rain, Hollywood Reporter,* 18 June 1957.

12. The Cleavers lived in two homes, which, as Haralovich has noted, were fairly different from each other. For the summation here, I will be referring to the Cleaver residence from 1959 to 1963, 211 Pine Street, the Universal Studios house and the one most familiar to viewers. Haralovich has done an extensive analysis of the floor plans of the homes of the Cleaver and Anderson families. See Haralovich, "Sitcoms and Suburbs," pp. 75–77.

13. Newcomb, *TV: The Most Popular Art,* pp. 29–30.

14. The fact that the furniture looked "used" was an important element of all the programs. For example, Jane Wyatt recalls a woman who approached her and demanded that "the Andersons" get a new davenport, since the shabby sofa was inferior to their living conditions. Ms. Wyatt explained that the purpose was for the furniture to look abused and comfortable and that if the furniture were "too new" looking, it wouldn't fit the aura of the program. Wyatt, interview.

15. *My Three Sons* was sponsored solely by Chevrolet during its first two years, and after that by Pontiac. Consequently, all the cars used on the program were of the make provided by the sponsor. The Douglas family car, as well as cars parked on the street or used by friends, were all provided by the sponsor, and therefore served as visual and continual advertising.

16. A crucial exception to this inconspicuous attire was the housewife's dress, heels, and pearls. Popular myth has claimed that the women's formal dress was deliberate and typical, but this was not quite the case. First, Donna, Margaret, and Harriet often wore slacks, and even June was seen in pants during the first two years of the program. Harriet, Margaret, and Donna nearly always wore flat shoes when doing housework, as did June for the first two years of the program. June's attire changed drastically in the 1959 season, when Tony Dow and Jerry Mathers grew so fast that actress Barbara Billingsley needed the heels for authoritative height. The pearls (worn consistently by June, but rarely by the other moms) were necessitated by lighting problems with Billingsley, whose slender neck created a distracting reflection. Barbara Billingsley, interview.

17. Molly Haskell, *From Reverence to Rape,* p. 160.

18. This analysis by no means contradicts the predominant theme of the rich daddy who neglects his son. Indeed, the argument between fathers and sons in the typical adolescent weepy scene consists of men who see themselves as hard-working upper-middle-class executives, who demonstrate their nouveau-riche attitude with the assortment of "things" they purchase, and who feel that their tenuous foothold in the upper class demands their continued vigilance.

19. This valuation of the middle class is discussed in the next section.

20. It is significant that Bud's financial dilemmas always stem from his attempts to impress the opposite (evil) sex.

21. Interestingly, the Douglas family's consumerism is focused entirely on automobiles, a crucial point in light of their sponsorship by Chevrolet (1960–1964) and Pontiac (1964 onward).

22. I am grateful to Tom Schatz for pointing out this thematic principle.

23. Richard De Cordova, "A Case of Mistaken Legitimacy: Class and Generational Difference in Three Family Melodramas," in *Home is Where the Heart Is,* ed. Christine Gledhill, p. 265.

24. John Fisk and John Hartley, *Reading Television,* p. 102.

25. Cooper Foote, letter.

26. T. B. Bottomore, *Classes in Modern Society,* p. 103, quoted in Darrell Hamamoto, p. 57.

27. This is in sharp contrast to a Gothic film—such as *Rebecca* (1940), for example—in which

the disadvantaged young bride becomes the new mistress of the mansion, ascending into the wealthy class and usually suffering for it. It is also quite distinct from melodrama's turn-of-the-century roots, wherein it was the wealthy class, not the middle class, that was valued, and whose emphasis on peripitous elevation of status belied melodrama's supposedly classless outlook. Grimsted notes: "Such [class-oriented] twists of plot . . . [contradicted] melodrama's egalitarian argument. All the talk about nature's nobleman and love leveling all differences rang hollow when the dramatists felt obliged to resort to such absurdities [as paupers turning out to be princes] to salvage class distinctions. In part the convention showed democracy's ambivalence toward class distinctions, but, perhaps more importantly, the revelation that the peasant hero was really a prince suggested the excitement and surprises that life might have in store for anyone." Grimsted, *Melodrama Unveiled*, p. 209.

28. Tom's initial response is, "I try, if I can get them away from the television set." Ralph responds: "Kick it in and throw it away." This blast at television as yet another reason for family isolation is fairly common in 1950's film-family melodrama. In *No Down Payment* Troy kicks in the television set in frustration and Isabel can't get Mike away from the TV to eat his lunch. In *All That Heaven Allows* Carey Scott's children present her with a television set as a surrogate friend and lover; the visual image of her reflection in the cold, dark screen has been discussed extensively as a criticism of film's chief economic competitor.

29. Crucially, Tom has inherited a great deal of land from his grandmother and, with his wife's business acumen, will subdivide it into a housing tract and make a fortune. It is relatively simple for Tom to live by the principle of fewer working hours when he is making additional income without doing any additional work.

30. Jim Anderson—like Tom Rath in *The Man in the Gray Flannel Suit*—can afford, quite literally, to be smug. His limited work schedule has nonetheless provided him with a beautiful, spacious home in a well-apportioned neighborhood; he will send his children effortlessly to college; his furniture and other material possessions are up to date and in good working condition.

8 Conclusion

1. This scene, in which Mr. Loomis tells Deanie of Bud's whereabouts despite Frieda's neurotic protests, is unfailingly met with applause every time I screen it for a college audience.

2. Ernie's status as outsider was granted the ultimate in melodramatic excess when his family was killed in a car accident and he was adopted by the Douglas family. Once he became one of the three sons of the title, replacing Mike in 1965, he could no longer be as troublesome, and new guest-stars were required to bear the burden of rebellion.

3. Of course, my sisters and I watched both programs, mainly because of the romantic appeal of the leading men.

Bibliography

Books

Adler, Richard. *Television as Cultural Force*. New York: Praeger, 1976.

Allen, Jeanne. "The Social Matrix of Television: Invention in the United States." In *Regarding Television*, ed. E. Ann Kaplan, pp. 109–119. Los Angeles: American Film Institute, 1983.

Allen, Robert C. *Speaking of Soap Operas*. Chapel Hill: University of North Carolina Press, 1985.

Althusser, Louis. "Ideology and Ideological State Apparatuses." In his *Lenin and Philosophy,* pp. 23–70. New York: Monthly Review Press, 1971.

Altman, Rick. "Television Sound." In *Studies in Entertainment: Critical Approaches to Mass Culture,* ed. Tania Modleski, pp. 39–54. Bloomington: Indiana University Press, 1986.

Anderson, Christopher. "Negotiating the Television Text: The Transformation of *Warner Bros. Presents.*" In *Making Television: Authorship and the Production Process,* ed. Robert Thompson and Gary Burns, pp. 95–116. New York: Praeger, 1990.

Applebaum, Irwin. *The World according to Beaver*. New York: Bantam Books, 1984.

"As We See It: An Open Letter to Newton H. Minow, New Chairman of the Federal Communications Commission." In *TV Guide: The First 25 Years*, ed. J. S. Harris, p. 54. New York: New American Library, 1980. Originally published in *TV Guide*, 8 April 1961.

Balio, Tino, ed. *The American Film Industry*. Madison: University of Wisconsin Press, 1985.

———, ed. *Hollywood in the Age of Television*. Cambridge, Mass.: Unwin Hyman, 1990.

Barnouw, Erik. *The Sponsor: Notes on a Modern Potentate*. New York: Oxford University Press, 1978.

———. *Tube of Plenty: The Evolution of American Television*. New York: Oxford University Press, 1975.

Barthes, Roland. *Image, Music, Text*. New York: Hill and Wang, 1975.

———. *S/Z*. New York: Hill and Wang, 1974.

Baughman, James L. "The Weakest Chain and the Strongest Link." In *Hollywood in the Age of Television,* ed. Tino Balio, pp. 91–114. Cambridge, Mass.: Unwin Hyman, 1990.

Benson, Leonard. *Fatherhood, A Sociological Perspective*. New York: Random House, 1968.

Besen, S. M. *Misregulating Television: Network Dominance and the FCC*. Chicago: University of Chicago Press, 1984.

Biskind, Peter. *Seeing is Believing: How Hollywood Taught Us to Stop Worrying and Love the Fifties*. New York: Pantheon, 1983.

Boddy, William. *Fifties Television: The Industry and Its Critics.* Urbana and Chicago: University of Illinois Press, 1990.

———. "From the 'Golden Age' to the 'Vast Wasteland': The Struggles over Market Power and Dramatic Formats in 1950's Television." Ph.D. diss., New York University, 1984.

Bordwell, David, Kristin Thompson, and Janet Staiger. *The Classical Hollywood Cinema.* New York: Columbia University Press, 1985.

Bottomore, T. B., *Classes in Modern Society.* New York: Vintage Books, 1966.

Brooks, Peter. *The Melodramatic Imagination: Balzac, Henry James, Melodrama, and the Mode of Excess.* New York: Columbia University Press, 1985.

Brooks, Tim, and Earle Marsh. *The Complete Directory to Prime Time Network Television Shows.* New York: Ballantine, 1981.

Byars, Jackie. *All That Hollywood Allows: Re-Reading Gender in 1950s Melodrama.* Chapel Hill: University of North Carolina Press, 1990.

———. "Gender Representation in American Family Melodramas of the 1950s." Ph.D. diss., University of Texas, 1983.

Cahiers du Cinéma, "Young Mr. Lincoln." In *Movies and Methods I,* ed. Bill Nichols, pp. 493–528. Berkeley: University of California Press, 1976. Originally published in Cahiers du Cinéma no. 223 (1970).

Campbell, Robert. *The Golden Years of Broadcasting: A Celebration of the First 50 Years of Radio and Television on NBC.* New York: Scribners, 1976.

Cantor, Muriel. "Audience Control." In *Television: The Critical View,* 3d ed., ed. Horace Newcomb, pp. 311–334. New York: Oxford University Press, 1982.

Carmen, Ira H. *Movies, Censorship, and the Law.* Ann Arbor: University of Michigan Press, 1966.

Carroll, Noël, "The Family Plot and Magnificent Obsession." In *Melodrama,* ed. Daniel C. Gerould, pp. 197–206. New York: New York Literary Forum, 1980.

Castleman, Harry, and Walter J. Podrazik. *Watching TV: Four Decades of American Television.* New York: McGraw-Hill, 1984.

Cawelti, John G. *Adventure, Mystery, and Romance: Formula Stories as Art and Pop Culture.* Chicago: University of Chicago Press, 1976.

Ciment, Michel. *Kazan on Kazan.* London: Secker and Warburg, 1973.

Cole, Barry, and Mal Oettinger. *Reluctant Regulators: The FCC and the Broadcast Audience.* Reading, Mass.: Addison-Wesley, 1978.

Conant, Michael. *Antitrust in the Motion-Picture Industry.* Berkeley: University of California Press, 1960.

Considine, David M. *The Cinema of Adolescence.* Jefferson, N.C.: McFarland, 1985.

Cowan, Geoffrey. *See No Evil: The Backstage Battle over Sex and Violence on Television.* New York: Simon and Schuster, 1979.

Dalton, David. *James Dean: American Icon.* New York: St. Martin's, 1984.

———. *James Dean: The Mutant King.* New York: Dell, 1974.

Davidson, Sara. "A Nice Normal Family." In her *Real Property,* pp. 113–140. New York: Pocket Books, 1971, 1981.

De Cordova, Richard. "A Case of Mistaken Legitimacy: Class and Generational Difference in Three Family Melodramas." In *Home Is Where the Heart Is: Studies in Melodrama and the Woman's Film,* ed. Christine Gledhill, pp. 255–267. London: British Film Institute, 1987.

Doane, Mary Ann, Patricia Mellencamp, and Linda Williams, eds. *Re-Vision, Essays in Feminist Film Criticism.* Los Angeles: American Film Institute, 1984.

Doherty, Thomas. *Teenagers and Teenpics: The Juvenilization of American Movies in the 1950s.* Cambridge, Mass.: Unwin Hyman, 1988.

Dombkowski, Dennis J. "Film and Television: An Analytical History of Economic and Creative Integration." Ph.D. diss., University of Illinois, 1982.

Donzelot, Jacques. *The Policing of Families.* New York: Pantheon, 1979.

Efron, Edith. "Television: America's Timid Giant." In *TV Guide: The First 25 Years,* ed. J. S. Harris, pp. 75–78. New York: New American Library, 1980. Originally published in *TV Guide,* 18 May 1963.

Eisner, Joel, and David Krinsky. *Television Comedy Series: An Episode Guide to 153 TV Sitcoms in Syndication.* Jefferson, N.C.: McFarland, 1984.

Eliot, Marc. *American Television, The Official Art of the Artificial.* New York: Doubleday, 1981.

Elliot, William Y. *Television's Impact on American Culture.* East Lansing: Michigan State University Press, 1956.

Ellis, John. *Visible Fictions: Cinema, Television, Video.* London: Routledge and Kegan Paul, 1982.

Facey, Paul W. *The Legion of Decency: A Sociological Analysis of the Emergence and Development of a Pressure Group.* New York: Arno, 1974.

Farber, Stephen. *The Movie Rating Game.* Washington, D.C.: Public Affairs Press, 1972.

Fass, Paula. "Television as Cultural Document: Promises and Problems." In *Television as a Cultural Force,* ed. Richard Adler, pp. xx–xx. New York: Praeger, 1976.

Feuer, Jane. *The Hollywood Musical,* 2d ed. Bloomington: Indiana University Press, 1993.

Fisk, John, and John Hartley. *Reading Television.* New York: Methuen, 1978.

Fletcher, James. *Handbook of Radio-TV Broadcasting: Research Procedures in Audience, Program, and Revenues.* New York: Van Nostrand-Reinhold, 1981.

French, Brandon. *On the Verge of Revolt: Women in American Films of the Fifties.* New York: Frederick Unger, 1978.

Freud, Sigmund. *The Interpretation of Dreams,* trans. James Strachey. New York: Avon Books, 1967.

———. *Three Essays on the Theory of Sexuality,* trans. James Strachey. New York: Basic Books, 1962.

Friedan, Betty. "Television and the Feminine Mystique." In *TV Guide: The First 25 Years,* ed. J. S. Harris, pp. 93–98. New York: New American Library, 1980. Originally published in two parts in *TV Guide,* 1 February 1964 and 8 February 1964.

Gerould, Daniel C. *American Melodrama.* New York: Performing Arts Journal Publications, 1983.

———. *Melodrama.* New York: New York Literary Forum, 1980.

Gianakos, Larry James. *TV Drama Series Programming: A Comprehensive Chronicle.* Metuchen, N.J.: Scarecrow, 1980.

Gitlin, Todd. "Prime Time Ideology: The Hegemonic Process in Television Entertainment." In *Television: The Critical View,* 3d ed., ed. Horace Newcomb, pp. 426–454. New York: Oxford University Press, 1982.

———, ed. *Watching Television: A Pantheon Guide to Popular Culture.* New York: Pantheon, 1986.

Gledhill, Christine, ed. *Home Is Where the Heart Is: Studies in Melodrama and the Woman's Film.* London: British Film Institute, 1987.

———. "The Melodramatic Field: An Investigation." In her *Home Is Where the Heart Is: Studies in Melodrama and the Woman's Film,* pp. 5–42. London: British Film Institute, 1987.

Goldman, Eric. *The Crucial Decade and After: America 1945–1960.* New York: Alfred Knopf, 1971.

Goodhardt, G. J., A. Ehrenberg, and M. Collins. *The Television Audience: Patterns of Viewing.* Farnsborough University, England: Saxon House, 1975.

Gow, Gordon. *Hollywood in the Fifties.* New York: Barnes, 1971.

Greenfield, Jeff. *Television: The First Fifty Years.* New York: Abrams, 1977.

Grimsted, David. *Melodrama Unveiled.* Chicago: University of Chicago Press, 1968.

Habegger, Alfred. *Gender, Fantasy, and Realism.* New York: Columbia University Press, 1982.

Halliday, Jon. *Sirk on Sirk.* London: Secker & Warburg in association with the British Film Institute, 1971.

Hamamoto, Darrell Y. *Nervous Laughter: Television Situation Comedy and Liberal Democratic Ideology.* New York: Praeger, 1989.

———. "Television Situation Comedy and Post-War Liberal Ideology: 1950–1980." Ph.D. diss., University of California, 1981.

Harris, J. S., ed. *TV Guide: The First 25 Years.* New York: New American Library, 1980.

Haskell, Molly. *From Reverence to Rape: The Treatment of Women in the Movies,* 2d ed. Chicago: University of Chicago Press, 1987.

Heath, Stephen. *Questions of Cinema.* Bloomington: Indiana University Press, 1981.

Heath, Stephen, and Patricia Mellencamp. *Cinema and Language.* Los Angeles: American Film Institute, 1983.

Hirsch, Paul M. "The Role of Television and Popular Culture in Contemporary Society." In *Television: The Critical View,* 3d ed., ed. Horace Newcomb, pp. 280–310. New York: Oxford University Press, 1982.

Johnson, Catherine E. *TV Guide 25 Year Index: By Author and Subject.* Radner, Pa.: Triangle Publications, 1979.

Jowett, Garth. *Film, The Democratic Art.* Boston: Little, Brown, 1976.

Kaplan, E. Ann. "Mothering, Feminism and Representation: The Maternal in Melodrama and the Woman's Film, 1910–1940." In *Home Is Where the Heart Is: Studies in Melodrama and the Woman's Film,* ed. Christine Gledhill, pp. 113–137. London: British Film Institute, 1987.

———. *Regarding Television.* Los Angeles: American Film Institute, 1983.

———. *Women and Film, Both Sides of the Camera.* New York: Methuen, 1983.

Keniston, Kenneth. "Social Change and Youth in America." In *Youth: Change and Challenge,* ed. Erik Erikson, pp. 161–187. New York: Doubleday, 1963.

Krasnow, Erwin, et al. *The Politics of Broadcast Regulation.* New York: St. Martin's, 1982.

Kuhn, Annette. "Women's Genres: Melodrama, Soap Opera, and Theory." In *Home Is Where the Heart Is: Studies in Melodrama and the Woman's Film,* ed. Christine Gledhill, pp. 309–349. London: British Film Institute, 1987.

———. *Women's Pictures: Feminism and Cinema.* London: Routledge and Kegan Paul, 1982.

Lang, Robert. *American Film Melodrama: Griffith, Vidor, Minnelli.* Princeton: Princeton University Press, 1989.

La Place, Maria. "Producing and Consuming in the Woman's Film: Discursive Struggle in *Now, Voyager.*" In *Home Is Where the Heart Is: Studies in Melodrama and the Woman's Film,* ed. Christine Gledhill, pp. 138–166. London: British Film Institute, 1987.

Larson, Allan. "Integration and Attempted Integration between the Motion Picture and Television Industries through 1956." Ph.D. diss., Ohio University, 1979.

Laurent, Lawrence. "Commercial Television: What Are Its Educational Possibilities and Limits?" In *Television's Impact on American Culture,* ed. William Y. Elliot, pp. 125–173. East Lansing: Michigan State University Press, 1956.

Lewis, Jon. *The Road to Romance and Ruin: Teen Films and Youth Culture.* New York: Routledge, Chapman and Hall, 1992.

MacCann, Richard Dyer, ed. *Film and Society.* New York: Charles Scribner's Sons, 1964.

————. *Hollywood in Transition.* Boston: Houghton Mifflin, 1962.

Manvell, Roger. "The Cinema in Society." In *Film and Society,* ed. Richard Dyer MacCann, pp. 241–252. New York: Charles Scribner's Sons, 1964.

Marc, David. *Comic Visions: Television Comedy and American Culture.* Boston: Unwin Hyman, 1989.

————. *Demographic Vistas: Television in American Culture.* Philadelphia: University of Pennsylvania Press, 1984.

————. "Screen Gems: Prime-Time Story-Telling." In *Making Television: Authorship and the Production Process,* ed. Robert Thompson and Gary Burns, pp. 137–144. New York: Praeger, 1990.

McCarthy, Todd, and Charles Flynn, eds. *Kings of the B's.* New York: E. P. Dutton, 1975.

McGee, Mark Thomas, and R. J. Robertson. *The J. D. Films.* London: McFarland, 1982.

Meehan, Diana. *Ladies of the Evening: Women Characters of Prime-Time Television.* Metuchen, N.J.: Scarecrow, 1983.

Mellen, Joan. *Big Bad Wolves: Masculinity in American Film.* New York: Pantheon, 1977.

Mellencamp, Patricia. "Situation Comedy, Feminism, and Freud, Discourse of Gracie and Lucy." In *Studies in Entertainment: Critical Approaches to Mass Culture,* ed. Tania Modleski, pp. 80–98. Bloomington: Indiana University Press, 1986.

Meyer, Martin. "The Impact of TV on Other Media," In *TV Guide: The First 25 Years,* ed. J. S. Harris, pp. 61–63, New York Library, 1980. Originally published in *TV Guide,* 21 July 1962.

Miller, Mark Crispen. "Prime Time: Deride and Conquer." In *Watching Television,* ed. Todd Gitlin, pp. 183–228. New York: Pantheon, 1986.

Minow, Newton H. "FCC's Reply to TV Guide." In *TV Guide: The First 25 Years,* ed. J. S. Harris, p. 54, New York Library, 1980. Originally published in *TV Guide,* 13 May 1961.

Mitz, Rick. *The Great TV Sitcom Book.* New York: Richard Marek, 1980.

Modleski, Tania, ed. *Studies in Entertainment: Critical Approaches to Mass Culture.* Bloomington: Indiana University Press, 1986.

Montgomery, Kathryn. *Target: Prime Time; Advocacy Groups and the Struggle over Entertainment Television.* New York: Oxford University Press, 1989.

Mulvey, Laura. "Melodrama Inside and Outside the Home." In her *Visual and Other Pleasures,* pp. 63–77. Bloomington: Indiana University Press, 1989. Originally published in Colin MacCabe, ed., *High Theory/Low Culture* (St. Martin's, 1986).

————. *Visual and Other Pleasures.* Bloomington: Indiana University Press, 1989.

————. "Notes on Sirk and Melodrama." In her *Visual and Other Pleasures,* pp. 39–44. Bloomington: Indiana University Press, 1989. Originally published in *Movie* no. 25 (1977): n.p.

Neale, Stephen. *Genre.* London: British Film Institute, 1980.

Nelson, Ozzie. *Ozzie.* Englewood Cliffs, N.J.: Prentice-Hall, 1973.

Newcomb, Horace, ed. *Television: The Critical View,* 3d ed. New York: Oxford University Press, 1982.

————. *TV: The Most Popular Art.* New York: Anchor-Doubleday, 1974.

Nichols, Bill, ed. *Movies and Methods I.* Berkeley: University of California Press, 1976.

Perkins, V. F. "The Cinema of Nicholas Ray." In *Movies and Methods I,* ed. Bill Nichols, pp. 251–261. Berkeley: University of California Press, 1976.

Randall, Richard S. "Censorship: From *The Miracle* to *Deep Throat*. In *The American Film Industry*, ed. Tino Balio, pp. 510–536. Madison: University of Wisconsin Press, 1985.

——. *Censorship of the Movies*. Madison: University of Wisconsin Press, 1968.

Rodowick, David N. "Madness, Authority and Ideology: The Domestic Melodrama of the 1950's." In *Home Is Where the Heart Is: Studies in Melodrama and the Woman's Film*, ed. Christine Gledhill, pp. 268–282. London: British Film Institute, 1987.

Roffman, Peter, and Jim Purdy. *The Hollywood Social Problem Film*. Bloomington: Indiana University Press, 1981.

Rosen, Marjorie. *Popcorn Venus*. New York: Avon Books, 1973.

Rosenblatt, Roger. "Growing Up on Television." In *Television: The Critical View*," ed. Horace Newcomb, pp. 373–385. New York: Oxford University Press.

Schatz, Thomas. *Hollywood Genres: Formulas, Filmmaking, and the Studio System*. New York: McGraw-Hill, 1981.

Sklar, Robert. *Movie-Made America: A Cultural History of American Movies*. New York: Random House, 1975.

Staehling, Richard. "From Rock Around the Clock to the Trip: The Truth about Teen Movies (1969)." In *King of the B's*, ed. Todd McCarthy and Charles Flynn, pp. 220–251. New York: E. P. Dutton, 1975.

Steiner, George. *The Death of Tragedy*. New York: Oxford University Press, 1961, 1980.

Strecker, Edward A. *Their Mothers' Sons*. Philadelphia: J. B. Lippincott, 1946.

Stuart, Frederic. *The Effects of Television on the Motion Picture Industries*. New York: Arno, 1975.

Taflinger, Richard. "Sitcom: A Survey and Findings of an Analysis of the TV Situation Comedy." Ph.D. diss., Washington State University, 1980.

Taylor, Ella. *Prime-Time Families: Television Culture in Postwar America*. Berkeley: University of California Press, 1989.

Thompson, Robert, and Gary Burns, eds. *Making Television: Authorship and the Production Process*. New York: Praeger, 1990.

Thorburn, David. "Television Melodrama." In *Television as Cultural Force*, ed. Richard Adler. New York: Praeger, 1976.

Vicinus, Martha. *Suffer and Be Still*. Bloomington: Indiana University Press, 1972.

Walker, Janet. "Hollywood, Freud, and the Representation of Women: Regulation and Contradiction, 1945–early 60's." In *Home Is Where the Heart Is: Studies in Melodrama and the Woman's Film*, ed. Christine Gledhill, pp. 197–216. London: British Film Institute, 1987.

Warner, Harry P. *Radio and Television Rights*. New York: Matthew Bender, 1953.

White, Timothy R. "Hollywood's Attempt at Appropriating Television: The Case of Paramount Pictures." In *Hollywood in the Age of Television*, ed. Tino Balio, pp. 145–164. Cambridge, Mass.: Unwin Hyman, 1990.

Wylie, Philip. *A Generation of Vipers*. New York: Holt, Rinehart and Winston, 1942.

Articles

"The abc of ABC." *Forbes*, 15 June 1959.

Alley, Robert S. and Irby B. Brown. "The Family on Television." *Caucus Quarterly* (August 1984): 17–27.

"Barbara Billingsley's Advice to Homemakers." *TV Guide*, 25 February 1961, 10–11.

"Barbara Billingsley's Fashions." *TV Guide*, 13 May 1961, 24–25.

Bassler, Paul. "Connelly's Kids Provide the Plots." Los Angeles *Herald Examiner, TV Weekly,* 24 February 1963.

"Beaver, Magnificent Moppet." *Catholic Preview of Entertainment* (August 1958): 20–22.

Bernstein, Fred. "Where Are They Now?" *People,* 4 May 1985, 96–103.

"The Big Lug Has Something." *TV Guide,* 17 August 1963, 15–17.

"Billingsley Returns to 'Beaver' Role." *TV Week Features,* 12 August 1984.

"Billion Dollar Whipping Boy." *Television Age,* 4 November 1957, 29–31.

"'Blue Denim' Ending Sad, Not Happy; Critics Crazy, Thinks Chas Brackett." *Variety,* 11 August 1959.

Brown, Judy. "Leave It to Bill: The Huxtables Are the Cleavers of the '80's." *L.A. Weekly,* 27 December 1985, 20.

Camper, Fred. "The Films of Douglas Sirk." *Screen* 12, no. 2, (Summer 1971): 44–62.

———. "The Tarnished Angels." *Screen* 12, no. 2 (Summer 1971): 68–93.

Crandell, Robert W. "The Postwar Performance of the Motion Picture Industry." *The Antitrust Bulletin* 20, no. 1 (Spring 1975): 49–85.

Dern, Marion. "Sweet, Sincere, and Solvent." *TV Guide,* 20 June 1964, 10–13.

Dunn, Angela Fox. "TV's Perfect Wife, Jane Wyatt Lashes Out at Modern Marriages." *Star,* 10 May 1983.

Eddy, Bob. "Private Life of a Perfect Papa." *Saturday Evening Post,* 27 April 1957.

Elsaesser, Thomas. "Tales of Sound and Fury: Observations of the Family Melodrama." *Monogram* no. 4 (1972): 12–15.

"An Expert on the Male." *TV Guide,* 25 February 1961.

"The Family Spirit." *TV Guide,* 24 December 1954, 17–19.

"Father Does Know Best—Robert Young Proves a TV Dad Doesn't Have to Be Stupid." *TV Guide,* 6 June 1956, 8–10.

Film Daily [article on Production Code changes] 110, no. 112 (12 December 1956).

Fitzgerald, John E. "The Indestructible Beaver." *St. Jude: A National Catholic Monthly,* January 1963, 24–29.

"The Girl Who Walks Alone." *Look,* 20 May 1958, 91–95.

Gomery, Douglas. "The Coming of Television and the 'Lost' Motion Picture." *The Journal of Film and Video* 37, no. 3 (summer 1985): 5–11.

Hagerty, Steward. "Censorship." *Show Business,* 28 November 1961.

Hall, Bob. "Beaver Series Merely Too True." Los Angeles *Herald and Express,* 14 February 1958.

Halliday, Jon. "All That Heaven Allows." *Monogram* no. 4 (1972): 30–32.

Haralovich, Mary Beth. "Sitcoms and Suburbs: Positioning the 1950's Homemaker." *Quarterly Review of Film and Video* 11, no. 1 (May 1989): 61–83.

———. "Suburban Family Sitcoms and Consumer Product Design: Addressing the Social Subjectivity of Homemakers in the 1950's." Paper presented at the International Studies Conference, London, July 1986.

Hift, Fred. "Mull Pix Classification System" *Variety,* 1957.

Hoffman, Irving, "Tales of Hoffman." *Hollywood Reporter,* 24 April 1952, 3.

Holland, Jack. "Need a Mother? Call Barbara." *TV Life,* 12 July 1958.

Horowitz, Susan. "Sitcom Domesticus: A Species Endangered by Social Change." *Channels,* September/October 1984.

Hueng, Marina. "What's the Matter with Sara Jane?: Daughters and Mothers in Douglas Sirk's *Imitation of Life.*" *Cinema Journal* 26, no. 3 (1987): 21–43.

Irvin, Bill. "She's Lived her TV Role." *Chicago American TV Pictorial*, 4 June 1961.

"It's Not Always Father Who 'Knows Best' for Backstage Problems." *TV Guide*, 16 February 1957, 17–19.

Jaffe, Louis F. "The Scandal in TV Licensing." *Harpers*, September 1957, 79–84.

"Jane Wyatt's Triple Threat." *Good Housekeeping*, October 1959, 48.

Johnson, Erslene. "They'll Leave it to Beaver Again for Third Year." *NEA Newsletter*, 6 November 1959.

Johnson, Rob. "What Makes Ricky Tick." *TV Guide*, 28 December 1957, 17–19.

Kern, Janet. "Success Was Built In." *Chicago American TV Pictorial*, 4 June 1961.

Leibman, Nina. "The Rock 'n Roller Coaster: Popular Music in 1950s Film and Television." Paper presented at the annual meeting of the University Film and Video Association, Bozeman, Mont., 1988.

———. "Sexual Misdemeanor/Psychoanalytic Felony." *Cinema Journal 26*, no. 2 (1987): 26–38.

———. "The Way We Weren't: Abortion 1950s Style in *Blue Denim* and *Our Time*." *Velvet Light Trap* no. 29 (Spring 1992): 31–42.

Lipsitz, George. "The Meaning of Memory: Family, Class and Ethnicity in Early Network Television." *Camera Obscura* no. 16 (January 1988): 79–118.

London, Michael. "Beaver Sinks Teeth into TV Reunion." Los Angeles *Times*, 19 September 1982.

Lowe, Herman. "How TV Affects the USA." *TV Guide*, 2 May 1954, 18–19.

MacKaye, Milton. "The Big Brawl: Hollywood vs. Television." Parts 1–3. *Saturday Evening Post*, 19 January 1952; 26 January 1952; 2 February 1952.

Matheson, Richard. "Religious Group Aids Movies in Claremont." Los Angeles *Times*, 19 January 1959.

"Men Are Getting Smarter." *TV Guide*, 13 November 1956, 4–6.

Miletich, Steve, and John Snell. "Leave it Two Beaver." *University of Washington Daily*, 2 June 1976, 14–16.

Miller, De M. "It's Tough Losing Your Innocence." *The Kansan*, 20 August 1982.

Mills, Nancy. "Donahue Returns to '50's as TV Mom." Los Angeles *Times*, 31 August 1987.

"More Than a Stick of Furniture." *TV Guide*, 29 June 1963, 16.

"Motion Picture Industry Should Stay Out of TV Programming." *TV Guide*, 12 January 1957, inside front cover.

"Movies Now Active in Telefield," *Radio-Television Daily*, 15 June 1954, 5, 7.

Mulvey, Laura. "Douglas Sirk and Melodrama." *Australian Journal of Screen Theory* no. 3 (1977): 26–30.

———. "Visual Pleasure and Narrative Cinema." *Screen* 16, no. 3 (1975): 6–18.

Nowell-Smith, Geoffrey. "Minnelli and Melodrama." *Australian Journal of Screen Theory* 3 (1977): 31–35.

———. "Minnelli and Melodrama." *Screen* (Summer 1977): 113–119.

Ohmer, Susan. "Like/Dislike/Like Very Much: Reception Theory and Audience Research of the 1940's." Paper presented at the annual meeting of the UFVA/Society for Cinema Studies Conference, 1988.

"Old Stars Making Love in Pix Opposed by Fans in U.S. Poll." *Hollywood Reporter*, 24 June 1957.

"Paul and Patty Petersen of *The Donna Reed Show*." Picture feature, *TV Guide*, 1 August 1964, 8–9.

Pedell, Kathy. "To Kiss or Not to Kiss." *TV Guide*, 21 August 1954, 4–6.

"Perversion in Pix De-Coded." *Variety*, 14 October 1961.

Petersen, Paul. "The Story of My Life." *16 Magazine*, January 1963, 4–5.

Porter, Thomas. "'Donna Reed Show' Making TV Comeback—As a Movie." *Enquirer*, n.d., n.p.

"P.S. We Want Father!" *TV Guide*, 3 September 1955, 20–21.

Ray, Nicholas. "Story into Script." *Sight and Sound* (Autumn 1956): 70–74.

"Reader's Poll." *16 Magazine*, November 1962.

Reddicliffe, Steven. "Beaver's Grown Up Now and May Get His Own Show." *Miami Herald*, 6 January 1982.

Rosenbaum, Jonathan, "Circle of Pain: The Cinema of Nicholas Ray." *Sight and Sound* (Autumn 1973): 218–221.

Scott, Vernon. "A Nice Normal Family." *TV Guide*, 21 September 1963, 10–13.

Selig, Michael E. "Contradiction and Reading: Social Class and Sex Class in *Imitation of Life*." *Wide Angle* 10, no. 4 (1988): 13–23.

"Shelley Fabares Answers 40 Intimate Questions." *16 Magazine*, November 1962.

"She's Still the Girl Next Door." *TV Guide*, 9 January 1960, 17–19.

"Softened Script in Abortion Theme; Pros and Cons Follow 'Blue Denim.'" *Variety*, 5 August 1959.

Spigel, Lynn. "Installing the Television Set: Popular Discourses on Television and Domestic Space, 1948–1955." *Camera Obscura* no. 16 (January 1988): 11–48.

Stengel, Richard. "When Eden Was in Suburbia." *Time*, 9 August 1982, 76.

Stern, Michael. "Patterns of Power and Potency, Repression and Violence: Sirk's Films of the 1950s." *Velvet Light Trap* (Fall 1976): 15–21.

"Teen-age Girls Our Best Customers." *Film Daily*, 19 February 1964.

"Television's Tight Little Band." *TV Guide*, 11 January 1964, 18–21.

"10 Things You Never Knew About Rick Nelson." *16 Magazine*, January 1963, 24.

"TV's Eager Beaver." *Look*, 27 May 1958, 67–70.

"TV's Mother's Days." *TV Guide*, 7 May 1954, 10–12.

White, Lyle. "Tony Dow—TV's Favorite Big Brother." *Progress*, December 1962.

Whitney, Dwight. "The Anatomy of Success." *TV Guide*, 31 July 1965, 15–18.

"Who Needs the Social Register?" *TV Guide*, 21 November 1955, 13–15.

"Why Father Still Has His Day." *TV Guide*, 14 June 1958, 17–20.

Willeman, Paul. "Distanciation and Douglas Sirk." *Screen* 12 no. 2 (Summer 1971): 63–67.

Winters, Georgia. "Stop Those Nasty Rumors About Rick." *16 Magazine*, August 1961.

Wood, Robin. "Film Favorites: Bigger Than Life." *Film Comment* (September–October 1972): 56–61.

"Wow! All Those Beautiful TV Wives!" *Chicago American TV Pictorial*, 19 February 1961.

Reviews

Amory, Cleveland. Review of *The Adventures of Ozzie and Harriet*. *TV Guide*, 6 June 1964, 3.

Amory, Cleveland. Review of *My Three Sons*. *TV Guide*, 7 May 1966, 26.

Canby, Vincent. Review of *Blue Denim*. *Motion Picture Daily*, 22 July 1959.

Gertner, Richard. Review of *Cat on a Hot Tin Roof*. *Motion Picture Daily*, 13 August 1958.

Gertner, Richard. Review of *No Down Payment*. *Motion Picture Daily*, 30 September 1957.

Leyendecker, Frank. Review of *Blue Denim*. *Box Office*, 3 August 1959.

Moffitt, Jack. Review of *Picnic*. *Hollywood Reporter*, 5 December 1955.

Moffitt, Jack. Review of *A Summer Place*. *Hollywood Reporter*, 7 October 1959.

Review of *About Mrs. Leslie*. *Variety*, 5 May 1954.

Review of *All Fall Down*. *Variety*, 26 May 1962.

Review of *All That Heaven Allows*. *Variety*, 26 October 1955.

Review of *Blue Denim*. *America*, 22 August 1959.

Review of *Blue Denim*. *Film Daily*, 21 August 1959.

Review of *Blue Denim*. *Hollywood Reporter*, 29 July 1959.

Review of *Blue Denim*. *Variety*, 29 July 1959.

Review of *The Courtship of Eddie's Father*. *Motion Picture Daily*, 4 April 1963.

Review of *The Courtship of Eddie's Father*. *Time*, 5 April 1963.

Review of *The Courtship of Eddie's Father*. *Variety*, 3 March 1963.

Review of *Father Knows Best*. *TV Guide*, 20 November 1954.

Review of *A Hatful of Rain*. *Hollywood Reporter*, 18 June 1957.

Review of *A Hatful of Rain*. *Variety*, 18 June 1957.

Review of *Leave It to Beaver*. *Variety*, 9 October 1957.

Review of *Magnificent Obsession*. *Variety*, 11 May 1954.

Review of *The Man in the Gray Flannel Suit*. *Hollywood Reporter*, 30 March 1956.

Review of *Marty*. *Variety*, 23 March 1955.

Review of *Never Say Goodbye*. *Variety*, 15 February 1956.

Review of *No Down Payment*. *Variety*, 30 September 1957.

Review of *Peyton Place*. *Variety*, 13 December 1957.

Review of *Picnic*. *Motion Picture Daily*, 5 December 1955.

Review of *Return to Peyton Place*. *Variety*, 1 May 1961.

Review of *Stranger in My Arms*. *Variety*, 11 March 1959.

Review of *A Summer Place*. *Variety*, 7 October 1959.

Review of *There's Always Tomorrow*. *Hollywood Reporter*, 12 January 1956.

Steen, Al. Review of *All That Heaven Allows*. *Motion Picture Daily*, 25 October 1955.

Trade Journals

Film Daily Year Book of Motion Pictures, 1957–1962. New York: Film and Television Daily.

Film Daily, vol. 110, no. 112, 12 December 1956.

International Television Almanac, 1956–1965. New York: Quigley Publications.

Motion Picture Almanac, 1953–1965. New York: Quigley Publications.

Primary and Nonprint Sources

Alley, Robert S., and Irby B. Brown. "Genuine or Counterfeit?: Television's Portrayal of the American Family." Virginia Public Television, 1984.

Audience Files, The Margaret Herrick Library, Academy of Motion Picture Arts and Sciences.

CBS Files, Theater Arts Library, University of California at Los Angeles.

Eugene Rodney Collection, Theater Arts Library, University of California at Los Angeles.

FCC Interim Report, 1960.

FCC Interim Report, 1965.

Hallonquist, Tore. CBS-TV Research Department Program Analysis Division Report No. 20-57, August 1957. Arnold Becker's personal files.

Mark Robson Collection, Theatre Arts Library, University of California at Los Angeles.

Nielsen Newscast. Vol. 11, no. 4, August 1962.

Nielsen Newscast. Vol. 11, no. 5, December 1962.

Nielsen Newscast, Vol. 12, no. 3, August, 1963.

Production Files of the Production Code Administration (MPAA).
"To Improve Public Attendance Towards the American Motion Picture at Home and Abroad."
 MPAA report, October 1962.
Twentieth Century Fox Collection, University of California at Los Angeles.

Interviews and Correspondence

Harry Ackerman, 1 February 1988
Col. Grover Asmus III, 16 March 1989
Frank Bank, 17 September 1987
Arnold Becker, 5 April 1989
Jerry Bernstein, 28 January 1988
Barbara Billingsley, 17 September 1987
Tim Considine, 12 July 1989
Dick Conway, 1 July 1989
Dorothy Cooper Foote, 18 April 1989
Phil Davis, 12 March 1989
Ed Dewey, 7 March 1989
Elinor Donahue, 1 February 1988
Tony Dow, 17 September 1987
Richard Dwan, 3 May 1989
Shelley Fabares, 29 June 1989
Don Fedderson, 9 September 1987
Robert Fisher, 10 February 1989
Don Grady, 27 June 1989
Bill Gray, 2 February 1988
Barbara Hammer Avedon, 6 March 1989
Ed Hartmann, 13 July 1989
Brian Levant, 15 September 1987
David Levy, 28 April 1989
Fred MacMurray, 17 July 1989
Jerry Mathers, 15 September 1987
Andrew McCullough, 1 June 1989
John McGreevey, 6 July 1989
Nate Monaster, 10 March 1989
David Nelson, 8 February 1988
Gene Nelson, 22 March 1989
Ken Osmand, 15 September 1987
Paul Petersen, 14 March 1989
Arnold and Lois Peyser, 7 June 1989
Alan Press, 9 September 1989
Winnie Rich, 26 September 1987
William Roberts, 5 March 1989
Mrs. Eugene Rodney, 20 April 1989
Roswell Rogers, 8 March 1989
Doug Roth, 23 May 1989
Henry Sharp, 19 March 1989

John Stephens, 11 July 1989
Peter Tewksbury, 25 June 1989
Tom Watson, 23 May 1989
Paul West, 23 March 1989
John Whedon, 9 March 1989
Jane Wyatt, 9 May 1989
Robert Young, 11 March 1989

Filmography

Of the original 199 films targeted as family melodramas, I screened the following 104 (the remaining 95 being unavailable). Eighty-nine of these fell within the family-melodrama genre. The 15 films marked with an asterisk do not qualify as family melodrama; the brief description with each title explains why. The films included here, however, do not constitute all family melodramas available for the period. While I have sufficient knowledge to recognize their generic status, I did not include films which I did not screen. Films are listed by title, director, and studio.

1954
About Mrs. Leslie (not enough family; love affair), Daniel Mann, Paramount
Executive Suite, Wise, MGM
It's a Woman's World, Negules, TCF
Last Time I Saw Paris, Brooks, MGM
Magnificent Obsession, Sirk, Universal
This is My Love, Heisler, RKO
Track of the Cat (setting; rural mystery), Wellman, Warner Bros.

1955
All That Heaven Allows, Sirk, Universal
The Blackboard Jungle (major focus on school, juvenile delinquents), Brooks, MGM
The Cobweb, Minnelli, MGM
The Desperate Hours (crime thriller), Wyler, Paramount
East of Eden, Kazan, Warner Bros.
The Man with the Golden Arm (drug problem/love affair), Preminger, Preminger
One Desire, Hopper, Universal
Picnic, Logan, Columbia
Rebel without a Cause, Ray, Warner Bros.
The Shrike, Ferrer, Universal

1956
Autumn Leaves, Aldrich, Columbia
The Bad Seed (horror thriller), LeRoy, Warner Bros.

Bigger Than Life, Ray, TCF
The Bottom of the Bottle, Hathaway, TCF
The Catered Affair, Brooks, MGM
Come Next Spring, Springsteen, Republic
Crime in the Streets, Siegel, Allied Artists
Giant, Stevens, Warner Bros.
Hilda Crane, Dunne, TCF
A Kiss Before Dying (thriller mystery), Oswald, UA
The Man in the Gray Flannel Suit, Johnson, TCF
Rock, Rock, Rock, Price, Distributor Corp.
Tea and Sympathy, Minnelli, MGM
There's Always Tomorrow, Sirk, Universal
* *These Wilder Years* (home for unwed mothers), Rowland, MGM
The Unguarded Moment, Keller, Universal
Written on the Wind, Sirk, Universal

1957

April Love, Levin, TCF
Bernardine, Levin, TCF
Dino, Carr, Allied Artists
Fear Strikes Out, Mulligan, Paramount
A Hatful of Rain, Zinneman, TCF
Man on Fire, Ruttenberg, MGM
No Down Payment, Ritt, TCF
Peyton Place, Robson, TCF
Tammy and the Bachelor, Pevney, Universal
The Tarnished Angels, Sirk, Universal
That Night, Newland, RKO
The Three Faces of Eve, Johnson, TCF
The Young Stranger, Frankenheimer, RKO

1958

Another Time/Another Place, Allen, Paramount
Cat on a Hot Tin Roof, Brooks, MGM
Desire Under the Elms (too dated), Delbert Mann, Paramount
God's Little Acre, Anthony Mann, Security
Home Before Dark, LeRoy, Warner Bros.
Houseboat, Shavelson, Paramount
Kings Go Forth, Daves, UA
Lonelyhearts, Donehue, UA
The Long Hot Summer, Ritt, TCF
Marjorie Morningstar, Rapper, Warner Bros.
Some Came Running, Minnelli, MGM
Ten North Frederick, Dunne, TCF
The Tunnel of Love, Kelly, MGM

1959

Blue Denim, Dunne, TCF
*Gidget (too teen-restricted), Wendkos, Columbia
Imitation of Life, Sirk, Universal
Night of the Quarter Moon, Haas, MGM
The Remarkable Mr. Pennypacker, Levin, TCF
Stranger in My Arms, Kautner, Universal
Suddenly Last Summer, Mankiewicz, Columbia
A Summer Place, Daves, Warner Bros.

1960

All the Fine Young Cannibals, Anderson, MGM
Butterfield 8, Daniel Mann, MGM
From the Terrace, Robson, TCF
Home from the Hill, Minnelli, MGM
Please Don't Eat the Daisies, Walters, MGM
Strangers When We Meet, Quine, Columbia
*Where the Boys Are (too teen-restricted), Levin, MGM

1961

The Explosive Generation, Kulik, UA
Gidget Goes Hawaiian, Wendkos, Columbia
*Madison Avenue (workplace only/love affair), Humberstone, TCF
The Parent Trap, Swift, Disney
The Pleasure of his Company, Seaton, Paramount
Return to Peyton Place, Ferrer, TCF
Splendor in the Grass, Kazan, Warner Bros.

1962

All Fall Down, Frankenheimer, MGM
Bon Voyage, Neilsen, Disney
Boys' Night Out, Gordon, MGM
David and Lisa, Perry, Continental
The Days of Wine and Roses, Edwards, Warner Bros.
Five Finger Exercise, Daniel Mann, Columbia
Four Horsemen of the Apocalypse, Minnelli, MGM
If a Man Answers, Levin, Universal
Mr. Hobbs Takes a Vacation, Koster, TCF
Period of Adjustment, Hill, MGM
State Fair, Ferrer, TCF

1963

All the Way Home, Segal, Paramount
*Beach Party (too teen-restricted), Asher, American Int'l.
A Child is Waiting, Cassevetes, UA
The Courtship of Eddie's Father, Minnelli, MGM

A Gathering of Eagles, Delbert Mann, Universal
***Gidget Goes to Rome* (too teen-restricted), Wendkos, Columbia
***Long Day's Journey into Night* (too dated), Lumet, Landau
Love with the Proper Stranger, Mulligan, Paramount
Move Over Darling, Sher, TCF
Take Her—She's Mine, Koster, TCF
The Thrill of it All, Jewison, Universal

Studio Totals
20th Century–Fox (TCF) = 21 films
MGM = 19 films
Universal = 14 films
Warner Bros. = 8 films
Paramount = 6 films
Columbia = 6 films
UA = 4 films
RKO = 3 films
Disney = 2 films
Others = 6 films

Frequent Directors
Douglas Sirk = 6 films
Vincent Minnelli = 5 films
Henry Levin = 5 films
Richard Brooks = 4 films
Philip Dunne = 3 films
Jose Ferrer = 3 films
John Frankenheimer = 2 films
Irwin Koster = 2 films
Elia Kazan = 2 films
Daniel Mann = 2 films
Nicholas Ray = 2 films
Mark Robson = 2 films

Videography

The Adventures of Ozzie and Harriet
ABC, October 1952–September 1966. Created and produced by Ozzie Nelson and his brother
Don, with Bill Davenport and Ben Gershman, under the name "Stage Five Productions." Most
episodes were written by the Nelsons, Davenport, and Gershman, occasionally joined by Jay
Sommers, Dick Bensfield, and Perry Grant. All early episodes were directed by Ozzie Nelson.
After 1961 David Nelson occasionally directed.

Episodes Screened
1952–1953: "Riviera Ballet," "The Rover Boys," "Harriet's Hairdo," "The Dental Receptionist," "Day
After Thanksgiving," "The Hallowe'en Party," "Whistler's Daughter," "Curiosity," "Oscillating
Ozzie," "Monetary System," "Baby Sitter," "Who's Walter?"
  1953–1954: "The Initiation," "The Credit Reference," "No Noise," "David Writes a Column,"
"The Swimming Pool," "Ozzie's Night Out," "Ricky's Lost Letter," "An Evening with Hamlet,"
"Too Many Children."
  1955–1956: "David's Engagement," "The Volunteer Fireman."
  1956–1957: "Like Father, Like Son," "Ozzie, the Treasurer."
  1957–1958: "Tutti Frutti Ice Cream," "The Trophy," "The Top Gun," "The Closed Circuit,"
"Ozzie's Triple Banana Surprise," "The Dating System," "The Old Band Pavilion," "The Bachelor," "A Cruise for Harriet," "The Magic of Three," "The Safe," "The Record Trout," "David and
the Men's Club," "Who is Betty?" "The Code of Honor," "Picture in Rick's Notebook," "David
and the Stewardess."
  1958–1959: "Rick's Scientific Date," "David Loses His Poise," "The Pony," "The Runaways,"
"The Motorcycle," "Togetherness," "The Buckingham," "Always a Bridegroom," "The Costume
Dance."
  1959–1960: "Bad Day at Blueberry Rock," "The Gas Station," "The Uninvited Guests," "An
Interesting Evening," "The T-Shirts," "Big Plans for Summer," "The Magic Dishes," "David and
the School Teacher," "No News for Harriet," "The Professor's Experiment."
  1960–1961: "David Gets Discouraged," "His Brother's Girl," "Ozzie, the Boatkeeper," "A Piano
for the Fraternity," "Bowling with the Wives," "Our Man in Alaska," "Two Small Boys and a
Dog," "Dave's Golf Story," "Rick's Broken Arm," "The Boy's Portraits," "The Pen and Pencil Set,"
"The Fraternity Junk Drive," "Selling Ricky's Drums," "Extra Sensory Perception," "The Built-In
Television Set," "The Manly Arts," "The Table and the Painting."
  1961–1962: "The Backyard Pet Show," "The Special Cake," "The Barking Dog," "Ten for the

Tigers," "The Savings Stamps," "Lending Money to Wally," "The High Cost of Dating."

1962–1963: "Any Date in a Storm," "The Adventurers."

1963–1964: "Wally's TV Set," "The Torn Dress," "Rick's Wedding Ring," "The Blue Moose," "The Secret Agent," "Ozzie's Hidden Trophy," "David Takes a Client to Dinner," "The Lawyers' Convention," "June is Always Late," "Wally's Pen Pal," "The Dean's Birthday."

1964–1965: "Early Rush Party," "The Exotic Housemother."

1965–1966: "The Secret Passage," "Ozzie, the Sitter," "An Honor for Oz," "Rick's Assistant."

Father Knows Best

CBS, October 1954–March 1955; NBC, August 1955–September 1958; CBS, October 1958–September 1962; ABC,* October 1962–April 1963. Created by Eugene Rodney. Produced by Eugene Rodney and Robert Young under the name Cavelier Productions, in association with Columbia's Screen Gems. Roswell Rogers was head writer, and Dorothy Cooper Foote, Phil Davis, and Paul West contributed scripts. Directors included William D. Russell (1954–1956) and Peter Tewksbury (1956–1960).

Note: Original programs ended at the end of the 1959–1960 season. After that, reruns were presented in prime time.

Episodes Screened

1954–1955: "Bud Takes up the Dance," "Lesson in Citizenship," "The Motor Scooter," "Football Tickets," "Live My Own Life," "Grandpa Jim's Rejuvenation," "Typical Father," "Second Honeymoon," "Margaret Goes Dancing," "Boy's Week," "Bud, the Snob," "The Promised Playhouse," "Jim, the Farmer," "Father of the Year," "The Mink Coat," "The Matchmaker," "Proud Father," "Father Delivers the Papers," "No Partiality," "Close Decision."

1955–1956: "Art of Salesmanship," "Father's Private Life," "Lessons in Civics," "First Disillusionment," "Woman in the House," "New Girl at School," "Kathy Makes Magic," "Advantage to Betty," "The Big Test," "Father is a Dope," "Bud, the Lady Killer," "Margaret's Premonition," "Bad Influence," "Betty Hates Carter," "Jim, the Tyrant," "Betty's Brother," "Betty Earns a Formal," "The House Painter," "Bud, the Wallflower," "The Bus to Nowhere," "The $10 Question," "Kathy, the Indian Giver," "The Historical Andersons," "The Grass is Greener," "The Persistent Guest," "Family Reunion," "Family Dines Out," "Bud, the Boxer," "Betty, Girl Engineer," "The Martins and the Coys," "Dilemma for Margaret," "Father, the Naturalist," "Hero Father," "The Spirit of Youth."

1956–1957: "Spaghetti for Margaret," "Margaret Disowns the Family," "Homing Pigeon," "Shoot for the Moon," "Brief Vacation," "Betty Goes to College," "Betty Goes Steady."

1957–1958: "Kathy's Big Chance," "Mother Goes to School," "A Medal for Margaret," "The Rivals," "Big Sister."

1958–1959: "Frank's Family Tree," "Second Wedding," "Bud, the Carpenter," "Big Shot Bud," "Betty, the Pioneer Woman," "The Great Experiment," "The Basketball Coach," "Kathy, Girl Executive," "The Good Samaritan," "Ideal Father," "Hard Luck Leo," "Bud, the Campus Romeo," "Crisis Over a Kiss," "Kathy Grows Up," "A Man of Merit," "Betty Makes a Choice," "It's a Small World," "An Extraordinary Woman," "Formula for Happiness," "Bud, the Debutante," "The Meanest Professor," "Bud Has a Problem," "The Great Anderson Mystery," "Vine Covered Cottage," "The Gold Turnip."

1959–1960: "A Day in the Country," "Bud Branches Out," "The Gardener's Big Day," "The Imposter," "Bud Plays it Safe," "Bicycle Trip for Two," "Margaret's Old Flame," "Kathy Becomes a

Girl," "Bud, the Willing Worker," "Turn the Other Cheek," "Good Joke on Mom," "Betty's Double," "Bud Hides Behind a Skirt," "Time to Retire," "Bud, the Speculator," "The $500 Letter," "Family Contest," "Betty's Career Problem," "Blind Date," "Bud Lives It Up," "Not His Type," "Second Best," "Kathy's Big Deception," "Cupid Knows Best," "Jim's Big Surprise."

Leave It to Beaver

CBS, October 1957–August 1958; ABC, September 1958–September 1963. Created and produced by Joe Connelly and Bob Mosher under the name Gomalco Productions. Originally shot at the Republic lot. George Gobel and Dave O'Malley (as Gomalco) were executive producers the first two years. Beginning in September 1958, *Leave It to Beaver* was produced for MCA and aired on ABC as a Kayro production (named for Connelly and Mosher's wives, Kathryn and Rose). All stories and most scripts in the first two years were by Connelly and Mosher. Later writers included the team of Dick Conway and Roland MacLane, as well as that of John Whedon and Robert Fisher. Directors included Norman Tokar, Norman Abbot, and David Butler.

Episodes Screened

1957–1958: "Capt. Jack," "Water Anyone," "Beaver Gets 'spelled," "New Neighbors," "Lonesome Beaver," "The Broken Window," "Train Trip," "Beaver's Bad Day," "Wally's Girl Trouble," "Part-Time Genius," "The Haircut," "Brotherly Love," "Beaver's Short Pants," "Beaver's Crush," "Voodoo Magic," "Party Invitation," "Child Care," "Tenting Tonight," "Beaver's Old Friend," "Wally's Job," "Lumpy Rutherford," "New Doctor," "Boarding School," "Beaver's Poem," "Cat Out of the Bag," "Beaver and Henry," "The Bank Account," "Beaver and Pancho."

1958–1959: "Beaver and Gilbert," "Dance Contest," "Beaver Runs Away," "The Lost Watch," "Ward's Problem," "Her Idol," "The Grass is Always Greener," "Beaver's Hero," "Wally's New Suit," "The Shave," "The Visiting Aunts," "The Tooth," "The Bus Ride," "A Horse Named Nick," "The Pipe," "Wally's Present," "Beaver's Ring," "Beaver Gets Adopted," "Eddie's Girl," "Price of Fame," "The Boat Builders," "Beaver Plays Hookey," "The Garage Painters," "Beaver's Pigeons," "Wally's Haircomb," "Beaver's Sweater," "The Cookie Fund."

1959–1960: "Beaver's Fortune," "Beaver Takes a Walk," "School Sweater," "Wally, the Businessman," "Blind Date Committee," "Wally's Play," "Beaver Makes a Loan."

1960–1961: "Wally and Dudley," "Eddie's Double Cross," "Beaver Becomes a Hero," "Beaver's Freckles," "Beaver Won't Eat," "Wally's Glamor Girl," "Beaver's Big Contest," "Beaver's I.Q.," "Beaver Goes in Business," "Miss Landers' Fiancé," "Chuckie's New Shoes," "Ward's Millions," "Beaver and Kenneth," "The Dramatic Club," "Mother's Helper."

1961–1962: "Beaver Takes a Drive," "Nobody Loves Me," "Beaver's Long Night," "Beaver's First Date," "Wally Stays at Lumpy's," "Beaver's Typewriter," "Beaver's Jacket," "Sweatshirt Monsters," "A Night in the Woods."

1962–1963: "Beaver the Caddy," "Wally's Dinner Date," "More Blessed to Give?" "Box Office Attraction," "Don Juan Beaver," "Beaver's Graduation," "Wally's Practical Joke," "The All-Night Party," "Family Scrapbook," "Beaver's Good Deed," "The Credit Card," "The Moustache," "Wally and the Fraternity," "Beaver Sees America."

The Donna Reed Show

ABC, October 1959–September 1966. Created by William Roberts. Produced by Donna Reed and her husband Tony Owen in association with Screen Gems' Irving Brisken, under the name Todon-Brisken. Writers included Nate Monaster, John Whedon, Robert Fisher, Paul West (also a co-producer), Tom and Helen August, John Elliotte, David Adler, Barbara Hammer, and Phil Davis. Directors included Oscar Rudolph, Gene Nelson, Lawrence Dobkin, Norman Tokar, Andrew McCullough, Robert Ellis Miller, and Jeffrey Hayden.

Episodes Screened

1958–1959: "Weekend Trip," "Pardon My Gloves," "The Hike," "The Male Ego," "The Football Uniform," "The Foundling," "Three Part Mother," "Change Partners and Dance," "Guest in the House," "The Baby Contest," "The Beaded Bag," "The Busy Body," "Mary's Double Date," "Jeff's Double Life," "Nothing But the Truth," "Have Fun," "Jeff vs. Mary," "It's the Principle of the Thing," "Donna Plays Cupid," "Love Thy Neighbor," "The Report Card," "Boys Will Be Boys," "The Ideal Wife," "Mary's Campaign," "April Fool," "The Parting of the Ways," "The Hero," "Do You Trust Your Child?" "The Grateful Patient," "The Flowered Dress," "The Testimonial," "Tomorrow Comes Too Soon," "Advice to Young Lovers," "Operation Deadbeat," "That's Show Business," "Sleep No More, My Lady."

1959–1960: "A Penny Earned," "Nothing Like a Good Book," "Miss Lovelace Comes to Tea," "A Friend Indeed," "The First Child," "Going Steady," "The Neighborly Gesture," "Flowers for the Teacher," "All Mothers Worry," "Jeff Joins a Club," "The Punishment," "A Difference of Opinion," "The Homecoming Dinner," "Lucky Girl," "The Broken Spirit," "The New Mother," "The Secret," "Just a Housewife," "The Free Soul," "The First Quarrel," "A Place to Go," "A Night to Howl," "The Editorial," "The Gentle Dew," "The Fatal Leap," "Perfect Pitch," "Pickles for Charity," "Mary's Growing Pains," "Alex Runs the House," "The Career Woman," "Jeff, the Financial Genius," "Mary's Crusade," "The First Time We Met," "The Gossip," "Love's Sweet Awakening," "The Wedding Present," "Cool Cat," "Weekend," "The Mystery Woman."

1960–1961: "The Love Letter," "How the Other Half Lives," "The Model Daughter," "Decisions, Decisions, Decisions," "Donna Goes to a Reunion," "A Rose is a Rose."

1961–1962: "The Mouse at Play."

1962–1963: "Mrs. Stone and Dr. Hyde," "To Be a Boy," "Fine Feathers," "Rebel with a Cause," "Big Star," "Man to Man," "The Soft Touch," "Jeff Stands Alone," "Just a Little Wedding," "A Woman's Place," "Three is a Family," "Big Sixteen," "Pioneer Woman," "The House on the Hill," "The Handy Man."

1965–1966: "Calling Willie Mays," "Is There a Small Hotel?" "No More Parties—Almost," "So You Really Think You're Young At Heart."

My Three Sons

ABC, September 1960–September 1965; CBS, September 1965–August 1972. Created by Don Fedderson and George Tibbles; produced by Don Fedderson Productions (which was owned jointly by Fred MacMurray and Fedderson). Writers included George Tibbles, Ed Hartmann (both also co-producers), John McGreevey, Gail Ingram Clement, Arnold and Lois Peyser, Dorothy Cooper Foote, Phil Davis, and Kitty Buehler Bradley. Directors included Peter Tewksbury (1960–1961), Richard Wharf (1961–1962), Gene Reynolds (1962–1964), and James V. Kern (1964–1965).

Episodes Screened

1960–1961: "Adjust or Bust," "My Three Strikers," "The Elopement," "Domestic Trouble," "Bub Leaves Home," "The Bully," "Organization Woman," "Other People's Houses," "The Delinquent," "Man in a Trench Coat," "The Lostling," "Soap-Box Derby," "Unite or Sink," "Chip—Off the Old Block," "The Little Ragpicker," "Bub in the Ointment," "Brotherly Love," "Lady Engineer," "Raft on the River," "Lonesome George," "Spring Will Be a Little Late."

1961–1962: "The Birds and the Bees," "Weekend in Tokyo."

1962–1963: "Almost the Sound of Music," "Moment of Truth," "Daughter for a Day," "Pretty as a Picture," "What's Cookin'?" "Chip's Last Fight," "The Beauty Contest," "Doctor in the House," "Going Steady," "Mother Bub," "Honorable Grandfather," "High on the Hog," "First Things First," "Bub's Butler," "Francesca," "The Rug," "The System," "Let's Take Stock," "Total Recall."

1963–1964: "A Car of His Own," "How Do You Know," "Will Success Spoil Chip Douglas?" "Stage Door Bub," "Never Look Back," "House for Sale," "The Ballad of Lissa Stratmeyer," "The Stone Frog," "Fish Gotta Swim—Birds Gotta Fly," "Cherry Blossoms in Bryant Park," "The People House," "The Tree," "The Substitute Teacher," "Mike Wears the Pants," "The Guys and the Dolls," "Tramp Goes Hollywood," "Huckleberry Douglas," "Guest in the House," "My Friend Ernie," "The End of You Know What," "The Toupee," "The Ever Popular Robbie Douglas," "Dear Robbie," "Stage Door Bub."

1964–1965: "Caribbean Cruise," "Women's Work," "Be My Guest," "Hawaiian Cruise," "Chip o' the Island," "Divorce, Bryant Park Style," "Lady in the Air," "Fountain of Youth," "Steve and the Computer," "The Teenager," "One of Our Moose is Missing," "Charley and the Kid," "The Sure Thing," "Here Comes Charley," "Tramp and the Prince," "All the Weddings," "A Serious Girl," "The Practical Shower," "Dublin's Fair City, Part I," "Lady President," "A Touch of Larceny," "The Coffeehouse Set," "The Lotus Blossom," "You're in my Power," "Robbie and the Nurse."

Index

DATE DUE

GAYLORD   PRINTED IN U.S.A.